Southern Living

Homestyle
Cookbook

©2008 by Oxmoor House, Inc.
Book Division of Southern Progress Corporation
P. O. Box 2262, Birmingham, Alabama 35201-2262

Southern Living® is a federally registered trademark belonging to Southern Living, Inc.

ISBN-13: 978-0-8487-3182-3
ISBN-10: 0-8487-3182-4
Library of Congress Control Number: 2007941803
Printed in the United States of America
Second Printing 2008

Oxmoor House, Inc.
Editor in Chief: Nancy Fitzpatrick Wyatt
Executive Editor: Susan Carlisle Payne
Art Director: Keith McPherson
Managing Editor: Allison Long Lowery

Southern Living® **Homestyle Cookbook**
Editor: Elizabeth Taliaferro
Digital Production Editor: Julie Boston
Senior Designer: Melissa Jones Clark
Nutrition Editor: Rachel Quinlivan, R.D.
Copy Chief: L. Amanda Owens
Copy Editor: Donna Baldone
Editorial Assistant: Amelia Heying
Director, Test Kitchens: Elizabeth Tyler Austin
Assistant Director, Test Kitchens: Julie Christopher
Test Kitchens Professionals: Jane Chambliss; Kathleen Royal Phillips;
    Catherine Crowell Steele; Ashley T. Strickland; Kate Wheeler, R.D.
Photography Director: Jim Bathie
Photographers: Ralph Anderson, Mary M. Chambliss, Van Chaplin, Gary Clark,
    Joe Descoise, William Dickey, Beth Dreiling, Meg McKinney, Art Meripol,
    Emily Minton, Bruce Roberts, Allen Rokach, Mark Sandlin, Charles Walton IV
Senior Photo Stylist: Kay E. Clarke
Associate Photo Stylist: Katherine Eckert
Director of Production: Laura Lockhart
Production Manager: Terri Beste-Farley
Production Assistant: Faye Porter Bonner

Contributors
Designer: Carol Loria
Indexer: Mary Ann Laurens
Editorial Assistant: Cory Bordonaro
Writer: Deborah Garrison Lowery
Interns: Tracey Apperson, Carol Corbin, Erin Loudy, Maggie Lane Marlin, Patricia Michaud
Food Stylists: Ana Price Kelly, Debby Maugans
Recipe Consultant: Leah Marlett
Photographers: J. Savage Gibson, Beau Gustafson, Lee Harrelson, Vince Lupo, Blake Sims
Photo Stylists: Melanie Clarke, Katie Stoddard

To order additional publications, call 1-800-765-6400.
For more books to enrich your life, visit **oxmoorhouse.com**

To search, savor, and share thousands of recipes, visit **myrecipes.com**

Cover: Mile-High White Chocolate Hummingbird Cake (page 243)
Left (center): Iced Mint Tea (page 204)
Right: Fresh Corn Salad (page 311)
Back Cover (clockwise from top left): Fresh Mozzarella and Basil Pizza (page 61),
    Apple-Broccoli Salad (page 310), Apple Stack Cake (page 40),
    Shrimp and Grits (page 18), Fried Okra (page 371)

Southern Living
Homestyle
Cookbook

Oxmoor
House.

contents

homestyle flavors

These chapters define the South's culinary evolution. You'll find traditional recipes to savor as well as new favorites brought by immigrants to our region through the years. Twenty menus will tempt your taste buds, whether you're stirring up simple weeknight family meals or casually cooking for friends.

homestyle favorites

Flip through these chapters to find delicious offerings of family fare, festive food, fantastic desserts, and even food gifts just waiting for you to sample and share. Fun and historical Southern food stories nestled among the recipes offer the perfect trivia for table talk.

a homestyle welcome

One of the true culinary hallmarks of *Southern Living* is its strong connection to millions of devoted readers. That's because over the past 42 years, the vast majority of our recipes have come straight out of Southern kitchens just like yours. We've learned from this special relationship that, among other things, you treasure classic, comforting, down-home recipes, which is why we're so excited about the all-new Homestyle Cookbook.

With more than 400 delectable recipes, this cookbook is a virtual feast for any food lover. Jump right into Southern Heritage Treasures to discover iconic gems from the Lowcountry to the Chesapeake Bay to Cajun country and more. Be sure to reference the prep and cook times for each soul-soothing recipe to help you plan your schedule, as well as the specialty text boxes sprinkled throughout, which are chock-full of tips, secrets, and good ol' Southern lore.

Don't miss chapters such as Healthy Homestyle Cooking, Weeknight Family Meals, and Casual Entertaining Menus, which truly speak to the needs of today's home cooks. As an added bonus, we've layered in our staff's collective expertise on everything from lightening recipes and make-ahead suggestions to exclusive tips from our Test Kitchens. So whether you need a dish for a quick and easy supper or special weekend get-together, we hope this cookbook will be your guide.

Happy cooking!

Scott Jones
Executive Editor

Hearty Oat and Walnut Bread, page 227

homestyle flavors

Southern heritage treasures

Pan-fried Crab Cakes and East Coast Tarter Sauce, page 20

Cajun, Creole and jazz

At the edge of the French Quarter wafts of sweet fried beignets, brewing chicory coffee, and the sugary scent of warm pralines cooling on marble slabs are as traditional as the tinkling of jazz tunes heard 'round the clock. And that's just New Orleans. The rich heritage of the region goes beyond the Quarter to swampy bayous, where spicy, rustic peasant-style Cajun meals of alligator meat, wild game, tasso ham, and crawfish étouffée are rampant. It meshes with the more cultured tomato-infused Creole favorites, such as red beans and rice, and the influence of Africans, who settled here years ago. It's a region where dining style ranges from an elegant Fat Tuesday dinner party to a down-home crawfish boil with plenty of loud laughter and zydeco music for all. Throw in Louisiana food staples such as Tabasco sauce, sweet potatoes, rice, and pecans for a culinary heritage as colorful as the crowns of the many kings who ruled over the land. And, talk about good! (a favorite Cajun expression): Even with the arrival of the Nouvelle Creole trend toward lighter fare, these new versions of old favorites have remained true to the heritage of a region that knows how to *laissez les bons temps rouler* (let the good times roll)!

Creole Red Beans and Rice

makes 8 servings • prep: 20 min., cook: 3 hr., other: 8 hr.

test kitchen tip: To quick-soak kidney beans, place them in a Dutch oven; cover with water 2 inches above beans, and bring to a boil. Boil 1 minute; cover, remove from heat, and let stand 1 hour. Drain beans, and rinse thoroughly.

1 (16-oz.) package dried red kidney beans
1 lb. smoked sausage, thinly sliced
2 Tbsp. vegetable oil
3 celery ribs, sliced
1 green bell pepper, chopped
1 large onion, chopped
3 green onions, chopped
3 garlic cloves, minced
1 (14½-oz.) can diced tomatoes

1 (32-oz.) container chicken broth
3½ cups water
2 bay leaves
1 Tbsp. Worcestershire sauce
1 tsp. sugar
½ tsp. salt
½ tsp. pepper
⅛ tsp. ground red pepper
Hot cooked rice
Garnish: thinly sliced green onions

1. Rinse and sort beans according to package directions. Place beans in a Dutch oven; add water 2 inches above beans, and let soak 8 hours. Drain beans, and rinse thoroughly; drain again, and set aside.

2. Sauté sausage in hot oil in Dutch oven over medium heat 5 to 7 minutes or until sausage is golden brown. Drain sausage on paper towels, reserving drippings in Dutch oven. Refrigerate sausage until ready to stir into bean mixture. Add celery and next 4 ingredients to hot drippings; sauté 5 minutes or until vegetables are tender. Add tomatoes, and simmer, stirring occasionally, 7 minutes.

3. Stir in beans, broth, and next 7 ingredients; increase heat to medium-high, and bring to a boil. Boil 10 minutes; reduce heat, and simmer, uncovered, stirring occasionally, 1½ to 2 hours or until beans are tender. Stir in sausage, and simmer 30 more minutes. Discard bay leaves. Serve beans over hot cooked rice. Garnish, if desired.

If it was Monday, then red beans and rice were on the menu in the early days of New Orleans. That's because it was the traditional wash day, and this was one dish that could be made with little effort and occasional stirring while women were busy with the laundry.

Deep-Fried Turkey

makes 20 servings • prep: 40 min., cook: 1 hr., other: 45 min.

Turkey was so plentiful in the colonial days that Ben Franklin argued that instead of the eagle, the turkey should be the national bird. The Louisiana-born method of frying whole turkeys began in the early 1980s and has swept the country in popularity. The reason—fried turkey is incredibly moist, succulent, and amazingly has no greasy taste.

1   (12- to 15-lb.) turkey
2   Tbsp. ground red pepper (optional)
4   to 5 gal. peanut oil

Garnishes: fresh sage, parsley, thyme sprigs, kumquats with leaves

1. Remove giblets and neck, and rinse turkey with cold water. Drain cavity well; pat dry. Place turkey on fryer rod; allow all liquid to drain from cavity (20 to 30 minutes). Rub outside of turkey with red pepper, if desired.

2. Pour oil into a deep propane turkey fryer 10 to 12 inches from top; heat to 375° over a medium-low flame according to manufacturer's instructions. Carefully lower turkey into hot oil with rod attachment.

3. Fry 55 minutes or until a meat thermometer inserted in turkey breast registers 165° or to desired doneness. (Keep oil temperature at 340°.) Remove turkey from oil; drain and let stand 15 minutes before slicing. Garnish, if desired.

test kitchen tip: Frying a turkey is simple but requires observance of these important safety tips. Always follow the manufacturer's instructions. Place the propane deep fryer outdoors on a level grassy or dirt area. Never fry turkeys using a propane fryer indoors, in a garage, or in any structure attached to a building. And always have a fire extinguisher nearby. It's crucial to add just enough oil needed to fry the turkey. Our Test Kitchens suggest filling the fryer with oil to a level approximately 10 to 12 inches below the top of the fryer.

Crawfish Jambalaya

makes 4 to 6 servings • prep: 20 min., cook: 40 min.

In rural south Louisiana, jambalaya is usually cooked in a cast-iron pot, turning the sauce a brownish color. In New Orleans the stew is red, due to the Creole preference for tomatoes.

1   medium onion, chopped
4   garlic cloves, minced
½   cup chopped green pepper
½   cup chopped celery
½   cup butter, melted
1   (14.5-oz.) can stewed tomatoes, undrained

1   lb. frozen crawfish tails, thawed
1   cup chopped green onions
3   cups cooked long-grain rice
¼   tsp. salt
⅛   tsp. pepper

1. Sauté first 4 ingredients in butter in a large skillet over medium-high heat until tender. Add tomatoes; reduce heat, and simmer, uncovered, 20 minutes.

2. Add crawfish, and cook 10 minutes. Stir in green onions, rice, salt, and pepper.

Charlotte Champagne

Nun Better: Tastes and Tales from Around a Cajun Table
St. Cecilia School ~ Broussard, Louisiana

test kitchen tip: For more flavor, cook rice in chicken broth instead of water. If you do, omit the salt in the jambalaya.

Shrimp and Sausage Gumbo

makes 11 cups • prep: 30 min.; cook: 2 hr., 10 min.

Gumbo comes from the African word "ngombo," which means okra, but not all gumbos contain okra. Though the ingredients vary, all start with the "holy trinity" of celery, onion, and bell pepper.

2   lb. unpeeled, large raw shrimp
2   (32-oz.) containers chicken broth
1   lb. andouille or smoked sausage,
    cut into ¼-inch slices
Vegetable oil
1   cup all-purpose flour
1   medium onion, chopped
1   green bell pepper, chopped
3   celery ribs, sliced
3   garlic cloves, minced
2   bay leaves
2   tsp. Creole seasoning
½   tsp. dried thyme
1   Tbsp. Worcestershire sauce
2   to 3 tsp. hot sauce
½   cup chopped green onions
Hot cooked rice

make it ahead: Most soups taste better after stored in the refrigerator overnight, and this one is no exception. Prepare the recipe through Step 5, and refrigerate up to 24 hours. The following day, bring it to a boil over medium-high heat, stirring frequently. Reduce heat to a simmer, and continue with Step 6.

1. Peel shrimp, reserving shells, and devein, if desired. Store shrimp in refrigerator until ready to stir into gumbo.

2. Combine shrimp shells and chicken broth in a large Dutch oven; bring to a boil. Reduce heat, and simmer, uncovered, 20 minutes. Pour mixture through a wire-mesh strainer into a large bowl, discarding shells. Set broth aside, and keep warm.

3. Sauté sausage in a Dutch oven over medium heat until browned. Remove sausage with a slotted spoon, and drain on paper towels. Store sausage in refrigerator until ready to stir into gumbo. Measure drippings, adding enough vegetable oil to measure ½ cup. Gradually whisk in flour, and cook, whisking constantly, over medium-low heat about 35 to 40 minutes, until roux is chocolate colored.

5. Stir in onion and next 3 ingredients; cook 7 minutes or until vegetables are tender, stirring often. Gradually stir in warm broth; bring mixture to a boil. Stir in bay leaves and next 4 ingredients; reduce heat, and simmer, uncovered, 50 minutes, stirring occasionally.

6. Stir in shrimp, sausage, and green onions; cook 5 to 7 minutes or until shrimp turn pink. Discard bay leaves. Serve gumbo over hot rice.

Bread Pudding With Whiskey Sauce

makes 16 servings • prep: 25 min., cook: 1 hr., other: 10 min.

Made with leftover cornbread, biscuits, or even saltines, bread pudding is possibly the most Southern pudding of all. In French-influenced Louisiana, French bread is the main ingredient for a dessert revered in even the most upscale restaurants.

test kitchen tip: In the Whiskey Sauce, there's no need to further cook the sauce after adding the hot syrup to the beaten eggs. Our testing revealed that the mixture easily reached the USDA's recommended temperature (160°) for cooking eggs.

1	(1-lb.) loaf French bread		2	apples, peeled, cored, and cubed
4	cups milk		1	(8-oz.) can crushed pineapple,
4	large eggs, beaten			drained
2	cups sugar		¼	cup butter, melted
2	Tbsp. vanilla extract			Whiskey Sauce
1	cup raisins			

1. Preheat oven to 350°.

2. Tear bread into small pieces; place in a large bowl. Add milk to bowl; let mixture stand 10 minutes.

3. Stir mixture well with a wooden spoon. Add eggs, sugar, and vanilla; stir well. Stir in raisins, apple, and pineapple.

4. Pour butter into a 13- x 9-inch pan; tilt pan to coat evenly. Spoon pudding mixture into pan. Bake, uncovered, at 350° for 55 to 60 minutes. Remove from oven, and cool slightly.

5. Cut into squares; spoon Whiskey Sauce over each serving.

Whiskey Sauce

makes 2⅔ cups • prep: 5 min., cook: 6 min., other: 4 min.

1	cup butter		⅔	cup bourbon, divided
2	cups sugar		2	large eggs

1. Melt butter in a 2-qt. heavy saucepan over medium-low heat. Stir in sugar and ⅓ cup bourbon. Bring to a boil over medium-high heat, stirring occasionally; reduce heat, and simmer 3 minutes, stirring often. Remove from heat, and let stand about 4 minutes or until a thermometer reaches 185°.

2. While syrup cooks, whisk eggs until thick and pale in a medium bowl. Gradually add hot syrup, whisking constantly, until smooth. Whisk in remaining ⅓ cup bourbon.

King Cake

makes 18 servings • prep: 50 min.; cook: 20 min.; other: 1 hr., 10 min.

King Cake has been a New Orleans tradition dating back to the 1800s. A coin, bean, or tiny plastic baby pressed into the risen dough before baking is said to bring the recipient good luck and once determined the Mardi Gras queen. Colored sugar toppings in the traditional colors of purple, green, and gold stand for justice, faith, and power.

4¾ cups all-purpose flour, divided	½ cup water
1 cup granulated sugar, divided	2 large eggs
1½ tsp. salt	1 Tbsp. ground cinnamon
2 (¼-oz.) envelopes rapid-rise yeast	2 cups sifted powdered sugar
¾ cup butter or margarine, divided	3 Tbsp. milk
¾ cup milk	Colored sugars

test kitchen tip: This sweet yeast cake is an ideal part of a breakfast or brunch menu as well as a fitting end to a Mardi Gras dinner celebration.

1. Combine 1½ cups flour, ¼ cup sugar, salt, and yeast in a large bowl.

2. Melt ½ cup butter in a small saucepan over low heat. Add ¾ cup milk and water, and heat until hot (120° to 130°). Add milk mixture to flour mixture, and beat at medium speed with an electric mixer 2 minutes. Add eggs, beating well. Stir in remaining 3¼ cups flour. Turn dough out onto a well-floured surface, and knead until smooth and elastic (about 10 minutes).

3. Place in a well-greased bowl, turning to grease top. Cover and let rise in a warm place (85°), free from drafts, 45 minutes or until doubled in bulk.

4. Stir together remaining ¾ cup sugar and cinnamon.

5. Preheat oven to 375°.

6. Punch dough down, and let dough rest 6 minutes. Divide dough into 3 portions. Roll each portion into a 28- x 4-inch rectangle. Melt remaining ¼ cup butter; brush evenly over rectangles. Sprinkle each rectangle with ¼ cup sugar mixture leaving a 1-inch margin around edges.

7. Roll up each dough rectangle, jelly-roll fashion, starting at 1 long side; pinch edges together to seal. Pinch ropes together at 1 end to seal, and braid. Cover and let rise in a warm place (85°), free from drafts, 15 minutes or until doubled in bulk.

8. Bake at 375° for 18 to 20 minutes or until golden. Transfer to a wire rack to cool completely.

9. Combine powdered sugar and 3 Tbsp. milk in a small bowl, stirring until smooth. Drizzle over cake, and sprinkle with colored sugars.

Atchafalaya Legacy
Melville Woman's Club ~ Melville, Louisiana

Chesapeake Bay bounty

Ocean waves gently lick the Chesapeake shore, and the breeze smells of salt air and fish. In the bay, fishermen on 90-year-old skipjacks harvest shrimp, oysters, famous blue crabs, and fish the same way they have for years. It's the starting point of the South geographically in both lifestyle and food, and it's on these shores that the Native Americans taught the settlers how to survive . . . to bake clams in earthen ovens, spear crabs, mix corn and lima beans for succotash, and harvest native wild rice. Staples of corn, sweet potatoes, and cornbread complemented the diet heavy in seafood. Today, sounds of laughter and the smell of food feasts for fun, not just sustenance, punctuate the air—at any time there may be a beachside clam bake or a crab boil, where tables lined with grocery sacks and cracked crabs provide feasting time with friends. In summer, homemade barbecue pits line highways to the beaches where the business of selling plates of barbecued chicken quarters, in a nod to Maryland's poultry population, is brisk. Restaurants feature favorite seafood chowders, Maryland crab cakes, and fried soft shell crabs reflecting the heritage still treasured by those who make their life and their living from the waters of the Chesapeake Bay.

Shrimp and Grits

makes 4 servings • prep: 30 min., cook: 40 min.

make it a meal: This recipe for Shrimp and Grits is a great entertaining option for brunch or dinner. Either way, round out the menu with a salad of Boston lettuce, fresh melons and a balsamic vinaigrette, French bread, and Sweet Potato Praline Pie (page 21).

2	cups water	1	lb. unpeeled, medium-size raw
1	(14-oz.) can chicken broth		shrimp, peeled and deveined
¾	cup half-and-half	¼	tsp. black pepper
¾	tsp. salt	⅛	tsp. salt
1	cup regular uncooked grits	1	cup sliced mushrooms
¾	cup (3 oz.) shredded Cheddar	½	cup chopped green onions
	cheese	2	garlic cloves, minced
¼	cup grated Parmesan cheese	2	Tbsp. all-purpose flour
2	Tbsp. butter	2	Tbsp. fresh lemon juice
½	tsp. hot sauce	½	cup chicken broth
¼	tsp. ground white pepper	¼	tsp. hot sauce
3	bacon slices		

1. Bring first 4 ingredients to a boil in a medium saucepan; gradually whisk in grits. Reduce heat, and simmer, stirring occasionally, 10 minutes or until thickened. Add Cheddar cheese and next 4 ingredients. Keep warm.

2. Cook bacon in a large skillet until crisp; remove bacon, and drain on paper towels, reserving 1 Tbsp. drippings in skillet. Crumble bacon, and set aside.

3. Sprinkle shrimp with pepper and salt.

4. Sauté mushrooms in hot drippings in skillet 5 minutes or until tender. Add green onions, and sauté 2 minutes. Add shrimp and garlic, and sauté 2 minutes or until shrimp turn pink. Whisk together flour and lemon juice until smooth. Add flour mixture, chicken broth, and hot sauce, and cook 2 more minutes until mixture is slightly thickened, stirring to loosen particles from bottom of skillet.

5. Serve shrimp mixture over hot cheese grits, and top with crumbled bacon.

The simple mixture of shrimp, grits, and bacon drippings is known historically as a "fisherman's breakfast" during shrimp season. In the 1990s shrimp and grits went upscale like the recipe here.

Pan-fried Crab Cakes

(pictured on page 11)

makes 4 servings • prep: 15 min.; cook: 16 min.; other: 1 hr., 3 min.

Most people can't agree on what makes a traditional Maryland crab cake, but many say it's usually spicier than other versions.

test kitchen tip: Lump crabmeat, the pricier of all varieties of fresh crabmeat, includes pieces of white body meat with no fin or claw meat included. While making the crab cakes, handle the mixture as little and as gently as possible so the large chunks stay intact.

½	cup mayonnaise	1	lb. fresh lump crabmeat, drained
2	egg yolks, lightly beaten	1	cup crushed saltines (about 20 crackers)
1	Tbsp. Dijon mustard		
1	Tbsp. white wine Worcestershire sauce	3	Tbsp. butter
			East Coast Tartar Sauce
½	tsp. hot sauce		Garnish: Parsley sprigs, lemon wedges

1. Stir together first 5 ingredients; fold in crabmeat and saltines. Let stand 3 minutes. Shape mixture into 8 patties. Place on a wax paper-lined baking sheet; cover and chill 1 hour.

2. Melt butter in a large skillet over medium-high heat; add crab cakes, and cook 3 to 4 minutes on each side until golden. Drain on paper towels. Serve with East Coast Tartar Sauce. Garnish, if desired.

East Coast Tartar Sauce

makes 1½ cups • prep: 5 min., other: 1 hr.

1	cup mayonnaise	2	Tbsp. minced shallots
2	Tbsp. lemon juice	2	Tbsp. capers
1	tsp. Worcestershire sauce	⅛	tsp. salt
	Dash of hot sauce	⅛	tsp. pepper
¼	cup finely chopped dill pickle		
¼	cup finely chopped fresh flat-leaf parsley		

1. Stir together first 4 ingredients in a medium bowl. Add dill pickle and remaining ingredients; stir gently. Cover and chill at least 1 hour.

Grilled Oysters With Cocktail Sauce

makes 6 appetizer servings • prep: 5 min., grill: 20 min.

Laws to protect the oyster harvest in the Chesapeake Bay have been enacted since the early 1800s. Today, a law states that oysters from the bay can be harvested only by skipjacks, sail-powered boats.

test kitchen tip: Serve Grilled Oysters with our recipe for Cocktail Sauce or a splash of hot sauce and vinegar.

2	dozen fresh oysters (in the shell)
	Cocktail Sauce

1. Preheat grill to 300° to 350° (medium heat).

2. Grill oysters, covered with grill lid, over medium heat (300° to 350°) for 20 minutes or until oysters open. Serve with Cocktail Sauce.

Cocktail Sauce

makes 1½ cups • prep: 5 min., chill: 30 min.

1	(12-oz.) jar chili sauce	2	tsp. Worcestershire sauce
½	cup cider or white vinegar	1	tsp. lemon juice
2	tsp. pepper		

1. Stir together all ingredients. Cover and chill at least 30 minutes.

Sweet Potato Praline Pie

makes 8 servings • prep: 30 min., cook: 49 min.

Sweet potatoes are sometimes called yams, a name given to them by Africans who thought they resembled "nyami," a root vegetable in their native land.

3	large eggs, lightly beaten	¼	tsp. ground nutmeg
1½	cups cooked, mashed sweet potato	1⅓	cups all-purpose flour
		½	tsp. salt
1	cup evaporated milk	½	cup shortening, chilled
½	cup granulated sugar	5	to 6 Tbsp. ice water
½	cup firmly packed dark brown sugar	3	Tbsp. butter or margarine, softened
½	tsp. salt	⅓	cup firmly packed dark brown sugar
1	tsp. ground cinnamon	⅓	cup chopped pecans
¼	tsp. ground cloves		Garnish: whipped cream

test kitchen tip: Baking whole sweet potatoes takes about 45 minutes, but you can do other things while they bake. Plus, there are no dirty pots or pans. Scrub medium-size sweet potatoes, pat dry, and brush with vegetable oil. Arrange potatoes directly on oven rack, and bake at 425° for 45 minutes or until tender. Cool completely before peeling and mashing.

1. Preheat oven to 425°.

2. Whisk eggs in a large bowl. Add sweet potato and next 7 ingredients, whisking until smooth. Set aside.

3. Combine flour and ½ tsp. salt in a medium bowl; cut in shortening with a pastry blender until mixture is crumbly. Sprinkle ice water, 1 Tbsp. at a time, evenly over surface; stir with a fork until dry ingredients are moistened. Shape into a ball.

4. Roll dough into an 11-inch circle on a lightly floured surface. Fit into a 9-inch deep-dish pie plate; trim off excess pastry along edges. Fold edges under, and crimp.

5. Combine butter and ⅓ cup brown sugar, stirring until creamy. Gently spread mixture in pastry shell; sprinkle with pecans. Bake at 425° on lowest oven rack for 9 minutes.

6. Carefully open oven, and pull out oven rack, leaving pie plate on rack. Pour sweet potato filling into crust. Carefully slide rack back into oven. Reduce temperature to 350°, and bake 40 more minutes or until pie is set. Let cool completely on a wire rack. Garnish, if desired.

Florida's catch

In Miami's Little Havana, the coffee is strong, the cigar smoke pungent, beans are black, chorizo is spicy, and Cuban family ties are tight. Old men play checkers and dominos on street corners and young ones form Congo lines in the streets, especially during "Calle Oche," an annual street party. Travel to the Keys and the preferred beans are red in Caribbean island-style cuisine, where blistering pepper-flavored hot sauces and jerk seasonings are favored. Refreshing tropical fruits such as mango tame the heat. And, of course, creamy Key lime pie is king. Central Florida is horse, cattle, and rodeo country, where tables are laden with traditional Deep South favorites. The Panhandle tends toward French-Cajun-style flavors. Despite the diversity of ethnic origin, seafood is the common thread throughout the state's culinary regions. Mullet, considered a trash fish to most, is revered and smoked in the Panhandle. On the Gulf Coast, locals go "cooning" for oysters, "soft-shelling" for crabs at night, "gigging" for flounder, and seining for shrimp, all by hand like the early Native Americans did. In the 1990s a Nuevo Latino cuisine emerged to create another tie among the cultures. It was the creation of inventive chefs, who pulled together Caribbean, Latin American, and Asian flavors in fruit salsas, mojitos, and more, to continue the culinary adventure that is Florida.

Florida Clambake

makes 4 servings • prep: 20 min., cook: 30 min.

make it a meal: Whether your clambake is a seashore party or in your own backyard, offer light appetizers and icy beverages while preparing for the clambake, which is a one-dish meal in itself. Our number one dessert choice—Rum-Coconut Key Lime Pie (page 25).

4	large lettuce leaves
4	small ears fresh corn
4	(3- to 4-oz.) Florida lobster tails, split
12	littleneck clams, scrubbed
8	new potatoes, halved
1	cup unsalted butter, melted
1	(1-oz.) envelope dry onion soup mix
2	garlic cloves, pressed
2	tsp. dried oregano

1. Preheat grill to medium–high heat (350° to 400°).

2. Cut 4 large sheets of aluminum foil. Place 1 lettuce leaf in the center of each sheet. Pull back husks from corn, leaving husks attached at base of cob; remove silks. Rinse corn, and pat dry. Pull husks up over corn. Arrange 1 lobster tail, 3 clams, 1 ear of corn, and 4 potato halves over each lettuce leaf.

3. Combine butter and next 3 ingredients; drizzle over seafood mixture. Fold aluminum foil loosely around seafood mixture, sealing edges. Grill, covered with grill lid, over medium–high heat (350° to 400°) for 20 to 30 minutes or until clams open. (Discard any clams that do not open.)

Made in the Shade
The Junior League of Greater Fort Lauderdale, Florida

For a traditional clambake, clams and other seafood are baked on rocks over seaweed. This beach tradition usually means a party, as Elvis demonstrated in his movie "Clambake," filmed in Florida.

Sunshine State Salsa

makes 3½ cups • prep: 30 min., other: 24 hr.

In the 1990s when Miami chefs blended Latino and Caribbean flavors in their Nuevo Latino cuisine, fruit salsas were one of their popular creations.

test kitchen tip: Fresh jalapeño peppers give this sweet-hot salsa its kick. When you've finished removing the seeds and chopping the peppers, be careful not to touch your eyes before washing hands well with soap and water.

1   cup diced fresh mango
1   cup diced fresh papaya
¾   cup diced fresh pineapple
½   cup diced red onion
⅓   cup peeled and diced tomato
¼   cup chopped fresh cilantro
2   jalapeño peppers, seeded and chopped
⅓   cup red wine vinegar
2   Tbsp. olive oil

1. Combine all ingredients in a bowl; stir well. Serve at room temperature, or cover and chill up to 24 hours.

Jill Shockett

Signature Cuisine
Miami Country Day School Parents' Association ~ Miami, Florida

Stone Crab Bisque

makes about 8 cups • prep: 15 min., cook: 20 min.

Stone crabs are more prolific in Florida than anywhere else and just the claw is eaten. A large stone crab claw can weigh up to a half pound.

test kitchen tip: Stone crab is in season October 15 to May 15. You can order it from Joe's Stone Crab in Miami Beach, Florida, at www.joesstonecrab.com, or from your local fish monger.

½   cup butter or margarine, divided
½   cup finely chopped onion
½   cup finely chopped green bell pepper
¼   cup chopped fresh parsley
2   green onions, finely chopped
1   (8-oz.) package fresh mushrooms, chopped
¼   cup all-purpose flour
2   cups milk
3   cups half-and-half
2   tsp. salt
¼   tsp. pepper
1   tsp. hot sauce
2½ cups stone crab claw meat (22 medium claws)
¼   cup dry sherry

1. Melt ¼ cup butter in a skillet over medium-high heat; add onion and next 4 ingredients, and cook, stirring constantly, 5 minutes or until tender. Remove from skillet; set aside.

2. Melt remaining ¼ cup butter in Dutch oven over low heat; add flour, whisking until smooth. Cook 1 minute, stirring constantly. Gradually stir in milk. Cook over medium heat, stirring constantly, until thickened and bubbly.

3. Add onion mixture, half-and-half, and next 3 ingredients. Bring to a boil, stirring constantly; reduce heat, and stir in crab claw meat. Simmer 5 minutes, stirring often. Stir in sherry.

A Ritzy Mojito

makes 1 serving • prep: 5 min.

To prepare a mojito traditionally, you'll need a muddler—a wooden dowellike stick used to crush or bruise the leaves so they release refreshing mint oil. A small wooden spoon works just as well.

10 mint leaves	Ice
2 Tbsp. sugar	Splash of club soda
Juice from ½ lime	Garnish: fresh mint sprig
1½ oz. rum	

test kitchen tip: Chill a highball or Collins tumbler in the freezer before filling with this Caribbean rum drink.

1. Mix 10 mint leaves, sugar, and lime juice in a small mortar bowl; crush mint. Add rum, and stir.

2. Pour into a glass with ice. Add a splash of club soda, and garnish with a mint sprig, if desired.

Rum–Coconut Key Lime Pie

makes 8 servings • prep: 20 min., other: 4 hr.

Fresh milk wasn't easy to get in the Florida Keys before the Overseas Highway was built, so cooks depended on sweetened condensed milk. An inventive cook teamed the milk with the area's plentiful Key limes and came up with one of the state's most famous claims to fame.

1 (8-oz.) package cream cheese, softened	1 tsp. rum
	Coconut Crust
1 (14-oz.) can sweetened condensed milk	Garnish: whipped cream, grated lime rind, shredded coconut
½ cup fresh Key lime juice (about 10 Key limes)	

test kitchen tip: Real Key limes are sometimes hard to find, but bottled Key lime juice is available in the produce department of most grocery stores.

1. Beat cream cheese and milk at medium speed with an electric mixer until smooth. Add lime juice and rum, stirring to combine. Pour filling into Coconut Crust. Cover and chill at least 4 hours or until set. Garnish, if desired.

Coconut Crust

makes 1 (9-inch) piecrust • prep: 5 min., cook: 12 min.

15 cream-filled vanilla sandwich cookies, finely crushed (about 1½ cups)	1 cup sweetened flaked coconut, toasted
	6 Tbsp. butter or margarine, melted

1. Preheat oven to 350°.

2. Combine all ingredients; firmly press on bottom and up sides of a 9-inch pie plate. Bake at 350° for 12 minutes or until lightly browned. Let cool completely.

the heart of dixie

Silver is set, dainty finger foods are plated, and Mississippi women in hoop skirts wait for Natchez pilgrimage guests. The tailgate meal is spread, school colors are waved, and couples sit waiting for the game to start. The water is calm, the hook is baited, and the fisherman thinks about family dinner that night. The Deep South is today as it was in times past: a place where food is intertwined with celebration, comfort, and everyday life. Talented African-American slaves on plantations set the stage for the go-home-to-mama foods Southerners crave today—fluffy biscuits, crispy cornbread, and collard greens. Fried favorites such as okra, chicken, potatoes, and ham. Chicken and dumplings, deviled eggs, buttery grits, creamed corn, iced tea, and juicy peaches. Now it's the chefs with Southern roots who are preserving these links to the past by spotlighting them on menus in their top-rated restaurants, and finding ways to keep the flavor, yet lighten calories and fat. And, by admitting to the world that they are proud of their culinary roots. Grab a bottle of Coke—for that's something worth toasting.

Pecan–Peach Cobbler

makes 8 to 10 servings • prep: 35 min., cook: 50 min., other: 10 min.

test kitchen tip: Substitute 3 (16-oz.) packages frozen unsweetened sliced peaches if fresh peaches are out of season.

12 cups peeled, sliced fresh peaches (about 10 medium)
2   cups sugar
⅓   cup all-purpose flour
¼   tsp. ground nutmeg
2   (15-oz.) packages refrigerated piecrusts

½   cup chopped toasted pecans, divided
¼   cup sugar
1   tsp. vanilla extract
½   cup butter or margarine
Vanilla ice cream

1. Preheat oven to 475°.
2. Combine first 4 ingredients in a Dutch oven; let stand 10 minutes.
3. Unfold 2 piecrusts. Sprinkle ¼ cup pecans and 2 Tbsp. sugar evenly over 1 piecrust; top with other piecrust. Roll stacked piecrusts into a 12-inch circle, gently pressing pecans between pastry. Repeat procedure with remaining piecrusts, pecans, and sugar. Cut into 1½-inch strips. Refrigerate 9 of the longest pastry strips for top of cobbler. Place remaining strips on an ungreased baking sheet. Bake at 475° for 15 minutes or until lightly browned. Cool on a wire rack.
4. Bring peach mixture to a boil; reduce heat to low, and simmer 10 minutes or until tender. Remove from heat; add vanilla and butter, stirring until butter melts.
5. Spoon half of peach mixture into a lightly greased 13- x 9-inch baking dish. Top with baked pastry strips. Spoon remaining peach mixture over baked pastry strips. Arrange unbaked pastry strips in a lattice design over peach mixture.
6. Bake at 475° for 20 minutes or until lightly browned. Serve warm with vanilla ice cream.

Though cobblers made with meat were popular in England, colonial Southerners learned to make cobbler for dessert using what was available—peaches, apples, and berries. The best place to cool a juicy cobbler was on a wide windowsill, where the tantalizing aroma attracted possible buyers or enticed kids to come in for supper on time.

Grilled Marinated Venison Tenderloin With Blueberry Barbecue Sauce

makes 4 servings • prep: 10 min.; cook 10 min.; other: 5 hr., 10 min.

Game hunting success is a cause for celebration in the South, where the abundance of whitetail deer makes venison the game of choice.

¾	cup vegetable oil	1	Tbsp. chopped fresh parsley
¼	cup plus 2 Tbsp. soy sauce	1½	tsp. freshly ground pepper
¼	cup red wine vinegar	1	tsp. salt
3	Tbsp. fresh lemon juice	1	garlic clove, minced
2	Tbsp. Worcestershire sauce	1½	lb. venison tenderloin
1	Tbsp. dry mustard		Blueberry Barbecue Sauce

1. Combine first 10 ingredients in a large zip-top plastic freezer bag; add venison. Seal and chill 4 to 5 hours, turning bag occasionally.

2. Preheat grill to medium-high heat (350° to 400°).

3. Remove tenderloin from marinade, discarding marinade. Grill, covered with grill lid, over medium-high heat (350° to 400°) 10 minutes on each side or until meat thermometer registers 160° or to desired degree of doneness, turning once. Let stand 10 minutes before slicing. Serve tenderloin with Blueberry Barbecue Sauce.

Blueberry Barbecue Sauce

makes ⅔ cup • prep: 10 min., cook: 23 min.

2	Tbsp. minced onion	1½	Tbsp. brown sugar
1½	tsp. chopped fresh jalapeño pepper	1½	Tbsp. Dijon mustard
1½	tsp. olive oil	½	tsp. hot sauce
1	cup fresh blueberries	2	Tbsp. unsalted butter
2	Tbsp. rice vinegar	⅛	tsp. salt
2	Tbsp. ketchup	⅛	tsp. freshly ground pepper

1. Sauté onion and jalapeño pepper in hot oil in a medium saucepan over medium-high heat until tender. Add blueberries and next 5 ingredients; bring to a boil. Reduce heat, and simmer, uncovered, 15 minutes, stirring often.

2. Add butter, salt, and pepper to blueberry mixture; cook over medium heat until butter melts, stirring occasionally.

Buttermilk Batter-Fried Onion Rings

makes 4 servings • prep: 20 min., cook: 4 min. per batch

For early cooks, buttermilk was what was left of milk after butter was churned. Using it in biscuits, cornbread, and batter-fried vegetables was a great way to add flavor to favorite Southern foods.

1	lb. large Spanish onions	1	tsp. baking powder
1	cup all-purpose flour	½	tsp. salt
1	cup buttermilk		Peanut oil
1	Tbsp. sugar		

1. Cut onions into ½-inch slices, and separate into rings. Set aside.

2. Combine flour and next 4 ingredients in a medium bowl, stirring with a wire whisk until smooth.

3. Pour oil to a depth of 2 inches into a Dutch oven; heat to 375°. Dip rings into batter. Fry, in batches, 2 minutes on each side until golden, turning once. Drain on paper towels. Serve immediately.

test kitchen tip: For crisp, evenly cooked onion rings, carefully add them to the hot oil in batches and leave plenty of space between each piece. If too many onion rings are added at once, the temperature will drop and the food will absorb the oil.

Peach Butter

makes 1½ cups • prep: 15 min., cook: 33 min.

Though all states in the South grow peaches, the fruit is most associated with Georgia, thanks to an early minor league baseball team named the Georgia Peaches.

3	cups sliced fresh peaches (about 4 large)	2	Tbsp. honey
¼	cup orange juice	½	tsp. grated orange rind
¾	cup sugar	⅛	tsp. ground allspice

test kitchen tip: It's easiest to grate the orange rind before juicing the orange. Serve this silky condiment with pancakes, biscuits, or toast.

1. Combine peaches and orange juice in a saucepan; bring to a boil. Cover, reduce heat, and simmer 8 minutes or until tender, stirring occasionally. Cool slightly. Transfer mixture to a blender or food processor; process until smooth, stopping to scrape down sides.

2. Return peach mixture to saucepan; add sugar and remaining ingredients. Bring to a boil; reduce heat, and simmer, uncovered, 25 minutes or until thickened, stirring occasionally. Cool completely. Cover and store in refrigerator up to 2 weeks.

Flavors of Fredericksburg
St. Bonnabus Episcopal Church ~ Fredericksburg, Texas

lowcountry cookin'

The Gullah women sit cross-legged on the ground at Charleston's seaside market contentedly weaving their famous sweetgrass baskets. Occasionally, the dialect of their unique language is caught on the humid breeze that blows in from the bay. Down the street tourists and locals alike are getting their fill of hoppin' John and famous she-crab soup, the city's signature dish. It was the West African ancestors of these Gullah island women who brought with them staples of rice, sweet potatoes, okra, and sesame seeds, teamed them with native seafood and game, smoked meats from the German settlers, and the English immigrants' desire for sophisticated menus to fashion what is today Lowcountry cuisine along the coast from North Carolina to north Florida. It's actually a type of Creole cuisine, appearing here long before it reached New Orleans. Deep South favorites, also influenced by African cooks, spill over to the coastal cuisine. Still the sea is center of the culinary culture here, whether you're dining at a sophisticated Hilton Head restaurant or sitting cross-legged on the shore while digging into a pot of traditional Frogmore Stew rich with shrimp, corn on the cob, and red potatoes. Here, it's okay to lick your fingers.

Smothered Quail

makes 4 servings • prep: 10 min., cook: 45 min.

test kitchen tip: A savory gravy of sherry and chicken broth smothers these quail and makes a delicious sauce to serve over rice. It's important to use a good quality sherry, not cooking sherry, for this gravy.

½	cup butter or margarine
8	quail, dressed
¼	cup all-purpose flour
2	cups chicken broth

½	cup dry sherry
1	tsp. salt
¾	tsp. pepper

1. Melt butter in a large skillet over medium–high heat; add 4 quail, and brown on all sides. Repeat procedure with remaining quail.

2. Add flour to skillet, whisking until smooth. Cook 2 minutes, whisking constantly over medium heat. Gradually stir in broth and sherry; cook over medium heat, stirring constantly, until mixture is thickened and bubbly. Stir in salt and pepper.

3. Return quail to skillet; cover and simmer, stirring occasionally, 30 minutes or until tender.

V.V. Thompson

'Pon Top Edisto
Trinity Episcopal Church ~ Edisto Island, South Carolina

Quail, the game bird most associated with the South, has been important on the region's tables since the days of cotton plantations. In the early days the elite roasted them with the skin on, and the rural cooks served them skinned and fried.

Creamy Crab Soup

makes 6 cups • prep: 15 min., cook: 15 min.

She-crab soup was considered to be the perfect prelude to an elegant dinner in early Charleston society. The orange crab roe (eggs) was added simply to make it more colorful. She-crab soup is a seasonal specialty because fresh crab roe is produced only in the spring. This soup omits the roe, as most restaurants do today, to ensure that a steady crop of crab remains.

test kitchen tip: To accommodate taste preferences, stir a spoonful of sherry into individual servings rather than into the whole batch.

¼	cup butter	¼	tsp. paprika
3	Tbsp. minced onion	2	tsp. Worcestershire sauce
¼	cup all-purpose flour		Dash of Old Bay seasoning
4	cups half-and-half	1	lb. fresh lump crabmeat
½	tsp. salt	2	hard-cooked eggs, finely chopped
½	tsp. freshly ground pepper		Sherry (optional)

1. Melt butter in a Dutch oven over low heat; add onion, and cook over medium heat, stirring constantly, 5 minutes or until tender. Whisk in flour until smooth. Cook 1 minute, whisking constantly. Gradually whisk in half-and-half; cook over medium heat, whisking constantly, until mixture is thickened and bubbly. Stir in salt and next 4 ingredients.
2. Add crabmeat and hard-cooked eggs. Add sherry to taste, if desired.

Red Rice

makes 6 to 8 servings • prep: 15 min.; cook: 1 hr., 30 min.

This traditional Lowcountry dish celebrates the mixed heritages of European, African, and Native American peoples.

test kitchen tip: You can prepare this recipe in an ovenproof Dutch oven instead of a cooktop rice steamer. To do so, prepare recipe as directed through Step 2. Add uncooked rice to tomato mixture in skillet, and bring to a boil. Stir in bacon pieces. Pour mixture into a lightly greased ovenproof Dutch oven; cover and bake at 350° for 1 hour or until rice is tender.

9	bacon slices	2	tsp. sugar
1	small onion, chopped	1	tsp. salt
1	(12-oz.) can tomato paste	½	tsp. pepper
3½	cups chicken broth	2	cups uncooked long-grain rice

1. Cook bacon slices in a large skillet over medium-high heat until crisp. Remove bacon, and drain on paper towels, reserving 2 Tbsp. drippings in skillet. Crumble bacon, and set aside.
2. Sauté chopped onion in hot drippings in skillet over medium-high heat 3 minutes or until tender. Add tomato paste to skillet, stirring until mixture is smooth. Gradually stir in chicken broth, stirring to loosen particles from bottom of skillet. Stir in sugar, salt, and pepper. Bring to a boil; reduce heat, and simmer, stirring occasionally, 10 minutes.
3. Combine tomato mixture and rice in top portion of a cooktop rice steamer. Stir in crumbled bacon. Add water to bottom of steamer, and bring to a boil over high heat. (We used 4½ cups water, but amounts may vary with different steamers. Follow manufacturer's instructions.) Place the top of steamer over boiling water. Reduce heat to medium-high; cover and cook 1 hour or until rice is tender, stirring every 15 minutes.

Lane Cake

makes 16 to 24 servings • prep: 30 min., cook: 20 min., other: 10 min.

When she created this bourbon-laced fruit and nut cake in the late 1800s, Emma Rylander Lane never knew what a tradition her namesake cake would become for weddings and special occasions.

1	cup butter or margarine, softened	1	cup milk
2	cups sugar	1	tsp. vanilla extract
3½	cups sifted cake flour	8	egg whites
1	Tbsp. plus ½ tsp. baking powder		Fruit and Nut Filling
¾	tsp. salt		Fluffy White Frosting (following page)

1. Preheat oven to 375°.

2. Grease 4 (9-inch) round cake pans; line with wax paper. Grease wax paper. Set aside.

3. Beat butter at medium speed with an electric mixer until creamy; gradually add sugar, beating well.

4. Combine flour, baking powder, and salt; add to butter mixture alternately with milk, beginning and ending with flour mixture. Mix at low speed after each addition until blended. Stir in vanilla.

5. Beat egg whites at high speed until stiff peaks form. Gently fold into flour mixture. Pour batter into prepared pans.

6. Bake at 375° for 20 minutes or until a wooden pick inserted in center comes out clean. Cool in pans on wire racks 10 minutes; remove from pans, and let cool completely on wire racks.

7. Spread Fruit and Nut Filling between layers and on top of cake. Spread Fluffy White Frosting on sides of cake.

Fruit and Nut Filling

makes enough for 1 (4-layer) cake • prep: 20 min., cook: 35 min., other: 5 min.

1½	cups raisins	12	egg yolks, lightly beaten
1½	cups red candied cherries, quartered	1¾	cups sugar
1½	cups pecan halves, coarsely chopped	¾	cup butter, cut into small pieces
1½	cups flaked coconut	½	tsp. salt
		½	cup bourbon

1. Place raisins in a small saucepan, and cover with water. Bring to a boil; cover, remove from heat, and let stand 5 minutes. Drain and pat dry. Combine raisins, cherries, pecans, and coconut in a large bowl; set aside.

2. Combine egg yolks, sugar, butter, and salt in a large saucepan; cook over medium-low heat, stirring constantly, 20 minutes or until butter melts and mixture is very thick. Add bourbon; stir well. Pour over fruit and nut mixture, stirring well; cool completely.

test kitchen tip: Lining cake pans with wax paper is easy and ensures that the baked layers will release from the pans effortlessly. Before preparing batter, turn cake pan upside down, and cover completely with a sheet of wax paper. Holding the wax paper in place with one hand, gently scrape the corner of the pan with a small knife, leaving a faint line on the wax paper. Using the line as a guide, cut the wax paper into a circle to fit.

Fluffy White Frosting

makes 7 cups • prep: 15 min., cook: 15 min.

1½	cups sugar	½	tsp. cream of tartar
½	cup water	½	tsp. vanilla extract
4	egg whites		

1. Combine sugar and water in a heavy saucepan. Cook over medium heat, stirring constantly, until clear. Cook, without stirring, until mixture reaches soft-ball stage or a candy thermometer registers 240°.

2. While syrup cooks, beat egg whites and cream of tartar until soft peaks form; continue to beat, adding syrup in a heavy stream. Add vanilla; continue beating just until stiff peaks form and frosting is thick enough to spread.

Spoonbread

makes 8 servings • prep: 5 min., cook: 56 min.

The original spoonbread was more of a cornmeal pudding popular with Native Americans in the Northeast. When the recipe traveled farther south, eggs and butter were added to make this richer version.

test kitchen tip: For the richest and creamiest spoonbread, use whole milk.

4	large eggs	1½	tsp. salt
4	cups milk	3	Tbsp. butter or margarine
1	cup white cornmeal		Melted butter

1. Preheat oven to 425°.

2. Whisk eggs until thick and pale in a medium bowl; set aside.

3. Cook milk in a 3-qt. heavy nonaluminum saucepan over medium heat, stirring often, about 8 minutes or just until bubbles begin to appear around edges of pan (do not boil). Gradually whisk in cornmeal. Add salt and 3 Tbsp. butter. Cook, whisking constantly, 8 minutes or until very thick.

4. Gradually whisk about one-fourth of hot mixture into eggs; add to remaining hot mixture, whisking constantly. Pour mixture into a lightly greased 2-qt. baking dish. Bake at 425° for 40 minutes or until golden. Serve with melted butter.

Benne Seed Wafers

makes 10 dozen • prep: 45 min., cook: 15 min., other: 1 hr.

West African slaves grew benne (sesame) seeds in their slave gardens in the 1700s and considered them good luck. They added the seeds to cookies, crackers, and sweet brittle.

½ cup sesame (benne) seeds.
½ cup butter or margarine, softened
1 cup sugar
1 large egg
½ tsp. vanilla extract

1¾ cups all-purpose flour
2 tsp. baking powder
½ tsp. baking soda
½ tsp. salt

freeze it: Layer crisp Benne Seed Wafers between sheets of wax or parchment paper in an airtight container, and freeze up to 6 weeks.

1. Preheat oven to 325°.
2. Cook sesame seeds in a heavy skillet over medium heat, stirring often, 5 minutes or until toasted. Cool completely.
3. Beat butter at medium speed with an electric mixer until creamy; gradually add sugar, beating well. Stir in sesame seeds, egg, and vanilla.
4. Combine flour and next 3 ingredients; stir into butter mixture. Cover dough, and chill at least 1 hour.
5. Shape into ½-inch balls; place on lightly greased baking sheets. Flatten to ¹⁄₁₆-inch thickness with floured fingers or a flat-bottomed glass.
6. Bake at 325° for 10 minutes or until lightly browned. Transfer to wire racks to cool.
Note: Natural food stores sell sesame seeds in bulk.

mountain heritage

It was hard work farming in the mountains. But the determined group of Scots-Irish, Brits, and Germans settling along the Appalachian Mountains chain from West Virginia to north Georgia fished and hunted; dried pork, apples, and beans; churned fresh butter; and formed the foundation of Appalachian-mountain cuisine with staples of pork, chicken, apples, beans, potatoes, honey, blackberries, and corn. Travel difficulties kept the settlers home, and visitors and traders at bay, so spices were rare, ingredients were grown or foraged, and friendships were made with the Cherokees. Despite the hardscrabble life, the mountaineers found ways to celebrate while making molasses or apple butter, killing hogs, stringing beans, shucking corn, or sewing quilts. And when the work was done, strains of plunky banjos echoed between the peaks while cloggers resembling Irish dancers stepped in doubletime as they do today. Instead of abandoning the heritage of hard times, the region is now a magnet for tourists looking for a bluegrass festival or a fried apple pie at the gas station on the hairpin curve. Upscale restaurant menus reflect the region's culinary heritage, but for a true taste of the past, it's the church cookbooks that preserve the stories and stack cakes, the mountain remedies, and the delicious secrets of "making do."

Kentucky Burgoo

makes 11 qt. • prep: 1 hr., 50 min.; cook: 5 hr., 10 min.; other: 8 hr.

test kitchen tip: Chilling the soup overnight allows the fat to solidify and rise to the surface, making it easier to skim.

1	(3- to 4-lb.) cut-up whole chicken	2	cups frozen whole kernel corn
1	(2-lb.) beef chuck roast	1	cup frozen baby lima beans
2	lb. pork loin chops, trimmed	1	cup frozen English peas
5	qt. water	3	garlic cloves, minced
1	rabbit, dressed (optional)	2	(32-oz.) containers beef broth
1	lb. tomatoes	1	(32-oz.) bottle ketchup
5	large potatoes	2	cups dry red wine
5	celery ribs	1	(10-oz.) bottle Worcestershire sauce
4	carrots	¼	cup white vinegar
2	onions	1	Tbsp. salt
2	green bell peppers	1	Tbsp. pepper
1	small cabbage	1	Tbsp. dried thyme

1. Bring first 4 ingredients and rabbit, if desired, to a boil in a 4-gal. heavy stockpot. Cover, reduce heat, and simmer 1 hour or until tender. Remove meats from stockpot, and cool. Skin, bone and shred meats; return meats to stockpot.
2. Cover and chill soup overnight. Skim solidified fat from surface. Chop tomatoes and next 5 ingredients. Shred cabbage. Add prepared vegetables, corn, and remaining ingredients to soup; cook over low heat, stirring often, 4 hours.
Note: Portion leftovers into individual servings in airtight containers, and freeze up to 2 months.

In Kentucky, burgoo is a favorite church supper or fund-raiser dinner that's cooked by a crowd and eaten by a crowd. Traditionally, it contained mutton that was raised in the state.

Bluegrass BBQ Chicken

makes 3 to 4 servings • prep: 5 min., cook: 25 min., other: 8 hr.

Chicken is the most widely available source of meat in the world. And no where is there a better dish than the South's barbecued chicken.

make it a meal: Serve Bluegrass BBQ Chicken with corn-on-the-cob, slaw, and Blackberry Cobbler (page 41).

¾	cup Worcestershire sauce	½	(8-oz.) jar horseradish mustard
½	cup water	2	tsp. salt
½	cup apple cider vinegar	1	tsp. chili powder
½	cup butter or margarine	1	(3-lb.) cut-up whole chicken

1. Combine first 7 ingredients in a medium saucepan; bring to a boil, stirring occasionally. Remove marinade from heat, and cool.

2. Place chicken pieces in an ungreased 13- x 9-inch dish. Pour marinade over chicken. Cover and chill 8 hours.

3. Preheat grill to medium heat (300° to 350°).

4. Remove chicken from marinade, discarding marinade. Grill chicken, covered with grill lid, over medium heat (300° to 350°) about 10 minutes on each side or until done.

Creating a Stir
The Fayette County Medical Auxiliary ~ Lexington, Kentucky

Tabb's Barbecue Pork

makes 8 servings • prep: 30 min.; cook: 8 hr.; other: 9 hr., 15 min.

"Long and slow" is the motto of North Carolina pitmaster Jim "Trim" Tabb when it comes to barbecue. His recipe below will convince you.

test kitchen tip: Transform leftover barbecue pork into Brunswick stew, barbecue pizza, or a main-dish salad.

1	(6-lb.) bone-in pork shoulder roast (Boston butt)	Hickory wood chunks
1	cup Barbecue Rub	Apple juice

1. Trim fat on pork shoulder roast to about ⅛ inch thick. Sprinkle pork evenly with Barbecue Rub; rub thoroughly into meat. Wrap pork tightly with plastic wrap, and chill 8 hours.

2. Discard plastic wrap. Let pork stand at room temperature 1 hour.

3. Soak hickory chunks in water 1 hour.

4. Prepare smoker according to manufacturer's instructions, bringing internal temperature to 225° to 250°; maintain temperature for 15 to 20 minutes.

5. Drain wood chunks, and place on coals. Place pork on lower cooking grate, fat side up. Spritz pork with apple juice each time charcoal or wood chunks are added to the smoker.

6. Smoke pork roast, maintaining the temperature inside smoker between 225° and 250°, for 6 hours or until a meat thermometer inserted horizontally into thickest portion of pork registers 170°.

7. Remove pork from smoker, and place on a sheet of heavy-duty aluminum foil; spritz with apple juice. Wrap tightly, and return to smoker, and smoke 2 hours or until thermometer inserted into the thickest portion of pork registers 190°. Remove pork from smoker, and let stand 15 minutes. Remove bone, and chop pork.

Barbecue Rub

makes about 3 cups • prep: 15 min.

1¼	cups firmly packed dark brown sugar	1	Tbsp. ground cumin
⅓	cup kosher salt	1	Tbsp. lemon pepper
¼	cup granulated garlic	1	Tbsp. onion powder
¼	cup paprika	2	tsp. dry mustard
1	Tbsp. chili powder	2	tsp. ground black pepper
1	Tbsp. ground red pepper	1	tsp. ground cinnamon

1. Combine all ingredients. Store in an airtight container.

Bourbon Pound Cake

makes 20 to 24 servings • prep: 40 min.; cook: 1 hr., 20 min.; other: 15 min.

Southern cooks loved making pound cakes because the recipe was easy to remember—one pound each of flour, sugar, butter, and eggs. Cakes were flavored with whatever ingredients were regionally available. In Kentucky, that meant bourbon.

½	cup chopped pecans	⅓	cup bourbon
8	large eggs, separated	2	tsp. vanilla extract
3	cups granulated sugar, divided	2	tsp. almond extract
2	cups butter, softened		Sifted powdered sugar
3	cups all-purpose flour		

test kitchen tip: Before beating egg whites in Step 3, make sure the bowl and beaters are clean and free of fat. Even a small amount of fat, such as egg yolk or butter, can prevent egg whites from whipping properly.

1. Preheat oven to 350°.

2. Generously grease a 10-inch tube pan; sprinkle pecans in pan.

3. Beat egg whites at high speed with an electric mixer until soft peaks form. Gradually add 1 cup granulated sugar, 1 Tbsp. at a time, beating until stiff peaks form and sugar dissolves (2 to 4 minutes). Set aside.

4. Beat butter in a separate large mixing bowl at medium speed about 2 minutes or until creamy; gradually add remaining 2 cups granulated sugar, beating at medium speed 5 to 7 minutes. Add egg yolks, 1 at a time, beating just until yellow disappears.

5. Add flour to butter mixture alternately with bourbon, beginning and ending with flour. Mix at low speed just until blended after each addition. Stir in flavorings. Fold in one-third of beaten egg white mixture. Gently fold in remaining egg white mixture, and spoon into prepared pan.

6. Bake on bottom rack of oven at 350° for 1 hour and 20 minutes or until a wooden pick inserted in center comes out clean. (Cover with aluminum foil to prevent excessive browning, if necessary.) Cool in pan on a wire rack 10 to 15 minutes; remove from pan, and let cool completely on wire rack. Sprinkle top of cake with powdered sugar.

Apple Stack Cake

makes 12 to 16 servings • prep: 25 min., cook: 30 min., other: 2 days

Cooks in the Appalachians found a great way to use dried sweet apples as filling for cakes with up to 8 thin layers. Some cooks poured batter into cake pans to bake, and others rolled out the dough and cut it into rounds.

test kitchen tip: Don't be tempted to eat the cake until it has stood for 2 days. This standing time allows the moisture from the filling to seep throughout the cake and fill it with moist, slightly spicy goodness.

⅓	cup shortening	½	tsp. salt
½	cup sugar	½	cup buttermilk
1	large egg	½	cup molasses
4	cups all-purpose flour	2½	tsp. sugar
1	tsp. baking powder		Dried Apple Filling
1	tsp. baking soda		

1. Preheat oven to 400°.

2. Beat shortening at medium speed with an electric mixer 2 minutes or until creamy. Gradually add ½ cup sugar, beating 5 to 7 minutes. Add egg, beating until yellow disappears.

3. Combine flour and next 3 ingredients. Stir together buttermilk and molasses in a large measuring cup. Gradually add flour mixture to shortening mixture alternately with buttermilk mixture, beginning and ending with flour mixture. Beat at low speed just until blended after each addition.

4. Divide dough into 5 equal portions; place each portion in a 9-inch greased and floured cakepan, and firmly press with floured fingers into pan. Prick dough several times with a fork. Sprinkle each layer evenly with ½ tsp. sugar.

5. Bake at 400° for 10 minutes or until golden brown. (Only bake layers on 1 rack at a time.) Repeat procedure as needed to bake in pans. Remove layers from pans; cool completely on wire racks.

6. Spread 1½ cups Dried Apple Filling between each layer to within ½ inch of edge, beginning and ending with a cake layer. (Save your prettiest cake layer for the top.) Loosely cover cake, and let stand 2 days at room temperature.

Dried Apple Filling

makes 6 cups • prep: 5 min., cook: 55 min.

3	(6-oz.) packages dried sliced apples	1	tsp. ground cinnamon (optional)
1	cup firmly packed brown sugar	½	tsp. ground allspice (optional)
1	tsp. ground ginger (optional)	½	tsp. ground nutmeg (optional)

1. Stir together apples and 6 cups water in a large saucepan or Dutch oven. Bring to a boil; reduce heat, and simmer 30 minutes or until tender. Stir in sugar, and, if desired, spices. Return mixture to a boil; reduce heat, and simmer, stirring occasionally, 10 to 15 minutes or until most of liquid has evaporated. Cool completely.

Blackberry Cobbler

makes 8 servings • prep: 16 min.; cook: 1 hr., 4 min.; other: 10 min.

Blackberry bushes grow wild throughout the South on road-sides, in fields, near seashores, and in the mountains. Though some thornless bushes are now cultivated, it's worth fighting thorny, untamed branches for the sweet purple juice.

7	(6-oz.) containers fresh blackberries (about 9 cups)	1	(15-oz.) package refrigerated piecrusts
2¼	cups sugar	¼	cup butter or margarine, cut up
⅓	cup all-purpose flour		Sugar
1	tsp. lemon juice		Vanilla ice cream (optional)

test kitchen tip: We baked half the pastry in Step 3 until it was browned and crisp before assembling the cobbler. That way, the pastry remained flaky even when nestled between layers of juicy blackberries.

1. Preheat oven to 425°.

2. Stir together first 4 ingredients; let mixture stand 10 minutes or until sugar dissolves.

3. Unroll 1 piecrust, and cut into 1½-inch-wide strips. Place strips on a lightly greased baking sheet. Bake at 425° for 9 minutes or until lightly browned. Remove to a wire rack, and cool. Break strips into 2-inch pieces.

4. Reduce oven to 350°.

5. Spoon half of blackberry mixture into a lightly greased 13- x 9-inch baking dish; top with baked pastry pieces. Spoon remaining blackberry mixture over pastry; dot with butter.

6. Unroll remaining piecrust; cut into 1-inch strips, and arrange in a lattice design over filling. Sprinkle piecrust with additional sugar. Bake at 350° for 55 minutes or until crust is golden and center is bubbly. Serve with vanilla ice cream, if desired.

Texan treasures

Tall pitchers of cold, sweet iced tea, platters of fried chicken, and bowls of black-eyed peas let you know that East Texas is part of the traditional South. But a short journey southward to the bluebonnet-covered Hill Country and you may think you've arrived in Germany as you pass through the towns of Ekhert, New Braunfels, and Gruene, and smell sausage as it sizzles on flaming grills. Keep going south and accordion notes turn into mariachi music in San Antonio, home of tamales, huevos rancheros, homemade tortillas, and blistering salsa. Travel west across the vast treeless lands to cowboy country, where sourdough biscuits bake soft and crusty in cast-iron pots and a chili cook-off is probably around the corner. Still, there are several things Texans—from the Neiman-Marcus shopper to the dusty rodeo cowboy—can agree on: Barbecue means beef. Beef is king. It's a ranch, not a farm. Boots and cowboy hats are formal dress. Don't criticize religion or mess with someone's mama. And there ain't no beans in chili!

Hot Tamales

makes 8 to 12 servings • prep: 1 hr.; cook: 1 hr., 40 min.; other: 2 hr.

test kitchen tip: Find dry corn husks in the produce section of large supermarkets or in Hispanic specialty markets.

½	(8-oz.) package corn husks or about 9 whole dried corn husks (we tested with Don Enrique)	2	Tbsp. ground cumin
		1	Tbsp. ground red pepper
		1	tsp. black pepper
¾	cup yellow cornmeal	3	lb. lean ground beef
½	cup plus 1 Tbsp. chili powder	1	(8-oz.) can tomato sauce
3	Tbsp. onion powder	¾	cup water
1	Tbsp. plus 1 tsp. salt	1	large egg
1	Tbsp. garlic powder		Tamale Sauce

1. Place whole corn husks in a large bowl (each husk should contain several layers); cover with hot water. Let stand 1 to 2 hours or until softened. Remove any silks; rinse husks well. Drain well, and pat dry. Separate layers of corn husks; set aside.

2. Combine cornmeal and next 11 ingredients; stir well. Roll meat mixture into 24 (4-inch) logs. Place 1 log in center of 1 layer of corn husk; wrap husk tightly around meat. Twist ends of husks; tie securely with narrow strips of softened corn husk or pieces of string. Cut off long ends of husks, if necessary.

3. Layer tamales in a Dutch oven; drizzle with Tamale Sauce. Bring to a boil; reduce heat, and simmer, uncovered, 1½ hours, turning tamales every 30 minutes.

Tamale Sauce

makes 9½ cups sauce • prep: 10 min.

1	(6-oz.) can tomato paste	1	Tbsp. salt
¼	cup chili powder	1	Tbsp. ground cumin
2	Tbsp. onion powder	2	tsp. garlic powder

1. Combine all ingredients and 9 cups water in a large bowl, stirring until smooth.

Many Southerners embrace the Mexican tamale party tradition of gathering with friends and family for a long day of tamale making the day before Christmas.

Grandmother's Texas Barbecued Brisket

makes 8 servings • prep: 15 min.; cook: 5 hr.; other: 8 hr., 10 min.

In addition to beef, traditional central Texas barbecue includes smoked sausage and is served with slices of white loaf bread to make a sandwich or sop up the savory juices.

make it a meal: In Texas, must-have barbecue sides include coleslaw, potato salad, pinto beans, pickles, onions, tea, soda, and beer.

1	(3- to 4-lb.) beef brisket	½	cup barbecue sauce
1	tsp. celery salt	2	Tbsp. ketchup
1	tsp. garlic powder	2	Tbsp. Worcestershire sauce
1	tsp. onion salt	½	tsp. liquid smoke

1. Trim fat from brisket to ⅛-inch thickness.

2. Combine celery salt, garlic powder, and onion salt. Sprinkle brisket evenly with mixture, and rub thoroughly into meat.

3. Stir together barbecue sauce and next 3 ingredients until blended. Brush barbecue sauce mixture evenly onto brisket. Wrap brisket in heavy-duty aluminum foil; place in a roasting pan. Chill 8 hours.

4. Preheat oven to 300°.

5. Bake at 300° for 5 hours or until a meat thermometer inserted in thickest portion registers 190°. Let stand 10 minutes. Slice brisket thinly across the grain.

Blue Corn Muffins With Cheddar Cheese and Pine Nuts

makes 1 dozen • prep: 20 min., cook: 35 min.

Blue corn, a variety with bluish kernels, was a favorite of the southwestern Native Americans for making tortillas. Ground into meal and baked into breads, it has a nuttier flavor and courser texture than yellow cornmeal.

test kitchen tip: Blue cornmeal can be found in the specialty section of most supermarkets. If you can't find it, substitute plain white or yellow cornmeal.

1¼	cups all-purpose flour	2	tsp. salt
½	cup blue cornmeal	¾	cup buttermilk
1	tsp. baking soda	¾	cup (3 oz.) shredded white Cheddar
1	tsp. baking powder		cheese
1	large egg, lightly beaten	2	green onions, thinly sliced
½	cup vegetable oil	½	cup pine nuts, toasted
⅓	cup sugar		

1. Preheat oven to 350°. Combine first 4 ingredients in a large bowl; make a well in center of mixture. Combine egg, oil, sugar, salt, and buttermilk; add to dry ingredients, stirring just until moistened. Add Cheddar cheese and remaining ingredients, and stir just until blended.

2. Spoon batter into greased muffin pans, filling two-thirds full. Bake at 350° for 30 to 35 minutes or until lightly browned and a wooden pick inserted in center comes out clean.

Settings on the Dock of the Bay
Assistance League of the Bay Area ~ Houston, Texas

Fresh Salsa

makes 3½ cups • prep: 10 min., other: 1 hr.

Salsa dates back to the 1500s when Aztec lords mixed tomatoes and chili peppers to put on their meat and seafood. The word salsa is Spanish for "sauce."

1	jalapeño pepper, seeded and minced	2	Tbsp. vinegar
1	medium cucumber, peeled and diced	2	Tbsp. olive oil
4	large plum tomatoes, chopped	1	tsp. sugar
½	cup finely chopped fresh cilantro	1	tsp. ground cumin
		½	tsp. salt
			Tortilla chips

test kitchen tip: This highly rated recipe pairs perfectly with tortilla chips but you can also serve it with grilled pork, chicken, or fish.

1. Stir together first 9 ingredients in a small bowl. Cover and chill at least 1 hour. Serve with tortilla chips.

Virginia's jewels

Just minutes away from the Tidewater Coast, where watermen pull in their haul of fresh crabs and oysters, pepper-coated country hams hang from wooden rafters in famous Smithfield, as they have for centuries. Nearby, pork barbecue soaked in tangy sauce feeds the locals, who wash it down with a glass of sweet tea. Up the road, 5-star restaurants do what Thomas Jefferson encouraged his African cooks to do: Incorporate local specialties of country ham, seafood, game, peanuts, and garden vegetables into classic French cuisine. Here, down home meets sophisticated—buy boiled peanuts at the gas station or dine on creamy peanut soup at the best restaurant. Grab a country ham biscuit at the local diner, or savor a brown sugar-crusted country ham roast for a holiday meal. Hunt deer and turkey in camo or don a scarlet jacket and join a fox hunt club. In central Virginia the cuisine is much like the Deep South's, and in the western part of the state, tables are spread Appalachian mountain-style. Virginians are the best at paying homage to the past and keeping with the times. Country ham companies now ship cooked, sliced hams to your door, the state's wine industry has come into its own with awards and festivals galore, and the nation's top chefs never cease to find new ways to add to the state's unsurpassed culinary history.

Country Ham With Red-Eye Gravy and Beaten Biscuits

makes 4 servings • prep: 5 min., cook: 15 min.

test kitchen tip: Expect red-eye gravy to be slightly thicker than the natural juices served with roast beef, referred to as au jus (ah ZHOO). We suggest simmering red-eye gravy until reduced by half.

3   (⅛- to ¼-inch-thick) country ham
     slices
¼   cup butter or margarine
¼   cup firmly packed light brown sugar
     (optional)

1   cup strong brewed coffee
     Beaten Biscuits (page 48)

1. Cut ham slices into serving-size pieces. Make cuts in fat to keep ham from curling.
2. Melt butter over low heat in a heavy skillet; add ham, and cook, in batches, 3 to 5 minutes on each side or until lightly browned. Remove ham from skillet, and keep warm. Reserve drippings in skillet.
3. Stir brown sugar into hot drippings until dissolved, if desired. Add coffee, and bring to a boil; reduce heat, and simmer 5 minutes. Serve with ham and Beaten Biscuits.

Thrifty mountain cooks added coffee to ham drippings to make a cheap sauce to go with meat. One story says that the gravy got its name when Andrew Jackson asked his drunken cook to bring him a gravy as "red as your eyes." Other stories trace the red-eye concept to the eye-opening jolt one gets from the strong hot coffee in the gravy.

Beaten Biscuits

makes 28 • prep: 15 min., cook: 20 min.

Cooks originally beat these thin little biscuits up to 45 minutes by hand to develop their hard, crisp texture. This food processor version simplifies the process.

2 cups all-purpose flour
1 tsp. salt
½ cup cold butter, cut into small pieces
⅓ cup ice water

1. Preheat oven to 400°.
2. Process flour and salt in food processor 5 seconds; add butter, and process 10 seconds or until mixture is crumbly.
3. With food processor running, pour water through food chute in a slow, steady stream; process until mixture forms a ball.
4. Turn dough out onto a lightly floured surface. Roll dough to a ⅛-inch thickness. Fold dough in half; cut with a 1-inch round biscuit cutter. Place on an ungreased baking sheet. Prick top of each biscuit with a fork 3 times. Bake at 400° for 20 minutes or until lightly browned.

Old Virginia Peanut Pie

makes 8 servings • prep: 20 min., cook: 50 min., other: 1 hr.

Peanuts have been a cash crop in Virginia for more than 400 years. You'll find pies like this one with a crunchy layer of nuts over a creamy, sweet filling in homestyle diners around the state.

test kitchen tip: Once opened, vacuum-packed peanuts keep at room temperature for about a month or in the refrigerator for up to 6 months.

1 cup dark corn syrup
⅔ cup sugar
⅓ cup butter or margarine, melted
3 large eggs, lightly beaten
1 tsp. vanilla extract
⅛ tsp. salt
1 cup unsalted roasted peanuts
1 unbaked deep-dish 9-inch piecrust shell
1 cup whipping cream, whipped

1. Preheat oven to 350°.
2. Whisk together first 6 ingredients in a large bowl until thoroughly blended; stir in peanuts. Pour into piecrust shell.
3. Bake at 350° for 50 minutes or until a knife inserted in center comes out clean, shielding edges with aluminum foil after 25 minutes to prevent excess browning, if necessary. Cool on a wire rack 1 hour or until completely cool. Serve with whipped cream.

The William & Mary Cookbook
Society of the Alumni, College of William and Mary ~ Williamsburg, Virginia

a world of flavors

Fresh Mozzarella and Basil Pizza, page 61

a world of flavors

Early immigrants, particularly European and African settlers, brought their heritage homestyle cooking as well as agricultural ideas to this vast region to shape the oldest Southern food traditions. In addition, those traditions have been richly flavored by new waves of immigrants with unique food heritages, worldwide influences broadcast by mass media, new cooking techniques fueled by technology, and an ever-increasing availability of global ingredients. Just in recent decades, Mexican, Thai, Vietnamese, and other ethnic cuisines, have seduced our taste buds and forever tweaked the seasonings of the South. Celebrate this glorious ever-changing melting pot that is Southern cuisine with some of our favorite worldly homestyle recipes featured here.

Quick Baba Ghanoujh

makes 1⅓ cups • prep: 15 min., cook: 10 min.

make it ahead: This dip can be refrigerated up to 5 days or frozen up to 1 month. If frozen, thaw it overnight in the refrigerator and allow it to return to room temperature before serving.

1	large eggplant (about 1 to 1½ lb.)
3	garlic cloves, minced
3	Tbsp. tahini
2	Tbsp. lemon juice
½	tsp. salt
⅛	tsp. ground cumin
2	Tbsp. olive oil

Garnishes: kalamata olives, fresh parsley sprigs

1. Remove and discard ends of eggplant (do not peel). Prick eggplant with a fork. Microwave at HIGH 7 to 10 minutes or until eggplant is tender; cool completely.

2. Cut eggplant in half lengthwise, and scrape out soft pulp; discard shell. Process pulp, garlic, tahini, lemon juice, salt, and cumin in a food processor until smooth. Add water to reach desired consistency, if necessary. Place mixture in a shallow serving dish; drizzle with olive oil. Garnish, if desired. Serve with pita bread.

Classically Kiawah
The Alternatives Kiawah Island, South Carolina

Middle Eastern foods such as this garlicky eggplant dip have come to be common across the South as folks try to eat more healthfully. Tahini, a key ingredient in this Middle Eastern puree, is a paste made of sesame seeds. Find it on the ethnic foods aisle.

Moravian Sugar Cake

makes 15 servings • prep: 20 min.; cook: 15 min.; other: 1 hr., 20 min

Moravians traditionally used boiled and mashed potatoes in this dough to give it a distinctive, moist texture. Our updated version uses instant potato flakes instead.

test kitchen tip: If your kitchen is cool and drafty, use your oven to proof the dough in Steps 2 and 3. To do so, turn on the oven to its lowest temperature setting for 2 minutes or until it's barely warm. Turn off oven, and add the dough to rise.

2   (¼-oz.) envelopes active dry yeast
½   tsp. granulated sugar
½   cup warm water (105° to 115°)
1   cup butter or margarine, melted and divided
¾   cup water
½   cup granulated sugar

¼   cup instant potato flakes
2   Tbsp. instant nonfat dry milk powder
½   tsp. salt
2   large eggs
3   cups all-purpose flour
1   cup firmly packed brown sugar
1   tsp. ground cinnamon

1. Combine first 3 ingredients in a 1-cup liquid measuring cup, and let stand 5 minutes.

2. Combine yeast mixture, ½ cup melted butter, ¾ cup water, and next 5 ingredients in a large mixing bowl. Add 1 cup flour; beat at low speed with an electric mixer 2 minutes. Stir in enough remaining 2 cups flour to make a soft dough. Cover and let rise in a warm place (85°), free from drafts, 45 minutes or until doubled in bulk.

3. Punch dough down; spread in a greased 15- x 10-inch jelly-roll pan. Cover and let rise in a warm place (85°), free from drafts, 30 minutes.

4. Preheat oven to 375°. Make shallow indentations in dough at 1-inch intervals, using the handle of a wooden spoon. Drizzle with remaining ½ cup butter. Combine brown sugar and cinnamon; sprinkle over dough.

5. Bake at 375° for 12 to 15 minutes. Cut into squares.

three centuries of sweet tradition
The sight of ooey, gooey Moravian Sugar Cakes and the scent of cinnamon-and-ginger-spiced paper-thin molasses cookies tempt those passing by the Moravian bakery in the living history village of Old Salem, North Carolina. With each sniff, the food traditions of the Protestant Moravians, who emigrated as missionaries from modern-day Czechoslovakia in the 1700s, are still evident. Thriving yet in the 24 churches in the area is the "Lovefeast" on Christmas Eve, a service of hymns that includes a ritual serving of mace, lemon, and orange-flavored sweet buns and coffee or cider. "It's this sort of custom that is the glue of any group and keeps us together," says Moravian archivist Richard Starbucks. Though busy Moravians now get buns from the local bakery instead of making them, the heritage of a people lives on in every bite.

Black Fruitcake

makes 20 to 24 servings • prep: 30 min.; cook: 2 hr., 10 min.; other: 10 days

Sharon Green of Atlanta always serves this luscious rum-soaked fruitcake, which reflects her Jamaican origin as she celebrates Kwanzaa. Kwanzaa means "first fruits." Sharon says the key is in the soaking. "The longer you soak it, the better the flavor and texture of the cake. Some of my family start soaking the fruit months ahead," she confides.

1¾ cups currants

1½ cups raisins

1½ cups pitted prunes

1   (8-oz.) package candied cherries

½   (7-oz.) package mixed dried fruit

2   cups dark rum

6   large eggs

⅛   tsp. ground cinnamon

⅛   tsp. ground nutmeg

1   cup butter

½   lb. dark brown sugar

2   cups all-purpose flour

1½ tsp. baking powder

¼   cup burnt sugar syrup
     (see note below)

2   cups tawny port wine, divided

Whipped cream

Garnish: ground nutmeg

test kitchen tip: As the cake cools, cut a piece of triple-thickness cheesecloth big enough to completely wrap the entire cake for soaking.

1. Combine first 6 ingredients in a large bowl; cover fruit mixture, and chill 8 hours or up to 1 week.

2. Preheat oven to 300°.

3. Process fruit mixture, in batches, in a food processor until smooth, stopping to scrape down sides; set aside fruit puree.

4. Whisk together eggs, cinnamon, and nutmeg until foamy.

5. Beat butter and brown sugar at medium speed with an electric mixer until creamy. Add egg mixture, beating until blended. Add fruit puree; blend well.

6. Combine flour and baking powder; stir into fruit mixture. Stir in burnt sugar syrup. Spoon batter evenly into a greased and floured 10-inch springform pan.

7. Bake at 300° for 2 hours and 10 minutes or until a wooden pick inserted in center comes out clean. Cool in pan on a wire rack 1 hour; remove from pan, and cool completely on wire rack.

8. Carefully brush 1 cup port wine evenly over top of cake, and let stand 10 minutes. Soak cheesecloth in remaining 1 cup wine, wrap around cake, and place in an airtight container. Let stand 2 to 3 days. (Do not refrigerate.)

9. Serve cake with whipped cream, and garnish, if desired.

Note: Burnt sugar syrup is available online at evesales.com or by mail order from Eve Sales Corporation at 945 Close Avenue, Bronx, NY 10473; or call (718) 589-6800. The syrup costs $1.75 plus shipping.

Linzer Cookies

makes about 3 dozen • prep: 25 min., cook: 15 min. per batch, other: 1 hr.

These Austrian Christmas cookies have ingredients similar to the famous linzertorte. Black currant jam is the traditional filling for the sandwich cookies.

1¼ cups butter, softened
1 cup powdered sugar, sifted
2½ cups all-purpose flour
½ cup finely chopped pecans, toasted
¼ tsp. salt

¼ tsp. ground cloves
¼ tsp. ground cinnamon
1 tsp. grated lemon rind
¼ cup seedless raspberry jam
Powdered sugar

1. Beat butter at medium speed with an electric mixer; gradually add 1 cup powdered sugar, beating until light and fluffy.

2. Combine flour and next 5 ingredients; gradually add to butter mixture, beating just until blended. Divide dough into 2 equal portions. Cover and chill 1 hour.

3. Preheat oven to 325°.

4. Roll each portion to ⅛-inch thickness on a lightly floured surface; cut with a 3-inch star-shaped cutter. Cut centers out of half of cookies with a 1½-inch star-shaped cutter. Place all stars on lightly greased baking sheets.

5. Bake at 325° for 13 to 15 minutes; cool on wire racks. Spread 3-inch solid cookies with jam, and top with hollow cookie stars. Sprinkle remaining stars with additional powdered sugar.

Tiramisù Toffee Trifle Pie

makes 8 to 10 servings • prep: 25 min., other: 8 hr.

Tiramisù, an Italian dessert, means "pick me up." It's traditionally made with delicate ladyfingers, but this highly rated version instead uses a Southern phenomenon—pound cake.

1½ Tbsp. instant coffee granules

¾ cup warm water

1 (10.75-oz.) frozen pound cake, thawed

1 (8-oz.) package mascarpone or cream cheese, softened

½ cup powdered sugar

½ cup chocolate syrup

1 (12-oz.) container frozen whipped topping, thawed and divided

2 (1.4-oz.) English toffee candy bars, coarsely chopped

test kitchen tip: Mascarpone (mas-kar-POHN or mas-kahr-POH-nay) cheese is a luxurious, triple-cream Italian cheese made from cow's milk. Find it with specialty cheeses in your grocer's dairy case. If it's unavailable, substitute cream cheese.

1. Stir together coffee granules and ¾ cup warm water until granules are dissolved. Cool.

2. Cut pound cake into 14 slices. Cut each slice in half diagonally. Place triangles on bottom and up sides of a 9-inch deep-dish pie plate. Drizzle coffee over cake.

3. Beat mascarpone cheese, sugar, and chocolate syrup at medium speed with an electric mixer until smooth. Add 2½ cups whipped topping, and beat until light and fluffy.

4. Spread cheese mixture evenly over coffee-soaked cake. Dollop remaining whipped topping around edges of pie. Sprinkle with chopped candy. Chill 8 hours.

the "wurst" of days

You can find bratwurst, knockwurst, bockwurst, bierwurst, blutwurst, and every other kind of wurst at the Wurstfest in New Braunfels, Texas, where it's held each year to keep the area's German heritage alive. Besides the sausage, mustard, and beer, you're likely to hear polka music, join in a chicken dance, and generally enjoy the Gemutlichkeit or "fun and fellowship, German-style." That camaraderie can be found at Oktoberfests and other German celebrations throughout the South, where German settlers flocked in the 1700s and 1800s. In Covington, Kentucky, 30% of the population claim German heritage; in upland South Carolina, mustard-based barbecue sauce is a gift from the Bavarians. In northeast Virginia, the Appalachian valleys, Huntsville, Alabama, and even Roberts Cove, a spot deep in Acadiana, Louisiana, residents share German roots and celebrate each year with food, fun, and plenty of lederhosen.

Easy Chicken Cassoulet

makes 8 to 10 servings • prep: 12 min., cook: 1 hr., other: 10 min.

Cassoulet, a hearty French casserole containing white beans, can literally take days to prepare the old-fashioned way, which starts out with cooking and boning a duck. This streamlined method (minus the duck) offers great flavor in a fraction of the time. Cassoulet is considered by many to be the origin of our Southern "casserole."

make it a meal: This hearty French casserole is practically a meal in itself. Pair it with a light salad of mesclun greens with a balsamic vinaigrette, French bread, and a crisp Chardonnay.

8	skinned and boned chicken thighs	3	(15-oz.) cans navy beans, drained
3	Tbsp. olive oil	1	cup shredded Parmesan cheese
2	cups sliced fresh mushrooms	1	cup fine, dry breadcrumbs
2	to 3 tsp. minced fresh or dried rosemary	1	tsp. salt
½	cup vermouth or chicken broth	½	tsp. pepper
1	(12-oz.) jar mushroom gravy	2	Tbsp. butter or margarine, cut up

1. Preheat oven to 350°.

2. Brown chicken on both sides in hot oil in a 12-inch cast-iron skillet over medium-high heat. Add mushrooms and rosemary, and cook, stirring constantly, 3 minutes or until tender. Stir in vermouth, and cook 5 minutes.

3. Spoon mushroom gravy in a lightly greased 2½-qt. baking dish. Top with beans and chicken thighs. Spoon mushroom mixture over chicken. Sprinkle with Parmesan cheese, breadcrumbs, salt, and pepper; dot with butter.

4. Bake at 350° for 35 to 40 minutes. Let stand 10 minutes before serving.

Shepherd's Pie

makes 6 servings • prep: 30 min.; cook: 1 hr., 25 min.

Shepherd's Pie is a traditional English way to use lamb—the meat with gravy is in the bottom and the top crust is a layer of mashed potatoes. This version uses ground beef instead; it's a play on our favorite Southern combo—meat loaf and mashed potatoes.

make it ahead: Prepare Shepherd's Pie through Step 5 just before baking. Cover with plastic wrap, and refrigerate overnight. Uncover and bake at 350° for 35 to 40 minutes or until lightly browned.

1	lb. ground round	1½	tsp. salt, divided
1	large onion, chopped	½	tsp. pepper, divided
3	medium carrots, chopped	1	Tbsp. cornstarch
1	large green pepper, chopped	1	Tbsp. cold water
1	medium tomato, chopped	1½	lb. baking potatoes, peeled and cubed
¼	cup chopped fresh parsley		
½	cup plus 2 Tbsp. chicken broth	2	Tbsp. butter or margarine
3	Tbsp. Worcestershire sauce	¼	cup milk

1. Preheat oven to 350°.

2. Brown beef and onion in a large skillet, stirring until meat crumbles. Add carrot, and cook until tender; drain. Add green pepper, tomato, parsley, broth, Worcestershire sauce, ¾ tsp. salt, and ¼ tsp. pepper. Bring to a boil;

reduce heat, and simmer, uncovered, 15 minutes.

3. Combine cornstarch and water, stirring until smooth. Stir into meat mixture. Cook, stirring constantly, until mixture is thickened and bubbly; cook 1 more minute, stirring constantly. Remove from heat; keep warm.

4. Cook potato in boiling water to cover 15 minutes or until tender; drain well. Return to pan. Add butter, and mash with a potato masher. Stir in milk, remaining ¾ tsp. salt, and remaining ¼ tsp. pepper. Mash until smooth.

5. Spoon meat mixture into a greased 11- x 7-inch baking dish. Spread potato mixture over meat, sealing edges. Bake, uncovered, at 350° for 30 minutes or until lightly browned.

Laura Perry

Designer's Recipes for Living
East Tennessee Interior Design Society ~ Knoxville, Tennessee

Roasted Chicken With 40 Cloves of Garlic

makes 4 to 6 servings • prep: 25 min.; cook: 1 hr., 50 min.

Garlic cloves baked whole and slow give a sweet nutty flavor to food such as this roasted chicken. Don't be overwhelmed by the amount of garlic in this traditional French dish. The intense flavor of raw garlic mellows and sweetens as it roasts slowly.

1	(4- to 5-lb.) roasting chicken	½	tsp. freshly ground black pepper
3	fresh thyme sprigs	1	large onion, quartered
1	fresh rosemary sprig	2	celery ribs, cut into 2-inch pieces
1	lemon, halved	2	Tbsp. olive oil
2	Tbsp. butter or margarine, softened	40	garlic cloves, peeled
1	tsp. salt		

test kitchen tip: To peel garlic cloves, place them on a cutting board, and press each firmly with the flat side of a chef's knife. The skins will slip off easily. Or for an even quicker alternative, purchase already-peeled garlic cloves in a jar from your supermarket's produce department.

1. Preheat oven to 375°.

2. Remove and discard giblets from chicken; rinse under cold water, and pat dry. Trim excess fat. Place thyme and rosemary sprigs into cavity of bird. Squeeze lemon halves over chicken and inside cavity of bird; place lemon halves inside cavity of bird. Rub chicken with softened butter, and sprinkle with salt and pepper. Tie ends of legs together with string. Lift wing tips up and under chicken. Set aside.

3. Combine onion, celery, olive oil, and garlic in a well-greased shallow roasting pan; toss to coat evenly. Nestle chicken, breast side up, in vegetable mixture. Bake at 375° for 1 hour and 50 minutes or until juices run clear or a meat thermometer inserted into the thigh registers at least 165°, basting every 30 minutes. Serve chicken with vegetables and garlic.

Pastitsio

makes 8 servings • prep: 30 min.; cook: 1 hr., 25 min.

Greek-born-and-bred Catherine and Angelo Petelos of Birmingham, Alabama, make this Greek white lasagnalike casserole lightly spiced with cinnamon as part of their year-round entertaining. It overflows with Greek goodness and Southern charm.

lighten up: Switching from whole milk to 1% low-fat milk in this family-style Greek casserole makes a velvety cream sauce and saves 160 calories and 22 grams of fat in the entire recipe.

8   oz. ziti, cooked
3   Tbsp. butter or margarine
2   (3-oz.) packages shredded Parmesan cheese, divided
1½   lb. ground round
1   medium onion, diced
2   garlic cloves, minced
2   (8-oz.) cans tomato sauce
1½   tsp. salt, divided
½   tsp. ground cinnamon
¼   tsp. pepper
½   cup butter or margarine
⅔   cup all-purpose flour
4   cups milk
2   large eggs

1. Preheat oven to 350°.

2. Toss pasta with 3 Tbsp. butter and ½ cup Parmesan cheese.

3. Cook ground round, onion, and garlic in a large skillet over medium-high heat, stirring until beef crumbles and is no longer pink; drain. Stir in tomato sauce, 1¼ tsp. salt, cinnamon, and pepper.

4. Melt ½ cup butter in a heavy saucepan over low heat. Whisk in flour. Cook, whisking constantly, 1 minute. Whisk in milk; cook over medium heat, whisking constantly, until thickened and bubbly. Add remaining ¼ tsp. salt. Remove from heat.

5. Whisk eggs until thick and pale. Whisk about one-fourth milk mixture into eggs; add to remaining milk mixture, whisking constantly.

6. Spoon pasta mixture into a greased 13- x 9-inch baking dish. Spoon beef mixture over pasta; sprinkle with remaining Parmesan cheese. Top with cream sauce. Bake at 350° for 1 hour or until golden.

Mediterranean Salmon With White Beans

makes 4 servings • prep: 15 min., cook: 10 min.

Cannellini beans, olive oil, fresh basil, and olives give this recipe a Tuscan twist. If you can't find cannellini beans, use large white butter beans instead.

1	medium onion, coarsely chopped	2	Tbsp. chopped fresh basil
2	Tbsp. olive oil, divided	4	(6-oz.) salmon fillets
1	(15-oz.) can cannellini beans, rinsed and drained	½	tsp. salt
		½	tsp. pepper
½	cup chopped pitted kalamata olives		Garnish: fresh basil
1	cup halved grape tomatoes		

1. Sauté onion in 1 Tbsp. hot oil in a saucepan over medium heat 2 minutes or until slightly softened. Add beans, olives, and tomatoes; cook over medium heat, stirring occasionally, 2 minutes or until thoroughly heated. Remove from heat, and stir in basil.

2. Sprinkle salmon fillets evenly with salt and pepper. Cook salmon in a large nonstick skillet in remaining 1 Tbsp. hot oil over medium-high heat 3 minutes on each side or until fish flakes easily. Spoon bean mixture evenly over salmon fillets, and serve immediately. Garnish, if desired.

Spicy Fish Tacos With Mango Salsa and Guacamole

makes 4 to 6 servings • prep: 20 min., fry: 3 min. per batch

Cumin, an essential spice in chili powder and Mexican cuisine, was once said to keep chickens and lovers from straying.

lighten up: Bake these fillets in the oven instead of frying them, omitting vegetable oil from Spicy Fish Tacos recipe, if you'd like. Assemble as directed through Step 3. Spray the cornmeal-coated fish with vegetable cooking spray. Bake at 350° on a lightly greased rack on a baking sheet 12 minutes or until fish flakes with a fork. Proceed with recipe in Step 5.

6 (6-oz.) flounder fillets	Vegetable oil
1 lime	4 to 6 flour or corn tortillas
2 Tbsp. chili powder	Mango Salsa
2 tsp. salt	Guacamole
2 tsp. ground cumin	Toppings: shredded iceberg lettuce,
½ tsp. ground red pepper	chopped tomato
1½ cups yellow cornmeal	

1. Place fish in a shallow dish. Squeeze juice of 1 lime over fillets.

2. Combine chili powder and next 3 ingredients. Sprinkle 1½ Tbsp. seasoning mixture evenly over fish, coating both sides of fillets. Reserve remaining seasoning mixture.

3. Combine cornmeal and reserved seasoning mixture in a shallow dish. Dredge fish fillets in cornmeal mixture, shaking off excess.

4. Pour oil to a depth of 1½ inches in a Dutch oven; heat to 350°. Fry fillets, in batches, 2 to 3 minutes or until golden brown. Drain fillets on wire racks over paper towels.

5. Break each fillet into chunks, using a fork. Place fish in warmed tortillas, and serve with Mango Salsa, Guacamole, and desired toppings.

Mango Salsa

makes 1 cup • prep: 15 min.

1 mango, chopped	1 Tbsp. fresh lime juice
1 jalapeño, seeded and finely chopped	1 Tbsp. finely chopped red onion
	1 Tbsp. chopped fresh cilantro
1 garlic clove, minced	¼ tsp. salt

1. Stir together all ingredients. Cover and chill salsa until ready to serve.

Guacamole

makes 1⅓ cups • prep: 15 min.

2 ripe avocados	¼ cup sour cream
1 jalapeño, seeded and finely chopped	1 Tbsp. lime juice
	½ Tbsp. finely chopped red onion
1 garlic clove, minced	½ tsp. salt

1. Cut avocados in half, and discard pits. Scoop pulp into a medium bowl, and mash into chunks with a fork. Stir in chopped jalapeño and remaining ingredients, stirring well. Cover and chill avocado mixture until ready to serve.

Fresh Mozzarella and Basil Pizza

(pictured on page 49)

makes 1 (6- to 8-inch) pizza • prep: 30 min., cook: 10 min., other: 32 min.

Considered a peasant's meal in Italy for centuries, pizza made its Southern debut when returning World War II GIs came home with tales of "the meal on a bread plate."

1	(4-oz.) portion Pizza Dough	4	thin slices (2 oz.) fresh mozzarella
½	tsp. extra virgin olive oil	1	(1-oz.) slice country ham or smoked
1	large plum tomato, thinly sliced		ham, cut into thin strips
1	Tbsp. sliced fresh basil	¼	tsp. pepper

1. Preheat oven to 450°.

2. Shape Pizza Dough ball into a 6- to 8-inch circle on a lightly floured surface. (Dough doesn't need to be perfectly round.) Place dough on a piece of parchment paper. Fold up edges of dough, forming a 1-inch border. Brush oil evenly over dough using a pastry brush.

3. Cover pizza dough circle loosely with plastic wrap, and let rise in a warm place (85°), free from drafts, 15 to 20 minutes.

4. Heat pizza stone or heavy baking sheet 10 to 12 minutes in oven. Remove and discard plastic wrap from dough. Layer tomato and next 3 ingredients evenly over dough. Sprinkle with pepper. Carefully transfer dough on parchment paper to pizza stone.

5. Bake at 450° for 10 minutes or until crust is golden.

test kitchen tip: If you don't have time to prepare fresh Pizza Dough, buy it from the deli department of the supermarket. Bake pizza on a pizza stone or heavy baking sheet that withstands high baking temperatures. High heat makes the crust crisp.

Pizza Dough

makes 6 (4-oz.) portions • prep: 15 min., other: 1 hr., 37 min.

1	cup warm water (100° to 110°)	1½	tsp. salt
⅛	tsp. sugar	1	Tbsp. extra virgin olive oil
1	(¼-oz.) envelope active dry yeast		Vegetable cooking spray
3	to 3½ cups all-purpose flour		

1. Stir together 1 cup warm water and sugar in a 2-cup measuring cup. Sprinkle with yeast, and let stand 5 to 7 minutes or until mixture is bubbly.

2. Place 3 cups flour and salt in food processor bowl. With motor running, add yeast mixture and olive oil; process mixture until dough forms. (If dough is too sticky, add more flour, 2 Tbsp. at a time.) Place dough in a large bowl coated with cooking spray; lightly coat dough with cooking spray. Cover with a clean cloth, and let rise in a warm place (85°), free from drafts, 1 hour or until doubled in bulk.

3. Punch dough down. Turn dough in bowl, and coat with cooking spray; cover with cloth, and let rise in a warm place, 30 minutes or until doubled in bulk. Cut dough into 6 equal portions, shaping each portion into a 3-inch ball immediately or wrap in wax paper, place in a zip-top freezer bag, and freeze up to 1 month. Let thaw overnight in refrigerator.

So-Easy Paella

makes 6 to 8 servings • prep: 20 min., cook: 50 min., stand: 10 min.

This Spanish dish of saffron rice with meats and shellfish is named after the pan in which it's cooked and served. Bright yellow (and expensive) threads of saffron are a must in traditional paellas.

test kitchen tip: Rinse fresh mussels, and then pull off any remaining pieces of the stringlike beard. Discard any mussels that don't close when you tap them. If you can't find mussels at your local seafood counter, add an extra half pound of shrimp.

1   lb. unpeeled, large raw shrimp
1   (32-oz.) container chicken broth
½   lb. chorizo sausage, sliced
1   (10-oz.) package frozen diced onion, red and green bell pepper, and celery, thawed
2   tsp. minced garlic
1   (10-oz.) package saffron rice
½   tsp. freshly ground black pepper
3½ cups chopped cooked chicken
1   cup frozen small green peas
18 fresh mussels (about ¾ lb.)
2   lemons, cut into wedges

1. Peel shrimp, reserving shells, and set shrimp aside.

2. Bring shrimp shells and chicken broth to a boil in a large saucepan over medium-high heat; reduce heat, and simmer 5 minutes. Remove from heat, and let stand 10 minutes. Pour shrimp broth through a fine wire-mesh strainer into a bowl; discard shells.

3. Sauté sausage and vegetables in a paella pan or large heavy skillet over medium heat until vegetables are tender; add garlic, and cook 1 minute. Stir in rice; cook, stirring gently, 1 minute. Stir in shrimp broth and pepper; cover, reduce heat, and simmer 15 minutes.

4. Remove pan from heat; stir in shrimp and chicken. Sprinkle peas evenly over mixture; arrange mussels around outside of pan, hinge ends down.

5. Cook, covered, over medium-low heat 20 minutes or until liquid is absorbed and mussel shells are open. (Discard any unopened mussels.) Serve paella with lemon wedges.

Chicken-Artichoke Pasta With Rosemary

makes 4 servings • prep: 25 min., cook: 25 min.

Italian recipes often call for plum or Roma tomatoes. These egg-shaped tomatoes pack a powerful sweet tomato flavor year-round and are available in red and yellow versions.

test kitchen tip: If fresh rosemary is not available, substitute an equal amount of dried rosemary.

4   skinned and boned chicken breasts, cut into 1-inch pieces
½   tsp. salt
1   tsp. freshly ground pepper
½   cup butter or margarine, divided
1   small sweet onion, halved and sliced
2   garlic cloves, pressed
6   plum or Roma tomatoes, seeded and chopped
1   (8-oz.) package sliced fresh mushrooms
1   (12-oz.) jar marinated artichoke heart quarters, drained
1   to 2 Tbsp. chopped fresh rosemary
⅓   cup dry white wine
2   cups whipping cream
1   (9-oz.) package refrigerated fettuccine, cooked
¾   cup freshly grated Parmesan cheese
Garnish: fresh rosemary

Chicken-Artichoke Pasta With Rosemary

1. Sprinkle chicken evenly with salt and pepper.

2. Melt ¼ cup butter in a Dutch oven over medium-high heat; add chicken, and cook 5 minutes or until lightly browned. Remove chicken with a slotted spoon, and set aside.

3. Add onion and next 5 ingredients to Dutch oven; sauté 10 minutes or until vegetables are tender. Drain and remove from Dutch oven.

4. Add remaining ¼ cup butter, wine, and whipping cream to Dutch oven. Cook over medium heat, stirring constantly, 10 minutes or until thickened. Add chicken, vegetables, cooked fettuccine, and Parmesan cheese, tossing gently. Garnish, if desired.

Sweet–Hot Asian Noodle Bowl

makes 8 servings • prep: 35 min., cook: 15 min.

¾ cup rice wine vinegar
⅓ cup lite soy sauce
⅓ cup honey
2 Tbsp. minced fresh ginger
2 Tbsp. dark sesame oil
1 Tbsp. Asian chili-garlic sauce
16 oz. uncooked spaghetti
1 (15-oz.) can cut baby corn, rinsed and drained

1 (8-oz.) can sliced water chestnuts, rinsed and drained
1 large red bell pepper, thinly sliced
1 cup (about 4 oz.) thinly sliced snow peas
⅓ cup finely chopped green onions
¼ cup chopped fresh cilantro
1 Tbsp. toasted sesame seeds (optional)

1. Whisk together first 6 ingredients in a medium bowl; set aside.

2. Cook pasta according to package directions in a large Dutch oven; drain and return to pan. Pour vinegar mixture over pasta. Add corn and next 5 ingredients; toss. Sprinkle with sesame seeds, if desired. Serve hot or cold.

test kitchen tip: Dark sesame oil has a distinctive flavor—rich, toasted, and nutty. It's perishable, so store it in the refrigerator. When chilled, the oil will solidify; let it come to room temperature before measuring.

Summer Rolls With Thai Dipping Sauce

makes 12 appetizer servings • prep: 30 min., other: 8 hr.

Cilantro, a pungent herb with a distinctive (some say "soapy") taste, is a common flavoring in Asian dishes.

2½ cups shredded carrot
½ lb. cabbage, shredded
2 cups bean sprouts
1 cup minced fresh cilantro
¼ cup chopped green onions
3 Tbsp. minced fresh ginger
¼ cup rice wine vinegar

2 Tbsp. sesame oil
2 Tbsp. soy sauce
1½ tsp. Chinese five spice
1 tsp. dried crushed red pepper
18 rice paper sheets
Thai Dipping Sauce

1. Combine first 11 ingredients. Cover and chill at least 8 hours. Drain well. Soak a rice paper sheet in warm water for 30 to 45 seconds or until softened; place on a flat surface. Spoon ¼ cup vegetable mixture below center of wrapper. Fold bottom corner over filling; fold in both sides, and roll up.

2. Place, seam side down, on a serving plate; cover with a damp towel. Repeat procedure. Serve with Thai Dipping Sauce.

test kitchen tip: You'll find rice paper sheets at large supermarkets in the produce section with tofu and won ton wrappers.

Thai Dipping Sauce

makes ⅔ cup • prep: 5 min.

½ cup fresh lime juice
2½ tsp. brown sugar
2 tsp. minced fresh ginger
1 tsp. minced fresh cilantro

1 tsp. diced dry-roasted peanuts
1 tsp. minced green onions
1 tsp. fish sauce

1. Combine all ingredients, stirring well.

This dish is traditionally served with chopsticks in an Asian noodle bowl. A large shallow soup bowl and a dinner fork will work just as well.

Sweet-Hot Asian Noodle Bowl

Gorditas With Turkey Mole

makes 12 servings • prep: 40 min., cook: 4 min. per batch, other: 30 min.

make it a meal: Serve Gorditas With Turkey Mole buffet-style alongside chili con carne, tortilla chips, salsa, guacamole, and icy margaritas.

2 cups masa harina
1¼ cups chicken broth
¼ cup shortening
½ cup plus 1 Tbsp. all-purpose flour
½ tsp. salt
1 tsp. baking powder
Vegetable oil

1½ cups refried beans
Turkey Mole
Toppings: 1 (15-oz.) can black beans, rinsed and drained; shredded romaine lettuce; chopped tomato; sour cream
Garnishes: lime wedges

1. Stir together masa harina and broth in a large mixing bowl. Cover and let stand 30 minutes. Add shortening, flour, salt, and baking powder; beat at medium speed with an electric mixer until smooth.

2. Divide dough into 12 golf-size balls. Arrange on wax paper, and cover with damp towels. Pat each ball of dough into a 3-inch circle. (Lightly oil fingers to keep mixture from sticking.) Pinch edges of circles to form a ridge, and press a well into each center to hold toppings. Cover with a damp towel to prevent dough from drying.

3. Pour oil to a depth of 1 inch into a large skillet; heat to 350°. Fry gorditas, in batches, 2 minutes on each side, or until golden brown. Drain on paper towels.

4. Top each gordita with 2 Tbsp. refried beans; spoon 1 Tbsp. Turkey Mole over beans on each gordita. Top with desired toppings, and garnish, if desired.

Note: Masa harina is corn flour traditionally used to make corn tortillas. It can be found in the ethnic foods section of larger grocery stores.

Turkey Mole

makes 6½ cups • prep: 15 min., cook: 15 min.

1 (8¼-oz. to 9¼-oz.) can mole sauce
1 (10-oz.) can enchilada sauce
4 cups chicken broth
1 Tbsp. creamy peanut butter
2 (1-oz.) unsweetened dark chocolate baking squares

1½ lb. cooked turkey, shredded (about 5 cups)
½ tsp. salt

1. Combine mole and enchilada sauces in a medium saucepan, and stir in chicken broth. Bring mixture to a boil; reduce heat, and simmer 5 minutes.

2. Add peanut butter and chocolate, stirring until melted and smooth. Stir in turkey and salt; cook until thoroughly heated.

Note: Freeze extra Turkey Mole in 1-cup portions. Thaw, reheat, and serve over enchiladas and soft tacos.

Gorditas With Turkey Mole

Dotty Griffith of Dallas often entertains with this recipe, which salutes the authentic Mexican cuisine south of the Lone Star State. A bit of chocolate is the signature ingredient in Mexican mole (moe LAY), a smooth sauce of cooked onion and garlic. This Turkey Mole gets a head start with a can of already-prepared mole sauce.

Hot Sesame Pork on Mixed Greens

makes 8 servings • prep: 40 min., cook: 25 min.

The wok is the most popular utensil in Asian cooking. It provides excellent heat control like a large heavy skillet, which we used to test this recipe.

test kitchen tip: Partially freeze pork loin about 30 minutes before cutting into strips. An electric knife speeds up the slicing process.

½	(16-oz.) package won ton wrappers	¼	cup dark sesame oil, divided
2	lb. boneless pork loin, trimmed	⅓	cup soy sauce
¾	cup sesame seeds, divided	¼	cup rice wine vinegar
1	cup vegetable oil, divided	10	to 12 small green onions, sliced
½	cup all-purpose flour	1	(10-oz.) package mixed salad
1	tsp. salt		greens
½	tsp. pepper	1	bok choy, shredded

1. Cut won ton wrappers into ½-inch strips, and cut pork into 3- x 1-inch strips; set aside.

2. Toast ½ cup sesame seeds in a large heavy skillet over medium-high heat, stirring constantly, 2 to 3 minutes; remove from skillet.

3. Pour ½ cup vegetable oil into skillet; heat to 375°. Fry won ton strips in batches until golden. Drain on paper towels; set aside. Drain skillet.

4. Combine remaining ¼ cup sesame seeds, flour, salt, and pepper in a zip-top plastic freezer bag; add pork. Seal and shake to coat.

5. Pour 2 Tbsp. sesame oil into skillet; place over medium heat. Fry half of pork in hot oil, stirring often, 6 to 8 minutes or until golden. Remove pork, and keep warm. Repeat procedure with remaining 2 Tbsp. sesame oil and pork.

6. Process toasted sesame seeds, remaining ½ cup vegetable oil, soy sauce, and vinegar in a blender 1 to 2 minutes or until smooth.

7. Combine pork and green onions; drizzle with soy sauce mixture, tossing gently. Combine mixed greens and bok choy; top with pork mixture and fried won ton strips. Serve immediately.

Tabbouleh Salad

makes 5 cups • prep: 20 min.; other: 1 hr., 30 min.

A Middle Eastern staple, bulgur wheat is steamed, dried, and crushed wheat kernels with a tender, somewhat chewy, texture. It's traditionally used in salads like this one.

test kitchen tip: Substitute 2 cups cooked brown rice in place of bulgur and boiling water, if you prefer.

1	cup uncooked bulgur wheat	½	tsp. grated lemon rind
1	cup boiling water	⅓	cup fresh lemon juice
2	medium tomatoes, chopped	3	Tbsp. olive oil
4	green onions, thinly sliced	½	tsp. salt
¼	cup minced fresh parsley	½	tsp. pepper
¼	to ½ cup chopped fresh mint		Lettuce leaves

1. Place bulgur in a large bowl, and add boiling water. Cover and let stand 30 minutes. Stir in tomato and next 8 ingredients. Cover and chill 1 hour. Serve on lettuce leaves.

Sweet Noodle Kugel

makes 12 servings • prep: 25 min., cook: 50 min.

Noodle "pudding" is a Jewish tradition served on the Sabbath and Jewish holidays. Savory versions are often served as a side dish and sweet ones as dessert.

1   (16-oz.) package wide egg noodles
1   (8-oz.) package cream cheese, softened
1   (8-oz.) container sour cream
1   cup sugar
4   large eggs
1   (20-oz.) can crushed pineapple in juice, drained
½   cup butter or margarine, melted and divided
3   cups frosted flaked cereal, coarsely crushed
1½ tsp. ground cinnamon

test kitchen tip: Noodles need plenty of room to boil; use 6 qts. rapidly boiling water for this recipe. After draining the noodles, there's no need to rinse them.

1. Preheat oven to 350°.

2. Cook noodles according to package directions; drain and set aside.

3. Beat cream cheese and next 3 ingredients at high speed with an electric mixer in a large mixing bowl until smooth. Stir in pineapple. Add noodles and ¼ cup melted butter, stirring until blended. Spoon mixture into a lightly greased 13- x 9-inch baking dish.

4. Stir together cereal, cinnamon, and remaining ¼ cup melted butter; sprinkle over noodle mixture. Bake at 350° for 45 to 50 minutes or until set.

shalom y'all

"Being a Jew in the South means you are different from 99.9% of the people you know," says Southern born-and-bred Diane Slaughter, of Birmingham, Alabama. She keeps a commitment to cook kosher and tries to find ways to make Southern recipes fit her lifestyle. Today, it's easy to blend Southern cuisine and kosher cooking, which requires meat and dairy products to be cooked and eaten separately. In her book, *Matzoh Ball Gumbo: Culinary Tales of the Jewish South*, author Marcie Cohen Ferris highlights the new products and mindsets that may be the start of a Southern Jewish cuisine trend with recipes such as Sabbath Fried Chicken, Matzoh Meal Fried Green Tomatoes, and Rosh Hashanah Jam Cake. Let the trend begin!

African Peanut Stew

makes 14 cups • prep: 25 min., cook: 55 min.

Traditionally, this spicy African stew combines okra, peanuts, and sweet potatoes—all the favorites of West Africa that the enslaved natives brought to our southern coast. And it's perfect for company; it makes almost a gallon.

make it a meal: Serve this hearty stew over couscous and alongside spinach salad and flatbread.

1	lb. boneless leg of lamb, cut into 1-inch pieces	1	large onion, chopped
½	tsp. salt	2	garlic cloves, minced
¼	tsp. freshly ground black pepper	1	large jalapeño pepper, finely chopped
2	Tbsp. vegetable oil	6	cups chicken broth, divided
2	large tomatoes, chopped	½	cup natural crunchy peanut butter
2	medium-size sweet potatoes, peeled and cut into 1-inch cubes	2	Tbsp. tomato paste
2	medium carrots, peeled and cut into 1-inch pieces	2	cups frozen cut okra, thawed
			Hot cooked couscous

1. Sprinkle lamb evenly with salt and pepper. Heat oil in large Dutch oven over medium-high heat until hot. Add lamb, and cook, stirring frequently, 5 minutes or until browned on all sides; remove lamb from pan, and set aside.

2. Add tomatoes and next 5 ingredients to pan; cook, stirring often, about 10 minutes or until caramel colored. Whisk together 1 cup broth, peanut butter and tomato paste. Add peanut butter mixture and remaining broth to pan, stirring well.

3. Return lamb to pan; bring mixture to a boil. Reduce heat, and simmer 30 minutes, stirring occasionally, until vegetables are tender. Stir in okra; cook 5 more minutes. Serve over hot cooked couscous.

Gazpacho Blanco

makes 9 cups • prep: 15 min., other: 2 hr.

Gazpacho is a fresh, uncooked, cold Spanish soup made with tomatoes, bell peppers, cucumbers, and garlic, and pureed until smooth or left chunky. This version is "white" since the tomatoes are served on top instead of blended in the soup.

test kitchen tip: Peeled and seeded cucumber gives this chilled soup fresh flavor and a velvety consistency. To remove the seeds after peeling, cut the cucumber in half lengthwise. Using a melon baller or small spoon, scrape out the seeds in short, gentle motions.

3	small cucumbers, peeled, seeded, and chopped	3	Tbsp. white vinegar
1	garlic clove, pressed	½	tsp. salt
2	cups chicken broth, divided	¼	tsp. pepper
1	(16-oz.) container sour cream		Toppings: diced tomato, sliced green onions, chopped fresh parsley
1	(8-oz.) container plain low-fat yogurt		

1. Process cucumber, garlic, and 1 cup broth in a blender or food processor until smooth, stopping to scrape down sides.

2. Pour into a bowl; whisk in remaining 1 cup broth, sour cream, and next 4 ingredients. Cover and chill at least 2 hours. Sprinkle with desired toppings.

healthy homestyle cooking

Baked Spinach-and-Artichoke Dip, page 74

Polenta With Black-Eyed Pea Topping

makes 6 appetizer servings • prep: 15 min., cook: 11 min.

test kitchen tip: For testing purposes only, we used Melissa's Organic Sun-Dried Tomato Polenta. You'll find it in the produce section of the supermarket.

½ (16-oz.) tube refrigerated sun-dried tomato polenta, cut into 6 even slices

Vegetable cooking spray

1 (15-oz.) can black-eyed peas, rinsed and drained

½ cup finely chopped onion

¼ cup water

¼ tsp. ground red pepper

¼ tsp. salt

½ cup diced tomatoes

3 Tbsp. chopped fresh cilantro

¼ cup light sour cream

1 Tbsp. chopped fresh cilantro

1. Cook polenta rounds in a large nonstick skillet coated with cooking spray over medium-high heat 4 minutes on each side or until lightly browned. Remove from heat, and keep warm.

2. Wipe pan with paper towel, and spray with cooking spray. Add peas and next 4 ingredients; cook over medium heat 3 minutes or until water evaporates. Remove from heat; stir in tomatoes and 3 Tbsp. cilantro. Spoon warm black-eyed pea mixture over polenta rounds, and top evenly with sour cream. Sprinkle with 1 Tbsp. cilantro.

Per serving: Calories 74; Fat 1g (sat 0.6g, mono 0g, poly 0.1g); Protein 3.2g; Carb 13.5g; Fiber 2.2g; Chol 3mg; Iron 0.6mg; Sodium 263mg; Calc 14mg

eating for luck
Every culture claims to have food that ensures health, wealth, and luck, and the South is no exception. It's said that when a Union raid during the Civil War left nothing but black-eyed peas to eat, the peas from then on were considered lucky. Today they are a must for New Year's Day to ensure luck. For some, a washed coin in the pot of peas promises extra fortune. Eating greens—collards, cabbage, spinach, turnip, or mustard—is the Southern guarantee of enough money in the year to come. The lucky plastic baby in today's Mardi Gras King Cake stems from centuries of European tradition. And in Texas it's a toss up as to whether the menudo, the pungent stew made from calf stomach, is consumed more as a remedy for hangovers or the luck it's said to bring!

It's said that black-eyed peas (also called cowpeas) became a Southern staple during the Civil War when Union soldiers who burned crops didn't bother with the cowpeas because they considered them to be animal feed. Southerners quickly adapted the high-calcium legume into their diets.

Baked Spinach-and-Artichoke Dip

(pictured on page 71)

makes 11 servings • prep: 10 min., cook: 22 min.

Artichoke hearts, actually the flower bud of the plant, add a distinct nutty flavor to this dip. Artichokes tend to be pricey because they are harvested completely by hand.

make it ahead: For easy entertaining, assemble this dish a day ahead. Cover and store in the refrigerator. Uncover and bake just before serving.

2	(6-oz.) packages fresh baby spinach	1	(14-oz.) can artichoke hearts,
1	Tbsp. butter		drained and chopped
1	(8-oz.) package ⅓-less-fat cream	½	cup light sour cream
	cheese	½	cup shredded part-skim mozzarella
1	garlic clove, chopped		cheese, divided

1. Preheat oven to 350°.

2. Microwave spinach in a large microwave-safe bowl at HIGH 3 minutes or until wilted; drain well. Press spinach between paper towels to remove excess moisture. Chop spinach.

3. Melt butter in a nonstick skillet over medium-high heat. Add cream cheese and garlic, and cook 3 to 4 minutes, stirring constantly, until cream cheese melts. Fold in spinach, artichokes, sour cream, and ¼ cup mozzarella cheese; stir until mozzarella cheese melts.

4. Transfer mixture to a 1-qt. shallow baking dish. Sprinkle with remaining ¼ cup mozzarella cheese. Bake at 350° for 15 minutes or until hot and bubbly. Serve immediately with fresh pita wedges or baked pita chips.

Per ¼-cup (not including pita wedges or pita chips): Calories 111; Fat 7g (sat 4.7g, mono 0.5g, poly 0.1g); Protein 5.4g; Carb 8.1g; Fiber 2.2g; Chol 24mg; Iron 1mg; Sodium 316mg; Calc 85mg

No-Cook Eggnog

makes 6 servings • prep: 10 min.

Old World recipes for "grog" often used wine, but once the recipe traveled to American soil, the spike of choice was rum. Southerners replaced rum with bourbon in this rich holiday drink that's commonly known today as eggnog.

test kitchen tip: Using egg substitute in this recipe allows you to skip the usually required cooking process. For testing purposes, we used Egg Beaters egg substitute and Silk Vanilla Soymilk.

1½	cups 2% reduced-fat milk or vanilla-flavored soymilk	½	cup sweetened condensed milk
¾	cup fat-free half-and-half	2	Tbsp. bourbon
¾	cup egg substitute	1	tsp. vanilla extract
		⅛	tsp. ground nutmeg

1. Whisk together all ingredients in a bowl or pitcher. Cover and chill until ready to serve.

Per ¾-cup: Calories 159; Fat 3.8g (sat 2.4g, mono 1.1g, poly 0.2g); Protein 7.8g; Carb 20.1g; Fiber 0g; Chol 15mg; Iron 0.6mg; Sodium 169mg; Calc 186mg

Smoky-Hot Buffalo Chicken Pizzas

makes 8 appetizer servings • prep: 12 min., cook: 10 min.

Buffalo chicken has nothing to do with bison. It refers to the hot sauce-coated chicken that has become a rage across the country and is named for the city where it originated— Buffalo, New York.

2 cups diced deli-roasted chicken breast

3 Tbsp. chipotle hot sauce

1 tsp. butter

¼ cup refrigerated light blue cheese dressing

2 (7-inch) prebaked pizza crusts

½ cup (2 oz.) shredded 2% Colby-Jack cheese blend

2 green onions, thinly sliced

test kitchen tip: For testing purposes only, we used Mama Mary's Gourmet Pizza Crusts. For a softer crust, bake pizza on a pizza pan or baking sheet.

1. Preheat oven to 450°.

2. Stir together first 3 ingredients in a microwave-safe bowl. Microwave at HIGH 45 seconds or until thoroughly heated.

3. Spread 2 Tbsp. blue cheese dressing evenly over each pizza crust, leaving a 1-inch border around edges. Top evenly with chicken mixture. Sprinkle with cheese and green onions.

4. Bake directly on oven rack at 450° for 10 minutes or until crusts are golden and cheese melts. Cut each pizza into 4 wedges.

Per appetizer serving: Calories 194; Fat 5.9g (sat 2g, mono 0.6g, poly 0.3g); Protein 15.7g; Carb 18.8g; Fiber 1.7g; Chol 35mg; Iron 0.4mg; Sodium 352mg; Calc 108mg

Banana-Peach Buttermilk Smoothie

makes 4 servings • prep: 10 min.

In the Appalachian Mountains, peach trees were important for more than just the fruit. "Water witches" claimed that the forked branch of a peach tree was essential for helping them find water to locate wells.

2 large ripe bananas, sliced and frozen

2 cups frozen peaches

1 cup fat-free buttermilk

¼ cup fresh orange juice

1 Tbsp. honey

test kitchen tip: Cultured dairy products—such as buttermilk and yogurt—are good for maintaining healthy digestion.

1. Process all ingredients in a blender until smooth, stopping to scrape down sides. Serve immediately.

Per 1-cup: Calories 139; Fat 0.5g (sat 0.1g, mono 0.1g, poly 0.1g); Protein 3.9g; Carb 33.1g; Fiber 3.1g; Chol 1mg; Iron 0.4mg; Sodium 61mg; Calc 86mg

Whole Wheat Popovers

makes 6 popovers • prep: 10 min., cook: 30 min., other: 6 min.

Also called Laplanders and puff pops, popovers are considered to be an Americanized version of England's Yorkshire pudding.

test kitchen tip: These light and airy popovers have a crisp crust and offer the healthy benefits of whole wheat flour. They are delicious on their own, but we also liked them dipped in olive oil (moderation is the key) or topped with honey or low-fat yogurt.

½ cup all-purpose flour
½ cup whole wheat flour
¼ tsp. salt
1 cup 2% reduced-fat milk

2 large eggs
2 egg whites
1 Tbsp. vegetable oil
Vegetable cooking spray

1. Preheat oven to 425°.

2. Combine first 3 ingredients in a medium bowl. Whisk together milk and next 3 ingredients. Whisk milk mixture into flour mixture, whisking until smooth.

3. Place popover pan or 6 (8-oz.) custard cups heavily coated with cooking spray on a baking sheet. Place in a 450° oven 3 minutes or until hot. Remove baking sheet from oven, and fill cups half full with batter.

4. Bake at 425° for 30 minutes. Turn oven off; remove pans from oven. Cut a small slit in popover tops; return to oven. Let popovers stand in closed oven 3 minutes. Serve immediately.

Per popover: Calories 142; Fat 5.1g (sat 1.3g, mono 1.9g, poly 1.4g); Protein 7.1g; Carb 17.4g; Fiber 1.5g; Chol 74mg; Iron 1.2mg; Sodium 160mg; Calc 64mg

Whole Kernel Corn Sticks

makes 20 corn sticks • prep: 10 min., cook: 15 min., other: 5 min.

Old timers sometimes refer to cornbread as corn pone, a term which comes from "appone" or "suppone," Indian words for the bread made from cornmeal. In the early days, hog or bear grease was used to make the bread. This recipe minimizes the fat to keep the corn sticks healthful.

1	cup all-purpose flour		¼	tsp. ground red pepper
1	cup yellow cornmeal		¾	cup 1% low-fat milk
1	Tbsp. baking powder		½	cup egg substitute
1	tsp. salt		2	egg whites
1	(11-oz.) can sweet whole kernel corn, drained		1	Tbsp. vegetable oil
2	Tbsp. minced red bell pepper			Vegetable cooking spray

test kitchen tip: Sweet yellow corn makes these corn sticks slightly sweet without adding sugar or artificial sweetener.

1. Preheat oven to 450°.

2. Combine first 7 ingredients; make a well in center. Stir together milk and next 3 ingredients. Add to flour mixture, stirring just until moistened.

3. Spoon batter into cast-iron corn stick pans coated with cooking spray. Bake at 450° for 15 minutes. Remove from pans immediately; cool slightly on wire racks.

Per corn stick: Calories 68; Fat 1.2g (sat 0.2g, mono 0.4g, poly 0.4g); Protein 2.7g; Carb 11.8g; Fiber 0.9g; Chol 0mg; Iron 0.9mg; Sodium 328mg; Calc 77mg

cooking with cast iron

It's hard to imagine what Southern cooking would be without cast-iron cookware. The high heat it holds makes the crunchiest cornbread crust, fries the crispiest chicken, is ideal for blackening meats, and bakes the softest biscuits over cowboy fires. It even contributes to good health because it adds iron to the food that's cooked in it. And if you have a well-seasoned pan, it works as nonstick cookware. Allowing water to stand in the cookware during storage will cause rust, and if that happens, just re-season as you would new cookware by coating it in vegetable shortening and baking it at 350° for an hour. For cooks who want a seasoned pan right away, Lodge Manufacturing Co. in Tennessee has the answer. "The newest thing is preseasoned cast iron with stainless handles," says Lodge representative Gayle Grier.

Blueberry Sherbet

makes 6 servings • prep: 15 min., other: 8 hr.

If it's summer in the South, then there is a blueberry festival nearby. Check for festivals in June in Alabama, Georgia, Mississippi, North Carolina, Florida, and Texas. Virginia and Maryland host their festivals in July.

test kitchen tip: A food processor fitted with the knife blade works just as well as a blender to blend this icy concoction. With either appliance, stop and scrape down the sides as needed.

2 cups fresh or frozen blueberries, thawed
1 cup fat-free buttermilk
½ cup sugar
1 Tbsp. fresh lemon juice
½ tsp. vanilla extract
Garnish: fresh mint sprigs

1. Process first 5 ingredients in a blender until smooth. Pour mixture into a 9-inch square pan; cover and freeze 4 hours or until firm.

2. Break frozen blueberry mixture into chunks using a fork. Process frozen mixture, in batches, in a blender until smooth. Cover and freeze 4 hours or until frozen. Garnish, if desired.

Per ½-cup: Calories 109; Fat 0.2g (sat 0g, mono 0g, poly 0.1g); Protein 1.9g; Carb 26.4g; Fiber 1.2g; Chol 0mg; Iron 0.2mg; Sodium 41mg; Calc 53mg

Banana Pudding

makes 10 servings • prep: 25 min., cook: 33 min., other: 30 min.

In the early days, Charleston and New Orleans were lucky enough to get boatloads of bananas. Cooks used the bountiful shipments to make what is now one of the South's most popular puddings.

⅓	cup all-purpose flour	2	tsp. vanilla extract
Dash of salt		3	cups sliced ripe banana
2½	cups 1% low-fat milk	45	reduced-fat vanilla wafers
1	(14-oz.) can fat-free sweetened condensed milk	4	egg whites
2	egg yolks	¼	cup sugar

test kitchen tip: Beat the meringue at least 2 minutes or until there's no appearance of any sugar granules. It's ready when a tiny bit of the meringue rubbed between your thumb and forefinger feels silky with no evidence of undissolved sugar.

1. Combine flour and salt in a medium saucepan. Gradually stir in milks and yolks, and cook over medium heat, stirring constantly, 8 minutes or until thickened. Remove from heat; stir in vanilla.

2. Preheat oven to 325°.

3. Arrange 1 cup banana slices in bottom of a 2-qt. baking dish. Spoon one-third pudding mixture over bananas; top with 15 vanilla wafers. Repeat layers twice, ending with pudding; arrange remaining 15 wafers around inside edge of dish. Gently push wafers into pudding.

4. Beat egg whites at high speed with an electric mixer until foamy. Add sugar, 1 Tbsp. at a time, beating until stiff peaks form and sugar dissolves (2 to 4 minutes). Spread meringue over pudding, sealing to edge of dish.

5. Bake at 325° for 25 minutes or until meringue is golden. Let cool at least 30 minutes.

Per serving: Calories 300; Fat 2.9g (sat 0.8g, mono 0.6g, poly 0.2g); Protein 8.5g; Carb 59.6g; Fiber 1.3g; Chol 49mg; Iron 0.9mg; Sodium 172mg; Calc 185mg

Chocolate Parfaits

makes 6 servings • prep: 20 min., other: 1 hr.

1	(1.4-oz.) package fat-free, sugar-free chocolate instant pudding mix	¾	cup chocolate graham cracker crumbs (4 cracker sheets)
2	cups 1% low-fat milk	1	Tbsp. grated chocolate
½	cup light sour cream		
1	(8-oz.) container fat-free frozen whipped topping, thawed and divided		

test kitchen tip: To keep whipped topping light and fluffy, thaw it overnight in the refrigerator. For testing purposes only, we used Cool Whip fat-free frozen whipped topping.

1. Whisk together first 3 ingredients in a bowl until blended and smooth. Fold in 1½ cups whipped topping.

2. Spoon 1 Tbsp. crumbs into each of 6 (4-oz.) glasses, and top with ⅓ cup pudding mixture. Repeat layers with remaining crumbs and pudding mixture. Top each parfait evenly with remaining whipped topping and grated chocolate. Cover and chill at least 1 hour.

Per serving: Calories 213; Fat 7.3g (sat 4.5g, mono 1.9g, poly 0.3g); Protein 5.2g; Carb 31.8g; Fiber 0.8g; Chol 10mg; Iron 1.4mg; Sodium 302mg; Calc 139mg

Brown Sugar Bread Pudding With Crème Anglaise

makes: 9 servings • prep: 30 min., cook: 35 min., other: 10 min.

4   egg whites
1   large egg
1¼   cups 2% reduced-fat milk
¾   cup evaporated fat-free milk
½   cup firmly packed light brown sugar
1   tsp. ground cinnamon
¼   tsp. ground nutmeg
⅛   tsp. salt
⅛   tsp. ground allspice

2   tsp. vanilla extract
1   (12-oz.) day-old French bread loaf, cut into 1-inch cubes (about 8 cups)
Vegetable cooking spray
4   tsp. light brown sugar
½   Tbsp. butter, cut into small pieces
¼   cup sliced almonds, toasted
Crème Anglaise

1. Preheat oven to 350°. Whisk together egg whites and egg in a medium bowl until blended. Whisk in reduced-fat milk and next 7 ingredients.

2. Arrange bread cubes in an 8-inch square pan coated with cooking spray. Pour egg mixture evenly over bread. Sprinkle evenly with 4 tsp. brown sugar, butter, and almonds. Press down gently on bread cubes, and let stand 10 minutes.

3. Bake at 350° for 30 to 35 minutes or until a knife inserted in center comes out clean. Serve warm with 2 Tbsp. chilled Crème Anglaise per serving.

Per 1 serving bread pudding and 2 Tbsp. Crème Anglaise: Calories 319; Fat 10.8g (sat 5.2g, mono 3.5g, poly 0.9g); Protein 10.7g; Carb 43g; Fiber 1.3g; Chol 87mg; Iron 1.8mg; Sodium 372mg; Calc 156mg

Crème Anglaise

makes 2⅔ cups • prep: 10 min., cook: 15 min.

1   vanilla bean
1⅓   cups whipping cream
⅔   cup milk

4   egg yolks
½   cup sugar
½   cup Irish cream liqueur

1. Cut a 2-inch piece of vanilla bean, and split lengthwise. Reserve remaining bean for other uses. Combine vanilla bean, whipping cream, and milk in a medium-size heavy saucepan. Cook over medium heat, stirring constantly, until mixture reaches 185°.

2. Combine yolks and sugar in a bowl; beat with a wire whisk until blended. Gradually stir about one-fourth of hot mixture into yolks; add to remaining hot mixture, stirring constantly. Cook over low heat, stirring constantly, 6 minutes or until thickened. Discard vanilla bean, and stir in liqueur. Cover and chill.

Per 2 Tbsp.: Calories 99; Fat 6.9g (sat 3.9g, mono 1.9g, poly 0.1g); Protein 1.8g; Carb 7.2g; Fiber 0g; Chol 59mg; Iron 0.1mg; Sodium 9mg; Calc 23mg

In the hundreds of versions of this classic dessert, sweeteners vary from sugar to molasses, and breads from biscuits to French bread. Stale bread is the one factor they all have in common.

Creamy Beef Stroganoff

makes 6 servings • prep: 30 min., cook: 30 min.

The traditional stroganoff recipe of thinly sliced beef, mushrooms, and onions in sour cream sauce was named for Russian diplomat Count Paul Stroganov.

make it a meal: Creamy Beef Stroganoff makes a welcomed weeknight meal. Serve it with steamed baby carrots and a spinach salad from an all-inclusive salad kit.

1 (8-oz.) package egg noodles
1½ lb. sirloin steak, cut into thin strips
2 tsp. olive oil
Vegetable cooking spray
1 large sweet onion, diced
1 (8-oz.) package sliced fresh mushrooms
2 Tbsp. all-purpose flour
1 (14.25-oz.) can low-sodium fat-free beef broth

3 Tbsp. tomato paste
3 Tbsp. dry sherry
½ tsp. salt
½ tsp. pepper
¼ tsp. dried tarragon
1 (8-oz.) container fat-free sour cream
2 Tbsp. chopped fresh parsley

1. Cook noodles according to package directions, omitting salt and fat; keep noodles warm.

2. Cook beef, in 2 batches, in hot oil in a large nonstick skillet coated with cooking spray over medium–high heat 3 to 4 minutes or just until browned. Remove from skillet, and set aside.

3. Add onion to skillet, and sauté over medium–high heat 2 minutes. Add mushrooms, and sauté 3 minutes. Sprinkle with flour, and stir until blended. Add beef broth and tomato paste; cook, stirring constantly, 2 to 3 minutes or until thickened.

4. Return beef to skillet; add sherry and next 3 ingredients. Reduce heat to low; simmer 5 minutes. Remove from heat; stir in sour cream. Sprinkle with parsley. Serve over hot cooked noodles.

Per serving: Calories 396; Fat 14.3g (sat 5.3g, mono 6.1g, poly 0.7g); Protein 33.2g; Carb 32.4g; Fiber 2.1g; Chol 77mg; Iron 3.4mg; Sodium 520mg; Calc 80mg

Flank Steak Soft Tacos With
Molasses Barbecue Glaze

makes 6 servings • prep: 10 min., cook: 12 min., other: 2 hr.

Molasses, the dark, thick syrup once made from grind-
ing sugar cane in mills run by horses or mules, is making a
comeback. Kentucky and Tennessee produce more of it than
any other state.

½	cup molasses	1	cup shredded lettuce	
¼	cup coarse grained mustard	1	large tomato, chopped	
1	Tbsp. olive oil	¾	cup (3 oz.) reduced-fat shredded	
1	(1½-lb.) flank steak		Cheddar cheese	
6	(8-inch) flour tortillas	½	cup light sour cream	

test kitchen tip: To cut the grilled flank steak, use a sharp chef's knife or an electric knife, and cut at an angle. Cutting thin slices diagonally across the meat fibers or grain produces tender results.

1. Whisk together first 3 ingredients; remove and reserve ¼ cup marinade
for basting.

2. Place steak in a large shallow dish or zip-top plastic freezer bag. Pour remaining molasses mixture over steak. Cover or seal, and chill 2 hours, turning
occasionally. Remove meat from marinade, discarding marinade.

3. Preheat grill to medium-high heat (350° to 400°).

4. Grill, covered with grill lid, over medium-high heat (350° to 400°) 6
minutes on each side or to desired degree of doneness, brushing often with
reserved marinade. Cut steak diagonally across the grain into very thin strips.

Per serving: Calories 412; Fat 14.1g (sat 6.2g, mono 3.4g, poly 1.4g); Protein 33.7g; Carb 38.3g; Fiber 3.9g;
Chol 65mg; Iron 4.2mg; Sodium 475mg; Calc 292mg

Grillades and Grits

makes 4 servings • prep: 15 min., cook: 35 min.

Pronounced *gree odds and grits*, this famous Louisiana brunch dish contains pork or beef, grits, and vegetables.

make it a meal: This slimmed down version of the New Orleans favorite is a quick, good-for-you dinner served with a green salad. It also doubles as a well-balanced morning meal with grapefruit halves sprinkled with a touch of brown sugar.

3   Tbsp. all-purpose flour
1   tsp. Creole seasoning, divided
1   lb. lean breakfast pork cutlets, trimmed
2   tsp. olive oil, divided
1   cup finely diced onion
1   cup finely diced celery
½   cup finely diced green bell pepper
1   (14.5-oz.) can no-salt-added diced tomatoes
1   (14-oz.) can low-sodium fat-free chicken broth
Creamy Grits

1. Combine flour and ½ tsp. Creole seasoning in a shallow dish. Dredge pork in flour mixture.

2. Cook pork, in 2 batches, in ½ tsp. hot oil per batch in a large skillet over medium-high heat 2 minutes on each side or until done. Remove from skillet, and keep warm.

3. Add remaining 1 tsp. oil to skillet. Sauté diced onion, celery, and bell pepper in hot oil 3 to 5 minutes or until vegetables are tender. Stir in remaining ½ tsp. Creole seasoning. Stir in diced tomatoes and chicken broth, and cook 2 minutes, stirring to loosen particles from bottom of skillet. Simmer 15 to 18 minutes or until liquid reduces to about 2 Tbsp. Serve tomato mixture over Creamy Grits and pork.

Per 1 serving pork mixture and ½ cup Creamy Grits: Calories 357; Fat 9.1g (sat 2.8g, mono 4.6g, poly 0.9g); Protein 33g; Carb 35.4g; Fiber 3.6g; Chol 66mg; Iron 2.2mg; Sodium 864mg; Calc 145mg

how many ways can you fix grits?

In Charleston and along the Atlantic Coast, what was once a simple fisherman's breakfast has become shrimp-'n'-grits, a Southern icon. In Louisiana, the tradition is grillades-and-grits, a beef brunch entrée. Some areas serve quail and grits as a traditional holiday breakfast. But in the "grits belt" from Louisiana to North Carolina, the traditional ingredients paired with the ground corn staple are butter, salt, cheese, sausage, and bacon. These days you'll find grits in one form or another served at five-star restaurants in creative ways or simply served in place of potatoes or rice beside a fancy entrée. But the one thing that will send most grits-lovin' Southerners into a tailspin is to see someone stir sugar into the hot, creamy mixture as if it were a cereal!

Creamy Grits

makes 2 cups • prep: 5 min., cook: 20 min.

1	(14-oz.) can low-sodium, fat-free chicken broth	1	cup fat-free milk
		½	cup quick-cooking grits

1. Bring broth and milk to a boil in a medium saucepan over medium-high heat; reduce heat to low, and whisk in ½ cup grits. Cook, whisking occasionally, 15 to 20 minutes or until creamy and thickened.

Per ½-cup: Calories 104; Fat 0.3g (sat 0.1g, mono 0.1g, poly 0.1g); Protein 5.4g; Carb 20g; Fiber 0.4g; Chol 1mg; Iron 0.8mg; Sodium 314mg; Calc 80mg

Chicken and Dumplings

makes 6 servings • prep: 15 min., cook: 15 min.

Slick or doughy? That's the debate when it comes to dumplings. A biscuit-type dough like in this recipe produces a soft-centered dumpling. A pie crust-type dough will produce the "slick" dumplings that some people prefer.

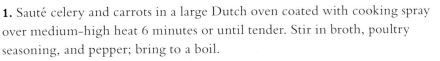

3	celery ribs, sliced	½	tsp. poultry seasoning
2	carrots, sliced	½	tsp. pepper
Vegetable cooking spray		1⅔	cups reduced-fat baking mix
3	(14½-oz.) cans low-sodium fat-free chicken broth	⅔	cup fat-free milk
		3	cups chopped cooked chicken

test kitchen tip: Chicken and Dumplings is best served just after it's prepared. When reheating leftovers, add a little water or chicken broth to regain the stewlike consistency.

1. Sauté celery and carrots in a large Dutch oven coated with cooking spray over medium-high heat 6 minutes or until tender. Stir in broth, poultry seasoning, and pepper; bring to a boil.

2. Stir together baking mix and milk until blended.

3. Turn dough out onto a heavily floured surface; roll or pat dough to ⅛-inch thickness. Cut into 3- x 2-inch strips.

4. Drop strips, 1 at a time, into boiling broth; stir in chicken. Cover, reduce heat, and simmer, stirring occasionally, 8 minutes.

Per serving: Calories 287; Fat 7.2g (sat 1.4g, mono 3.1g, poly 1.6g); Protein 27.2g; Carb 28.2g; Fiber 1.6g; Chol 63mg; Iron 2.3mg; Sodium 1066mg; Calc 189mg

Quick Collard Greens and Beans Risotto

makes 6 servings • prep: 20 min., cook: 30 min.

Known mostly as a Deep South staple, collard greens cooked in fatback have long been served with hog jowls, hoppin' John, and cornbread as a traditional New Year's Day meal. As the greens cook, the scent can be unpleasant, but it's said that dropping a whole pecan in the cooking collards will help.

test kitchen tip: This Southern variation of a classic Italian risotto uses quick-cooking brown rice instead of Arborio rice. It's much quicker than the classic, too.

1	Tbsp. salt	1	(15.5-oz.) can cannellini beans, rinsed and drained
1	(16-oz.) package chopped fresh collard greens	½	tsp. salt
1	cup chopped onion (about 1 large)	¼	tsp. freshly ground black pepper
3	large garlic cloves, minced	1	(3.5-oz.) bag quick-cooking brown rice
1	Tbsp. canola oil	½	tsp. dried crushed red pepper
3	cups low-sodium fat-free chicken broth	¾	cup grated Parmesan cheese, divided
2	Tbsp. all-purpose flour		

1. Bring 4 qt. water to a boil in a large Dutch oven. Add 1 Tbsp. salt, and stir until dissolved. Add collard greens, and cook 2 minutes or until wilted.

Drain greens in a colander; rinse with cold water. Drain and pat dry with paper towels. Set aside.

2. Sauté onion and garlic in hot oil in Dutch oven over medium heat 3 to 4 minutes or until tender.

3. Whisk together chicken broth and flour; add to Dutch oven, and bring to a boil. Add cannellini beans, ½ tsp. salt, pepper, and collard greens. Simmer, uncovered, 5 minutes. Reduce heat to low, and stir in rice and red pepper. Simmer, stirring frequently, 10 minutes or until greens and rice are tender. Remove from heat, and stir in ½ cup Parmesan cheese.

4. Sprinkle each serving with remaining ¼ cup cheese. Serve immediately.

Per serving: Calories 214; Fat 6.1g (sat 2g, mono 2.2g, poly 1.2g); Protein 11.2g; Carb 29.8g; Fiber 5.9g; Chol 9mg; Iron 1.4mg; Sodium 966mg; Calc 246mg

Chicken Fingers With Honey–Horseradish Dip

makes 8 servings • prep: 25 min., cook: 20 min.

Horseradish, a large white root that's peeled and grated to use, is one of the five bitter roots traditionally served at Jewish Passover.

16	saltine crackers, finely crushed	4	(6-oz.) skinned and boned chicken breasts
¼	cup pecans, toasted and ground	1	egg white
½	tsp. salt		Vegetable cooking spray
½	tsp. pepper		Honey-Horseradish Dip
2	tsp. paprika		

make it a meal: This recipe coupled with apple slices and milk makes an ideal meal for families with small children.

1. Preheat oven to 425°.

2. Stir together first 5 ingredients.

3. Cut each breast into 4 strips. Whisk egg white until frothy; dip chicken strips into egg white, and dredge in saltine mixture.

4. Place a wire rack coated with cooking spray in a broiler pan. Coat chicken strips on each side with cooking spray, and place on rack.

5. Bake at 425° for 18 to 20 minutes or until golden brown. Serve with Honey-Horseradish Dip.

Per 1 serving Chicken Fingers and 2 Tbsp. Honey-Horseradish Dip: Calories 200; Fat 4.4g (sat 0.6g, mono 2.1g, poly 1.1g); Protein 22.2g; Carb 17.2g; Fiber 1.8g; Chol 50mg; Iron 1.4mg; Sodium 412mg; Calc 48mg

Honey–Horseradish Dip

makes 1 cup • prep: 5 min.

½	cup plain nonfat yogurt	¼	cup honey
¼	cup coarse grained mustard	2	Tbsp. prepared horseradish

1. Stir together all ingredients.

Per Tbsp.: Calories 27; Fat 0.1g (sat 0g, mono 0g, poly 0g); Protein 0.6g; Carb 6g; Fiber 0.5g; Chol 0mg; Iron 0.1mg; Sodium 70mg; Calc 15mg

Broiled Salmon With Lemon and Olive Oil

makes 4 servings • prep: 20 min., cook: 12 min., other: 30 min.

If you believe some of the superstitions about herbs, you may want to save some of the fresh rosemary used in this entrée to place under a pillow to ward off nightmares or to wear in your hair to help your memory.

4	(6-oz.) salmon fillets	1	tsp. fresh or dried rosemary
½	tsp. salt		Vegetable cooking spray
½	tsp. coarsely ground pepper	2	cups hot cooked brown rice
1	tsp. grated lemon rind	4	cups arugula or uncooked baby
3	Tbsp. fresh lemon juice, divided		spinach
2	Tbsp. extra virgin olive oil, divided		Garnishes: lemon slices, rosemary sprigs

1. Sprinkle salmon fillets evenly with salt and pepper.

2. Place fillets, lemon rind, 1 Tbsp. lemon juice, 1 Tbsp. oil, and rosemary in a large zip-top plastic freezer bag. Seal and turn to coat. Chill 30 minutes.

3. Preheat broiler.

4. Remove fillets from marinade, discarding marinade. Place fillets, skin side down, on a rack coated with cooking spray in an aluminum foil–lined broiler pan. Broil fish 5½ inches from heat 10 to 12 minutes or until fillets flake with a fork.

5. Arrange rice and arugula on a serving platter; top with fillets. Whisk together remaining 2 Tbsp. lemon juice and 1 Tbsp. oil; drizzle evenly over fillets. Garnish, if desired.

Per serving: Calories 437; Fat 19.3g (sat 4g, mono 10g, poly 4g); Protein 39g; Carb 24.7g; Fiber 2.2g; Chol 87mg; Iron 1.4mg; Sodium 377mg; Calc 65mg

Roasted Potato-and-Bacon Salad

makes 8 servings • prep: 25 min., cook: 1 hr.

Though some people think of new potatoes as any small, waxy potato, the term actually refers to potatoes harvested in spring or early summer. You can tell new potatoes by their skin; it's thin and papery and easy to peel off by bits with your fingers.

2	lb. new potatoes, quartered	3	Tbsp. olive oil
2	tsp. olive oil	1	Tbsp. sugar
2	Tbsp. chopped fresh rosemary	2	garlic cloves, pressed
1	tsp. salt, divided	1	(6-oz.) package fresh spinach
1	tsp. freshly ground pepper, divided	1	(5-oz.) package mixed salad greens
	Vegetable cooking spray	¼	cup freshly shredded Parmesan
8	turkey bacon slices		cheese
¼	cup red wine vinegar		

1. Preheat oven to 400°.

2. Combine potatoes, oil, rosemary, ½ tsp. salt, and ½ tsp. pepper, tossing gently.

Roasted Potato-
and-Bacon Salad

Spread mixture in a 15- x 10-inch jelly-roll pan coated with cooking spray.
3. Bake at 400° for 40 to 50 minutes or until potatoes are tender and lightly browned. Sprinkle with ¼ tsp. salt and ¼ tsp. pepper; keep warm.
4. Cook bacon in a large skillet until crisp; remove bacon, and drain on paper towels, reserving drippings in skillet. Crumble bacon, and set aside.
5. Add vinegar, next 3 ingredients, remaining ¼ tsp. salt, and remaining ¼ tsp. pepper to skillet; cook over medium heat, whisking occasionally, 3 to 4 minutes or until thoroughly heated. Keep dressing warm.
6. Place spinach and mixed greens in a large serving bowl; top with potatoes, bacon, and Parmesan cheese. Drizzle with warm dressing, tossing to coat.

Per serving: Calories 197; Fat 10.2g (sat 2.4g, mono 4.8g, poly 0.8g); Protein 6.1g; Carb 21.5g; Fiber 2.9g; Chol 15mg; Iron 1.8mg; Sodium 532mg; Calc 78mg

Chopped Vegetable Coleslaw

makes 6 servings • prep: 15 min., other: 2 hr.

Coleslaw, the shredded salad Southerners love to pile onto barbecue sandwiches, is derived from the Dutch words, *kool sla,* which means cabbage salad.

test kitchen tip: If you cut broccoli florets from a bunch, don't throw away the broccoli stalks. Peel them with a vegetable peeler, and enjoy them as a healthful snack.

¼	cup light mayonnaise	1	cup fresh broccoli florets, chopped
¼	cup light sour cream	1	cup fresh cauliflower florets, chopped
1	Tbsp. white vinegar		
1	tsp. salt	2	cups seeded, diced plum tomato
¼	tsp. pepper	½	cup chopped red onion
3	cups shredded cabbage		

1. Stir together first 5 ingredients in a large bowl. Add cabbage and remaining ingredients, tossing to coat. Cover and chill 2 hours.

Per serving: Calories 78; Fat 4.2g (sat 1.1g, mono 0g, poly 0.1g); Protein 2.2g; Carb 9.4g; Fiber 2.6g; Chol 7mg; Iron 0.6mg; Sodium 495mg; Calc 47mg

Wild Mushroom Soup

makes 8 servings • prep: 25 min., cook: 45 min., other: 30 min.

Morel mushrooms are a delicacy sniffed out by hogs in France, but they also grow wild in the Appalachian Mountains.

test kitchen tip: Look for dried wild mushrooms in the produce section of large supermarkets. Don't substitute fresh mushrooms; they'll make the soup watery.

2	vegetable bouillon cubes	1	(½-oz.) package dried chanterelle mushrooms, chopped
2	cups boiling water		
¾	cup Madeira wine	2	Tbsp. butter or margarine
4	cups fat-free low-sodium chicken broth, divided	6	green onions, sliced
		1	medium onion, diced
1	(½-oz.) package dried porcini mushrooms, chopped	3	Tbsp. all-purpose flour
		1	lb. fresh white mushrooms, quartered
1	(½-oz.) package dried morel mushrooms, chopped	¼	tsp. freshly ground pepper

1. Dissolve bouillon cubes in 2 cups boiling water. Set vegetable broth aside.

2. Bring wine, ½ cup chicken broth, and dried mushrooms to a boil in a small saucepan. Remove from heat, and let stand 30 minutes.

3. Melt butter in a Dutch oven over medium-high heat; add sliced green onions and diced onion. Sauté until tender. Stir in flour, and cook, stirring constantly, 1 minute. Gradually stir in vegetable broth and remaining 3½ cups chicken broth. Stir in wild mushroom mixture, white mushrooms, and pepper. Bring to a boil, stirring occasionally; reduce heat, and simmer, stirring occasionally, 30 minutes. Cool slightly.

4. Process mixture, in batches, in a blender or food processor until smooth, stopping to scrape down sides. Return to Dutch oven. Cook over low heat, stirring occasionally, 5 minutes or until thoroughly heated.

Per 1-cup: Calories 113; Fat 3.9g (sat 2.1g, mono 0.7g, poly 0.2g); Protein 5.3g; Carb 11.2g; Fiber 2.1g; Chol 8mg; Iron 1.4mg; Sodium 741mg; Calc 15mg

quick & easy
homestyle

Coconut-Sour Cream Cake, page 97

Bacon Appetizers

makes 2 dozen • prep: 10 min., cook: 27 min.

Only 4 ingredients, but put together just so, they pack a wallop of first-course pleasure.

1 lb. bacon

1¾ cups (7 oz.) shredded Gouda cheese

1 cup mayonnaise

½ (16-oz.) package cocktail rye bread, lightly toasted

Garnishes: sun-dried tomato slivers, sliced ripe olives, fresh herbs

1. Preheat oven to 350°.

2. Cook bacon in a large skillet over medium-high heat until crisp; remove bacon, and drain on paper towels. Crumble bacon. Combine bacon, cheese, and mayonnaise in a large bowl.

3. Spread mixture on rye bread slices. Place on ungreased baking sheets. Bake at 350° for 7 minutes or until cheese is bubbly. Garnish, if desired. Serve warm.

Look Who Came to Dinner
The Junior Auxiliary of Amory, Mississippi

Creamy Chipotle–Black Bean Dip

makes 1 cup • prep: 10 min.

Adobo sauce is a thick Mexican mixture made from chiles, vinegar, and spices that can be used as a marinade or as a sauce served on the side. Here, it packs a little punch into sour cream and prepared bean dip.

½   cup sour cream
½   cup prepared black bean dip
1   tsp. minced chipotle peppers in adobo sauce

1   tsp. adobo sauce from can
¼   tsp. salt

1. Combine all ingredients; stir well. Cover and chill up to 3 days. Serve with tortilla chips.

test kitchen tip: Chipotle peppers are smoked jalapeño peppers. They're typically packed in an adobo sauce. Store any remaining adobo sauce in an airtight container in the refrigerator. Use it in teaspoonfuls to jazz up soups and stews.

Dulce de Leche Coffee Shake

makes 4 servings • prep: 5 min.

The Latin American cooked sugar and milk mixture called dulce de leche makes this shake as rich tasting as the caramelized sauce.

1   cup dulce de leche ice cream
1   cup coffee ice cream

½   cup milk
1   Tbsp. coffee liqueur (optional)

1. Process first 3 ingredients, and, if desired, 1 Tbsp. coffee liqueur in a blender until smooth, stopping to scrape down sides as needed. Serve immediately.
Note: For testing purposes only, we used Häagen-Dazs Dulce de Leche and Coffee ice creams and Kahlúa coffee liqueur.

test kitchen tip: There's no need to soften the ice creams before blending this shake.

Raspberry-Orange-Mint Cooler

makes about 7 cups • prep: 10 min.

As a symbol of hospitality, fresh mint adds a refreshing taste to fruit drinks, iced tea, and even savory dishes. Experiment with some of the more than 30 species such as peppermint, spearmint, chocolate mint, apple mint, and pineapple mint.

make it ahead: Prepare this recipe a day in advance, and make ice cubes with a small portion of the mixture. The flavorful ice cubes will keep the drinks cold and prevent the beverage from diluting.

¼ cup packed fresh mint leaves
¼ cup honey
2 Tbsp. fresh lemon juice
6 cups pulp-free orange juice, chilled
1½ cups fresh or frozen raspberries, thawed
Garnish: mint leaves

1. Process ¼ cup mint leaves, honey, and lemon juice in a blender until mint leaves are finely chopped (about 30 seconds); pour into a pitcher. Add 2 cups orange juice and 1½ cups frozen raspberries to a blender, and process until smooth, stopping to scrape down sides as needed.

2. Pour raspberry mixture through a wire-mesh strainer into pitcher, discarding seeds. Stir in remaining 4 cups orange juice; serve over ice. Garnish, if desired.

cooling off–Southern style

Besides the South's number one beverage cooler—sweet iced tea, Southerners have managed to find plenty of ways to beat the humid summer heat. George Washington was one of the first to serve ice cream to his guests in Virginia. The general store in rural areas paid tribute to local soda brands—Royal Crown, Pepsi, and Atlanta's famous Coca Cola. In the early 1900s the soda fountain was a great place to get shakes, lemonade, limeade, and sodas. At Gilchrist's soda fountain in Mountain Brook, Alabama, it still is. "We make limeade, our specialty, and our shakes just like we did in 1928 when we first opened," says owner Leon Rosato. "On a good hot summer day, we'll make over 200 limeades—squeezing the fresh juice into the cup, just the way we used to."

Blueberry Muffins

makes 1 dozen • prep: 10 min., cook: 18 min.

In the early 1800s muffins were so popular that "muffin men" traveled the countryside ringing a bell at tea time to announce their muffins for sale.

2	cups self-rising flour		¼	cup vegetable oil
½	cup sugar		2	large eggs
1	cup milk		1	cup fresh or frozen blueberries

1. Preheat oven to 400°.

2. Combine flour and sugar in a large bowl; make a well in center of mixture. Whisk together milk, oil, and eggs until well blended. Add to flour mixture, and stir just until dry ingredients are moistened. Gently fold in blueberries.

3. Spoon mixture into lightly greased muffin pans, filling two–thirds full.

4. Bake at 400° for 15 to 18 minutes or until golden brown.

test kitchen tip: Be careful not to over-mix muffins. If you stir the batter until all the lumps have disappeared, the muffins will be tough and have pointed tops. For tender muffins, stir the batter just enough to moisten the dry ingredients, and no more.

Greek Bread

makes 6 servings • prep: 10 min., cook: 5 min.

Ripe black olives, essential in Mediterranean cooking, are too bitter to be eaten fresh. A curing process used before canning them mellows their flavor enough to nicely accent mild foods like this cheese toast.

1½	cups (6 oz.) shredded mozzarella cheese		1	(2¼-oz.) can sliced ripe olives, drained
¼	cup butter or margarine, softened		¼	tsp. garlic salt
2	Tbsp. mayonnaise		1	(1-lb.) loaf Italian bread
6	green onions, chopped			

1. Preheat broiler.

2. Stir together first 6 ingredients until well blended.

3. Cut bread in half lengthwise. Place bread on a baking sheet, cut sides up. Broil 6 inches from heat 1 minute or until lightly browned. Spread mozzarella cheese mixture on bread, and broil 3 more minutes or until melted and bubbly.

Kimm Looney

Cookin' with Pride
4th Infantry Division ~ Ft. Hood, Texas

make it a meal: A hefty slice of this gooey bread that's loaded with cheese, olives, and green onions is a perfect accompaniment with a dinner salad or soup.

Banana-Pecan Pancakes

makes 4 servings • prep: 10 min., cook: 8 min.

Pancakes aren't just for breakfast, and the variations are endless. So are the names they've been called—griddle cakes, hotcakes, and flapjacks all refer to the flat round skillet bread beloved in the South.

test kitchen tip: The Pancake Mix makes a welcomed gift from your kitchen. Include the Banana-Pecan Pancakes recipe on the gift card.

1½	cups Pancake Mix	1	Tbsp. vegetable oil
1	Tbsp. sugar	1	chopped banana
1½	cups buttermilk	¼	cup toasted chopped pecans
1	large egg, lightly beaten		

1. Combine Pancake Mix and sugar in a medium bowl.

2. Whisk together 1½ cups buttermilk, egg, and oil; add to dry ingredients, whisking just until lumps disappear. Stir in chopped banana and pecans.

3. Pour about ¼ cup batter for each pancake onto a hot, lightly greased griddle or large nonstick skillet. Cook 2 minutes or until tops are covered with bubbles and edges begin to look cooked; turn and cook 2 more minutes or until done.

Pancake Mix

makes 6 cups • prep: 10 min.

6	cups all-purpose flour	2	tsp. baking soda
3	Tbsp. baking powder	2	tsp. salt

1. Stir together all ingredients in a large bowl; store in a zip-top plastic bag up to 6 weeks.

Butter-Me-Nots

makes 3 dozen • prep: 10 min., cook: 15 min.

Muffins don't get any easier than this 3-ingredient recipe. These buttery poppers freeze well.

test kitchen tip: Self-rising flour is all-purpose flour that has leavening and salt added. If you need a substitute, use 1 cup all-purpose flour plus 1 tsp. baking powder and ¼ tsp. salt for every 1 cup of self-rising flour.

2	cups self-rising flour	1	cup butter, melted
1	(8-oz.) container sour cream		

1. Preheat oven to 400°.

2. Combine all ingredients in a medium bowl, stirring until blended. Spoon batter into lightly greased miniature (1¾-inch) muffin pans, filling full.

3. Bake at 400° for 15 minutes or until golden.

Simply Divine
Second-Ponce de Leon Baptist Church ~ Atlanta, Georgia

Cheesy Bacon Corn Muffins

makes 14 muffins • prep: 12 min., cook: 21 min.

Ranch dressing is the surprise flavor in these savory cornbread muffins. Be sure to use cornmeal mix, not cornbread mix.

2 cups self-rising white cornmeal mix
1 (8-oz.) container sour cream
½ cup Ranch dressing
1 large egg, beaten
¼ cup vegetable oil

1½ cups (6 oz.) shredded sharp Cheddar cheese
1 small onion, chopped
¼ cup cooked and crumbled bacon slices

make it a meal: These muffins are a perfect accompaniment with a bowl of steaming soup or a vegetable dinner, and also pair nicely with breakfast foods.

1. Preheat oven to 425°.

2. Generously grease 14 muffin pans; heat pans in a 425° oven while preparing muffin batter.

3. Place cornmeal mix in a medium bowl; make a well in center. Stir together sour cream, Ranch dressing, egg, and oil; add to cornmeal mix, stirring just until blended. Stir in cheese, onion, and bacon.

4. Remove muffin pans from oven; spoon batter evenly into hot muffin cups, filling three-fourths full. Bake at 425° for 21 minutes or until golden brown. Remove from pans immediately.

Coconut–Sour Cream Cake

(pictured on page 91)

makes 12 servings • prep: 25 min., cook: about 27 min., other: 9½ hr.

Butter-flavored cake mix gives you a head start on this elegant-looking 4-layer cake. The flavor gets better and the cake more moist the longer it chills.

1 (18.25-oz.) package butter-recipe cake mix (we tested with Pillsbury)
1 (16-oz.) container sour cream
2 cups sugar

4 cups sweetened flaked coconut
1½ cups frozen whipped topping, thawed

lighten up: You'll save calories and no one will notice a difference in this decadent cake by using light sour cream and reduced-fat whipped topping.

1. Prepare cake mix according to package directions, using 2 (9-inch) round cake pans. Slice each cake layer horizontally in half, using a long serrated knife.

2. Combine sour cream, sugar, and coconut in a bowl; stir well. Cover and chill 1½ hours. Reserve 1 cup sour cream mixture. Spread remaining sour cream mixture between layers.

3. Fold whipped topping into reserved sour cream mixture. Spread on top and sides of cake. Place cake in an airtight container. Cover and chill at least 8 hours.

Rocky Road Pie

makes 6 servings • prep: 10 min.; other: 8 hr., 10 min.

Stir together marshmallows, nuts, and chocolate in any dessert recipe, and the conglomeration looks like a rocky road. But, this is one road you'll want to take.

1½ cups half-and-half	⅓ cup semisweet chocolate morsels
1 (3.9-oz.) package chocolate instant pudding mix	⅓ cup miniature marshmallows
	⅓ cup chopped peanuts
1 (8-oz.) container frozen whipped topping, thawed	1 (6-oz.) graham cracker crust

1. Combine half-and-half and pudding mix in a large mixing bowl; beat with a wire whisk until blended. Fold in whipped topping, chocolate morsels, marshmallows, and peanuts.

2. Spoon into prepared crust. Cover and freeze 8 hours or until firm.

3. Let stand at room temperature 10 minutes before serving.   Bev Richmond

The Phoenix Zoo Auxiliary Cookbook
Phoenix Zoo Auxiliary ~ Phoenix, Arizona

Peanut Butter Squares

makes 2 dozen • prep: 15 min., other: 2 hr.

By the late 1800s in the South, locally made peanut butter was sold door to door in northeastern states. It wasn't until the 1920s that peanut butter was produced commercially.

4 cups sifted powdered sugar	1 cup butter or margarine, melted
1 (5⅓-oz.) package graham crackers, crushed (about 1⅔ cups)	1 cup semisweet chocolate morsels, melted
1 cup creamy peanut butter	

1. Stir together first 4 ingredients in a medium bowl. Firmly press mixture into an ungreased 13- x 9-inch pan. Spread melted chocolate evenly over cracker layer.

2. Let stand at room temperature 2 hours or until chocolate is set. Cut into squares.   Forest Bryant

A Little DAPS of This . . . A Little DAPS of That
Dallas Area Parkinsonism Society ~ Dallas, Texas

Caramel-Cashew Ice Cream

makes 1 qt. • prep: 10 min., other: 8 hr.

You won't need an ice-cream freezer for this rich butterscotch-caramel ice cream, just an airtight container. It's a great make-ahead dessert: Just mix, freeze, scoop, and enjoy!

2   cups whipping cream
1   (14-oz.) can sweetened condensed milk
½   cup butterscotch-caramel topping
1   cup salted cashews, chopped
Toppings: butterscotch-caramel topping, chopped cashews

1. Beat whipping cream at high speed with an electric mixer until firm peaks form.

2. Stir together sweetened condensed milk and ½ cup butterscotch-caramel topping in a large bowl. Fold in whipped cream and 1 cup cashews. Place in an airtight container; freeze 6 to 8 hours or until firm. Serve with desired toppings.

test kitchen tip: It's best to beat whipping cream in a chilled metal bowl with chilled beaters. If you overbeat whipping cream, it will turn into butter. So beat it just until firm peaks form when beaters are lifted straight up.

Turtle Cookies

makes 2 dozen • prep: 20 min.; cook: 20 min.; other: 2 hr., 2 min.

Georgia is the country's top producer of pecans, which come from the only major nut tree native to the U.S.

2   cups all-purpose flour
1   cup firmly packed brown sugar
½   cup butter or margarine, softened
1   cup pecan halves
⅔   cup butter or margarine
½   cup firmly packed brown sugar
1   cup milk chocolate morsels

1. Preheat oven to 350°.

2. Combine first 3 ingredients in a mixing bowl; beat at medium speed with an electric mixer until blended. Pat mixture firmly into an ungreased 13- x 9-inch pan. Arrange pecans over crust.

3. Combine ⅔ cup butter and ½ cup brown sugar in a saucepan; bring to a boil over medium-high heat, stirring constantly. Cook 3 minutes, stirring constantly. Pour mixture evenly over pecans. Bake at 350° for 15 to 17 minutes or until golden and bubbly.

4. Remove from oven; sprinkle with chocolate morsels. Let stand 2 minutes or until slightly melted. Gently swirl chocolate with a knife, leaving some morsels whole (do not spread); let cool on a wire rack at room temperature 2 hours or until chocolate is set. Cut into squares.   Helen Kelly

Over the Bridge
Corpus Christie Women's Guild ~ East Sandwich, Massachusetts

test kitchen tip: Arrange pecan halves in an even layer in Step 2 so that each cookie will have a pecan in it. Pecan halves make the prettiest cookies but chopped pecans taste just as delicious.

Salisbury Steak

makes 6 servings • prep: 14 min., cook: 28 min.

Canned soup simmers into a tasty sauce and simplifies comfort food at its best.

1	(10¾-oz.) can beefy mushroom soup, divided	½	cup fine, dry breadcrumbs
1½	lb. ground chuck	¼	cup finely chopped onion
1	large egg, beaten	⅛	tsp. pepper
		¼	cup water

make it a meal: Serve these savory patties with plenty of mashed potatoes or hot cooked rice to soak up every bit of the mushroom gravy.

1. Combine ¼ cup soup and next 5 ingredients, mixing well. Divide meat mixture evenly into 6 portions. Shape each portion into a ½-inch-thick patty.

2. Cook patties in a large nonstick skillet over medium-high heat 3 to 4 minutes on each side or until browned. Combine remaining soup and water, stirring well. Pour soup mixture over patties; cover, reduce heat, and simmer 20 minutes.

Stepping Back to Old Butler
Butler Ruritan Club ~ Butler, Tennessee

Ultimate Cheeseburger Pizza

makes 4 servings • prep: 15 min., cook: 18 min.

Though many Southerners prefer Cheddar cheese tinted orange with food coloring, Cheddar cheese is actually white. Either tastes great in this quick supper recipe that marries two favorite foods into one.

test kitchen tip: To avoid having to get out the cutting board, chop tomatoes while they are still in the can using kitchen shears.

½	lb. lean ground beef	1½	cups (6 oz.) shredded Cheddar cheese
1	(14.5-oz.) can whole tomatoes, drained and chopped	¼	cup chopped green onions
1	tsp. bottled minced garlic	½	tsp. salt
1	(12-inch) prebaked pizza crust		

1. Brown beef in a skillet over medium-high heat, stirring often, 4 minutes or until beef crumbles and is no longer pink; drain well.

2. Preheat oven to 450°.

3. Stir together tomatoes and garlic. Spread crust evenly with tomato mixture, and sprinkle with ground beef, cheese, green onions, and salt.

4. Bake at 450° directly on oven rack for 12 to 14 minutes or until cheese is melted.

Ultimate Cheeseburger Pizza

Cornflake-Coated Pork Chops

makes 6 servings • prep: 10 min., cook: 35 min.

These pork chops bake up so nice and crisp, you'll swear they're fried.

make it a meal: Serve Cornflake-Coated Pork Chops with steamed broccoli or green beans and microwaveable rice.

2	large eggs, lightly beaten		2	tsp. lemon pepper
2	Tbsp. milk		1	tsp. salt
5	cups cornflakes cereal, crushed (about 2 cups crushed)		1	tsp. garlic powder
6	boneless pork chops (about ¾ inch thick)		1	large lemon, halved
				Garnish: lemon slices

1. Preheat oven to 350°.

2. Stir together eggs and milk in a shallow dish. Place cornflakes crumbs in a separate shallow dish. Sprinkle pork evenly with lemon pepper, salt, and garlic powder. Dip pork chops in egg mixture, and dredge in cornflakes crumbs. Place chops on a lightly greased rack on a baking sheet.

3. Bake at 350° for 30 to 35 minutes or until done. Squeeze lemon juice evenly over chops, and garnish, if desired.

Orange-Ginger Grilled Chicken Thighs

makes 8 servings • prep: 13 min., cook: 8 min., other: 1 hr.

Fresh garlic and ginger, along with orange juice, soy sauce, and sesame oil, create a tasty marinade for these grilled chicken thighs.

lighten up: If you're watching calories, this recipe is a good choice. With only 146 calories per serving, it's considered low calorie. Team it with brown rice and roasted broccoli for a satisfying supper.

⅓	cup orange juice		1	Tbsp. dark sesame oil
3	Tbsp. rice wine vinegar		8	(4-oz.) skinned and boned chicken thighs
3	Tbsp. soy sauce			
1	Tbsp. minced garlic			Garnishes: fresh cilantro sprigs, orange slices
1	Tbsp. minced fresh ginger			

1. Combine first 6 ingredients in a shallow dish or large zip-top plastic freezer bag; add chicken. Cover or seal, and chill at least 1 hour, turning occasionally.

2. Preheat grill to medium-high heat (350° to 400°).

3. Remove chicken thighs from marinade, and discard marinade.

4. Grill, covered with grill lid, over medium-high heat (350° to 400°) for 4 minutes on each side or until done. Garnish, if desired.

Praline Chicken

makes 6 servings • prep: 14 min., cook: 28 min.

Speak of pralines, and most people think of the sugar-pecan candy icon of New Orleans. In this recipe, the traditional candy ingredients are drizzled over chicken for a delectable entrée.

6	skinned and boned chicken breasts	⅓	cup maple syrup
2	tsp. Creole seasoning	2	Tbsp. brown sugar
¼	cup butter, melted	1	cup chopped pecans, toasted
1	Tbsp. vegetable oil		

1. Sprinkle both sides of chicken breasts with Creole seasoning. Heat butter and oil in a large skillet over medium-high heat until hot. Add chicken, and cook 4 to 5 minutes on each side or until done. Remove chicken, reserving drippings in skillet. Place chicken on a serving platter; set aside, and keep warm.

2. Add maple syrup and sugar to drippings in skillet; bring to a boil. Stir in pecans, and cook 1 minute or until thoroughly heated. Spoon pecan mixture over chicken.

Among the Lilies
Women in Missions, First Baptist Church of Atlanta ~ Atlanta, Georgia

Sautéed Shrimp

makes 4 servings • prep: 10 min., cook: 10 min.

Put the pasta on to cook as you start the shrimp to have this mouthwatering dinner on the table in record time.

test kitchen tip: Dress up this recipe for company by adding slivered sun-dried tomatoes and pitted kalamata olives just after the shrimp turn pink.

¼   cup butter or margarine

1   (.7-oz.) envelope Italian dressing mix

1   lb. peeled and deveined medium-size raw shrimp

Hot cooked pasta

1. Melt butter in a large skillet over medium heat; stir in dressing mix. Add shrimp; cook, stirring constantly, 3 to 5 minutes or until shrimp turn pink. Serve immediately over pasta.

Good Food, Good Company
The Junior Service League of Thomasville, Georgia

jubilee in Alabama

"It's usually July or August, the winds come out of the east, and the bay gets real calm," explains Amy Dial of Fairhope, Alabama, as she describes conditions for Mobile Bay's unique phenomenon called jubilee. Deep in the night, the tide waters push flounder, crab, and shrimp onto the shore and into the shallow waters. In the old days, beachcombers alerted neighbors with shouts of, "Jubilee!" Today, locals count on their friends who live on the beach to call from cell phones. According to Amy, the essentials to take along are a kerosene "flounder light" that shines into the shallow waters, a stick with a nail in the end called a "gig" for collecting flounder, and a net for scooping crab and shrimp. "Depending upon how many hours the jubilee lasts," she says, "you can collect an ice chest full."

Fruit Salad With Honey-Pecan Dressing

makes 10 servings • prep: 25 min.

Pecans add a Southern touch to this sweet-tart dressing that's great over this fruit and lettuce salad or a bag of prepackaged greens.

2½	cups fresh orange sections	3⅓	cups sliced strawberries
2½	cups fresh grapefruit sections	10	cups Bibb lettuce leaves
1	avocado, sliced		Honey-Pecan Dressing

1. Arrange orange and grapefruit sections, sliced avocado, and sliced straw-berries on Bibb lettuce leaves; drizzle with Honey-Pecan Dressing.

Honey-Pecan Dressing

makes 2½ cups • prep: 10 min.

3	Tbsp. sugar	½	cup honey
1	Tbsp. chopped sweet onion	¼	cup red wine vinegar
½	tsp. dry mustard	1	cup vegetable oil
¼	tsp. salt	1	cup chopped pecans, toasted

1. Combine first 6 ingredients in a blender; pulse 2 or 3 times until blended. With blender running, pour oil through food chute in a slow, steady stream; process until smooth. Stir in pecans.

test kitchen tip: Ever wonder about the difference in the avocados in the produce section? Florida avocados have a slick green skin and are larger and more economical than black, pebbly-skinned California Hass avocados. The Hass variety is creamier and boasts a nutty flavor. Either works in this recipe as long as it's ripe—it yields to gentle pressure.

Oriental Chicken Salad

makes 4 servings • prep: 15 min., cook 8 min.

Cider vinegar, made from fermented apple cider, has a fruity taste that adds a delicious tang to salads and dressings. It's also a great way to get the odor from your hands or cutting surfaces after chopping pungent onions or garlic.

1	(3-oz.) package oriental-flavored ramen noodles	2	Tbsp. sugar	
½	cup slivered almonds	2	Tbsp. cider vinegar	
½	cup sunflower kernels	2	roasted chicken breasts, chopped	
½	cup canola or vegetable oil	1	(16-oz.) package coleslaw or salad mix	

1. Preheat oven to 350°.

2. Crumble uncooked noodles; set seasoning packet aside. Combine noodles, almonds, and sunflower kernels on a baking sheet. Bake at 350° for 7 to 8 minutes or until golden, stirring occasionally.

3. Combine seasoning packet, oil, sugar, and vinegar in a jar. Cover tightly, and shake vigorously. Combine chicken, coleslaw mix, toasted noodles, almonds, sunflower kernels, and dressing in a large bowl; toss well. Serve immediately.

Marsha Taylor

Somethin's Cookin' with Married Young Adults
Houston's First Baptist Church ~ Houston, Texas

Strawberry–Spinach Salad

makes 6 servings • prep: 10 min.

Besides adding lots of color to this salad, red onions have a sweeter flavor than some other onions, and also are good for you. Studies show that including them in your diet can help lower blood pressure.

¼	red onion, thinly sliced	½	cup sliced toasted almonds
2	(6-oz.) bags baby spinach		Bottled red wine vinaigrette
1	(16-oz.) container strawberries, quartered		Salt and freshly ground pepper to taste
1	(4-oz.) package crumbled blue cheese		

1. Toss together first 5 ingredients in a large bowl. Drizzle with red wine vinaigrette; sprinkle with salt and pepper to taste.

Green Peas With Crispy Bacon

makes 6 servings • prep: 15 min., cook: 20 min.

Rather than chase little round peas around the plate, be sure to serve this side with fluffy biscuits, or "pea pushers," to help you get every pea on your fork.

2   bacon slices
1   shallot, sliced
½   tsp. grated orange rind
½   cup fresh orange juice
½   tsp. pepper
¼   tsp. salt

1   (16-oz.) bag frozen sweet green peas, thawed
1   tsp. butter or margarine
1   Tbsp. chopped fresh mint
Garnishes: fresh mint sprig

1. Cook bacon in a medium skillet until crisp; remove and drain on paper towels, reserving 1 tsp. drippings in skillet. Crumble bacon, and set aside.

2. Sauté shallot in hot bacon drippings over medium-high heat 2 minutes or until tender. Stir in orange rind, orange juice, pepper, and salt. Cook, stirring occasionally, 5 minutes or until reduced by half.

3. Add peas, and cook 5 more minutes; stir in butter and chopped mint. Transfer peas to a serving dish, and sprinkle with crumbled bacon. Garnish, if desired.

Orange-Ginger-Glazed Carrots

makes 4 servings • prep: 10 min., cook: 40 min.

Flecks of orange rind, ginger, and pepper adorn these carrots that will complement most any entrée.

test kitchen tip: Ground ginger is more potent than fresh, so if you opt for the substitution, 1 tsp. will be plenty.

1 (1-lb.) package baby carrots, thoroughly washed	2 tsp. butter
1 cup water	2 tsp. honey
1 tsp. grated orange rind	1 to 3 tsp. freshly grated ginger
¼ cup fresh orange juice	¼ tsp. salt
	⅛ tsp. pepper

1. Combine all ingredients in a medium saucepan; bring to a boil over medium-high heat. Reduce heat, and simmer, stirring occasionally, 30 to 35 minutes or until liquid just evaporates and carrots are glazed.

Asparagus Amandine

makes 8 servings • prep: 10 min., cook: 15 min.

Tender asparagus is at its sweet flavor peak in early spring. Europeans tend to prefer white asparagus, now available in many Southern markets; it's actually grown underground to keep it from turning green.

test kitchen tip: If your asparagus is "pencil" thin, cook it only 1 minute in Step 1.

2 lb. fresh asparagus	1 Tbsp. fresh lemon juice
2 Tbsp. butter	½ tsp. salt
¼ cup sliced almonds	½ tsp. pepper
2 Tbsp. diced red bell pepper	

1. Snap off tough ends of asparagus. Cook asparagus in boiling salted water to cover in a large skillet 3 minutes or until crisp-tender; drain. Plunge asparagus into ice water to stop the cooking process; drain.
2. Melt butter in a large skillet over medium heat; add almonds, and sauté 2 to 3 minutes or until golden brown. Add asparagus and red bell pepper; cook 3 to 5 minutes. Toss with lemon juice, salt, and pepper. Serve immediately.

Blue Cheese–Bacon Slaw

makes 8 servings • prep: 15 min.

The gray-blue streaks in blue cheese are actually edible mold that helps to produce the crumbly cheese with a tangy flavor. Blending the cheese with bottled Ranch dressing makes a tasty and quick homemade dressing.

2	(12-oz.) packages broccoli coleslaw mix	6	bacon slices, cooked and crumbled	
1	small onion, chopped	1	(16-oz.) bottle Ranch dressing	
		1	cup crumbled blue cheese	

1. Rinse coleslaw mix with cold water; drain well. Combine coleslaw mix, onion, and bacon in a large bowl; toss to combine.

2. Stir together Ranch dressing and blue cheese. Add to coleslaw mixture just before serving.

test kitchen tip: After rinsing coleslaw mix with cold water, drain it very well to keep the shreds crisp. We like to drain it using a salad spinner.

better with bacon

That's always been the Southern train of thought. Wrap it around appetizers or a steak, chop it up and use it to season stove-cooked veggies, sprinkle crisp pieces over salads, slap slices on sandwiches, lay strips over game meat as it cooks to keep the lean meat moist, or use the drippings to bake cornbread. Bacon has been a staple in the South for centuries because it was easily smoked and cured for long storage and hogs were plentiful. Despite the healthy revolution, bacon hasn't lost its place in Southern cuisine. It's still a breakfast staple as well as popular on upscale menus. Leaner versions with less salt help Southerners satisfy the craving to bring home the bacon without guilt.

Ranch Potatoes

makes 4 servings • prep: 20 min., cook: 20 min.

Yukon gold potatoes have been around for centuries, but this variety is just beginning to be widely available in supermarkets. The buttery yellow tubers are moist and sweet, and good for boiling or mashing.

lighten up: Reduce calories with no taste sacrifice by using light butter, reduced-fat Ranch dressing, and turkey bacon.

1½ lb. Yukon gold potatoes (about 4 medium)
2 Tbsp. butter
¼ tsp. salt
½ tsp. pepper
⅓ cup Ranch dressing
2 bacon slices, cooked and crumbled

1. Bring potatoes and water to cover to a boil in a large Dutch oven; boil 15 to 20 minutes or until tender. Drain; peel, if desired.

2. Beat potatoes at low speed with an electric mixer just until mashed. Add butter, salt, and pepper, beating until butter is melted. Gradually add dressing, beating just until smooth. Top with crumbled bacon; serve warm.

Lemon Pilaf

makes 4 servings • prep: 10 min., cook: 10 min.

Whether you spell it pilau, perloo, pilaw, or pilaf, this Middle Eastern and South Asian specialty calls for rice mixed with vegetables and seasonings. The West African slaves introduced perloo to their new home in the Lowcountry, making it a specialty of the region today.

make it a meal: Turn this side dish into a main dish by stirring in 2 cups of chopped cooked chicken along with the rice in Step 2.

1 cup sliced celery
1 cup chopped green onions
2 Tbsp. butter or margarine, melted
3 cups cooked long-grain rice
1 Tbsp. grated lemon rind
1 tsp. salt
¼ tsp. pepper
Condiments: raisins, natural almonds, toasted flaked coconut, cooked and crumbled bacon

1. Cook celery and green onions in melted butter in a large skillet over medium-high heat, stirring constantly, until tender.

2. Add rice and next 3 ingredients to vegetable mixture; reduce heat, and cook 2 minutes or until thoroughly heated, stirring occasionally. Serve pilaf with desired condiments.

Gardener's Delight
Ohio Association of Garden Clubs ~ Grove City, Ohio

weeknight
family meals

Smothered Swiss Steak, page 112

Simply Satisfying

Smothered Swiss Steak

hot cooked rice

iceberg wedge salad with Ranch dressing

Black Bottom Cupcakes

serves 6

Smothered Swiss Steak

(pictured on previous page)

makes 6 servings • prep: 15 min.; cook: 1 hr., 35 min.

A cola soft drink is the secret ingredient for these slow-cooked steaks with a juicy tomato-based sauce. Start table talk by asking everyone to guess the surprise flavoring.

test kitchen tip: If you prefer, prepare this recipe early in the day in the slow cooker. See Note below recipe.

½	tsp. salt	1	medium-size green bell pepper, diced
6	(4-oz.) cube steaks		
½	cup all-purpose flour	1	(14.5-oz.) can petite diced tomatoes
1	tsp. seasoned pepper	1	(12-oz.) cola soft drink
4½	Tbsp. vegetable oil	1	Tbsp. beef bouillon granules
1	medium onion, diced	2	Tbsp. tomato paste

1. Sprinkle salt evenly on both sides of cube steaks. Combine flour and pepper in a shallow dish. Dredge steaks in flour mixture.

2. Brown 2 steaks in 1½ Tbsp. hot oil in a large nonstick skillet over medium-high heat 3 minutes on each side; drain on paper towels. Repeat procedure with remaining steaks and oil. Drain drippings from skillet, reserving 1 Tbsp. in skillet.

3. Sauté onion and bell pepper in hot drippings 7 minutes or until tender. Add diced tomatoes and next 3 ingredients to skillet. Bring to a boil, and cook, stirring often, 5 minutes or until slightly thickened. Return steaks to skillet; cover and cook over low heat 55 to 60 minutes or until tender.

Note: To prepare this recipe in the slow cooker, place seared cubed steaks in a 5-qt. slow cooker. After cola mixture has cooked 5 minutes, spoon it over seared cube steaks. Cover and cook on LOW 5 hours.

Black Bottom Cupcakes

makes 16 cupcakes • prep: 25 min., cook: 30 min.

Chocolate settles in the bottom of these cheesecakelike cupcakes to inspire the name.

1 (8-oz.) package cream cheese, softened	1 tsp. baking soda
1⅓ cups sugar, divided	½ tsp. salt
⅛ tsp. salt	¼ cup unsweetened cocoa
1 large egg	1 cup water
1 cup semisweet chocolate morsels	⅓ cup vegetable oil
1½ cups all-purpose flour	1 Tbsp. white vinegar
	1 tsp. vanilla extract

freeze it: Seal leftover cupcakes in an airtight plastic freezer bag, and freeze up to 1 month.

1. Preheat oven to 350°.

2. Beat cream cheese at medium speed with an electric mixer until creamy; gradually add ⅓ cup sugar, beating well. Add ⅛ tsp. salt and egg; beat well. Stir in chocolate morsels; set aside.

3. Combine remaining 1 cup sugar, flour and next 3 ingredients in a large bowl; make a well in center of mixture. Combine water and remaining 3 ingredients; add to flour mixture, stirring just until dry ingredients are moistened. Spoon batter evenly into paper-lined muffin pans, filling half-full. Spoon a heaping Tbsp. of cream cheese mixture over batter in each muffin cup.

4. Bake at 350° for 25 to 30 minutes or until a wooden pick inserted in center comes out clean. Remove from pans, and cool completely on wire racks.

Karla Hoff

Food for the Flock
Good Shepherd Presbyterian Church ~ Lincoln, Nebraska

slowing down

Southerners have historically had a reputation for speaking slowly and moving at a snail's pace in the region's oppressive heat. Today, most Southerners' lifestyles defy that image and are rushed to the point that cooking dinner can be stressful. Fortunately, a new trend called the "Slow Food Movement" is encouraging folks to fight the fast food track, take time to enjoy meals, and buy locally grown food. Slow cookers are one of the best ways to hop on this slow food train. Introduced in the early 1970s, slow cookers provide long cooking times that add flavor as well as the ability to let food cook unattended making meals simple. Slow cookers, now enjoying a popularity revival, are even more helpful with digital programming and multiple cooking containers. Take time to check them out.

Casserole Dinner

Chicken Cobbler Casserole
Fresh Spinach-and-Apple Salad With Cinnamon Vinaigrette
German Chocolate Sauce with pound cake or ice cream

serves 4

Chicken Cobbler Casserole

makes 4 servings • prep: 25 min., cook: 40 min.

Nope, this cobbler's not for dessert! Beneath chunks of cheesy sourdough croutons, a creamy mixture of chicken, mushrooms, and peppers offers up a delicious filling.

6	Tbsp. melted butter, divided	1	cup white wine
4	cups cubed sourdough rolls	1	(10¾-oz.) can cream of mushroom soup
⅓	cup grated Parmesan cheese		
2	Tbsp. chopped fresh parsley	½	cup drained and chopped jarred roasted red bell peppers
2	medium-size sweet onions, sliced		
1	(8-oz.) package sliced fresh mushrooms	2½	cups shredded cooked chicken

test kitchen tip: Substitute an equal amount of chicken broth or buttermilk for wine, if desired.

1. Preheat oven to 400°.

2. Toss 4 Tbsp. melted butter with next 3 ingredients; set aside.

3. Sauté onions in remaining 2 Tbsp. butter in a large skillet over medium-high heat 15 minutes or until golden brown. Add mushrooms; sauté 5 minutes. Stir in wine and next 3 ingredients; cook, stirring constantly, 5 minutes or until bubbly. Spoon mixture into a lightly greased 9-inch square baking dish; top evenly with bread mixture.

4. Bake at 400° for 15 minutes or until golden brown.

Fresh Spinach-and-Apple Salad With Cinnamon Vinaigrette

makes 4 servings • prep: 15 min.

A surprising dash of cinnamon flavors the honey-cider dressing that drapes tender spinach and crisp sweet apples for this salad. Let the kids tear the spinach and have fun using a salad spinner.

test kitchen tip: Apples ripen quickly at room temperature, so refrigerate them in the produce drawer until ready to use.

2	medium apples, thinly sliced	½	tsp. dry mustard
6	cups torn fresh spinach	¼	tsp. ground cinnamon
¼	cup honey	1	garlic clove, pressed
3	Tbsp. vegetable oil	⅛	tsp. salt
2	Tbsp. cider vinegar		

1. Combine apples and spinach in a serving bowl. Whisk together honey and next 6 ingredients until well blended. Pour mixture over salad, tossing gently. Serve immediately.

German Chocolate Sauce

makes 2 cups • prep: 5 min., cook: 15 min.

Serve this rich, buttery chocolate sauce over pound cake or ice cream, or as a dipping sauce with chunks of fresh fruit.

test kitchen tip: Seal remaining German Chocolate Sauce in a glass jar, and share with a neighbor or special friend.

½	cup butter	1	tsp. vanilla extract
1	(4-oz.) package sweet baking chocolate	⅛	tsp. salt
1½	cups sugar	1	(5-oz.) can evaporated milk

1. Melt butter and chocolate in a small saucepan over low heat, stirring until melted. Stir in sugar, vanilla, salt, and milk; bring to a boil over medium heat. Cook 7 minutes, stirring constantly. Serve warm over pound cake or ice cream.

Mediterranean Flair

Pan-Seared Trout With Italian-Style Salsa

Parmesan Cheese Grits

green salad with balsamic vinaigrette

serves 6

Pan-Seared Trout With Italian-Style Salsa

(pictured on following page)

makes 6 servings • prep: 5 min., cook: 4 min. per batch

Put on some Italian music when you serve these fork-tender trout fillets flash-seared in a pan of hot olive oil, and you'll feel you're in an Italian trattoria. A chunky chilled salsa of onion, tomatoes, balsamic vinegar, and feta cheese complements the delicate fish flavor.

6	(6-oz.) trout fillets	4	Tbsp. olive oil	
¾	tsp. salt		Italian-Style Salsa	
½	tsp. freshly ground pepper		Garnish: lemon wedges	

test kitchen tip: Substitute catfish or tilapia for trout. Both have a delicate fish flavor.

1. Sprinkle fillets with salt and pepper.

2. Cook 3 fillets in 2 Tbsp. hot oil in a large nonstick skillet over medium-high heat 1 to 2 minutes on each side or until fish flakes with a fork. Repeat with remaining fillets and oil. Top fish with salsa. Garnish, if desired.

Italian-Style Salsa

makes 2 cups • prep: 15 min.

Briny kalamata olives and feta cheese balance the sweet red onion and balsamic vinegar flavors for this salsa.

4	plum tomatoes, chopped	1	Tbsp. balsamic vinegar
½	small red onion, finely chopped	1	Tbsp. olive oil
12	kalamata olives, pitted and chopped	2	tsp. drained capers
		¼	tsp. salt
2	garlic cloves, minced	¼	tsp. freshly ground pepper
2	Tbsp. chopped fresh parsley	¼	cup crumbled feta cheese (optional)

1. Stir together first 10 ingredients, and, if desired, feta cheese, in a medium bowl. Cover and chill until ready to serve.

Pan-Seared Trout With Italian-Style Salsa, previous page
Parmesan Cheese Grits, opposite page

Parmesan Cheese Grits

makes 6 servings • prep: 10 min., cook: 15 min.

Grits aren't just for breakfast. Serve this creamy Southern comfort food instead of mashed potatoes or macaroni and cheese.

2	(14-oz.) cans chicken broth		2	cups freshly grated Parmesan cheese
3	cups milk		2	tsp. freshly ground pepper
1½	cups uncooked quick-cooking grits			
1	tsp. salt			

1. Bring chicken broth and milk just to a boil in a large saucepan. Slowly stir in grits and salt. Cover, reduce heat to medium-low, and cook, stirring occasionally, 6 to 7 minutes or until mixture is thickened. Add Parmesan cheese and pepper, stirring until cheese is melted.

test kitchen tip: If you prefer Cheddar cheese grits, cook grits as directed, reducing salt to ½ tsp., and substituting 3 cups (12 oz.) shredded extra-sharp Cheddar cheese for Parmesan cheese.

why eat together?
There was a time in Southern history when entire families ate together morning, noon, and night. Over the years, teens with jobs, both parents working late, long months of nice Southern weather for outdoor sports, and kids with more after-school activities led to a new norm. While it's a challenge to schedule dinners together during the week, it's worth it to do so. New studies show that kids who eat with their families at least three times a week tend to make better grades, eat healthier, and are less likely to drink alcohol or take drugs. They also are more likely to believe their parents are proud of them. The family meals don't always have to be home-cooked spreads. A simple breakfast, dinner at a restaurant, or even a hot dog at the ball park are fine options for getting the family together.

Fancy Fish 'n' Fixin's

Orange Roughy Parmesan

Pecan Pilaf

steamed asparagus

Pear Skillet Cake With Caramel-Rum Sauce

serves 4

Orange Roughy Parmesan

makes 4 servings • prep: 20 min., cook: 15 min., other: 10 min.

A creamy spread of mayonnaise and Parmesan tops these oven-broiled fillets. Since fish is good brain food, look up a few trivia questions to ask and get conversation started during the meal.

test kitchen tip: Catfish or tilapia substitute nicely for orange roughy fillets.

2	lb. orange roughy fillets	3	Tbsp. chopped green onions
2	Tbsp. lemon juice	¼	tsp. salt
½	cup grated Parmesan cheese	⅛	tsp. freshly ground pepper
¼	cup butter or margarine, softened		Dash of hot sauce
3	Tbsp. mayonnaise		Lemon wedges

1. Preheat broiler.

2. Place fillets on a greased pan. Brush fillets with lemon juice, and let stand at room temperature 10 minutes.

3. Combine Parmesan cheese and next 6 ingredients; set aside.

4. Broil fillets 8 inches from heat 8 minutes. Spread cheese mixture over fillets. Broil 5 more minutes or until fish flakes with a fork. Serve with lemon wedges.

Orange Roughy Parmesan, opposite page
Pecan Pilaf, following page

Pecan Pilaf

(pictured on previous page)

makes 4 servings • prep: 5 min., cook: 35 min.

This thyme-spiced dish teams two Southern favorites and pantry staples—rice and sweet, fragrant pecans.

¼	cup butter, divided	2	cups chicken broth
½	cup chopped pecans	½	tsp. salt
¼	cup chopped onion	⅛	tsp. dried thyme
1	cup uncooked long-grain rice	⅛	tsp. pepper

1. Melt 1½ Tbsp. butter in a large skillet over medium heat. Add pecans; sauté 8 minutes or until lightly browned. Remove pecans from skillet.

2. Melt remaining 2½ Tbsp. butter in skillet over medium heat; add onion, and cook until tender, stirring occasionally. Stir in rice and remaining ingredients. Bring mixture to a boil; cover, reduce heat, and simmer 20 minutes until liquid is absorbed and rice is tender. Remove from heat; stir in pecans.

Steve Stockton

Look Who Came To Dinner
The Junior Auxiliary of Amory, Mississippi

test kitchen tip: Aromatic basmati and Texmati rice are varieties of long-grain rice. They give this pilaf a sweet, nutty taste.

Pear Skillet Cake With Caramel-Rum Sauce

makes 8 servings • prep: 25 min.; cook: 1 hr., 8 min.; other: 20 min.

Flip this upside-down, sugar-soaked cake from the cast-iron skillet and the gooey molasses-colored topping makes the gingerbread cake irresistible.

1	cup firmly packed dark brown sugar	½	tsp. salt
6	Tbsp. unsalted butter, cut into pieces	2	tsp. ground cinnamon
4	pears, peeled and cut into 6 wedges each	2	large eggs
		½	cup vegetable oil
1⅓	cups all-purpose flour	1	small pear, unpeeled, cored, and coarsely grated
1⅓	cups granulated sugar	1	Tbsp. grated fresh ginger
1¼	tsp. baking soda		Caramel-Rum Sauce

1. Preheat oven to 325°.

2. Sprinkle brown sugar evenly in a 10-inch cast-iron skillet. Add butter, and place skillet in a 325° oven for 8 minutes. Remove skillet from oven; stir brown sugar mixture until blended. Arrange pear slices spoke-fashion on brown sugar mixture, working from the center of the skillet to the edge.

3. Combine flour and next 4 ingredients in a large bowl. Add eggs and oil, beating at low speed with an electric mixer until blended. Stir in grated pear and ginger. Spoon batter evenly over sliced pears in skillet.

4. Bake at 325° for 1 hour or until a wooden pick inserted in center comes out clean. Run a knife around edge to loosen from pan. Cool in pan on a wire rack 20 minutes. Invert onto a serving plate. Serve warm with Caramel-Rum Sauce.

test kitchen tip: A well-seasoned cast-iron skillet won't allow the sugary topping of the cake to stick, and its thick sides invite even cooking of the cake batter.

Caramel-Rum Sauce

makes 1½ cups • prep: 5 min., cook: 12 min., other: 5 min.

½   cup whipping cream

½   cup unsalted butter

½   cup granulated sugar

½   cup firmly packed dark brown sugar

3   Tbsp. dark rum

1. Combine first 4 ingredients in a medium saucepan; cook over medium heat until butter melts and sugars dissolve. Bring to a boil; cook 3 minutes or until slightly thickened. Stir in rum. Let stand 5 minutes.

Pear Skillet Cake With Caramel-Rum Sauce

Vegetable Night

Spaghetti and Cheese
Suppertime Turnip Greens
Black-eyed Peas
Delta Hot Chocolate
cornbread muffins

serves 6 to 8

Spaghetti and Cheese

makes 6 to 8 servings • prep: 20 min., cook: 45 min., other: 5 min.

Families who like macaroni and cheese will love this variation. Monterey Jack cheese and dry mustard give it a surprising flavor twist.

test kitchen tip: For a pimiento cheese version, substitute Cheddar cheese for Monterey Jack, and stir chopped pimiento into the milk mixture.

1   lb. spaghetti, cooked and drained
3   cups (12 oz.) shredded Monterey
        Jack cheese
1½   Tbsp. all-purpose flour
1½   tsp. salt
¾   tsp. dry mustard

¼   tsp. pepper
3¾   cups milk, divided
3   large eggs, lightly beaten
2   Tbsp. butter or margarine
Paprika

1. Preheat oven to 350°.

2. Place half of cooked spaghetti in a lightly greased 13- x 9-inch baking dish; sprinkle with half of cheese. Repeat procedure.

3. Combine flour, salt, dry mustard, and pepper in a small bowl. Whisk in 1 Tbsp. milk. Add remaining milk and eggs to flour mixture, stirring with a wire whisk until blended. Pour milk mixture over spaghetti mixture. Dot with butter, and sprinkle with paprika. Bake at 350° for 45 minutes or until set. Let stand 5 minutes before serving.

Spaghetti and Cheese, opposite page
Black-eyed Peas, following page
Suppertime Turnip Greens, following page

Suppertime Turnip Greens

(pictured on previous page)

makes 6 to 8 servings • prep: 20 min., cook: 50 min.

Even the kids will try turnip greens if you tell them that tradition promises plenty of money if greens are eaten on New Year's Day. They may want seconds of this savory version cooked with bacon, garlic, and red pepper.

test kitchen tip: Packages of prewashed greens take a fraction of the time to prepare compared to turnip greens purchased in bunches.

2	(1-lb.) packages fresh turnip greens	½	tsp. sugar
4	cups water	½	tsp. garlic powder
2	bacon slices, coarsely chopped	¼	to ½ tsp. ground red pepper
1	tsp. seasoned salt		

1. Remove and discard stems from greens; tear large pieces of greens into smaller pieces, if desired.

2. Combine water and bacon in a large Dutch oven; bring to a boil. Add greens, seasoned salt, and remaining ingredients. Cover and cook over medium heat 40 minutes or until greens are tender.

Black-eyed Peas

(pictured on previous page)

makes 6 to 8 servings • prep: 15 min., cook: 30 min.

Cooked crumbled bacon and a shake of hot sauce season this New Year's Day tradition said to bring good luck. To keep the meal really Southern, serve the peas with hot, crispy cornbread muffins.

lighten up: If you're taking steps to reduce sodium in your diet, rinse the peas with running water after draining. Use low-sodium chicken broth, and reduce or eliminate the salt.

4	bacon slices	1	(14-oz.) can chicken broth
1	medium onion, chopped	¼	tsp. hot sauce
1	garlic clove, minced	¼	tsp. salt
3	(15.8-oz.) cans black-eyed peas, drained	¼	tsp. pepper
		1	bay leaf

1. Cook bacon in a large skillet over medium-high heat until crisp. Remove bacon, reserving 1 Tbsp. drippings in pan. Crumble bacon, and set aside.

2. Sauté onion and garlic in bacon drippings in skillet. Add reserved bacon, black-eyed peas and remaining ingredients. Bring to a boil; reduce heat, and simmer 25 minutes. Discard bay leaf.

Delta Hot Chocolate

makes 7 cups • prep: 15 min., cook: 25 min.

This extra-rich hot chocolate made with cocoa and bitter-sweet chocolate bars makes an ordinary weeknight special. Serve it for dessert on a wintry night in front of the fireplace.

1	qt. milk	
2	cups whipping cream	
2	cinnamon sticks	
⅛	tsp. freshly ground nutmeg	
1	cup unsweetened cocoa	

¾	cup sugar	
1	Tbsp. vanilla extract	
2	(3-oz.) bars bittersweet chocolate, chopped	
Toasted marshmallows (optional)		

test kitchen tip: To make mint hot chocolate, omit cinnamon sticks, and substitute bittersweet chocolate with mint chocolate morsels; reduce sugar to ½ cup.

1. Cook first 4 ingredients in a Dutch oven over medium-low heat, stirring occasionally, 15 to 20 minutes or just until milk begins to steam. (Do not boil.) Remove from heat. Discard cinnamon sticks. Whisk in cocoa, sugar, and vanilla, whisking until blended.

2. Cook over low heat 5 minutes. Add chocolate, whisking until blended. Keep warm over low heat. Serve with toasted marshmallows, if desired.

Family-Pleasing Chicken

Buttermilk Picnic Chicken

Roasted Garlic Mashed Potatoes

green beans

biscuits

serves 6 to 8

Buttermilk Picnic Chicken

makes 6 to 8 servings • prep: 25 min., cook: 1 hr., other: 8 hr.

Think "picnic" when you prepare this seasoned chicken marinated in buttermilk. If you don't have time to pack one, spread a blanket on the den floor and have an indoor picnic.

test kitchen tip: Dredging the chicken in Step 3 can be messy, but a couple of options make it neater. Use tongs to transfer the wet chicken to the flour mixture. Or use disposable plastic gloves designed for use in food service. The gloves are inexpensive, available at large grocery stores or discount centers, and are ideal for promoting food safety.

¾	cup buttermilk	1	Tbsp. paprika
2	tsp. chicken bouillon granules	2	tsp. seasoned salt
1	tsp. poultry seasoning	¼	tsp. pepper
1	(3- to 4-lb.) package chicken pieces	¼	cup butter or margarine, melted
1	cup all-purpose flour		

1. Combine first 3 ingredients in a large zip-top plastic freezer bag. Add chicken. Seal and marinate in the refrigerator at least 8 hours, turning occasionally.

2. Preheat oven to 350°.

3. Remove chicken from marinade, discarding marinade. Combine flour and next 3 ingredients in a large zip-top plastic freezer bag. Add chicken, a few pieces at a time, shaking bag to coat. Arrange chicken on a 15- x 10-inch jelly-roll pan lined with aluminum foil. Drizzle chicken with melted butter.

4. Bake at 350° for 1 hour or until golden.

Buttermilk Picnic Chicken, opposite page
Roasted Garlic Mashed Potatoes, following page

Roasted Garlic Mashed Potatoes

(pictured on previous page)

makes 6 to 8 servings • prep: 35 min.; cook: 1 hr., 16 min.

Buttery roasted garlic cloves make these creamy, rich mashed potatoes taste like heaven. For family fun, give everyone small romaine lettuce leaves to use like spoons to eat the potatoes just like the ancient Greeks.

test kitchen tip: Adding warmed versus cold half-and-half to the potatoes in Step 5 assures a velvety texture.

3	large garlic bulbs	3	Tbsp. olive oil
3	lb. baking potatoes, cut into 3-inch pieces	¾	tsp. salt
		¼	tsp. ground white pepper
3	Tbsp. unsalted butter	1	cup half-and-half

1. Preheat oven to 350°.

2. Peel outer skins from garlic, and discard skins. Cut off and discard top one-fourth of each garlic bulb. Place garlic, cut side up, in center of a piece of heavy-duty aluminum foil; fold foil over garlic, sealing tightly. Bake at 350° for 1 hour or until garlic bulbs are soft. Remove from oven; let cool completely.

3. Squeeze pulp from garlic bulbs into a small bowl, and press with back of a spoon to make a paste. Set aside.

4. Cook potato in boiling water to cover 15 minutes or until tender; drain. Mash potatoes in a large bowl; stir in reserved garlic paste, butter, and next 3 ingredients.

5. Microwave half-and-half in a microwave-safe bowl at HIGH 1 minute. Gradually stir warm half-and-half into potato mixture.

fried chicken for family

Fried chicken has starred on family and company tables since the earliest days of the South. As the easiest and cheapest meat to raise, chicken was perfect for family meals and easy to carry in a lunch pail. It was also the Sunday dinner (as in midday) meat of choice for the traditional day of extended family gathering and eating. Big meals with lots of family are usually reserved for holidays now, but like in the past, fried chicken still takes center stage. While Southern fried chicken hasn't changed much, dining customs have. Families tended to eat together in the 1950s. Then, as they scattered to more activities and cooked less, the family meal became a special occasion in the next decades. Today, the resurgence of the family meal is on its way—and you can be sure fried chicken is still invited, sometimes as the traditional fried version and often as a more healthful oven-fried variation as on the previous page.

A Taste of Tex-Mex

salsa and tortilla chips
Mexican Lasagna
José Falcón's Slaw
Unbelievable Chocolate Ice Cream

serves 6

Mexican Lasagna

(pictured on following page)

makes 6 servings • prep: 25 min., cook 2 hr., other: 10 min.

Use a colorful tablecloth or runner and napkins in vivid hues
to give the table a Mexican flair.

1 lb. ground round	9 lasagna noodles
1 (16-oz.) can refried beans	1 (16-oz.) container sour cream
2 tsp. dried oregano	¾ cup thinly sliced green onions
1 tsp. ground cumin	1 (2¼-oz.) can sliced ripe olives,
¾ tsp. garlic powder	drained
2 cups picante sauce	1 cup (4 oz.) shredded Monterey Jack
1½ cups water	cheese

lighten up: Using a paper towel to wipe the skillet clean in Step 2 is an excellent tip to eliminate excess fat.

1. Preheat oven to 350°.

2. Cook ground beef in a large nonstick skillet, stirring until it crumbles and is no longer pink; drain. Wipe skillet clean. Return beef to skillet; stir in refried beans and next 3 ingredients.

3. Combine picante sauce and water. Pour 1⅓ cup picante mixture in a lightly greased 13- x 9-inch baking dish. Arrange 3 noodles over picante mixture. Spread half of beef mixture evenly over noodles. Pour 1 cup picante mixture over beef mixture, and top with 3 more noodles. Spread remaining beef mixture over noodles. Top with 3 remaining noodles. Pour remaining 1⅓ cups picante mixture evenly over noodles.

4. Cover and bake at 350° for 1½ hours.

5. Combine sour cream, green onions, and ripe olives in a small bowl. Remove lasagna from oven; spread sour cream mixture over lasagna, and sprinkle with cheese. Return to oven, and bake 10 more minutes. Let stand 10 minutes before serving.

Mexican Lasagna, previous page
José Falcón's Slaw, opposite page

José Falcón's Slaw

makes 6 servings • prep: 15 min., other: 1 hr.

In true Mexican tradition, bold colors from red and green cabbage and red bell pepper make this sweet cider slaw the star of the table. Cilantro adds an earthy flavor hint.

¼   cup mayonnaise

3   Tbsp. malt or cider vinegar

2   tsp. sugar

2   cups finely shredded red cabbage

1   cup finely shredded green cabbage

1   red bell pepper, thinly sliced

1   cup chopped fresh cilantro

¼   tsp. salt

test kitchen tip: Substitute a 16-oz. package of shredded coleslaw mix for red and green cabbages, if you'd like.

1. Stir together first 3 ingredients in a large bowl. Add red cabbage and remaining ingredients, tossing to coat. Cover and chill at least 1 hour.

Unbelievable Chocolate Ice Cream

makes 1 gal. • prep: 15 min., other: 1 hr.

Whether you use the old-fashioned hand-cranked ice cream maker using ice and rock salt or one of the new iceless, salt-less electric versions, let everyone have a hand in making the ice cream. Assign jobs to mix the ingredients, add salt or ice to the churn, or scoop the ice cream into serving bowls.

½   gal. chocolate milk

1   (14-oz.) can sweetened condensed milk

1   (12-oz.) container frozen whipped topping, thawed

2   Tbsp. unsweetened cocoa

¼   tsp. ground cinnamon (optional)

freeze it: Freeze any leftover ice cream in an airtight container up to 2 months. Before sealing, place a sheet of plastic wrap directly on the ice cream's surface to prevent freezer burn.

1. Pour all ingredients into freezer container of a 5-qt. hand-turned or electric freezer. Freeze according to manufacturer's instructions. (Instructions and freezing times may vary.)

Casual Night

Mustard-Glazed Pork Tenderloin

Parmesan Potato Sticks

steamed broccoli

Basil Batter Rolls

serves 4 to 6

Mustard-Glazed Pork Tenderloin

makes 4 to 6 servings • prep: 20 min., cook: 24 min., other: 40 min.

Spicy Creole seasoning, sweet orange juice, and a smoky grilled flavor make this tender pork cut a real treat. To make the meal seem extra special, turn off all the lights and eat by candlelight. You'll be surprised how sibling bickering sometimes ceases when the lights are low.

1	(8-oz.) jar Dijon mustard (1 cup)	2	Tbsp. Creole seasoning
⅓	cup orange juice	1½	pounds pork tenderloins

1. Stir together first 3 ingredients.

2. Place pork in a shallow dish or a zip-top plastic freezer bag; pour mustard mixture over pork. Cover or seal, and chill at least 30 minutes, turning occasionally.

3. Preheat grill to medium-high heat (350° to 400°).

4. Remove pork from marinade, discarding marinade.

5. Grill, covered with grill lid, over medium-high heat (350° to 400°) for 10 to 12 minutes on each side or until a meat thermometer inserted into thickest portion registers 155°. Remove from grill; let stand until thermometer registers 160°. Let stand 5 more minutes before slicing.

test kitchen tip: Removing the thick outer membrane called silver skin from pork tenderloin before cooking prevents it from curling and cooking unevenly. To do so, pull the end of the silver skin tight above the meat, and gently cut the layer away, making sure to keep the blade of the knife angled slightly upward and just underneath the silver skin. A trimmed pork tenderloin should be free of any visible fat and silver skin.

Mustard-Glazed Pork Tenderloin, opposite page
Basil Batter Rolls, page 137
Parmesan Potato Sticks, following page

Parmesan Potato Sticks

(pictured on previous page)

makes 4 to 6 servings • prep: 25 min., cook: 40 min., other: 5 min.

Kids can have fun measuring out the seasonings for the Parmesan Coating for these crispy home fries. Potato sticks with the cheese-spice coating bake to a golden brown.

6	small baking potatoes (about 3 lb.)	¾	cup butter or margarine, melted
3	to 4 cups cold water		Parmesan Coating
1	tsp. salt		

1. Scrub potatoes. Cut lengthwise into ½-inch slices; turn and stack potato slices, cut sides down. Cut lengthwise into ½-inch sticks. Place potato sticks in a large bowl. Combine cold water and salt; pour over potatoes to cover. Let stand 5 minutes.

2. Preheat oven to 400°.

3. Drain potatoes well; spread on paper towels to absorb water; pat dry. Dip potato sticks in melted butter; roll in Parmesan Coating. Place in a single layer on greased baking sheets. Bake at 400° for 30 minutes; turn potatoes, and bake 10 more minutes or until golden.

Parmesan Coating

makes 2¼ cups • prep: 5 min.

1	cup fine, dry breadcrumbs	½	tsp. paprika
1	cup grated Parmesan cheese	¼	tsp. garlic powder
1	tsp. salt	¼	tsp. pepper
1	tsp. dried parsley flakes		

1. Combine all ingredients in a bowl.

Basil Batter Rolls

(pictured on page 135)

makes 2 dozen • prep: 25 min.; cook: 16 min.; other: 1 hr., 20 min.

You won't have to call anyone to dinner when you bake these yeast rolls mixed with pesto. The herb and yeast bread aroma will linger longer in the air than the kids last at the table. Let family members help spoon the dough into the muffin pans to heighten the anticipation.

2 (¼-oz.) packages active dry yeast	1½ tsp. salt
1½ cups warm water (100° to 110°)	1 large egg
⅓ cup shortening	2 Tbsp. pesto
4 cups unbleached all-purpose flour	2 garlic cloves, minced
¼ cup sugar	Melted butter or margarine (optional)

freeze it: Seal and freeze leftover rolls in an airtight container up to 1 month.

1. Combine yeast and warm water in a 2-cup liquid measuring cup; let stand 5 minutes.

2. Combine yeast mixture, shortening, 2 cups flour, and next 3 ingredients in a large mixing bowl; beat at medium speed with an electric mixer until well blended. Stir in pesto and garlic. Gradually stir in enough remaining flour to make a soft dough. (Dough will be sticky.)

3. Cover and let rise in a warm place (85°), free from drafts, 40 minutes or until doubled in bulk.

4. Stir dough; spoon into greased muffin pans, filling half-full. Cover and let rise in a warm place (85°) for 35 minutes.

5. Preheat oven to 400°.

6. Bake at 400° for 15 to 16 minutes or until golden. Brush with melted butter, if desired.

Rogue River Rendezvous
The Junior Service League of Jackson County ~ Medford, Oregon

Better Than Takeout

Fried Noodles With Shrimp
Minted Sugar Snaps
orange wedges

serves 4

Fried Noodles With Shrimp

makes 4 servings • prep: 25 min., cook: 15 min.

When you serve this sweet-sour noodle dish with peanuts and shrimp, declare a "no-fork" night, and eat the entire meal with chopsticks.

test kitchen tip: Look for Thai rice noodles in the Asian section of larger grocery stores or at Asian markets.

1½	lb. uncooked, large raw shrimp	2	Tbsp. fish sauce
1	(8-oz.) package Thai rice noodles	2	Tbsp. Asian garlic-chili sauce
2	garlic cloves, minced	2	green onions, chopped
¼	cup vegetable oil	2	to 3 Tbsp. chopped peanuts
2	large eggs, lightly beaten	¼	cup chopped fresh cilantro
2	Tbsp. sugar		

1. Peel shrimp, and devein, if desired; set aside.

2. Cook noodles in boiling water 3 to 4 minutes; drain.

3. Sauté garlic in hot vegetable oil in a large nonstick skillet over medium heat 2 minutes. Add shrimp, and cook 2 minutes or just until shrimp turn pink. Add beaten egg to shrimp mixture in skillet. Cook over medium heat, without stirring, until egg begins to set. Stir until cooked, breaking up egg.

4. Stir in sugar, fish sauce, and garlic-chili sauce. Add noodles; cook 1 minute or until hot. Sprinkle with onions, peanuts, and cilantro.

Minted Sugar Snaps

makes 4 servings • prep: 5 min., cook: 5 min.

Fresh snap peas sautéed with garlic and mixed with mint add a fresh summer flavor to any meal. With kitchen scissors, chopping the mint and green onions is a snap.

test kitchen tip: Always check the freshness date on prepackaged produce for optimum quality. Sugar snap peas should be bright green, firm, and crisp.

	Vegetable cooking spray	1	large garlic clove, minced
1	(8-oz.) package fresh sugar snap peas, trimmed	2	Tbsp. minced fresh mint
		⅛	tsp. salt
2	green onions, chopped	¼	tsp. pepper

1. Coat a large nonstick skillet with cooking spray, and place over medium heat until hot. Add peas, green onions, and garlic; cook 3 minutes or until peas are crisp-tender, stirring often. Remove from heat; stir in mint, salt, and pepper.

Dinner in a Crust

Ham-and-Tomato Pie

Caesar salad

S'more Puffs

serves 6

Ham-and-Tomato Pie

makes 6 servings • prep: 20 min., cook: 28 min., other: 20 min.

Summer's best flavors are blended in this quiche-style recipe—sweet fresh basil, juicy plum tomatoes, and crisp green onions.

test kitchen tip: Use a traditional 9-inch pie shell, not a deep-dish. There's no need to thaw the crust before assembling.

1	(8-oz.) package diced cooked ham
½	cup sliced green onions
1	(9-inch) frozen unbaked pie shell
1	Tbsp. Dijon mustard
1	cup (4 oz.) shredded mozzarella cheese, divided
2	medium plum tomatoes, thinly sliced
1	large egg
⅓	cup half-and-half
1	Tbsp. chopped fresh basil
⅛	tsp. pepper

1. Preheat oven to 425°.

2. Sauté ham and green onions in a large nonstick skillet over medium heat 5 minutes or until ham is brown and any liquid evaporates.

3. Brush bottom of pie shell evenly with mustard; sprinkle with ½ cup mozzarella cheese. Spoon ham mixture evenly over cheese, and top with single layer of sliced tomatoes.

4. Beat egg and half-and-half with a fork until blended; pour over tomatoes. Sprinkle evenly with basil, pepper, and remaining ½ cup cheese.

5. Bake on lowest oven rack at 425° for 20 to 23 minutes or until lightly browned and set. Cool on a wire rack 20 minutes. Cut into wedges to serve.

S'more Puffs

makes 6 servings • prep: 5 min., cook: 8 min., other: 5 min.

Yes, you can have the famous Girl Scout campfire treat without the bonfire. When the rich melted marshmallow and chocolate flavor conjures up talk of camp days, encourage everyone to share a memorable camp experience.

test kitchen tip: Line the baking sheet with aluminum foil for easy cleanup. Watch the little ones—the centers of the marshmallows are very hot. The puffs will be just right for eating after the 5-minute cooling time.

12 round buttery crackers
12 milk chocolate kisses
6   large marshmallows, cut in half

1. Preheat oven to 350°.
2. Place crackers on a baking sheet. Top each with 1 milk chocolate kiss and 1 marshmallow half, cut side down.
3. Bake at 350° for 8 minutes or just until marshmallows begin to melt. Let cool on a wire rack 5 minutes.

casual
entertaining menus

Backyard Barbecue

Cox's Memphis-in-May Ribs

potato salad

Marinated Green Tomatoes

Thunder Valley Frozen Margaritas

chocolate ice cream

serves 4 to 6

Cox's Memphis-in-May Ribs

makes 4 to 6 servings • prep: 30 min.; cook: 1 hr., 30 min.; other: 3 hr.

When you serve ribs for company, make sure you have plenty of napkins and some moist towelettes for everyone. They're gonna be messy!

4	to 6 lb. spareribs or back ribs	2	tsp. ground white pepper
¼	cup paprika	2	tsp. black pepper
2	tsp. salt	1	tsp. ground red pepper
2	tsp. onion powder		Barbecue Sauce
2	tsp. garlic powder		

1. Place ribs in a large shallow dish. Combine paprika and next 6 ingredients in a small bowl; stir well. Rub paprika mixture over entire surface of ribs. Cover and chill 3 hours.

2. Preheat 1 side of charcoal or gas grill to medium heat (300° to 350°).

3. Place ribs on cool side of grill. Grill, covered with grill lid, over medium coals (300° to 350°) for 2 to 2½ hours, turning every 30 minutes. Brush ribs with Barbecue Sauce during last 30 minutes of grilling time. Serve with additional Barbecue Sauce.

Barbecue Sauce

makes 3 cups • prep: 10 min.; cook: 1 hr., 30 min.

2	cups water	3	Tbsp. salt
2	cups white vinegar	3	Tbsp. sugar
2	cups ketchup	3	Tbsp. chili powder
½	cup chopped onion	3	Tbsp. pepper

1. Combine all ingredients in a large saucepan. Bring to a boil; reduce heat, and simmer, uncovered, 1½ hours, stirring often.

Heart & Soul
The Junior League of Memphis, Tennessee

test kitchen tip: This recipe makes quite a bit of Barbecue Sauce. Set some aside before basting to serve with the ribs; then store any leftover sauce in an airtight container in the refrigerator up to a week.

Marinated Green Tomatoes

makes 4 to 6 servings • prep: 20 min., other: 1 hr.

Tomatoes grow so well in the South that gardeners can't seem to give them away fast enough. For this recipe tangy tarragon vinegar and a little sugar complement the slightly acidic taste of green tomatoes for a great summer picnic buffet.

test kitchen tip: Red or yellow tomatoes may be substituted for green ones, or use a mixture of all three varieties for a colorful salad.

2	to 3 large green tomatoes	⅛	tsp. pepper
2	Tbsp. sugar	¼	cup tarragon vinegar
1	tsp. salt		

1. Cut tomatoes into ¼-inch-thick slices. Arrange half of slices in a large shallow serving dish; sprinkle with half each of sugar, salt, and pepper. Top with remaining tomato slices; sprinkle with remaining sugar, salt, and pepper. Drizzle vinegar evenly over tomatoes. Cover and chill 1 hour.

2. Turn tomato slices, coating with vinegar mixture, before serving.

Thunder Valley Frozen Margaritas

makes 16 cups • prep: 10 min., other: 24 hr.

This classic slushy concoction is guaranteed to liven up any party or celebration and quench everyone's thirst. For a festive touch, use colored margarita salt.

make it ahead: This popular drink needs to freeze at least 24 hours. Before serving, stir the frozen mixture and let stand until it reaches the desired slushy consistency. Spoon out desired number of servings, and keep the remainder in the freezer up to a month.

3	cups white tequila	1	(10-oz.) can frozen margarita mix,
8	cups water		thawed
1	cup Triple Sec		Lime juice
2	(12-oz.) cans frozen limeade		Coarse salt
	concentrate, thawed and undiluted		Garnish: lime wedges

1. Combine tequila, water, Triple Sec, limeade, and margarita mix in a very large plastic container. Cover and freeze at least 24 hours or until frozen to a slushy consistency.

2. Moisten rims of margarita glasses with lime juice, and dip into coarse salt. Pour margarita mixture into glasses. Garnish, if desired.

Start Your Ovens: Cooking the Way It Ought'a Be
The Junior League of Bristol, TN/VA ~ Bristol, Virginia

Southern Fish Fry

Classic Fried Catfish

Buttermilk Coleslaw

Hush Puppies

sweet iced tea

Rum-Coconut Key Lime Pie (page 25)

serves 6

Classic Fried Catfish

(pictured on following page)

makes 6 servings • prep: 15 min., cook: 6 min. per batch

Fresh catfish has inspired parties in the South for decades. For a large party, get a big outdoor fryer, and let your guests pitch in with the frying.

¾ cup yellow cornmeal
¼ cup all-purpose flour
2 tsp. salt
1 tsp. ground red pepper
¼ tsp. garlic powder
6 (4- to 6-oz.) farm-raised catfish
   fillets

¼ tsp. salt
Vegetable oil
Lemon wedges, tartar sauce or ketchup
   (optional)

test kitchen tip: To keep the oil from spattering and popping and for the crispiest crust, pat fillets with paper towels to remove excess moisture just before dredging them in the cornmeal coating.

1. Combine first 5 ingredients in a large shallow dish. Sprinkle fish with ¼ tsp. salt; dredge in cornmeal mixture, coating evenly.
2. Pour oil to a depth of 1½ inches into a deep cast-iron skillet; heat to 350°. Fry fish, in batches, 5 to 6 minutes or until golden; drain on paper towels. Serve with lemon wedges, tartar sauce or ketchup, if desired.

sensational Southern celebrations If you can eat it, there's probably a festival celebrating it. Although there's a food-based festival in almost every Southern town, some have become regional institutions. In fact, if you want to take a culinary tour of the South in one year, mark your calendar for these no-miss affairs: Belzoni, Mississippi, for the World Catfish Festival…Memphis-in-May for the best barbecue…Terlingua, Texas, for the International Chili Championship…Dothan, Alabama, for the National Peanut Festival…Breaux Bridge, Louisiana, Crawfish Festival for good Cajun fare…Cadiz, Kentucky, for the Country Ham Festival…South Pittsburg, Tennessee, for the National Cornbread Festival…the Chesapeake Bay for the Maryland Seafood Festival…Plant City for the Florida Strawberry Festival…Salley, South Carolina, for the Chitlin' Strut…Crowley, Louisiana, for the International Rice Festival…and many more.

Classic Fried Catfish, previous page
Buttermilk Coleslaw, opposite page
Hush Puppies, opposite page

Buttermilk Coleslaw

makes 6 servings • prep: 30 min.

Don't limit this colorful slaw to this menu. It's good eatin' with barbecue, ham, and great on your Christmas buffet since it can be made ahead.

⅔ cup buttermilk
⅔ cup mayonnaise
1 tsp. grated lemon rind
1½ Tbsp. fresh lemon juice
1 bunch green onions, diagonally sliced and divided
¼ cup chopped fresh dill

1 green cabbage, shredded (about 4½ cups)
½ red bell pepper, cut into thin strips
1 cup shredded carrot
½ tsp. salt
½ tsp. pepper

test kitchen tip: Omit cabbage and carrots, and substitute a 16-oz. package of preshredded coleslaw mix to save prep time. Most coleslaw mixes contain a blend of cabbage, carrots, and sometimes red cabbage.

1. Whisk together first 4 ingredients. Stir in green onions and dill. Cover and chill dressing.

2. Toss together green cabbage, red bell pepper, carrot, salt, and pepper. Add dressing; toss gently. Cover and chill.

Hush Puppies

makes 2 dozen • prep: 10 min., cook: 6 min. per batch

On his Carolina cuisine-inspired menu at Woods on South in Charlotte, North Carolina, Chef Marvin Woods updates this old-fashioned cornbread favorite by offering a hush puppy specialty of the day. The pups come filled with shrimp, oysters, fish filets, salmon, or mushrooms.

1½ cups self-rising white cornmeal
½ cup all-purpose flour
½ tsp. baking powder
1 small onion, diced (optional)

1½ tsp. sugar
1 cup plus 2 Tbsp. buttermilk
1 Tbsp. bacon drippings
Vegetable oil

test kitchen tip: It's fine to substitute ½ tsp. onion powder for the onion, if you'd prefer. But don't substitute any ingredient for the bacon drippings—they add extra flavor to these Hush Puppies.

1. Combine first 5 ingredients in a bowl; make a well in center of mixture. Add buttermilk and bacon drippings to dry ingredients, stirring just until dry ingredients are moistened.

2. Pour oil to a depth of 2 inches into a large Dutch oven; heat to 350°. Drop batter by tablespoonfuls into oil, and fry, in batches, 3 minutes on each side or until golden. Drain on paper towels.

Time to Tailgate

Barbecue Bean Dip   corn chips

Slow Cooker Beef and Pork Sandwiches

marinated vegetables

soft drinks

Grandma's Hint-of-Mint Chocolate Cake

serves 6

Barbecue Bean Dip

makes 6 to 8 servings • prep: 15 min., cook: 25 min.

Make this dip for any sporting affair.

make it ahead: Prepare this recipe through Step 2 the day before; cover and chill. Let stand at room temperature 30 minutes before baking.

4	bacon slices, cooked and crumbled	¼	cup spicy barbecue sauce
1	small sweet onion, chopped	¼	cup tomato sauce
1	(14.5-oz.) can great Northern beans, rinsed and drained	¼	tsp. garlic powder
		½	cup (2 oz.) shredded Cheddar cheese

1. Preheat oven to 350°.

2. Process first 6 ingredients in a food processor until smooth, stopping to scrape down sides. Spread bacon mixture into a 1-qt. baking dish.

3. Bake at 350° for 20 minutes; sprinkle cheese evenly over top, and bake 5 more minutes. Serve warm or at room temperature with corn chips.

Slow Cooker Beef and Pork Sandwiches

(pictured on opposite page)

makes 6 servings • prep: 15 min., cook: 8 hr.

Barbecue is best cooked slow anyway, so that makes this slow cooker recipe perfect for cooks who don't have time to tend the grill for hours.

make it ahead: Prepare recipe through Step 1, and refrigerate a couple of days in advance. Chilling it in advance also makes skimming the solidified fat from the surface easy.

1½	lb. beef stew meat	1	Tbsp. chili powder
1½	lb. lean cubed pork	2	tsp. salt
1	medium-size green pepper, chopped	1	tsp. dry mustard
1	small onion, chopped	2	tsp. Worcestershire sauce
1	(6-oz.) can tomato paste		Sandwich buns
½	cup firmly packed brown sugar		Sliced dill pickles (optional)
¼	cup white vinegar		

1. Combine all ingredients in a 5-qt. electric slow cooker. Cover and cook on HIGH 8 hours. Skim fat from juices. Shred meat with 2 forks.

2. Serve on sandwich buns with pickles, if desired.   Isabelle White

7 Alarm Cuisine

East Mountain Volunteer Fire Department ~ Gladewater, Texas

Grandma's Hint-of-Mint Chocolate Cake

makes 12 servings • prep: 25 min., cook: 46 min.

When you're bringing dessert for a potluck dinner, this is the cake to take. Garnish it with a few chocolate-covered peppermint patty candies to give a hint of the flavor.

test kitchen tip: A handy disposable 13- x 9-inch foil pan with a tight-fitting lid makes baking, transport, and cleanup easy.

2 cups all-purpose flour	1 tsp. vanilla extract
2 cups sugar	1 (12-oz.) package miniature chocolate-covered peppermint patties, unwrapped and halved crosswise
¼ cup unsweetened cocoa	
1 tsp. ground cinnamon	
1 cup butter or margarine	
1 cup water	Chocolate Frosting
1 tsp. baking soda	Garnish: miniature chocolate-covered peppermint patties
1 large egg, lightly beaten	
½ cup buttermilk	

1. Preheat oven to 350°.

2. Combine first 4 ingredients in a large bowl; set aside.

3. Combine butter and water in a saucepan; cook over low heat just until butter melts. Remove from heat; stir in baking soda. Add to flour mixture, stirring well.

4. Combine egg, buttermilk, and vanilla; stir into flour mixture. Pour batter into a greased and floured 13- x 9-inch pan. Bake at 350° for 40 minutes.

5. Top with peppermint patties, and bake 2 to 3 more minutes or until patties melt. Gently spread melted patties over top of cake. Let cool completely. Spread Chocolate Frosting over top of cake. Garnish, if desired.

Chocolate Frosting

makes 2 cups • prep: 5 min., cook: 3 min.

½ cup butter	¼ cup unsweetened cocoa
⅓ cup milk	1 tsp. vanilla extract
1 (16-oz.) package powdered sugar, sifted	

1. Combine butter and milk in a saucepan; cook over low heat until butter melts and mixture is hot. Remove from heat. Combine powdered sugar and cocoa in a large bowl; add butter mixture, stirring until smooth. Stir in vanilla.

Carol Gockel

Texas Sampler
The Junior League of Richardson, Texas

Game Night

Mango and Avocado Salsa   tortilla chips

White Bean Chili

**Blue Corn Muffins With Cheddar Cheese
and Pine Nuts (page 44)**

Butterscotch Oatmeal Cookies

serves 8 to 10

Mango and Avocado Salsa

makes 4 cups • prep: 15 min.

Sweet mangoes mixed with creamy avocado and a splash of
hot sauce makes this delicious salsa a tropical treat just right
for a Caribbean-inspired dinner.

2   large ripe mangoes, peeled and
    chopped

1   large avocado, peeled and chopped

1   cup chopped fresh cilantro

½   medium-size red onion, finely
    chopped

2   Tbsp. fresh lime juice

½   tsp. hot sauce

¼   tsp. salt

⅛   tsp. pepper

test kitchen tip: Serve leftovers as
a topping for fish, chicken, or Mexican
food.

1. Combine all ingredients in a large bowl; stir gently. Cover and chill. Serve
with tortilla chips.

Tammy Gahica

Cookin' in the Canyon
Jarbidge Community Hall ~ Jarbidge, Nevada

White Bean Chili, opposite page
Blue Corn Muffins With Cheddar Cheese and
Pine Nuts, page 44

White Bean Chili

(pictured on opposite page)

makes 13 cups • prep: 20 min.; cook: 2 hr., 30 min.; other: 8 hr.

Chicken and white beans make a great variation on the red chili first invented in San Antonio in 1840.

1	lb. dried great Northern beans	6	cups chicken broth
2	medium onions, chopped	5	cups chopped cooked chicken breast
1	Tbsp. olive oil	3	cups (12 oz.) shredded Monterey Jack cheese, divided
2	(4½-oz.) cans chopped green chiles, undrained	½	tsp. salt
4	garlic cloves, minced	½	tsp. black pepper
2	tsp. ground cumin		Toppings: sour cream, salsa, chopped fresh cilantro
1½	tsp. dried oregano		
	Dash of ground red pepper		

test kitchen tip: For a quick-cooking alternative, substitute 4 (15.8-oz.) cans drained great Northern beans for dried beans, and omit Step 1. Reduce chicken broth to 5 cups, omit salt, and reduce black pepper to ¼ tsp. Reduce simmer time in Step 2 with beans and broth to 30 minutes.

1. Rinse and sort beans according to package directions. Place beans in a Dutch oven; cover with water 2 inches above beans, and let soak 8 hours. Drain beans, and rinse thoroughly; drain and set aside.

2. Sauté onion in hot oil in Dutch oven over medium-high heat 4 minutes or until tender. Add green chiles and next 4 ingredients; cook, stirring constantly, 2 minutes. Add beans and chicken broth. Bring to a boil; cover, reduce heat, and simmer 2 hours or until beans are tender, stirring occasionally.

3. Add chicken, 1 cup cheese, salt, and pepper. Bring to a boil; reduce heat, and simmer, uncovered, 10 minutes, stirring often.

4. To serve, ladle chili into individual soup bowls. Top each serving evenly with remaining 2 cups cheese and desired toppings.

Mary Gartland

Immacolata Cookbook
Immacolata Church Ladies Society ~ St. Louis, Missouri

big pot stews for parties

Ever since Native Americans began sharing their secrets for one-pot cooking with settlers, Southerners have found ways to turn a pot of stew into a party. In fact, most of the region's hallowed camp stews are made by a group of men and eaten by a group of people at gatherings such as fund-raisers or festivals. Kentucky's burgoo made of meat and vegetables is similar to the Brunswick stew claimed by Georgia and Virginia. Instead of wild game, today the meat is chicken, pork, or beef. In South Carolina, Frogmore or Beaufort stew pots are full of potatoes, smoked sausage, ears of corn, and shrimp. Carolina hash is a lot like Brunswick stew served over rice or grits. North Carolina's muddle is fish or chicken, potatoes, and seasonings. And, of course, Louisiana has its gumbo and jambalaya.

Butterscotch Oatmeal Cookies

makes about 4 dozen • prep: 25 min., cook: 12 min. per batch, other: 10 min. per batch

Dutch immigrants were the first to bring cookies to America. They became a source of pride for colonial Southern cooks and were almost always called "tea cakes."

test kitchen tip: Coat the teaspoon for scooping the cookie dough with vegetable cooking spray. It helps the dough slip out easily onto the baking sheets.

¾	cup shortening		1	cup all-purpose flour
1	cup firmly packed light brown sugar		1	tsp. salt
½	cup granulated sugar		½	tsp. baking soda
1	large egg		3	cups uncooked quick-cooking oats
¼	cup water		1	(11-oz.) package butterscotch
1	tsp. vanilla extract			morsels

1. Preheat oven to 350°.

2. Beat shortening at medium speed with an electric mixer until fluffy; gradually add sugars, beating well. Add egg, water, and vanilla; beat well.

3. Combine flour, salt, and soda. Gradually add to shortening mixture, beating until smooth. Stir in oats and butterscotch morsels. Drop dough by heaping teaspoonfuls onto greased baking sheets.

4. Bake at 350° for 12 minutes or until edges are lightly browned. Cool on baking sheets 2 minutes; remove to wire racks to cool completely.   Linda Taylor

Cross Village: A Selection of Tastes, Art, and Memories
Cross Village Community Services ~ Cross Village, Michigan

Festive Holiday Dinner

Cranberry Gorgonzola Green Salad
Peppered Beef Tenderloin With Mustard Sauce
Wild Mushroom and Onion Risotto
Lemon-Rosemary Green Beans
dinner rolls
cranberry sorbet

serves 6

Cranberry Gorgonzola Green Salad

makes 6 servings • prep: 20 min.

Offer your company a flavorful twist to ordinary green salad by mixing the lettuce with cranberries, walnuts, apple, and Gorgonzola cheese.

⅓ cup vegetable oil
¼ cup seasoned rice vinegar
¾ tsp. Dijon mustard
1 garlic clove, pressed
1 small head Bibb lettuce, torn
1 small head green leaf lettuce, torn

1 Granny Smith or Pippin apple, thinly sliced
⅓ cup coarsely chopped walnuts, toasted
⅓ cup dried cranberries
⅓ cup crumbled Gorgonzola cheese

1. Combine first 4 ingredients; stir with a wire whisk until blended. Set aside.
2. Just before serving, combine Bibb lettuce and remaining 5 ingredients in a large bowl. Pour dressing over salad; toss gently.

Classic Favorites
P.E.O., Chapter SB ~ Moraga, California

test kitchen tip: To toast coarsely chopped walnuts or pecans, place in a single layer in a shallow pan. Bake at 350° for 6 to 8 minutes. To toast the nut halves, bake about 2 more minutes. You'll know they're ready when they appear lightly toasted and a nutty fragrance pours from the oven when you open the door.

Peppered Beef Tenderloin With Mustard Sauce, opposite page
Wild Mushroom and Onion Risotto, page 160
Lemony-Rosemary Green Beans, page 160

Peppered Beef Tenderloin With Mustard Sauce

makes 6 servings • prep: 15 min.; cook: 50 min.; other: 24 hr., 10 min.

For an impressive company meal, you can't go wrong with this tenderloin studded with three types of peppercorns, a spice once so prized it was used as money.

1	(8-oz.) container sour cream	2	tsp. coarse salt
2	Tbsp. prepared horseradish	1	cup chopped flat-leaf parsley
3	Tbsp. Dijon mustard	¼	cup butter, softened
2	tsp. whole white peppercorns	3	Tbsp. Dijon mustard
2	tsp. whole green peppercorns	1	(2-lb.) beef tenderloin, trimmed
2	tsp. whole black peppercorns		

test kitchen tip: To keep the beef juicy, let tenderloin stand 10 minutes before carving. This allows the juices to settle in the meat rather than pooling on the plate.

1. Combine first 3 ingredients; cover and chill.

2. Place peppercorns in a blender; pulse until coarsely chopped. Transfer to a shallow bowl, and stir in salt.

3. Combine parsley, butter, and 3 Tbsp. mustard; rub mixture evenly over tenderloin. Roll tenderloin in peppercorn mixture, coating thoroughly. Cover and chill up to 24 hours.

4. Preheat oven to 450°.

5. Place tenderloin on a lightly greased rack in a shallow roasting pan. Bake at 450° for 50 minutes or until a meat thermometer inserted in thickest portion of tenderloin registers 145° (medium rare) to 160° (medium). Transfer tenderloin to a platter, and cover loosely with aluminum foil. Let stand 10 minutes before slicing. Slice and serve with mustard mixture.

Cheyenne Frontier Days "Daddy of 'em All" Cookbook
Chuckwagon Gourmet ~ Cheyenne, Wyoming

Wild Mushroom and Onion Risotto

(pictured on page 158)

makes 6 servings • prep: 20 min., cook: 40 min.

Crimini mushrooms give risotto more flavor than the more common white mushrooms.

test kitchen tip: To ensure a creamy texture, never rinse the rice before cooking risotto. Rinsing washes away the starch that's needed to create risotto's creamy texture.

2½	cups chicken broth	1	cup sliced fresh crimini mushrooms
1	cup chopped onion	⅓	cup chopped fresh parsley
1	garlic clove, crushed	¼	cup freshly grated Parmesan
2	tsp. olive oil		cheese
1	cup Arborio or other short-grain rice, uncooked	2	Tbsp. dry white wine
1	(3.5-oz.) package fresh shiitake mushrooms, sliced		

1. Bring broth to a boil in a small saucepan. Cover and reduce heat to low.

2. Cook onion and garlic in oil in a large skillet over medium heat, stirring constantly, until onion is tender. Add rice, and cook 4 minutes, stirring constantly. Add mushrooms and ½ cup warm broth; cook, stirring constantly, until most of the liquid is absorbed.

3. Continue adding warm broth, ½ cup at a time, stirring constantly until rice is tender and mixture is creamy, allowing rice to absorb most of liquid each time before adding more broth. (The entire process should take about 25 minutes.) Stir in parsley, cheese, and wine. Serve immediately.

Stop and Smell the Rosemary: Recipes and Traditions to Remember
The Junior League of Houston, Texas

Lemon-Rosemary Green Beans

(pictured on page 158)

makes 6 servings • prep: 15 min., cook: 12 min.

For a birthday meal or get-together with special friends, a recipe with rosemary is especially appropriate. The herb represents remembrance.

test kitchen tip: If small stringless green beans are available, they'll save you prep time in Step 1. There's no need to trim the ends either.

2	lb. small fresh green beans	½	tsp. salt
3	Tbsp. butter	¼	tsp. freshly ground pepper
1	Tbsp. minced fresh rosemary		Garnish: grated lemon rind
½	tsp. grated lemon rind		

1. Wash beans; trim ends, and remove strings. Cook beans in boiling water to cover 8 minutes or until crisp-tender; drain. Plunge into ice water briefly to stop the cooking process; drain well. Transfer beans to a serving bowl.

2. Combine butter and next 4 ingredients in a small saucepan; cook over low heat until butter melts, stirring occasionally. Pour butter mixture over beans, and toss gently. Garnish, if desired.   Ardis McCain

A Culinary Tour of Homes
Big Canoe Chapel Women's Guild ~ Big Canoe, Georgia

St. Patrick's Day

Roasted Beet-and-Sugared Walnut Salad
Whiskey-Glazed Corned Beef With Cabbage and Potatoes
Irish Bread
Arant Clan's Cobbler

serves 12

Roasted Beet-and-Sugared Walnut Salad

makes 12 servings • prep: 50 min., cook: 25 min.

Guests will ooh and ahh over this colorful salad. For variety, use a mixture of golden and red beets. Just bake them separately to keep the colors pure.

1	tsp. grated orange rind	6	large fresh beets with tops
¼	cup fresh orange juice	1	Tbsp. olive oil
1	tsp. Dijon mustard	2	oranges, peeled and sectioned
1	tsp. salt, divided	1	(5-oz.) bag mixed salad greens
½	tsp. pepper, divided		Sugared Walnuts
½	cup olive oil		

1. Combine orange rind, orange juice, Dijon mustard, ½ tsp. salt, and ¼ tsp. pepper; gradually whisk in ½ cup oil until well blended. Set vinaigrette aside.
2. Preheat oven to 450°.
3. Cut tops from beets; slice 3 cups tops, and set aside. Discard remaining tops. Peel beets, and cut each into 8 wedges. Toss beets, 1 Tbsp. olive oil, remaining ½ tsp. salt, and remaining ¼ tsp. pepper; spread in an ungreased 15- x 10-inch jelly-roll pan. Bake at 450° for 25 minutes or until tender, turning once after 20 minutes. Cool.
4. Combine beets, oranges, and half of vinaigrette in a large bowl; toss to coat. Combine salad greens, sliced beet tops, and remaining vinaigrette in another large bowl; toss to coat. Arrange greens on salad plates; top with beets, oranges, and Sugared Walnuts.

Sugared Walnuts

makes 1 cup • prep: 5 min., cook: 20 min.

1	Tbsp. butter or margarine	1	Tbsp. orange juice
2	Tbsp. sugar	1	cup large walnut pieces

1. Preheat oven to 325°. Meanwhile, melt butter in a large skillet over medium heat; stir in sugar and orange juice. Add walnuts, stirring to coat. Cook over medium heat until liquid evaporates.
2. Spread walnuts on a lightly greased baking sheet. Bake at 325° for 15 minutes, stirring every 5 minutes. Cool completely.

test kitchen tip: Not only do the Sugared Walnuts jazz up this salad, but they're also perfect for munching or gift giving. You can easily double or triple the recipe.

Whiskey-Glazed Corned Beef
With Cabbage and Potatoes, opposite page
Irish Bread, page 164

Whiskey-Glazed Corned Beef With Cabbage and Potatoes

makes 12 servings • prep: 20 min.; cook: 4 hr., 10 min.

Corned beef and cabbage are traditional on the St. Patrick's Day menu of many Irish. Serve this recipe "Southernized" with bourbon, and celebrate your Irish roots.

1	(6- to 7-lb.) corned beef brisket	¾	cup firmly packed brown sugar
¾	cup bourbon, divided	¼	cup orange juice
4	whole cloves	1	tsp. yellow mustard
4	white peppercorns	2	lb. small round red potatoes
2	bay leaves	1	large cabbage, cut into thin wedges
1	garlic clove		

test kitchen tip: If your brisket is too long to fit inside the Dutch oven, cut it in half crosswise and stack the halves in the Dutch oven.

1. Place beef in a Dutch oven; add water to cover. Add ½ cup bourbon, cloves, and next 3 ingredients; bring to a boil. Cover, reduce heat, and simmer 3 hours or until beef is tender. Transfer beef to a roasting pan, reserving cooking liquid in Dutch oven. Set beef aside.

2. Preheat oven to 400°.

3. Combine 2 Tbsp. cooking liquid, remaining ¼ cup bourbon, brown sugar, orange juice, and mustard in a small saucepan; cook over low heat until sugar dissolves, stirring occasionally. Pour over beef. Bake, uncovered, at 400° for 30 minutes, basting every 10 minutes with bourbon mixture.

4. Meanwhile, pour cooking liquid through a wire-mesh strainer into a large bowl, discarding solids. Return strained cooking liquid to Dutch oven along with potatoes; bring to a boil. Cover, reduce heat, and simmer 10 minutes. Add cabbage; cover and cook 10 more minutes or until potatoes are tender.

5. Cut brisket diagonally across the grain into thin slices using a sharp knife. Serve brisket with potatoes and cabbage. Mary Rossi

60 Years of Serving
The Assistance League of San Pedro-Palos Verdes ~ San Pedro, California

Irish Bread

(pictured on page 162)

makes 12 servings • prep: 15 min., cook: 35 min.

This sweet raisin bread baked in cast-iron skillets or round cake pans is reminiscent of English scones. Serve wedges at breakfast, lunch, or tea.

test kitchen tip: Individual loaves of Irish Bread are a unique and convenient way to serve a crowd. We baked ours using preseasoned miniature cast-iron skillets for only 25 minutes. The same skillets we used are available at www.lodgemfg.com.

3	cups all-purpose flour	¼	cup shortening
½	cup sugar	¼	cup butter
1	Tbsp. baking powder	1	cup raisins
1	tsp. baking soda	2	large eggs
½	tsp. salt	1¼	cups buttermilk

1. Preheat oven to 350°.

2. Combine first 5 ingredients in a bowl. Cut shortening and butter into flour mixture with a pastry blender until mixture is crumbly. Stir in raisins.

3. Whisk together eggs and buttermilk; add to flour mixture, stirring just until moistened. Spoon batter into 2 greased 8-inch round cake pans.

4. Bake at 350° for 30 to 35 minutes or until golden.

Arant Clan's Cobbler

makes 12 servings • prep: 45 min., cook: 1 hr., other: 5 min.

Many traditional cobblers have a biscuit crust. In this update, the filling is rolled in the crust and sliced into pinwheels.

test kitchen tip: Vanilla, butter pecan, black walnut, and pralines 'n' cream are all excellent ice cream flavor choices with this cobbler.

2	cups sugar	2	cups finely chopped Granny Smith apple
2	cups water		
½	cup shortening	1	tsp. ground cinnamon
1½	cups self-rising flour	½	cup butter, melted
⅓	cup milk		Ice cream (optional)

1. Combine sugar and water in a small saucepan; cook over medium heat until sugar dissolves, stirring occasionally. Set sugar syrup aside.

2. Preheat oven to 350°.

3. Cut shortening into flour with a pastry blender until mixture is crumbly. Sprinkle milk over dry ingredients, stirring just until dry ingredients are moistened. Turn out dough onto a floured surface; knead 4 or 5 times. Roll dough into an 8- x 10-inch rectangle.

4. Sprinkle apple evenly over dough; sprinkle cinnamon over apple. Roll up dough, jelly-roll fashion, starting at long side; dampen edges of dough, and press together to seal. Cut into 12 slices.

5. Pour butter into an ungreased 13- x 9-inch baking dish. Place dough slices in pan, cut side down; pour reserved sugar syrup carefully around slices. Bake at 350° for 55 minutes or until golden brown. Let cool 5 minutes before serving. Serve with ice cream, if desired.

Food for Thought

Northeast Louisiana Chapter, Autism Society of America ~ Monroe, Louisiana

Derby Day Soiree

Tenderloin Steaks With Sherried Cream
Savory Roasted New Potatoes
Asparagus With Blue Cheese and Chive Vinaigrette
Mint Julep Martini
Blue Ribbon Chocolate Pecan Pie

serves 4

Tenderloin Steaks With Sherried Cream

(pictured on following page)

makes 4 servings • prep: 10 min., cook: 15 min., other: 30 min.

Skillet-grilled steaks in a decadent sherry cream sauce live up
to the lavish celebrations of Kentucky's Derby Days.

1	Tbsp. cracked pepper	¼	cup dry sherry
4	(4-oz.) beef tenderloin steaks	¼	cup whipping cream
	(1 inch thick)	2	Tbsp. Dijon mustard
1	Tbsp. butter		Garnish: minced fresh parsley
1	Tbsp. olive oil		

1. Press pepper into both sides of each steak. Cover and chill 30 minutes.

2. Heat butter and olive oil in a heavy skillet over medium-high heat. Cook steaks 10 minutes or to desired degree of doneness, turning once. Remove steaks from skillet, reserving drippings in skillet; keep steaks warm.

3. Add sherry, cream, and mustard to skillet; bring to a boil, stirring constantly. Pour over steaks. Garnish, if desired.

Symphony of Flavors
The Associates of the Redlands Bowl ~ Redlands, California

test kitchen tip: Some markets label beef tenderloin steaks as filet mignon. Our instructions in Step 2 result in tenderloin steaks cooked to medium rare (145°). If you prefer medium (160°) doneness, increase cooking time to 12 minutes.

Tenderloin Steaks With Sherried Cream, previous page
Savory Roasted New Potatoes, opposite page
Asparagus With Blue Cheese and Chive Vinaigrette, opposite page

Savory Roasted New Potatoes

makes 4 servings • prep: 15 min., cook: 50 min.

During the Alaska Gold Rush, potatoes were so valuable they were traded for gold. These spicy rosemary potatoes will be worth the trade.

12	small new potatoes, unpeeled and quartered	1	tsp. minced garlic
3	Tbsp. olive oil	½	tsp. hot Hungarian paprika
2	Tbsp. minced fresh rosemary	½	tsp. salt
1	Tbsp. Worcestershire sauce	¼	tsp. freshly ground pepper

1. Preheat oven to 375°.

2. Place potato in a large zip-top plastic freezer bag. Combine olive oil and next 6 ingredients; add to bag. Seal bag securely, and shake until potato is coated evenly.

3. Spread potato in a single layer in an ungreased 15- x 10-inch jelly-roll pan. Bake, uncovered, at 375° for 45 to 50 minutes or until potato is tender, stirring occasionally.

Colorado Collage
The Junior League of Denver, Colorado

test kitchen tip: Paprika is often used to garnish foods rather than as a flavor enhancer, but not so in this recipe. Hot Hungarian paprika not only blankets the potato wedges with a crimson color, it also gives them a touch of heat. Store paprika in a cool, dry place for up to 6 months to preserve the flavor.

Asparagus With Blue Cheese and Chive Vinaigrette

makes 4 servings • prep: 15 min., cook: 3 min.

Blue cheese and chives give a flavor punch to delicate fresh asparagus, which has been considered a luxury food since the days of ancient Greece and Rome.

2	Tbsp. olive oil	¼	tsp. salt
2	tsp. red wine vinegar	1	lb. fresh asparagus
¼	cup crumbled blue cheese		Ground white pepper
2	Tbsp. minced fresh chives		

1. Combine oil and vinegar in a small bowl; stir well with a wire whisk. Add cheese, chives and salt; stir well. Set vinaigrette aside.

2. Snap off tough ends of asparagus. Add water to a medium skillet to a depth of 1 inch; bring to a boil. Add asparagus in a single layer; cook 2 to 3 minutes or until crisp-tender. Drain asparagus, and arrange on a serving plate.

3. Drizzle vinaigrette over hot asparagus, sprinkle with white pepper, and serve immediately.

Our Sunrise Family Cookbook
Sunrise Drive Elementary School ~ Tucson, Arizona

test kitchen tip: Asparagus and blue cheese fans will also love this side dish served as a cold salad. After cooking the asparagus, plunge it immediately into ice water to stop the cooking process. Drain and keep it chilled until ready to serve with the vinaigrette.

Mint Julep Martini

makes 1 serving • prep: 5 min.

Here's an updated twist on an old Southern Derby classic. Crème de menthe stands in for fresh mint.

¼   cup bourbon
¼   cup orange liqueur
1   tsp. vanilla vodka

1   tsp. clear crème de menthe
6   ice cubes
Garnish: orange rind curl

1. Combine first 5 ingredients in a martini shaker. Cover with lid, and shake until thoroughly chilled. Remove lid, and strain into a chilled martini glass. Serve immediately. Garnish, if desired.

Blue Ribbon Chocolate Pecan Pie

makes 8 servings • prep: 10 min., cook: 50 min., other: 1 hr.

When the Derby party rounds start in Kentucky in May, a traditional rich chocolate-pecan pie is a must on the menu.

test kitchen tip: Pecans are harvested in the fall, and the freshest nuts arrive at retail stores during the Thanksgiving season. If shelled, the nuts can be kept in an airtight container in the refrigerator up to a month or the freezer up to a year.

¾   cup sugar
6   Tbsp. butter or margarine, melted
¾   cup light corn syrup
3   large eggs
1   tsp. vanilla extract
1   cup coarsely chopped pecans

½   cup semisweet chocolate
     mini-morsels
1   unbaked 9-inch pastry shell
Garnish: whipped cream, semisweet
     chocolate mini-morsels

1. Preheat oven to 350°.
2. Whisk together sugar and butter in a large bowl. Add corn syrup, eggs, and vanilla. Stir in pecans and chocolate mini-morsels; pour into pastry shell.
3. Bake at 350° for 45 to 50 minutes or until set and lightly browned. Shield edges of pastry with aluminum foil during the last 10 minutes of baking to prevent excessive browning, if necessary. Cool on a wire rack 1 hour or until completely cool. Garnish, if desired.

Linda Bonacorso

Fruits of Our Labor
St. Joseph Parish ~ Lincoln, Nebraska

Cinco de Mayo Brunch

Puffy Chile Rellenos Casserole

Fresh Tomatillo Salsa

bakery muffins

Creamy Pineapple Coolers

serves 6

Puffy Chile Rellenos Casserole

(pictured on following page)

makes 6 servings • prep: 25 min., cook: 45 min., other: 5 min.

Why not have a Mexican-themed brunch for friends? Egg-based chile rellenos (pronounced reah YEH nohs) make a hot, hearty entrée.

3 (4½-oz.) cans whole green chiles, drained
4 (6-inch) corn tortillas, cut into 1-inch strips
4 cups (16 oz.) shredded Monterey Jack cheese
1 large tomato, sliced
8 large eggs
½ cup milk
½ tsp. salt
½ tsp. garlic powder
½ tsp. ground cumin
½ tsp. pepper
¼ tsp. onion salt
Paprika

test kitchen tip: We preferred the rich-tasting results from using whole milk in this brunch favorite. If that's a staple you typically don't keep on hand, purchase a small carton for this recipe.

1. Preheat oven to 350°.

2. Make a lengthwise slit down each chile, and carefully remove seeds. Place half of chiles in a greased 8-inch square baking dish. Place half of tortilla strips over chiles, and sprinkle with half of cheese. Arrange tomato slices over cheese. Repeat layers with remaining chiles, tortilla strips, and cheese.

3. Whisk together eggs and next 6 ingredients in a bowl, beating with a wire whisk until blended. Pour over chile mixture; sprinkle with paprika. Bake at 350° for 40 to 45 minutes or until set and lightly browned. Let stand 5 minutes before serving.

Sheryl Dennis

Our Cherished Recipes, Second Edition
First Presbyterian Church ~ Skagway, Alaska

Puffy Chile Rellenos Casserole, previous page
Freesh Tomatillo Salsa, opposite page

Fresh Tomatillo Salsa

makes 1½ cups • prep: 15 min., other: 8 hr.

Walnut-sized tomatillos have a sharp lemony flavor that goes with egg dishes, fish, chicken, or any Mexican-style food.

8	fresh tomatillos, husks removed	2	Tbsp. fresh lime juice
2	jalapeño peppers, seeded and minced	1	garlic clove, minced
3	Tbsp. chopped fresh cilantro	½	tsp. salt

1. Coarsely chop tomatillos. Combine tomatillos, jalapeño peppers, and remaining ingredients. Cover; chill at least 8 hours.   Michael Anderson

Sharing Our Best
The Arrangement Hair Salon ~ Columbus, Ohio

Creamy Pineapple Coolers

makes 5½ cups • prep: 5 min.

The traditional piña colada (which means "strained pineapple") is spiked with rum. At a party, it's nice to have a nonalcoholic option as well. Dress up each drink with a skewer of fruit. The refreshing tropical flavors of this non-alcoholic piña colada are enhanced by the vanilla ice cream.

1	cup pineapple juice
½	cup cream of coconut
1	qt. vanilla ice cream

test kitchen tip: Transform this beverage for an adult brunch by adding ½ cup light rum to the blender with the remaining ingredients.

1. Process all ingredients in a blender until smooth, stopping to scrape down sides. Serve immediately.   Camille Mele

Watt's Cooking
Oasis Southern Company Services ~ Atlanta, Georgia

Beach Party

Garlicky Baked Shrimp

Fruit Salad With Fresh Mango Sauce

Grilled Vegetable Salad

French bread

Almond Sand Dollar Cookies

ice cream

serves 6

Garlicky Baked Shrimp

(pictured on page 143)

makes 6 servings • prep: 10 min., bake: 25 min.

Here's the perfect party recipe—guests peel their own shrimp and save you the work!

test kitchen tip: To bake this when you're on vacation at the beach, purchase a large disposable roasting pan for easy cleanup. French bread is perfect to sop up the savory sauce.

3	lb. unpeeled, large raw shrimp	2	lemons, halved
1	(16-oz.) bottle Italian dressing	¼	cup chopped fresh parsley
1½	Tbsp. freshly ground pepper	½	cup butter, cut up
2	garlic cloves, pressed		

1. Preheat oven to 375°.

2. Place first 4 ingredients in a 13- x 9-inch baking dish, tossing to coat. Squeeze juice from lemons over shrimp mixture, and stir. Add lemon halves to pan. Sprinkle shrimp with parsley; dot with butter.

3. Bake at 375° for 25 minutes, stirring after 15 minutes. Serve in pan.

Fruit Salad With Fresh Mango Sauce

makes 6 servings • prep: 40 min., other: 3 hr.

This colorful and naturally sweet salad is a perfect accompaniment with the garlicky entrée.

2	nectarines, sliced	1	cup seedless red grapes
2	peaches, peeled and sliced	¼	cup fresh lemon juice
2	plums, sliced	¼	cup fresh blueberries
1	mango, peeled and coarsely chopped		Fresh Mango Sauce
½	small honeydew melon, peeled, seeded, and cubed		

1. Combine first 6 ingredients in a large serving bowl; add lemon juice, and toss to coat. Cover and chill up to 3 hours before serving.

2. Sprinkle blueberries over fruit mixture. Serve with Fresh Mango Sauce.

Fresh Mango Sauce

makes 1⅓ cups • prep: 15 min., other: 2 hr.

1	large mango, peeled and chopped
1	Tbsp. grated orange rind
¾	cup fresh orange juice (about 2 oranges)
2	Tbsp. sugar

1. Process all ingredients in a blender until smooth, stopping to scrape down sides. Pour mixture through a wire-mesh strainer into a bowl, discarding solids. Cover and chill 2 hours.

Made In The Shade
The Junior League of Greater Fort Lauderdale, Florida

test kitchen tip: To ripen mangoes, place them in a paper bag at room temperature for a day or two. Once ripe, they can be placed in a plastic bag and refrigerated for several days.

Grilled Vegetable Salad

makes 6 servings • prep: 30 min.; cook: 20 min.; other: 8 hr., 30 min.

This top-rated recipe gets an earthy touch of sweetness from the molasses and colored bell peppers.

⅓	cup white balsamic vinegar	½	lb. carrots (about 4 medium)
2	Tbsp. olive oil	1	red bell pepper, seeded
2	shallots, finely chopped	1	yellow bell pepper, seeded
1	tsp. dried Italian seasoning	1	zucchini
¼	tsp. salt	1	yellow squash
¼	tsp. pepper	1	large onion
1½	tsp. molasses		

1. Combine first 7 ingredients in a large bowl. Cut carrots in half lengthwise. Cut carrot halves and remaining 5 ingredients into large pieces (about 1½ inches). Add vegetables to vinegar mixture, tossing to coat. Let stand 30 minutes, stirring occasionally.
2. Preheat grill to medium-high heat (350° to 400°).
3. Drain vegetables, reserving vinegar mixture. Arrange vegetables in a grill basket. Grill, covered with grill lid, over medium-high heat (350° to 400°) for 15 to 20 minutes, turning once. Return vegetables to reserved vinegar mixture. Cover and chill at least 8 hours.

Peggy Monroe

Cougar Bites
Crestline Elementary School ~ Birmingham, Alabama

test kitchen tip: If you don't have a grill basket, thread the marinated vegetables onto metal skewers and grill as directed, turning skewers once with tongs.

Almond Sand Dollar Cookies

makes 4 dozen • prep: 25 min., bake: 14 min. per batch, other: 2 hr.

Package a few sand dollar cookies for an extra treat to give to dinner guests when they leave. In Louisiana that's called a "lagniappe," meaning a little something extra.

make it ahead: To get ahead, chill the dough up to 3 days in advance. Before rolling, let it stand at room temperature about 30 minutes to soften.

1 cup butter, softened	½ tsp. baking powder
2 cups sifted powdered sugar	¼ cup granulated sugar
2 large eggs	1 tsp. ground cinnamon
1 large egg, separated	Sliced almonds
3⅓ cups all-purpose flour	

1. Beat butter at medium speed with an electric mixer until creamy; gradually add 2 cups sifted powdered sugar, beating until well blended. Add 2 eggs and 1 egg yolk, beating until blended.

2. Combine flour and baking powder. Add to butter mixture, beating at low speed until blended. Shape dough into a ball, and wrap in plastic wrap. Chill 2 hours.

3. Preheat oven to 350°.

4. Roll dough to ⅛-inch thickness on a lightly floured surface; cut with a 3-inch round cutter. Place on lightly greased, parchment paper-lined baking sheets; brush with lightly beaten egg white.

5. Stir together granulated sugar and cinnamon, and sprinkle evenly over cookies. Gently press 5 almond slices in a spoke design around center of each cookie.

6. Bake at 350° for 4 minutes; remove pan from oven, and gently press almonds into cookies again. Bake 10 more minutes or until edges are lightly browned. Remove cookies to wire racks to cool.

what's different about The Delta?

Flat fertile cotton fields, stately plantation homes, the wide Mississippi River rolling peacefully by. This is the Mississippi Delta stretching from Memphis to Vicksburg, and the image many have of the entire South. Here, despite income, wealth, or generation gap, there is a kinship that makes people more alike than different. Gardens are abundant and well kept. Cut flowers adorn the tables. Food tables groan. And, says Delta-raised Kim Jones of Starkville, "It's still very old school and very proper. It has a true old Southern charm not found anywhere else." This was evident in the days of house parties and garden receptions, and even today, though the landscape now includes tamale stands and casinos. If it's a formal reception, it will be done just so. If it's a catfish fry or hoedown, it will be as classy as they come. After all, it's the "Deltah."

Meat 'n' Three Dinner

deli-roasted whole chicken
White Cheddar-and-Squash Casserole
Creole-Style Green Beans
Fried Okra Salad
cornbread
Simple Peach Sorbet

serves 6

White Cheddar–and–Squash Casserole

makes 6 servings • prep: 20 min., cook: 50 min., other: 10 min.

Squash grows well in the South, where summers are hot and long. That's why you'll find at least one squash casserole at every reunion or church supper. This cheesy version is easy to make in advance for entertaining.

make it ahead: Prepare recipe as directed through Step 3 but do not top with breadcrumbs. Cover and chill overnight. Remove from refrigerator; let stand 45 minutes. Uncover and top with breadcrumbs; bake as directed.

4 Tbsp. butter, divided	1½ cups milk
1 medium onion, chopped	1 (10-oz.) block white Cheddar
3 lb. yellow squash, sliced	cheese, shredded
2 tsp. salt, divided	2 Tbsp. Italian-seasoned
¾ tsp. pepper	breadcrumbs
2 Tbsp. all-purpose flour	

1. Melt 2 Tbsp. butter in a large skillet over medium–high heat; add onion, and sauté 5 minutes or until tender. Add squash, 1½ tsp. salt, and pepper; cover and cook, stirring occasionally, 15 minutes or until squash is tender. Remove from heat; drain well.

2. Preheat oven to 400°.

3. Melt remaining 2 Tbsp. butter in a saucepan over medium–high heat; whisk in flour until smooth. Whisk in milk. Bring to a boil; reduce heat, and simmer 2 minutes. Remove from heat; stir in cheese and remaining ½ tsp. salt. Gently stir together squash and cheese mixture in a large bowl. Pour into a lightly greased 11- x 7-inch baking dish. Sprinkle breadcrumbs evenly over top.

4. Bake at 400° for 20 minutes or until bubbly. Let stand 10 minutes before serving.

Creole-Style Green Beans, following page
Fried Okra Salad, following page
White Cheddar-and-Squash Casserole, opposite page

Creole-Style Green Beans

(pictured on previous page)

makes 6 servings • prep: 10 min., cook: 35 min.

Creole style, in this recipe, simply means a dish has tomatoes added to it. To make this recipe even more Southern, sprinkle crunchy bacon on top.

test kitchen tip: Omit Step 1 by substituting 3 (14½-oz.) cans whole green beans if you'd like.

1½	lb. fresh green beans, trimmed	½	tsp. salt
4	bacon slices, diced	½	tsp. pepper
¾	cup chopped onion	¼	tsp. dry mustard
½	cup chopped green bell pepper	1	(14½-oz.) can stewed tomatoes
2	Tbsp. all-purpose flour	1	Tbsp. Worcestershire sauce
2	Tbsp. brown sugar		

1. Cook green beans in boiling water 9 minutes or until tender; drain and set aside.

2. Cook bacon in a large skillet until crisp; remove bacon, reserving 3 Tbsp. drippings in skillet. Crumble bacon, and set aside.

3. Sauté onion and green pepper in reserved drippings until tender. Stir in flour and next 4 ingredients. Stir in tomatoes and Worcestershire sauce; cook, stirring constantly, until thickened and bubbly. Stir in green beans; cook until thoroughly heated. Top with bacon.

Catherine Wisser

150 Years of Good Eating
St. George Evangelical Lutheran Church ~ Brighton, Michigan

Fried Okra Salad

(pictured on previous page)

makes 6 servings • prep: 20 min., cook: 2 min. per batch

All your favorite Southern favorites team up for this salad—tomatoes, bacon, and crispy fried okra. If you can't get enough okra, be sure to visit the South's biggest celebration of the vegetable, the Okra Strut, in Irmo, South Carolina.

test kitchen tip: To save time, substitute fully cooked bacon. Reheat it according to package directions before crumbling.

1½	cups self-rising yellow cornmeal	1	medium-size sweet onion, thinly sliced
1	tsp. salt		
1	lb. fresh okra	1	medium-size green bell pepper, chopped
1½	cups buttermilk		
Peanut oil		Lemon Dressing	
1	head Bibb lettuce, torn	3	bacon slices, cooked and crumbled
1	large tomato, chopped		

1. Combine cornmeal and salt. Dip okra in buttermilk; dredge in cornmeal mixture.

2. Pour oil to a depth of 2 inches into a Dutch oven; heat to 375°. Fry okra, in batches, 2 minutes or until golden, turning once. Drain well.

3. Arrange lettuce in a serving bowl; top with tomato, onion slices, and bell pepper. Add Lemon Dressing, tossing to coat. Top with fried okra, and sprinkle with crumbled bacon. Serve immediately.

Lemon Dressing

makes ¾ cup • prep: 5 min.

¼ cup fresh lemon juice
3 Tbsp. chopped fresh basil
1 tsp. salt
1 tsp. paprika
½ tsp. pepper
¼ cup olive oil

1. Combine first 5 ingredients in a bowl. Add oil, whisking until blended.

Simple Peach Sorbet

makes 4 cups • other: 3 hr., 10 min.

Just 3 ingredients, yet this satiny sorbet carries an intense ripe peach impact that belies its simplicity. This sorbet is as creamy as ice cream, but without the milk. In fact, sorbet was made from snow 1,000 years before the first ice cream was created.

4 or 5 fresh ripe peaches, peeled and chopped
¾ cup sugar
1 tsp. fresh lemon juice

1. Process all ingredients in a blender until smooth, stopping to scrape down sides. Pour mixture into a 9-inch square pan. Cover and freeze 3 hours or until firm.
2. Remove pan from freezer; let stand 10 minutes. Break frozen mixture into chunks; process in a food processor until smooth. Spoon into individual dessert dishes.

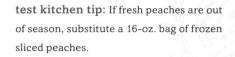

test kitchen tip: If fresh peaches are out of season, substitute a 16-oz. bag of frozen sliced peaches.

"...People just showed up and were always made welcome. To stay less than an hour was an insult, and there was always a meal...and nobody was ever let out of the house without the goodbye ritual...."

—*Shirley Abbott*
Memoirist and Novelist

homestyle favorites

appetizers and beverages

Gruyère and Onion Tarts, page 202

Sugar-and-Spice Pecans

makes about 5 cups • prep: 15 min., cook: 55 min.

Pecans dipped in beaten egg white and a sweet blend of spices are baked into crunchy-crusted nuts perfect for gift giving or party menus.

test kitchen tip: You can substitute 1 lb. of whole almonds or walnut halves to make this addictive snack, if you'd like.

¾	cup sugar		1	egg white
1	Tbsp. Sweet Spice Blend		1	Tbsp. water
¾	tsp. salt		1	lb. pecan halves

1. Preheat oven to 275°.

2. Combine first 3 ingredients in a medium bowl; set aside.

3. Whisk egg white and 1 Tbsp. water in a medium bowl until foamy. (No liquid should remain.) Add pecans, stirring until evenly coated.

4. Add pecans to sugar mixture, stirring until evenly coated. Place pecans in a single layer on a buttered 15- x 10-inch jelly-roll pan.

5. Bake at 275° for 50 to 55 minutes, stirring twice. Spread immediately on wax paper; cool. Store in an airtight container.

Sweet Spice Blend

makes 6 Tbsp. • prep: 5 min.

2	Tbsp. light brown sugar		1	tsp. ground nutmeg
2	Tbsp. ground cinnamon		½	tsp. ground cloves
4	tsp. dried ground ginger		½	tsp. ground cardamom

1. Combine all ingredients in a small bowl. Store in an airtight container.

Mexi Spiced Nuts

makes 4 cups • prep: 20 min., cook: 30 min.

For friends who prefer salty rather than sweet treats, this is the perfect food gift. Chili powder, red pepper, and hot sauce coat peanuts and pecans for southwestern-style roasted nuts.

make it ahead: Store Mexi Spiced Nuts in an airtight container for up to 2 weeks. They're ideal snacks for football season.

2	cups pecan halves		1	tsp. ground red pepper
2	cups salted roasted peanuts		½	tsp. garlic powder
1	egg white, lightly beaten		1	Tbsp. Worcestershire sauce
¼	cup butter or margarine, melted		1	tsp. hot sauce
1	Tbsp. chili powder			

1. Preheat oven to 350°.

2. Combine pecans and peanuts in an ungreased 13- x 9-inch pan.

3. Combine egg white and remaining 6 ingredients in a small bowl, stirring well; pour over nuts, stirring to coat. Bake, uncovered, at 350° for 30 minutes or until toasted; cool completely in pan on a wire rack. Store in an airtight container.

Honey-Cardamom Crunch

makes about 12 cups • prep: 20 min., cook: 45 min.

Coconut, cereal, dried cranberries, and almonds sweetened with honey and brown sugar make this easy snack mix the hit of any party.

6	cups crisp rice cereal squares		¼	cup butter or margarine
2	cups tiny pretzel twists		¼	cup honey
1	cup whole natural almonds		½	tsp. ground cardamom
1	cup sweetened flaked coconut		1	cup dried cranberries
⅓	cup firmly packed light brown sugar			

1. Preheat oven to 300°.

2. Combine first 4 ingredients in a large roasting pan; stir well.

3. Combine brown sugar and next 3 ingredients in a saucepan. Place over medium heat, and cook until blended, stirring often. Drizzle brown sugar mixture over cereal mixture; toss to coat. Bake at 300° for 40 minutes, stirring every 10 minutes.

4. Stir in cranberries; spread mixture on a baking sheet. Cool completely. Store in an airtight container.

Hilda Olson

Cooking with the Original Search Engine
Fort Worth Public Library All Staff Association ~ Fort Worth, Texas

Blue Cheese-Walnut Wafers

makes 4 dozen • prep: 20 min., cook: 15 min. per batch, other: 35 min.

Cheese wafers are a must on any Southern tea menu. The distinctive blue cheese flavor and crunchy walnuts make these cookie-sized morsels anything but ordinary.

test kitchen tip: If you're tempted to substitute margarine for butter in this recipe, don't. The butter makes these wafers wonderfully short and the dough easier to handle. Store the wafers in an airtight container up to 1 week.

1	(4-oz.) package blue cheese, softened	1¼	cups all-purpose flour
½	cup butter, softened	⅛	tsp. salt
		⅓	cup finely chopped walnuts

1. Position knife blade in food processor bowl; add first 4 ingredients. Process until blended, stopping once to scrape down sides. (Mixture will be sticky.) Transfer mixture to a bowl; stir in walnuts. Cover and chill 5 minutes. Divide dough in half. Shape each portion of dough into an 8-inch log. Wrap in heavy-duty plastic wrap, and chill 30 minutes or until firm.
2. Preheat oven to 350°.
3. Slice dough into ¼-inch slices; place on ungreased baking sheets. Bake at 350° for 15 minutes or until lightly browned.

Judy Bryson

Georgia Hospitality
Georgia Elks Aidmore Auxiliary ~ Conyers, Georgia

food gifts—the real southern comfort

Someone dies, a baby is born, the neighbor is hosting wedding guests, and a co-worker has the flu. You are a houseguest of a friend, decide to visit a shut-in member of your church, and notice a new family has moved in down the street. In the South, these are just some of the occasions that demand a food offering. For centuries, Southerners have used food to express emotion by leaving a pound cake with a note on the back porch of a grieving family or a tin of spiced nuts on the office desk of a friend with a birthday. In days when food supplies were short, food was the ultimate gift. Today, when time to make homemade gifts is short, it is still the ultimate gift.

Gouda–Cashew Bouchées

makes 2 dozen • prep: 25 min., cook: 18 min.

Bouchée is French for "little patty" or "mouthful." These little baked cheese bites topped with buttery cashews are a welcomed diversion from Cheddar cheese straws.

1½ cups (6 oz.) shredded Gouda cheese	1 tsp. dry mustard
½ cup butter or margarine, softened	⅛ tsp. salt
1½ cups all-purpose flour	24 whole cashews

1. Preheat oven to 375°.

2. Combine cheese and butter in a large mixing bowl; beat at medium speed with an electric mixer until blended.

3. Combine flour, mustard, and salt; add to cheese mixture, beating until dough is no longer crumbly. Shape into 24 (1-inch) balls. Place on lightly greased baking sheets; gently press a cashew on top of each ball. Bake at 375° for 16 to 18 minutes or until lightly browned. Let cool on wire racks.

Rebecca Hardaway King

The Summerhouse Sampler
Wynnton Elementary School PTA ~ Columbus, Georgia

test kitchen tip: If you like a smokier flavor, use smoked Gouda.

Orange–Sour Cream Dip

makes 2½ cups • prep: 15 min., other: 2 hr.

Make a centerpiece for a summer buffet by hollowing out a watermelon and filling it with chunks of fresh summer fruit to serve with this creamy pudding-based dip. Or dollop this sweet orange dip over fruit wedges for a simple salad.

1 (6-oz.) can frozen orange juice concentrate, thawed and undiluted	1¼ cups milk
1 (3¾-oz.) package vanilla instant pudding mix	¼ cup sour cream

1. Combine first 3 ingredients in a medium bowl, stirring with a wire whisk until blended. Stir in sour cream. Cover and chill at least 2 hours. Serve with fresh fruit.

Jean Merkle

Sweet Home Alabama Cooking
44th National Square Dance Convention ~ Montgomery, Alabama

lighten up: Using 1% low-fat milk instead of whole milk and light sour cream instead of regular reduces the percentage of calories from fat by half. Serving this version with fresh fruit makes it a healthy choice for snacking, too.

Dried Tomato Red Pesto

makes 1⅔ cups • prep: 15 min., other: 5 min.

As a twist on traditional pesto, this version uses parsley instead of basil along with dried tomatoes for a ruby-colored spread.

test kitchen tip: For a traditional use of this new-fashioned pesto, toss any leftovers with hot cooked pasta and Parmesan cheese for a simple supper.

1⅔ cups (3 oz.) dried tomatoes
¼ cup grated Parmesan cheese
1 cup loosely packed fresh flat-leaf parsley

4 garlic cloves
¾ cup extra virgin olive oil

1. Place dried tomatoes in a small bowl; add boiling water to cover, and let stand 5 minutes.

2. Drain tomatoes, and pat dry. Place tomatoes, cheese, parsley, and garlic in a food processor. With processor running, slowly pour oil through food chute, processing until smooth. Serve with toasted French baguette slices.

Always in Season
The Junior League of Salt Lake City, Utah

Corn–Walnut Dip

makes about 4⅓ cups • prep: 20 min., other: 1 hr.

Green chiles and cumin add a Southwest flavor to this cream cheese-based dip. Cumin is the traditional southwestern spice that adds a pungent, earthy taste.

test kitchen tip: We strongly recommend using fresh lemon juice in this highly rated dip. You'll need about 2 medium lemons.

2 (8-oz.) packages cream cheese, softened
¼ cup fresh lemon juice
1 Tbsp. ground cumin
1 tsp. salt
1 tsp. ground red pepper
1 tsp. black pepper

1 (8-oz.) can whole kernel corn, drained
1 cup chopped walnuts
1 (4.5-oz.) can chopped green chiles, undrained
3 green onions, chopped
Garnish: green onion curls

1. Beat cream cheese at medium speed with an electric mixer until smooth; gradually add lemon juice, beating well.

2. Add cumin and next 3 ingredients, beating well. Stir in corn and remaining ingredients. Cover and chill at least 1 hour. Serve with tortilla chips or corn chips. Garnish, if desired.

The Guild Collection: Recipes from Art Lovers
The Guild, The Museum of Fine Arts ~ Houston, Texas

Elegant Layered Torta

makes 15 to 20 appetizer servings • prep: 25 min., other: 8 hr.

Colorful layers of pine nuts, dried tomatoes, pesto, and a feta cheese mixture are chilled in a loaf pan, then inverted for a striking spread to serve with crackers.

2	garlic cloves, cut in half	½	cup dry vermouth or dry white wine
1	shallot, quartered	½	cup pine nuts, lightly toasted
1	cup butter, cut into small pieces	1	cup dried tomatoes in oil, drained and minced
12	oz. crumbled feta cheese		
1	(8-oz.) package cream cheese, cut into pieces	1	cup pesto

freeze it: Prepare recipe through Step 3, and freeze up to 1 month in advance. Thaw in refrigerator overnight before serving.

1. Lightly grease an 8- x 4-inch loaf pan. Line pan with plastic wrap, allowing it to extend slightly over edges of pan. Set pan aside.

2. With food processor running, drop garlic and shallot through food chute. Process 3 seconds or until minced. Add butter and next 3 ingredients; process until smooth, stopping to scrape down sides.

3. Layer half each of pine nuts, dried tomatoes, pesto, and cheese mixture in prepared pan, smoothing each layer to edges of pan. Repeat layers with remaining ingredients. Cover and chill at least 8 hours.

4. To serve, invert pan onto a serving platter; remove plastic wrap. Serve with crackers or baguette slices.

What Can I Bring?
The Junior League of Northern Virginia ~ McLean, Virginia

Tomato Chutney Cheesecake

makes 18 to 20 appetizer servings • prep: 15 min., other: 8 hr.

This savory no-cook appetizer will bring rave reviews. And the best part—it's make ahead.

4	(8-oz.) packages cream cheese, softened and divided	⅔	cup red tomato chutney
2	cups shredded Cheddar cheese	1	to 2 Tbsp. milk
½	tsp. ground red pepper		Garnishes: chopped fresh chives or green onions, cherry tomato halves
4	or 5 green onions, finely chopped		

test kitchen tip: Find red tomato chutney with pickles, chowchow, and relishes in your supermarket, or make your own using the Red Tomato Chutney recipe at myrecipes.com.

1. Beat 3 packages cream cheese, Cheddar cheese, and red pepper at medium speed with an electric mixer until blended and smooth. Stir in green onions.

2. Spread half of cream cheese mixture into an 8-inch round cake pan lined with plastic wrap; top with tomato chutney, leaving a ½-inch border of cream cheese around edge. Spread remaining cream cheese mixture over chutney layer. Cover and chill at least 8 hours.

3. Invert cheesecake onto a serving platter; remove plastic wrap. Spread remaining package cream cheese on top and sides of cheesecake. Serve with vegetables and crackers. Garnish, if desired.

Cranberry-Amaretto Chutney With Cream Cheese

makes 16 appetizer servings • prep: 15 min., cook: 20 min., other: 8 hr.

Chunky citrus-spiced cranberry chutney with a splash of amaretto is delicious spooned over cream cheese and served with crackers or gingersnaps. Or, spoon the chutney into pretty jelly jars and tie with a ribbon for a special home-made gift.

test kitchen tip: If time is tight, skip Steps 1 and 2 and spoon the rosy mixture over a block of softened cream cheese as we did in our Test Kitchens.

2	(8-oz.) packages cream cheese, softened	2	Tbsp. fresh lemon juice
1	(12-oz.) bag fresh cranberries (3 cups)	¾	tsp. grated lemon rind
1½	cups sugar	⅓	cup amaretto
		1	Tbsp. orange marmalade

1. Combine cream cheese in a small bowl; beat at medium speed with an electric mixer until smooth.

2. Line a 2-cup mold with cheesecloth, letting cloth hang over edge. Firmly press cream cheese mixture, 1 spoonful at a time, into mold. Fold cheesecloth over top; cover and chill 8 hours.

3. Combine cranberries, sugar, and lemon juice in a small saucepan. Bring to a boil over medium heat, stirring constantly. Reduce heat, and simmer 20 minutes. Remove from heat; stir in lemon rind, amaretto, and marmalade. Cool to room temperature.

4. Unmold cheese onto a serving platter; remove cheesecloth. Spoon cranberry sauce over cheese. Serve with crackers or gingersnaps.   Jacqueline Underwood

Savory Sweets
P.E.O. Chapter LR ~ St. Charles, Missouri

pimiento cheese, please

It's served at the epitome of genteel Southern sports events—the Masters Golf Tournament in Augusta, Georgia. It's packed in children's lunch boxes across the region. Stuffed in tomatoes. Spread on celery. Made into tiny sandwiches for tea rooms of the highest society. Whether in low- or high-brow settings, pimiento cheese spread, that luscious creamy mixture of mayo, shredded Cheddar cheese, and chopped sweet red pimiento peppers, has as many recipe variations as cornbread. Surprisingly, it's a Southern invention, which came about a century ago. At first, it was a special treat—about the only cheese Southerners could get was from the hoops at the general store. As cheese became more available, it became an economical staple. Now it's simply a favorite. Even Elvis loved it—if you added Worcestershire sauce.

Spicy Roasted Red Bell Pepper Pimiento Cheese

makes 4 cups • prep: 25 min.

Sharp Cheddar, roasted bell peppers, and a spoonful of Dijon mustard make this favorite Southern-born spread a bit different from classic pimiento cheese.

1¼ cups mayonnaise

½ (12-oz.) jar roasted red bell peppers, drained and chopped

2 tsp. finely grated onion

2 tsp. coarse grained Dijon mustard

½ tsp. ground red pepper

2 (10-oz.) blocks sharp Cheddar cheese, shredded

Freshly ground black pepper to taste

test kitchen tip: Stuff pimiento cheese into pretty celery ribs with leaves to serve on a relish tray during the holidays, or spread between slices of crustless bread for dainty tea sandwiches.

1. Stir together first 5 ingredients until well blended; stir in cheese and black pepper to taste. Store in the refrigerator in an airtight container up to 4 days.

Almond Ambrosia Spread

makes 12 appetizer servings • prep: 20 min., other: 6 hr.

The fruit dessert called ambrosia is more popular in the South than anywhere else. This congealed version works well for an appetizer buffet. It's best served with sturdy fruit, cookies, or sweet crackers.

make it ahead: Assemble recipe through Step 2; cover and refrigerate up to 3 days in advance.

1	envelope unflavored gelatin	1	Tbsp. grated orange rind
¼	cup cold water	½	cup golden raisins
12	oz. cream cheese, softened	½	cup currants
½	cup sugar	½	cup slivered almonds, toasted
½	cup butter, softened	½	cup chopped pecans
½	cup sour cream	¾	cup sliced almonds, toasted
1	Tbsp. grated lemon rind		

1. Sprinkle gelatin over cold water in a large bowl; let stand 1 minute. Microwave at HIGH 30 seconds; stir until gelatin dissolves. Add cream cheese and next 5 ingredients. Beat at medium speed with a mixer until creamy. Gently stir in raisins and next 3 ingredients.

2. Pour gelatin mixture into a lightly greased 1-qt. ring mold. Cover and chill at least 6 hours.

3. Unmold gelatin mixture; gently press sliced almonds around sides and top. Serve with gingersnaps, assorted crackers, or apple wedges. Jackie Marble

Seasonings Change
Ohio State University Women's Club ~ Columbus, Ohio

Garlic-Herb Cheese Spread

makes 5 cups • prep: 30 min., other: 8 hr.

Gardeners will love this creamy spread flavored with 6 different fresh herbs. Made ahead of time and garnished with edible flowers or fresh herb sprigs, it's perfect for spring celebrations or summer luncheons or showers.

test kitchen tip: This spread is also great with baked potatoes or tossed with steamed or grilled vegetables.

½	cup fresh parsley	⅓	cup sour cream
1	Tbsp. fresh thyme leaves	¼	cup butter or margarine, softened
1	Tbsp. fresh basil	¼	cup milk
1	Tbsp. fresh tarragon	3	Tbsp. fresh sage leaves
1	garlic clove	1	Tbsp. chopped fresh chives
2	(8-oz.) packages cream cheese	1	tsp. Dijon mustard
½	cup butter or margarine, softened	Garnishes: fresh herbs, fresh edible
1	tsp. Worcestershire sauce		flowers
½	tsp. red wine vinegar		
3	cups (12 oz.) shredded sharp Cheddar cheese		

1. Line a 1½-qt. soufflé dish with plastic wrap, leaving a 1-inch overhang around edges. Set aside.

2. Position knife blade in a food processor; add first 5 ingredients, and process until finely chopped, stopping to scrape down sides. Add cream cheese and next 3 ingredients; process until blended. Spoon cream cheese mixture into prepared dish, spreading evenly; set aside.

3. Combine Cheddar cheese and next 3 ingredients in processor; process until smooth, stopping to scrape down sides. Add sage, chives, and mustard; process until combined, stopping to scrape down sides. Spoon mixture over cream cheese layer, spreading evenly. Cover and chill at least 8 hours. Unmold onto a serving platter. Garnish, if desired. Serve with assorted crackers.

Baked Crab, Brie, and Artichoke Dip

makes 5 cups • prep: 30 min., cook: 30 min.

Serve this ideal Southern party recipe in an elegant soufflé dish. We promise the rich flavor will bring compliments to the cook. Sweet Vidalia onions grown only in Georgia make the creamy mixture of crabmeat, Brie, artichoke hearts, and spinach taste extra delicious.

½ (10-oz.) package frozen chopped spinach, thawed and drained
½ cup canned artichoke hearts, drained and coarsely chopped
1 (15-oz.) Brie round
1 medium leek, sliced
1 medium Vidalia onion, finely chopped
6 large garlic cloves, minced
2 Tbsp. olive oil
½ cup whipping cream
¼ cup dry white wine
1 lb. fresh jumbo lump crabmeat, drained
3 Tbsp. finely chopped fresh parsley
2 Tbsp. finely chopped fresh dill
1 Tbsp. finely chopped fresh tarragon
1 tsp. Dijon mustard
1 tsp. hot sauce
½ tsp. pepper

test kitchen tip: Leeks have a delicious onion-garlic flavor. They grow partly underground and need special attention in cleaning. Trim the root and tough tops of the green leaves. Then, cut the stalk in half, and rinse well under cold running water, gently separating the layers and rubbing the leaves to remove trapped dirt.

1. Preheat oven to 425°.

2. Press spinach and artichoke hearts between layers of paper towels to remove excess moisture; set aside.

3. Remove and discard rind from cheese with a vegetable peeler. Cut cheese into ¼-inch pieces; set aside.

4. Sauté leek, onion, and garlic in hot oil in a large skillet over medium-high heat 5 minutes or until tender. Stir in spinach and artichoke. Add whipping cream and wine; cook over high heat, stirring constantly, 5 minutes or until liquid evaporates. Remove from heat; add cheese, stirring until cheese melts.

5. Combine crabmeat and remaining 6 ingredients in a large bowl; stir well. Add hot cheese mixture; stir well. Spoon into a lightly greased 1½-quart soufflé dish. Bake at 425° for 20 minutes or until golden. Serve with crackers or thin toasted French baguette slices.

Susan Mason

From Black Tie to Blackeyed Peas: Savannah's Savory Secrets
St. Joseph's Foundation of Savannah, Inc. ~ Savannah, Georgia

Hot Seafood Dip

makes about 4¼ cups • prep: 25 min., cook: 27 min.

You'll need sturdy crackers for this hot and chunky seafood dip of shrimp, crabmeat, artichokes, and almonds.

test kitchen tip: Use prepeeled and deveined shrimp if you're in a hurry. Find them in the seafood section of your supermarket. You'll need about ⅓ lb. if they're already peeled.

½	lb. unpeeled, medium-size raw shrimp	1	tsp. fresh lemon juice
1	Tbsp. butter or margarine	2	drops of hot sauce
1	cup mayonnaise	½	lb. fresh lump crabmeat
1	cup freshly grated Parmesan cheese	1	(14-oz.) can artichoke hearts, drained and finely chopped
¼	cup chopped green onions	¼	tsp. salt
2	jalapeño peppers, seeded and minced	⅓	cup sliced almonds

1. Preheat oven to 375°.

2. Peel shrimp and, if desired, devein. Coarsely chop shrimp; set aside.

3. Melt butter in a medium skillet over medium-high heat; add shrimp, and cook 2 minutes, stirring constantly; drain and set aside.

4. Combine mayonnaise and next 5 ingredients in a large bowl. Add shrimp, crabmeat, artichoke hearts, and salt; stir well. Spoon mixture into a lightly greased 8-inch square baking dish; sprinkle with almonds.

5. Bake at 375° for 25 minutes or until mixture is bubbly around the edges. Serve with assorted hearty crackers.

Cathy Seymour

Cane River's Louisiana Living
The Service League of Natchitoches, Louisiana

Cocktail Meatballs

makes 3 dozen • prep: 20 min., cook: 25 min.

We can thank German immigrants for bringing tangy sauerkraut to the region. This pickled specialty is mixed with cranberry sauce and chili sauce to make a sweet-sour topping for these meatballs.

make it a meal: After the party, warm leftover meatballs, and drape them with melted Swiss cheese on a sandwich.

2	lbs. lean ground beef	1	(16-oz.) can whole-berry cranberry sauce
1	cup fine, dry breadcrumbs		
1	(1.4-oz.) envelope dry onion soup mix	1	(12-oz.) bottle chili sauce
3	large eggs	½	cup water
1	(16-oz.) can sauerkraut, drained	1	cup firmly packed light brown sugar

1. Combine ground beef, breadcrumbs, onion soup mix, and eggs in a large bowl, and stir until blended. Shape into 1-inch meatballs. Place meatballs in a greased 13- x 9-inch baking dish.

2. Preheat oven to 450°.

3. Stir together sauerkraut and remaining 4 ingredients. Spoon over meatballs. Bake, uncovered, at 450° for 25 minutes.

Tucson Treasures: Recipes & Reflections
Tucson Medical Center Auxiliary ~ Tucson, Arizona

Cheese Soufflé Sandwiches

makes 6 dozen • prep: 60 min., cook: 18 min. per batch, other: 24 hr.

They're cheesy, bite-sized, buttery, and they freeze easily. What appetizer could be easier to put on the menu for a shower or bunco night?

2	cups butter or margarine, softened	1½	tsp. Worcestershire sauce	
4	(5-oz.) jars sharp process cheese spread, softened	1	tsp. hot sauce	
1	tsp. onion powder	3	(16-oz.) loaves sandwich bread, chilled (we tested with Pepperidge Farm)	
1	tsp. Beau Monde seasoning			
1½	tsp. minced fresh dill			

1. Beat butter and cheese at medium speed with an electric mixer until light and fluffy. Add onion powder and next 4 ingredients.

2. Work with 1 loaf of bread at a time, leaving remainder chilled. Stack 3 slices of bread; using an electric knife or bread knife, remove crust from bread stack, and reserve crust for other uses. Spread cheese mixture between 3 bread slices, restacking slices. Cut stack into 4 squares, and spread cheese mixture on top, bottom, and sides of each square. Place stacks on ungreased baking sheets. Repeat procedure with remaining bread and cheese mixture. Place sandwiches in an airtight container, and freeze at least 24 hours or up to 1 month.

3. Preheat oven to 325°.

4. Bake desired amount on a greased baking sheet at 325° for 15 to 18 minutes or until edges are golden.

From Black Tie to Blackeyed Peas: Savannah's Savory Secrets
St. Joseph's Foundation of Savannah, Inc. ~ Savannah, Georgia

test kitchen tip: This party fare takes time to assemble, but its buttery goodness is well worth the effort. Chill the bread the night before you make these to make assembly easier. After assembling, you can freeze the unbaked sandwiches up to a month and bake them as you need them. And there's no need to thaw them before baking.

Garden Bruschetta

Garden Bruschetta

makes 2 dozen • prep: 20 min., cook: 3 min., other: 1 hr.

When the tomato plant bounty is ready to harvest, pull out this recipe. Blended with garlic and mellow-tasting balsamic vinegar, the chopped tomato mixture is great on crispy baguettes for a mouthful of summer flavor.

3	tomatoes, finely chopped (about 2 cups)	¼	tsp. salt	
⅓	cup finely chopped fresh basil	⅛	tsp. freshly ground pepper	
1	Tbsp. minced fresh garlic	1	French baguette, sliced diagonally into 24 (½-inch-thick) slices	
2	tsp. balsamic vinegar	2	Tbsp. olive oil	

1. Stir together first 6 ingredients in a bowl. Cover and chill 1 hour.

2. Preheat broiler.

3. Brush bread slices with oil; place on a baking sheet. Broil 5½ inches from heat 3 minutes or until lightly browned, turning once.

4. Spoon tomato mixture on bread slices just before serving.

The Bounty of Chester County: Heritage Edition
Chester County Agricultural Development Council ~ West Chester, Pennsylvania

make it a meal: For a beautiful, arranged luncheon salad, mound tender mesclun greens topped with grilled chicken or shrimp on a dinner-sized plate. Surround with 6 pieces of Garden Bruchetta and spears of steamed asparagus. Serve with a creamy Italian dressing.

Mustard-Dill Pancakes With Smoked Salmon and Caviar

makes 52 appetizers • prep: 25 min., cook: 3 min. per batch, other: 1 hr.

This upscale appetizer proves that pancakes do double duty as a sweet or savory dish.

1	cup all-purpose flour	3	Tbsp. butter or margarine, melted	
2	tsp. baking powder	2	Tbsp. chopped fresh dill	
1	large egg	1	lb. thinly sliced smoked salmon	
1¼	cups milk	½	cup sour cream	
3	Tbsp. Dijon mustard	1	(4-oz.) jar red or black caviar	
1	Tbsp. mustard seeds			

1. Combine flour and baking powder in a large bowl; set aside.

2. Whisk together egg and next 3 ingredients; add to flour mixture, whisking just until dry ingredients are moistened. Stir in butter and dill. Cover and chill 1 hour.

3. For each pancake, pour about ½ Tbsp. batter onto a hot, lightly greased griddle. Cook pancakes until tops are covered with bubbles and edges look cooked (about 1½ minutes); turn and cook other side. Keep warm. Repeat with remaining batter.

4. To serve, top each pancake with salmon, sour cream, and caviar. Wolfe Family

Cookin' with Friends
National Presbyterian School Class of 2000 ~ Washington, D.C.

test kitchen tip: Before using caviar, place it in a small wire-mesh strainer, and rinse under cold running water. Pat caviar dry with paper towels. This prevents the caviar's color from running.

Stuffed Mushrooms

makes 30 appetizers • prep: 35 min., cook: 25 min.

Feta cheese, dill, wine, olive oil, and Parmesan combine for a Greek-inspired filling to stuff into mushroom caps.

test kitchen tip: After giving mushrooms a quick rinse, clean them with a special mushroom brush or a damp paper towel.

30	large fresh mushrooms	¼	tsp. salt
2	Tbsp. butter or margarine, divided	1	cup crumbled feta cheese
2	Tbsp. olive oil, divided	1	Tbsp. chopped fresh dill
2	Tbsp. finely chopped green onions	2	Tbsp. whipping cream
2	Tbsp. dry white wine	¼	cup grated Parmesan cheese
½	tsp. pepper		

1. Rinse mushrooms; pat dry. Remove and discard stems. Melt 1 Tbsp. butter in a large skillet; add 1 Tbsp. olive oil. Sauté half of mushrooms over medium heat 5 minutes. Place mushrooms on an ungreased 15- x 10-inch jelly-roll pan, stem side up. Repeat procedure with remaining mushrooms, butter, and oil, reserving drippings in skillet; set pan aside.

2. Preheat oven to 350°.

3. Sauté green onions in drippings over medium heat 1 minute. Add wine, pepper, and salt; cook, uncovered, 30 seconds or until liquid evaporates. Remove from heat, and stir in feta cheese, dill, and whipping cream. Stuff mushroom caps with cheese mixture; sprinkle with Parmesan cheese, and bake at 350° for 10 minutes.

Blue Cheese Biscuits With Beef and Horseradish-Chive Cream

makes 20 appetizer servings • prep: 25 min., cook: 33 min., other: 15 min.

Putting meat in a biscuit has been a Southern tradition for centuries. Using strong-flavored blue cheese in the biscuits and a rich horseradish topping brings out the juicy tenderloin flavor.

2	cups self-rising flour	½	tsp. salt
1	(8-oz.) container sour cream	½	tsp. pepper
½	cup butter, melted	½	Tbsp. vegetable oil
1	(4-oz.) package crumbled blue cheese		Horseradish-Chive Cream
2	(6-oz.) beef tenderloin fillets (about 1½ inches thick)		

1. Preheat oven to 425°.

2. Stir together first 4 ingredients just until blended.

3. Turn dough out onto a lightly floured surface. Pat dough to a ½-inch thickness; cut with a 2-inch round cutter. Place on lightly greased baking sheets.

4. Bake at 425° for 12 to 15 minutes or until lightly browned.

5. Sprinkle fillets with salt and pepper. Heat oil in a small skillet over high heat; add fillets, and cook 8 to 9 minutes on each side or to desired degree of doneness. Remove fillets from pan; let stand 15 minutes.

6. Cut fillets into ¼-inch slices. Split biscuits in half, and top bottom half evenly with beef slices and Horseradish-Chive Cream. Top with remaining biscuit halves.

Horseradish-Chive Cream

makes 1 cup • prep: 5 min.

1	(8-oz.) container sour cream		1	Tbsp. Dijon mustard
1	Tbsp. prepared horseradish		1	Tbsp. chopped fresh chives

1. Stir together all ingredients. Chill until ready to serve.

make it ahead: Prepare biscuits, and store at room temperature in an airtight container up to a day in advance for easy assembly on the day of the party.

Mahogany Chicken Wings

makes 16 appetizer servings • prep: 40 min.; cook: 1 hr., 10 min.; other: 8 hr.

Have lots of napkins on hand when you serve these chicken wings marinated in a sweet-sour Asian sauce. A cup of hoisin sauce, a spicy chili mixture essential to Asian cuisine, gives the sauce its flavor punch.

1½	cups soy sauce		½	cup honey
¾	cup dry sherry		12	green onions, minced (about
¾	cup cider vinegar			2 cups)
1	cup hoisin sauce		6	large garlic cloves, minced
¾	cup plum sauce		32	chicken drummettes (6 to 7 lbs.)

1. Combine first 8 ingredients in a large saucepan. Bring to a boil; reduce heat, and simmer, uncovered, 5 minutes. Cool sauce. Reserve ½ cup sauce; cover and chill.

2. Place chicken in a large plastic container. Pour remaining sauce over chicken; cover and marinate in refrigerator at least 8 hours.

3. Preheat oven to 375°.

4. Remove chicken from marinade, discarding marinade. Place chicken into 2 lightly greased roasting pans. Bake chicken at 375° for 1 hour or until done, basting with reserved ½ cup sauce every 20 minutes. (Discard any remaining marinade.)

test kitchen tip: For easy cleanup, line roasting pans with aluminum foil before baking or, instead, grill chicken drummettes over medium-high heat (350° to 400°) for 35 to 40 minutes or until done, basting with reserved ½ cup sauce during the last 10 minutes.

President's House Miniature Crab Cakes With Pepper Sauce

makes 6 appetizer servings • prep: 25 min., cook: 16 min., other: 30 min.

Curry powder, a blend of 15 or more spices, seasons fresh crabmeat for these patties. Serve the bold Pepper Sauce drizzled over the hot cakes for a stunning sit-down appetizer.

1	large egg, lightly beaten	1	Tbsp. hot sauce
1	Tbsp. mayonnaise	1	Tbsp. fresh lemon juice
½	tsp. paprika	1	tsp. Worcestershire sauce
¼	tsp. salt	1	lb. fresh lump crabmeat, drained
¼	tsp. dry mustard	⅓	cup fine, dry breadcrumbs
¼	tsp. curry powder	¼	cup vegetable oil, divided
⅛	tsp. ground red pepper		Pepper Sauce
⅛	tsp. freshly ground black pepper		

1. Combine first 11 ingredients; stir well. Stir in crabmeat and breadcrumbs. Shape mixture into 18 (2-inch) patties; cover and chill 30 minutes.

2. Heat 2 Tbsp. oil in a large skillet over medium heat; cook half of patties on each side until golden. Drain on paper towels. Repeat procedure. Serve immediately with Pepper Sauce

Pepper Sauce

makes 1 cup • prep: 25 min., cook: 20 min.

½	large red bell pepper	¼	cup dry white wine
½	large yellow bell pepper	¼	cup white wine vinegar
½	jalapeño pepper	½	cup chicken broth
1	cup cold unsalted butter, divided	¼	cup whipping cream
½	cup chopped fresh mushrooms	1	Tbsp. fresh lemon juice
2	shallots, chopped	¼	tsp. freshly ground pepper
1	sprig fresh thyme, chopped		

make it ahead: Prepare Pepper Sauce through Step 2, and store peppers in the refrigerator in an airtight container up to a week. Or if time permits, prepare Pepper Sauce completely, and store in refrigerator in an airtight container up to 3 days ahead.

1. Preheat broiler.

2. Remove and discard seeds and membranes from peppers; place peppers, skin side up, on a baking sheet, and flatten with palm of hand. Broil 5½ inches from heat 15 to 20 minutes or until charred. Place peppers in ice water until cool. Remove from water; peel, chop, and set aside.

3. Melt 1 Tbsp. butter in a skillet over medium heat. Add mushrooms, shallot, and thyme; sauté until tender. Stir in wine, vinegar, and broth; cook over medium-high heat until mixture is reduced to ½ cup, stirring occasionally. Add cream; cook over medium-high heat until mixture is reduced to ½ cup, stirring occasionally. Reduce heat; add remaining butter, 1 Tbsp. at a time, stirring constantly with a wire whisk until sauce is smooth.

4. Pour sauce through a wire-mesh strainer into a small bowl, discarding solids. Stir in lemon juice, pepper, and chopped peppers.

The William & Mary Cookbook
College of William and Mary Alumni Society ~ Williamsburg, Virginia

Gruyère and Onion Tarts

(pictured on page 183)

makes 2 dozen • prep: 15 min., cook: 31 min.

Flaky little phyllo pastry tarts are filled with a creamy mixture of herbs, sweet caramelized onions, and nutty-tasting Gruyère cheese in this upscale-looking appetizer. They get a favorite Southern garnish of crumbled bacon on top.

test kitchen tip: To prevent tears while slicing onion, start with a chilled onion and avoid cutting off the root end.

1½	Tbsp. butter or margarine	⅛	tsp. dried rosemary
2	cups thinly sliced onion	¾	cup (3 oz.) shredded Gruyère cheese
2	garlic cloves, chopped	¼	cup whipping cream
¼	tsp. salt	24	frozen mini phyllo pastry shells, thawed
¼	tsp. dried sage	4	slices thick bacon, cooked and crumbled
¼	tsp. dried thyme		
¼	tsp. pepper		

1. Preheat oven to 350°.

2. Melt butter in a large skillet over medium heat. Add onion and next 6 ingredients. Cook, stirring often, 15 to 20 minutes or until lightly browned. Remove from heat; stir in cheese and whipping cream.

3. Place pastry shells on a baking sheet. Spoon onion mixture into shells. Sprinkle crumbled bacon on top. Bake at 350° for 9 to 11 minutes or until lightly browned. Serve immediately.

Key Ingredients
Le Bonheur Club, Inc. ~ Memphis, Tennessee

Lime-Garlic Shrimp With Mango-Mint Salsa

makes 4 to 6 appetizer servings • prep: 15 min., cook: 6 min., other: 45 min.

In many places in the region, it's warm enough to grill out all year long. This spicy grilled shrimp topped with a cooling salsa will have guests longing for the beach.

make it a meal: You'll love this recipe as a main dish as well as an appetizer. Just double the amount of shrimp to serve 4 as an entrée—the salsa recipe makes plenty without doubling. Serve the dish with mashed sweet potatoes.

12	unpeeled, jumbo raw shrimp	½	tsp. salt
2	Tbsp. fresh lime juice	¼	tsp. pepper
2	garlic cloves, crushed		Vegetable cooking spray
1	tsp. hot chili oil		Mango-Mint Salsa

1. Peel shrimp, leaving tails on, and if desired, devein; set aside.

2. Combine lime juice and next 4 ingredients in a medium bowl. Add shrimp, tossing to coat. Cover and chill 45 minutes.

3. Preheat grill to medium-high heat (350° to 400°).

4. Remove shrimp from marinade; discard marinade. Coat grill rack with cooking spray; place on grill over medium-high heat (350° to 400°). Place shrimp on rack; grill, uncovered, 3 minutes on each side or until shrimp turn pink. To serve, spoon salsa onto 6 individual serving plates. Arrange 2 shrimp on salsa on each plate.

Mango-Mint Salsa

makes 3½ cups • prep: 15 min.

2   cups diced mango (about 2 large)

¾   cup minced red onion

2   jalapeño peppers, seeded and minced

1   medium-size red bell pepper, seeded and diced

1   Tbsp. plus 1 tsp. chopped fresh mint

3   Tbsp. fresh lime juice

1. Combine all ingredients in a medium bowl, and toss well.

West of the Rockies
The Junior Service League of Grand Junction, Colorado

Elegant Shrimp Rounds

makes 2½ dozen • prep: 45 min., cook: 8 min., other: 1 hr.

Cut biscuit-size rounds from white sandwich bread, and top with a creamy dilled shrimp mixture to make a sensational appetizer from simple ingredients.

make it ahead: If you'd like to prepare this appetizer before guests arrive, spread the shrimp mixture on the toasted bread rounds, cover, and chill up to 4 hours before baking.

3	cups water	1	tsp. chopped fresh dill
1	lb. unpeeled, medium-size raw shrimp	1	cup plus 2 Tbsp. mayonnaise
30	slices sandwich bread, toasted	1	cup grated Gruyère cheese
1	garlic clove, minced	1	Tbsp. finely chopped green onions
2	Tbsp. butter or margarine, melted	2	tsp. finely chopped fresh parsley
1	Tbsp. dry white wine	¼	tsp. salt
1	tsp. grated lime rind	⅛	tsp. pepper

1. Bring water to a boil; add shrimp, and cook 3 to 5 minutes or until shrimp turn pink. Drain well; rinse with cold water. Chill.

2. Peel shrimp, and devein, if desired. Finely chop shrimp; set aside.

3. Cut 2½-inch rounds from each slice of bread; set aside.

4. Cook garlic in butter in a skillet over medium-high heat 30 seconds, stirring constantly. Remove from heat; stir in shrimp, wine, lime rind, and dill; cool. Add mayonnaise and next 5 ingredients; stir well. Cover and chill.

5. Preheat broiler.

6. Spread 1 heaping Tbsp. shrimp mixture on each bread round. Place on ungreased baking sheets; broil 3 inches from heat 3 minutes or until golden. Serve immediately.

Simply Heavenly
Woman's Synodical Union of the Associate Reformed Presbyterian Church
Greenville, South Carolina

Iced Mint Tea

makes 8½ cups • prep: 10 min.; cook: 5 min.; other: 1 hr., 50 min.

Southerners have steeped tea with mint or plunged a mint sprig in a glass of iced tea since the earliest days.

test kitchen tip: A good reason to drink tea is for its beneficial antioxidants, but be sure to select real tea leaves rather than herbal tea.

4	cups water	1	cup loosely packed fresh mint leaves
1	cup sugar		
⅓	cup lemon juice	4	cups cold water
2	family-size tea bags		Ice cubes

1. Bring 4 cups water to a boil over medium-high heat. Stir in 1 cup sugar, and cook, stirring constantly, 1 minute or until sugar dissolves; remove from heat. Stir in ⅓ cup lemon juice, tea bags, and mint leaves. Cover and let stand 10 minutes. Remove tea bags. Cover and let stand 40 minutes.

2. Pour tea mixture through a wire-mesh strainer into a 2-qt. pitcher, discarding mint leaves. Stir in 4 cups cold water. Cover and chill at least 1 hour. Serve over ice.

Iced Mint Tea

Strawberry Lemonade

makes 12 cups • prep: 20 min., cook: 5 min.

Lemonade has been a favorite Southern thirst quencher since the earliest colonial times. Adding strawberries makes this version pink and refreshingly fruity.

2   cups sugar, divided
1   cup water
1½ cups strawberries, halved
2   cups fresh lemon juice (about 15 lemons), chilled

6   cups sparkling water, chilled
Garnish: fresh mint leaves

1. Combine 1 cup sugar and 1 cup water in a small saucepan. Bring to a boil; reduce heat, and simmer, uncovered, 5 minutes or until sugar dissolves, stirring often. Cool.

2. Process strawberries, remaining 1 cup sugar, and sugar syrup in a blender or food processor until pureed. Pour mixture through a wire-mesh strainer into a large pitcher.

3. Stir in lemon juice and sparkling water just before serving. Serve over ice. Garnish, if desired.

Lori Moses

On Course
Women Associates of the Buffalo Power Squadron ~ Lancaster, New York

test kitchen tip: Substitute unsweetened frozen strawberries for fresh, and enjoy this refreshing drink all year long.

Tropical Smoothie

makes 3 cups • prep: 10 min., freeze: 30 min.

Fresh fruit—mango, banana and pineapple—teamed with coconut milk in this creamy drink will make you feel like you should be relaxing on a South Florida beach.

1   ripe banana
1   medium mango, cubed
1   cup cubed fresh pineapple
1   cup unsweetened pineapple juice, chilled

½   cup canned light coconut milk, chilled
1   tsp. fresh lime juice

1. Arrange first 3 ingredients in a single layer on a baking sheet lined with plastic wrap. Place in freezer for 30 minutes or until frozen solid.

2. Process frozen fruit, pineapple juice, coconut milk, and lime juice in a blender until thick and smooth, stopping to scrape down sides. Serve immediately.

Bea Westin

. . . And It Was Very Good
Temple Emeth ~ Teaneck, New Jersey

test kitchen tip: To cube mango, begin with the peel on. Stand the mango up so that the stem end points toward you. With a sharp knife, cut straight down about an inch to 1 side of the stem, just grazing the side of the pit. Repeat on the other side of the fruit. Peel and trim the fruit left around the pit. Then, carefully score the cut side of the mango in a crisscross pattern through the flesh, just down to the peel. Bend the peel back and turn the scored mango inside out, and cubes of fruit will pop forward. Cut across the bottom, next to the peel, to remove the cubes.

Frozen Pineapple Margarita Punch

makes about 2 gallons • prep: 10 min., other: 24 hr.

It's hard to eat out in Texas without seeing a salt-rimmed margarita go by on a waiter's tray. This refreshing pineapple version is ideal with spicy Mexican food. Invite plenty of friends when you stir up this recipe—it makes 2 gallons of sweet and puckery punch.

10 cups pineapple juice
8   cups water
6   cups white tequila
2   cups orange liqueur
3   (10-oz.) cans frozen margarita mix, thawed

1   (12-oz.) can frozen limeade concentrate, thawed and undiluted
Lime juice
Coarse salt
Garnish: lime wedges

make it ahead: Plan ahead because the mixture needs to freeze at least 24 hours before serving. Thaw it all at once for a large party, or stir it and spoon out portions for a glass or two at a time.

1. Combine pineapple juice, water, tequila, orange liqueur, frozen margarita mix, and limeade in a very large plastic container. Cover and freeze at least 24 hours or until frozen to a slushy consistency.

2. Moisten rims of margarita glasses with lime juice, and dip into coarse salt. Pour margarita mixture into glasses. Garnish, if desired.

front porch sippers

Even today the mention of Southern hospitality conjures up thoughts of high-columned porches, rocking chairs, and a sweaty glass of sweet iced tea or cold lemonade for visitors. In the early days, those of high social status were likely to make the porch offering a mint julep, thanks to the abundance of whiskey and mint that was stirred into a sugar syrup and served with ice. In fact, the mint julep became such a Southern icon that *Southern Living* magazine gave employees a sterling silver julep cup to honor the magazine's 25th anniversary in 1990. Super-sweet juleps are most often served today for nostalgia's sake, but not so sweet iced tea. So embedded is the sugar-saturated beverage in Southern everyday life, that visitors to northern states often are shocked to order it at a restaurant and find it's "not in season." Imagine.

Mocha Cappuccino Punch

makes 14 cups • prep: 15 min., other: 30 min.

Coffee, chocolate, and coffee ice cream make this a perfect punch for warm- or cold-weather parties. It's spiked with coffee liqueur, sweetened with chocolate syrup, and gets some fizz from chilled club soda.

test kitchen tip: This rich punch is delicious with or without the club soda.

2	Tbsp. instant coffee granules	4	cups milk or half-and-half
¼	tsp. ground cinnamon	¼	cup coffee liqueur
1	cup hot water	1	qt. coffee ice cream or chocolate
1	(14-oz.) can sweetened condensed		ice cream
	milk	2	cups club soda, chilled
½	cup chocolate syrup		

1. Combine coffee granules, cinnamon, and water in a bowl; stir until coffee granules dissolve. Stir in condensed milk and chocolate syrup. Cover and chill at least 30 minutes.

2. Combine coffee mixture, milk, and liqueur in a punch bowl; stir well. Scoop ice cream into coffee mixture. Stir in club soda just before serving. Garnish, if desired.

Picnics, Potlucks & Prizewinners
Indiana 4-H Foundation, Inc. ~ Indianapolis, Indiana

Peppermint Milk Shakes

makes 6 cups • prep: 5 min.

No need to wait for the seasonal peppermint ice cream to hit grocery stores to enjoy peppermint milk shakes. Just add crushed hard peppermint candies to vanilla ice cream to give it that cool, refreshing flavor any time of year.

test kitchen tip: This recipe is a soft pink with a hint of mint. Substitute chocolate ice cream for a completely different look and a chocolate-mint flavor.

2	cups milk, divided	4	cups vanilla ice cream, divided
½	cup crushed hard peppermint		Garnish: peppermint sticks
	candies (about 20 candies), divided		

1. Combine 1 cup milk and ¼ cup crushed candies in a blender; process 5 seconds. Add 2 cups ice cream; process until smooth, stopping to scrape down sides. Repeat procedure. Garnish each serving, if desired.   Mildred Orene Owen

Rainbow of Recipes, Volume I
The Dream Factory of Louisville, Kentucky

Whiskey Snowballs

makes 26 servings • prep: 10 min.; other: 8 hr., 30 min.

Use bourbon if you like in this sweet slushy drink full of fruit juices and maraschino cherries. But for a slightly sweeter flavor, use straight whiskey sometimes called "Tennessee whiskey." Like straight bourbon, it's aged in charred oak barrels, but it's also filtered through a sugar–maple charcoal for a sweet taste.

1	cup sugar
1	cup water
1	(750-milliliter) bottle bourbon
1	(48-oz.) bottle lemon-lime soft drink (we used 7UP)

1	(46-oz.) can pineapple juice
1	(6-oz.) can frozen orange juice concentrate, thawed and undiluted
2	(10-oz.) jars maraschino cherries, undrained

make it ahead: Mix up a batch of this slushy adult-only beverage, and it'll keep in the freezer up to a month.

1. Combine sugar and water in a large container, stirring until sugar dissolves. Stir in bourbon and remaining ingredients. Cover and freeze overnight in a large freezerproof pitcher. Let stand at room temperature 30 minutes before serving.   Carol Artall

Atchafalaya Legacy
Melville Women's Club ~ Melville, Louisiana

Hot White Russian

makes 3¾ cups • prep: 5 min., cook: 8 min.

Southerners have craved coffee beverages since before the Civil War, when coffee was a hard-won treat. It's still a special treat in beverages like this hot version of a White Russian, a vodka-coffee liqueur coffee drink traditionally served over ice.

test kitchen tip: To warm serving mugs, fill them with water, and microwave at HIGH until the water is very hot. Pour out the hot water, and fill with Hot White Russian.

2½ cups freshly brewed coffee
½   cup heavy cream
½   cup coffee liqueur
¼   cup vodka
    Whipped cream

1. Combine first 4 ingredients in a medium saucepan; cook over medium heat until thoroughly heated.

2. Divide mixture evenly among mugs, and top each serving with a dollop of whipped cream. Serve immediately.   Joyce Donovan

Our Sunrise Family Cookbook
Sunrise Drive Elementary School ~ Tucson, Arizona

December Cider

makes 12 cups • prep: 10 min., cook: 30 min.

Old-fashioned hot cider gets a toasty twist when it's spiked with rum or cinnamon schnapps.

test kitchen tip: For a party, keep the cider warm in a slow cooker, and let guests serve themselves.

1   (12-oz.) can frozen apple juice concentrate, undiluted
1   (11.5-oz.) can frozen cranberry-apple juice concentrate, undiluted
9   cups water
1   (6-oz.) can frozen lemonade concentrate, undiluted
5   (3-inch) cinnamon sticks
1   tsp. ground nutmeg
7   whole cloves
⅓   cup rum or cinnamon schnapps

1. Combine first 3 ingredients in a Dutch oven. Stir in lemonade concentrate, cinnamon sticks, nutmeg, and cloves; bring to a boil. Cover, reduce heat, and simmer 15 minutes. Remove and discard cinnamon sticks and cloves before serving. Stir in rum or schnapps. Serve warm.   Lindsey Lockett

Southern Elegance: A Second Course
The Junior League of Gaston County ~ Gastonia, North Carolina

breads, breakfasts, and brunches

Grits Soufflé With Caramelized Onions, page 237

Easy Pan Biscuits

makes 20 biscuits • prep: 15 min., cook: 15 min.

Soft drinks have a long history as ingredients in some deliciously novel recipes for pot roasts, glazed ham, barbecue sauce, sorbets, and granitas. Here, lemon–lime soft drink adds a touch of sweetness and sour cream adds a rich taste to these butter-brushed biscuits in a square pan.

2   cups all-purpose baking mix
½   cup sour cream
6   Tbsp. lemon-lime soft drink or diet lemon-lime soft drink
3   Tbsp. butter, melted and divided

1. Preheat oven to 425°.
2. Combine together first 3 ingredients, stirring to form a soft dough; lightly flour hands, and divide dough into 20 equal portions. Shape each portion into a ball, and place in a lightly greased 8-inch square pan. (Dough portions will touch.) Brush evenly with half of butter.
3. Bake at 425° for 15 minutes or until golden brown. Brush evenly with remaining half of butter. Serve immediately.
Note: For testing purposes, we used Bisquick All-Purpose Baking Mix and Sprite.

test kitchen tip: When making biscuits or other quick breads, it's important to preheat your oven. It typically takes about 10 minutes to reach the proper temperature.

Elsie's Biscuits

makes: about 3 dozen • prep: 20 min., cook: 9 min.

Customers of Laurey's Catering and Gourmet-to-Go in Asheville, North Carolina, rate these biscuits a favorite. The secret is sugar and vanilla in the dough.

3   cups all-purpose flour
2   Tbsp. baking powder
1   tsp. salt
½   cup butter or margarine
½   cup milk
½   cup buttermilk
⅓   cup sour cream
⅛   tsp. sugar
⅛   tsp. vanilla extract

1. Preheat oven to 450°.
2. Combine first 3 ingredients; cut in butter with a pastry blender until mixture is crumbly.
3. Combine milk and next 4 ingredients; add to dry ingredients, stirring just until dry ingredients are moistened.
4. Turn dough out onto a lightly floured surface; knead 3 or 4 times. Roll to ½-inch thickness; cut with a 1½-inch round cutter, and place on a lightly greased baking sheet. Bake at 450° for 7 to 9 minutes.

test kitchen tip: These biscuits are slightly sweet and dainty. If you prefer a heartier size, cut the dough with a 2½-inch round cutter, and bake at 450° for 10 to 12 minutes.

Sweet Potato Biscuits

makes 26 biscuits • prep: 15 min.; cook: 1 hr., 16 min.

These simple "raised" biscuits are sweetened with sugar as well as the natural taste of sweet potatoes. Serve the biscuits hot with honey butter or make them into ham biscuits—honey-glazed ham is the best with these.

2	medium-size sweet potatoes	½	cup butter
	Shortening	½	cup milk
4	cups self-rising flour		Honey butter (optional)
3	Tbsp. sugar		

test kitchen tip: Baked fresh sweet potatoes—versus boiled, steamed or canned—produce the best flavor for baked goods, especially biscuits.

1. Preheat oven to 450°.

2. Scrub potatoes, and pat dry with paper towels. Grease potatoes with shortening, and place on a foil-lined baking sheet. Bake at 450° for 1 hour or until tender when pierced with a small knife. Let cool completely. Peel potatoes, and mash with a potato masher until smooth. Measure 2 cups mashed potato, reserving any remaining potato for another use.

3. Whisk together flour and sugar in a large bowl. Cut in butter with a pastry blender until mixture is crumbly. Stir together sweet potato and milk. Add to dry ingredients, stirring to form a soft dough. (Dough will be very moist.) Turn dough out onto a floured surface, and knead 8 to 10 times or until smooth. Pat or roll dough to ¾-inch thickness; cut with a 2-inch round cutter. Place biscuits on lightly greased baking sheets. (It may be necessary to lift tender biscuits from work surface using a spatula.)

4. Bake at 450° for 16 minutes or until golden. Let stand 2 to 3 minutes before serving with honey butter, if desired.

why Southern biscuits are the best

Thank goodness flour prices fell in the 1880s or there might not be such a thing as a "Southern biscuit." Not long after flour became affordable, White Lily and Martha White companies began producing soft wheat flour in Tennessee, which led to the famous fluffy-style biscuits. Next to fried chicken, biscuits are probably the region's greatest culinary gift to the world, for almost every fast food restaurant sells them these days. Southerners have their preferences about how to eat one—as a sandwich for ham or sausage, drowned in cream or red eye gravy, or slathered with butter, jelly, or molasses. But, at some Southern tables, there is still a fight for the prize—the sometimes lumpy, large biscuit shaped from the dough scraps. Says Tennessean Clyde Garrison, "When I was growing up we all fought for the "cat head." It was the biggest biscuit and there was only one!"

Arleen's Herb Biscuits

makes 2½ dozen • prep: 20 min., cook: 11 min.

Three herbs flavor these rich biscuits that are perfect for serving with thinly sliced country ham.

make it a meal: Split any leftover biscuits, and fill with thinly sliced turkey and Swiss cheese. Serve them with a bowl of tomato soup for a quick lunch or supper.

4	cups all-purpose flour	1	tsp. pepper
1	Tbsp. plus 2 tsp. baking powder	½	tsp. dried thyme
½	tsp. baking soda	½	cup butter
¾	tsp. salt	1	cup milk
2	tsp. dried dillweed	1	(8-oz.) container sour cream
1	tsp. dried basil		

1. Preheat oven to 450°.

2. Combine first 8 ingredients in a large bowl. Cut in butter with a pastry blender until mixture is crumbly.

3. Combine milk and sour cream; add to flour mixture, stirring just until dry ingredients are moistened.

4. Turn dough out onto a floured surface; knead 4 or 5 times. Roll dough to ½-inch thickness; cut into rounds with a 2-inch biscuit cutter. Place on a lightly greased baking sheet. Bake at 450° for 11 minutes or until golden.

Cathy Cannon

Ka Mea 'Ai 'Ono Loa: Delicious Foods from the Honolulu Waldorf School
Honolulu Waldorf School ~ Honolulu, Hawaii

Cornmeal Biscuits

makes 3 dozen • prep: 20 min., cook: 15 min.

These buttery biscuits blend two Southern bread traditions. They have a slight nutty crunch from the cornmeal, but a texture more like biscuits.

test kitchen tip: Biscuits are considered "short," which means they have a high proportion of fat to flour making them tender, rich, flaky, and crisp. In this recipe, the butter needs to be cut into the flour mixture until crumbly; in other words, until it resembles coarse meal and you can't see any bits of butter.

4	cups self-rising flour	2	cups buttermilk
½	cup yellow cornmeal	¼	cup milk
1	cup butter, cut up		

1. Preheat oven to 425°.

2. Combine flour and cornmeal in a large bowl; cut in butter with a pastry blender or fork until crumbly. Add buttermilk, stirring just until dry ingredients are moistened.

3. Turn dough out onto a lightly floured surface; knead 2 or 3 times.

4. Pat or roll dough to a ½-inch thickness, and cut with a 2-inch round cutter. Place on lightly greased baking sheets. Reroll remaining dough, and proceed as directed. Brush tops with milk.

5. Bake at 425° for 13 to 15 minutes or until golden.

Ginger Scones

makes 8 scones • prep: 20 min., cook: 22 min.

Usually a breakfast or tea bread, Scottish scones are typically wedge-shaped such as this bread flavored with crystallized ginger. Top the scones with sweetened whipped cream.

2¾	cups all-purpose flour		¾	cup butter
2	tsp. baking powder		⅓	cup chopped crystallized ginger
½	tsp. salt		1	cup milk
½	cup sugar			

1. Preheat oven to 400°.

2. Combine first 4 ingredients in a large bowl; cut butter into flour mixture with a pastry blender until crumbly. Stir in ginger. Add milk, stirring just until dry ingredients are moistened. Turn dough out onto a lightly floured surface, and knead 10 to 15 times. Pat or roll dough to ¾-inch thickness; shape into a round, and cut dough into 8 wedges. Place wedges on a lightly greased baking sheet.

3. Bake at 400° for 18 to 22 minutes or until scones are barely golden. Cool slightly on a wire rack.

test kitchen tip: Crystallized ginger has been cooked in a sugar syrup and coated with sugar. Before you begin to chop the ginger, coat the knife blade with vegetable cooking spray to prevent the task from becoming unmanageably sticky.

Carrot-Zucchini Muffins

makes 1 dozen • prep: 20 min., cook: 20 min.

Once muffins were considered a breakfast-only bread. But with all the great flavor and nutrition from carrots, zucchini, walnuts, and raisins in these cinnamon-spiced muffins, you'll want to serve them anytime.

½	cup all-purpose flour		⅔	cup sugar
½	cup whole wheat flour		¼	cup vegetable oil
1	tsp. baking powder		½	tsp. vanilla extract
½	tsp. baking soda		¾	cup shredded zucchini
¼	tsp. salt		¾	cup shredded carrot
1	tsp. ground cinnamon		1	cup chopped walnuts
4	egg whites		½	cup raisins

1. Preheat oven to 400°.

2. Combine first 6 ingredients in a large bowl; make a well in center of mixture. Combine egg whites, sugar, oil, and vanilla; add to dry ingredients, stirring just until moistened. Stir in zucchini, carrot, walnuts, and raisins.

3. Spoon batter into greased muffin pans, filling two-thirds full. Bake at 400° for 18 to 20 minutes or until a wooden pick inserted in center of muffins comes out clean. Remove from pans immediately, and let cool on a wire rack.

Macadamia Nut Muffins

makes 1 dozen • prep: 25 min., cook: 25 min., other: 11 min.

Quick breads such as muffins have always been popular in the South—they don't heat up the kitchen as long as other breads. The fresh lemon glaze over these nutty muffins makes them special enough to take to the office or a potluck meal.

test kitchen tip: These tall muffins are prepared using an electric mixer. They have a cakelike texture and could double as dessert.

¼	cup plus 2 Tbsp. butter	4	tsp. baking powder
¼	cup plus 2 Tbsp. shortening	¾	tsp. salt
1	cup granulated sugar	½	cup chopped macadamia nuts
2	large eggs, beaten	½	cup sweetened flaked coconut
1	cup milk	2	cups sifted powdered sugar
2	tsp. vanilla extract	¼	cup fresh lemon juice
3	cups unbleached all-purpose flour		

1. Preheat oven to 350°.

2. Beat butter and shortening at medium speed with an electric mixer until creamy. Gradually add 1 cup granulated sugar, beating well.

3. Combine eggs, milk, and vanilla. Combine flour and next 4 ingredients. Add flour mixture to butter mixture alternately with egg mixture, beating after each addition. Spoon batter into greased muffin pans, filling almost full.

4. Bake at 350° for 25 minutes or until golden. Cool 1 minute; remove from pan, and cool 10 minutes on a wire rack.

5. Combine powdered sugar and juice. Drizzle over muffins. Cool on wire rack.

Cranberry-Orange Nut Bread

makes 1 loaf • prep: 7 min., cook: 1 hr., other: 10 min.

Sweet and moist quick breads have been a favorite gift from the Southern kitchens for decades. To give this recipe a nostalgic presentation, bake it in a large coffee can, and wrap the uniquely shaped loaf in brown craft paper.

lighten up: To encourage proper portion control, use an electric knife to cut the loaf into uniform slices. Wrap slices in individual portions; freeze in an airtight container or a zip-top plastic freezer bag.

3	cups all-purpose flour	1	large egg, lightly beaten
1	cup sugar	1½	cups milk
4	tsp. baking powder	½	cup butter, melted
¾	tsp. salt	1	Tbsp. grated orange rind
1½	cups chopped walnuts	2	tsp. vanilla extract
½	cup sweetened dried cranberries		

1. Preheat oven to 350°.

2. Whisk together first 4 ingredients until blended. Add nuts and cranberries, stirring to coat. Whisk together egg and remaining 4 ingredients in a medium bowl. Stir milk mixture into dry ingredients just until moistened. Pour batter into a greased and floured 9- x 5-inch loaf pan.

3. Bake at 350° for 1 hour or until a wooden pick inserted in center comes out clean. Cool in pan 10 minutes; remove from pan, and cool completely on a wire rack.

Sweet Potato Cornbread

makes 6 servings • prep: 10 min., cook: 30 min.

Two beloved Southern foods—sweet potatoes and cornbread—along with a time-honored cast-iron skillet produce a bread that's crisp on the outside and soft inside.

2	cups self-rising cornmeal mix	1	cup mashed cooked sweet potato
¼	cup sugar	¼	cup butter, melted
1	tsp. ground cinnamon	1	large egg, beaten
1½	cups milk		

1. Preheat oven to 425°.

2. Whisk together all ingredients just until dry ingredients are moistened. Spoon batter into a greased 8-inch cast-iron skillet or pan. Bake at 425° for 30 minutes or until a wooden pick inserted in center comes out clean.

Note: For testing purposes only, we used White Lily Self Rising Buttermilk Cornmeal Mix.

Vidalia Cheddar Spoonbread

makes 6 to 8 servings • prep: 15 min., cook: 40 min.

Corn muffin mix makes spoonbread super simple. Serve spoonbread as a side dish instead of grits at breakfast or brunch, or in place of potatoes or rice on lunch or supper menus.

make it a meal: Pair Vidalia Cheddar Spoonbread with link sausages, melon wedges, juice, and coffee for brunch or with grilled pork chops, collard greens, and sweet iced tea for supper.

1	large Vidalia onion, thinly sliced	1	cup cream-style corn
¼	cup butter or margarine, melted	1	(8-oz.) container sour cream
1	(8½-oz.) package corn muffin mix	½	tsp. salt
1	large egg, beaten	1	cup (4 oz.) shredded sharp Cheddar
⅓	cup milk		cheese, divided

1. Preheat oven to 425°.

2. Cook onion in melted butter in a large skillet over medium heat 10 minutes or until soft. Set aside.

3. Combine corn muffin mix and next 3 ingredients. Spoon into a greased 8-inch square pan. Stir together sour cream, salt, ½ cup cheese, and reserved onion. Spread evenly over corn mixture; sprinkle with remaining ½ cup cheese.

4. Bake at 425° for 30 minutes. Serve spoonbread immediately.

Cooking with Friends
Brunswick Community Hospital ~ Supply, North Carolina

confused about cornbread?
The South's oldest bread tradition has come a long way from the early "hoe cakes" made with bear grease and literally baked on a hoe over a fire. In fact, its many forms, including corn dodgers, corn cakes, ash cakes, griddle cakes, corn pone, Johnny cakes, corn sticks, hush puppies and spoonbread indicate the widespread evolution that gives us the cornbread choices we have today. Options include crispy, soft, yellow, white, sweet or not, pan-fried, deep-fried, or baked in a cast-iron skillet. Despite humble origins, upscale restaurants relish serving it in newfound ways, as in recipes such as crabmeat-cornbread-stuffed catfish or goat cheese and cornbread crostini. Still, in the Appalachians cornbread is a must with simple soup beans, in Texas with basic chili, and for many Southerners, crumbled into a glass of milk for a satisfying snack.

Apple-Peach Puff Pancake

makes 4 servings • prep: 15 min., cook: 25 min.

In England, the Tuesday before Ash Wednesday (known as Fat Tuesday in New Orleans) became designated as Pancake Day because cooks made pancakes to use up eggs and fats before the fasting period. Though the origins are European, the topping of juicy sweet peaches and applesauce makes this recipe pure Southern.

3	large eggs, lightly beaten	2	Tbsp. butter or margarine
½	cup milk	1	cup chunky applesauce
1	Tbsp. granulated sugar	1	cup sliced fresh peaches
¼	tsp. salt	½	tsp. ground cinnamon
½	cup all-purpose flour		Powdered sugar

1. Preheat oven to 425°.

2. Combine first 4 ingredients in a large bowl. Add flour, stirring with a wire whisk until blended. Melt butter in a 10-inch cast-iron skillet at 425° for 2 minutes or until butter melts. Remove skillet from oven; immediately pour batter into hot skillet. Bake at 425° for 15 to 20 minutes.

3. Meanwhile, combine applesauce, peaches, and cinnamon in a saucepan; cook over low heat until heated. Spoon mixture on baked pancake immediately after removing from oven. Sprinkle with powdered sugar. Cut into wedges.

test kitchen tip: If fresh peaches are out of season, substitute frozen peaches and add 1 Tbsp. sugar to the fruit mixture.

Autumn Apple Cakes

makes 18 pancakes • prep: 10 min., cook: 4 min. per batch

These pancakes, sweet and slightly crisp, yet soft and moist inside, are made with chunky applesauce in the batter. They taste great with a topping of sweetened applesauce or apple butter.

2	large eggs, beaten	2	cups biscuit mix
1	cup milk	1	tsp. ground cinnamon
1	cup chunky applesauce	4	to 5 Tbsp. vegetable oil, divided
¾	cup firmly packed light brown sugar		

1. Combine first 4 ingredients in a large bowl, stirring with a whisk until sugar dissolves. Combine biscuit mix and cinnamon; add to applesauce mixture. Stir with a wire whisk just until moistened.

2. Heat a 9-inch skillet or griddle over medium-low heat until hot. Heat 1 Tbsp. oil in skillet. Pour about ¼ cup batter for each pancake into skillet; cook 3½ to 4 minutes or until tops are covered with bubbles and edges look cooked. Turn and cook other side. Remove pancakes to a serving platter; keep warm. Repeat procedure with remaining batter, adding 1 Tbsp. oil to skillet per batch.

test kitchen tip: These pancakes contain more sugar than most, so it's important to cook over a lower heat than ordinary pancakes to prevent them from browning on the outside before they're done inside.

Gingery Banana Waffles

makes 12 waffles • prep: 15 min., cook: 8 min. per batch

Molasses, a favorite Southern syrup made of boiled ground sugar cane, adds a tangy taste to these tender, spicy-sweet waffles topped with bananas.

make it a meal: Use leftover waffles to make peanut butter and jelly sandwiches.

1½	cups all-purpose flour		¾	cup buttermilk
2	tsp. baking powder		¼	cup molasses
¾	tsp. salt		1	ripe banana, mashed
1	tsp. ground cinnamon		¼	cup butter, melted
¾	tsp. ground ginger		2	large bananas, sliced
⅓	cup firmly packed light brown sugar			Maple syrup
2	large eggs			

1. Combine first 5 ingredients in a large bowl; set aside.

2. Beat sugar and eggs at medium speed with an electric mixer until light and fluffy. Stir in buttermilk, molasses, and mashed banana. Add egg mixture to flour mixture; stir just until dry ingredients are moistened. Stir in melted butter.

3. Cook batter in a preheated, oiled waffle iron until lightly browned. Repeat procedure with remaining batter. Serve waffles with bananas and syrup.

Sue Mansfield

Plate & Palette: A Collection of Fine Art and Food
Beaufort County Arts Council ~ Washington, North Carolina

Baby Butter Rolls With Maple Glaze

makes 3 dozen • prep: 10 min., cook: 15 min., other: 15 min.

You can have homemade sweet rolls on the table in less than an hour with just 6 common ingredients.

test kitchen tip: To make a substitution for the self-rising flour, use 2 cups all-purpose flour, 2 tsp. baking powder, and 1 tsp. salt.

2	cups self-rising flour		1	cup powdered sugar
1	(8-oz.) container sour cream		2	Tbsp. maple syrup
1	cup butter, melted		1	Tbsp. milk

1. Preheat oven to 400°.

2. Combine flour, sour cream, and butter in a large bowl; stir until blended. Spoon batter into lightly greased miniature (1¾-inch) muffin pans, filling full. Bake at 400° for 15 minutes or until golden. Cool in pans on wire racks 5 minutes; remove from pans to wire racks, and cool 10 more minutes or until completely cool.

3. Combine powdered sugar, syrup, and milk in a small bowl, stirring until smooth. Drizzle glaze over rolls.

Herb Cheddar Rolls

makes 10 rolls • prep: 30 min.; cook: 20 min.; other: 1 hr., 30 min.

Italian seasoning and Cheddar and Romano cheeses make these pinwheel-shaped yeast rolls a special dinner treat.

2	(¼-oz.) envelopes active dry yeast	4	to 4½ cups all-purpose flour, divided	
¾	cup warm water (100° to 110°)			
¾	cup warm milk (100° to 110°)	¼	cup grated Romano cheese	
¼	cup vegetable oil	3	Tbsp. shredded sharp Cheddar cheese	
¼	cup sugar			
1	Tbsp. salt	1½	Tbsp. dried Italian seasoning	

test kitchen tip: Use vegetable cooking spray, shortening, or butter to grease the bowl for the dough in Step 2.

1. Combine yeast and warm water in a 2-cup glass measuring cup; let stand 5 minutes.

2. Combine yeast mixture, milk, oil, sugar, salt, and 2 cups flour in a large mixing bowl; beat at medium speed with an electric mixer until well blended. Gradually stir in enough of remaining 2½ cups flour to make a soft dough. Place in a well-greased bowl, turning to grease top.

3. Cover and let rise in a warm place (85°), free from drafts, 45 minutes or until doubled in bulk.

4. Punch dough down; turn out onto a lightly floured surface, and knead until smooth and elastic (about 3 minutes). Roll dough into a 12- x 8-inch rectangle; sprinkle with cheeses and Italian seasoning. Roll up dough, jelly-roll fashion, starting at short side. Slice dough into ¾-inch slices; place slices, cut side down, in a lightly greased 13- x 9-inch pan. Cover and let rise in a warm place, free from drafts, 40 minutes or until doubled in bulk.

5. Preheat oven to 400°.

6. Bake at 400° for 18 to 20 minutes or until lightly browned. Cool slightly in pan on a wire rack. Serve warm.

Splendor in the Bluegrass
The Junior League of Louisville, Kentucky

Light Wheat Rolls

makes 1½ dozen • prep: 25 min.; cook: 12 min.; other: 1 hr., 15 min.

These soft, slightly sweet rolls melt in your mouth even without butter.

test kitchen tip: A good test to see if you've kneaded a dough long enough is to push your fingertips into the dough. If the indentation springs back, the dough has been kneaded enough.

2   (¼-oz.) envelopes active dry yeast
½   cup sugar
1   tsp. salt
1¾ cups warm water (105° to 115°)
¼   cup butter or margarine, melted
1   large egg, lightly beaten
2¼ cups whole wheat flour
2¼ to 2¾ cups all-purpose flour
Melted butter

1. Combine yeast, sugar, and salt in warm water in a large mixing bowl; let stand 5 minutes. Add ¼ cup melted butter, egg, and whole wheat flour to yeast mixture, beating at medium speed with an electric mixer until well blended. Gradually stir in enough all-purpose flour to make a soft dough.

2. Turn dough out onto a well-floured surface, and knead until smooth and elastic (about 5 minutes). Place in a well-greased bowl, turning to grease top. Cover and let rise in a warm place (85°), free from drafts, 45 minutes or until doubled in bulk.

3. Punch dough down, and divide in half. Roll each portion into a 12- x 7-inch rectangle. Cut each portion into 12 (7- x 1-inch) strips. Roll each strip of dough into a spiral; place in well-greased muffin pans.

4. Brush with melted butter; let rise, uncovered, in a warm place, free from drafts, 20 to 25 minutes or until doubled in bulk.

5. Preheat oven to 400°.

6. Bake at 400° for 12 minutes or until lightly browned. Brush again with melted butter.

Cyndi Bradt

Moments, Memories & Manna
Restoration Village ~ Rogers, Arkansas

Orange Coffee Rolls

makes 2 dozen • prep: 40 min.; cook: 30 min.; other: 2 hr., 20 min.

These crescent-shaped yeast rolls feature a buttery sweet coconut-orange filling with a sugar glaze on top. Orange rolls served at The Club, a prominent dining club in Birmingham, Alabama, are similar to these, and so popular that patrons are known to take extras home in their purses.

1	(¼-oz.) envelope active dry yeast
¼	cup water (100° to 110°)
1	cup sugar, divided
2	large eggs
½	cup sour cream
¼	cup plus 2 Tbsp. butter or margarine, melted
1	tsp. salt

2¾	to 3 cups all-purpose flour
2	Tbsp. butter or margarine, melted and divided
1	cup flaked coconut, toasted and divided
2	Tbsp. grated orange rind
	Glaze

test kitchen tip: If the dough is too elastic as you are rolling it into a circle in Step 3, stop, cover the dough, and let it rest for about 5 minutes. This allows the gluten to relax, making the dough easier to handle.

1. Combine yeast and warm water in a large mixing bowl; let stand 5 minutes. Add ¼ cup sugar and next 4 ingredients; beat at medium speed with an electric mixer until blended. Gradually stir in enough flour to make a soft dough.

2. Turn dough out onto a well-floured surface, and knead until smooth and elastic (about 5 minutes). Place in a well-greased bowl, turning to grease top. Cover and let rise in a warm place (85°), free from drafts, 1½ hours or until doubled in bulk.

3. Punch dough down, and divide in half. Roll 1 portion of dough into a 12-inch circle; brush with 1 Tbsp. melted butter. Combine remaining ¾ cup sugar, ¾ cup coconut, and orange rind; sprinkle half of coconut mixture over dough. Cut into 12 wedges; roll up each wedge, beginning at wide end. Place in a greased 13- x 9-inch pan, point side down. Repeat with remaining dough, butter, and coconut mixture.

4. Cover and let rise in a warm place, free from drafts, 45 minutes or until doubled in bulk. Preheat oven to 350°.

5. Bake at 350° for 25 to 30 minutes or until golden. (Cover with aluminum foil after 15 minutes to prevent excessive browning, if necessary.) Spoon warm Glaze over warm rolls; sprinkle with remaining ¼ cup coconut.

Glaze

makes 1⅓ cups • prep: 5 min., cook: 5 min.

¾	cup sugar
½	cup sour cream

¼	cup butter or margarine
2	tsp. orange juice

1. Combine all ingredients in a small saucepan; bring to a boil. Boil 3 minutes, stirring occasionally. Let cool slightly.

Tastes and Traditions: The Sam Houston Heritage Cookbook
The Study Club of Huntsville ~ Huntsville, Texas

Sour Cream Cinnamon Buns

makes 1 dozen • prep: 30 min., cook: 25 min., other: 30 min.

Filled with a cinnamon-sugar blend and cut into pretty pinwheels, these rich-flavored buns are baked in muffin pans and topped with a powdered sugar glaze.

test kitchen tip: Store packets of active dry yeast in a cool, dry place. You'll need to use them before the expiration date, so check it before you begin.

1	(8-oz.) container sour cream	3	cups all-purpose flour, divided
2	Tbsp. butter or margarine	2	Tbsp. butter or margarine, softened
3	Tbsp. granulated sugar	½	cup firmly packed brown sugar
½	tsp. salt	2	tsp. ground cinnamon
⅛	tsp. baking soda	1½	cups sifted powdered sugar
1	large egg, lightly beaten	2	Tbsp. milk
1	(¼-oz.) envelope active dry yeast		

1. Heat sour cream in a saucepan over medium-low heat to 100° to 110°.

2. Combine warm sour cream, 2 Tbsp. butter, 3 Tbsp. granulated sugar, salt, and baking soda in a large mixing bowl. Add egg and yeast; blend well. Add 1½ cups flour; beat at medium speed with an electric mixer until well blended. Stir in enough remaining flour to make a soft dough.

3. Turn dough out onto a lightly floured surface, and knead 4 or 5 times. Cover and let rest 5 minutes.

4. Roll dough into an 18- x 6-inch rectangle; spread 2 Tbsp. softened butter over dough. Sprinkle brown sugar and cinnamon over dough. Roll up dough, starting at short side, pressing firmly to eliminate air pockets; pinch seam to seal.

5. Slice roll into 12 (1½-inch) slices. Place slices, cut side down, in greased muffin pans. Cover and let rise in a warm place (85°), free from drafts, 30 minutes or until doubled in bulk. Meanwhile, preheat oven to 375°.

6. Bake at 375° for 12 to 15 minutes or until golden. Remove buns from pan immediately; let cool on a wire rack. Combine powdered sugar and milk; drizzle glaze over buns.

Theo F. Bartschi

Montana Celebrity Cookbook
Intermountain Children's Home ~ Helena, Montana

Buttermilk Cinnamon Rolls

makes 1 dozen • prep: 35 min., cook: 20 min., other: 50 min.

Cinnamon rolls are a must for any Southern breakfast celebration. Dough rich with buttermilk encases a cinnamon, raisin, and walnut filling to make these rolls irresistible.

2	(¼-oz.) envelopes active dry yeast	¼	cup butter or margarine, softened
¼	cup warm water (100° to 110°)	¾	cup firmly packed brown sugar
1½	cups warm buttermilk (110°)	1½	tsp. ground cinnamon
½	cup vegetable oil	¾	cup raisins (optional)
3	Tbsp. granulated sugar	¼	cup chopped walnuts (optional)
1	tsp. salt	1½	cups sifted powdered sugar
½	tsp. baking soda	2	Tbsp. milk
4¾	cups all-purpose flour		

test kitchen tip: In Step 4, ordinary floss is perfect to quickly slice the dough roll into uniform pinwheels. Slide a 12-inch piece of floss under the roll about 1½ inches. Crisscross the floss over the top of the roll and quickly pull the floss to snip slices.

1. Combine yeast and warm water in a 1-cup liquid measuring cup; let stand 5 minutes. Combine buttermilk and next 4 ingredients in a large mixing bowl. Add yeast mixture; mix well. Add 2 cups flour, beating at medium speed with an electric mixer until well blended. Gradually stir in enough remaining flour to make a soft dough.

2. Turn dough out onto a lightly floured surface, and knead lightly 5 minutes. Cover and let rest 5 minutes.

3. Roll dough into an 18- x 9-inch rectangle; spread butter over dough. Sprinkle brown sugar and cinnamon over butter. If desired, sprinkle with raisins and walnuts. Roll up dough, starting at long side, pressing firmly to eliminate air pockets; pinch seam to seal.

4. Cut roll into 12 (1½-inch) slices. Place slices in a greased 13- x 9-inch pan. Cover and let rise in a warm place (85°), free from drafts, 30 minutes or until doubled in bulk.

5. Preheat oven to 350°.

6. Bake at 350° for 20 minutes or until golden. Cool 10 minutes. Combine powdered sugar and milk; drizzle over rolls.

Kathy Young

Past to Present: A Pictorial Cookbook
Washington School Restoration Committee ~ Oakland, Oregon

Lazy Maple Crescent Pull–Aparts

makes 1 dozen • prep: 15 min., cook: 23 min.

Golden maple topping drenches these rolls made from canned crescent dinner rolls. It's a great way to serve a special homemade bread with minimal effort.

lighten up: To save calories with no taste sacrifice, substitute reduced-fat crescent rolls for regular and reduced-calorie pancake syrup for maple syrup .

¼	cup firmly packed brown sugar	1	(8-oz.) package refrigerated
¼	cup butter or margarine		crescent dinner rolls
2	Tbsp. pure maple syrup	1	Tbsp. granulated sugar
¼	cup chopped pecans	½	tsp. ground cinnamon

1. Preheat oven to 375°.

2. Combine brown sugar, butter, and syrup in an 8-inch round cake pan. Bake at 375° for 5 minutes or until butter melts; stir gently to blend ingredients. Sprinkle pecans over butter mixture.

3. Remove dough from package (do not unroll dough). Slice roll into 12 slices. Combine 1 Tbsp. sugar and cinnamon. Dip both sides of each slice of dough into sugar mixture. Arrange slices, cut side down, in prepared pan. Sprinkle slices with remaining sugar mixture. Bake at 375° for 18 minutes or until golden. Invert pan immediately onto a serving platter, and serve rolls immediately.

Italian Biscuit Flatbread

makes 10 flatbreads • prep: 15 min., cook: 10 min.

A spread of Parmesan cheese, herbs, and green onions is a great way to dress up canned biscuits when you're short on time.

make it a meal: Italian Biscuit Flatbread is a perfect accompaniment with bowlfuls of creamy tomato soup and a garden salad, or alongside spaghetti or lasagna.

⅓	cup thinly sliced green onions	¼	tsp. dried basil
⅓	cup grated Parmesan cheese	¼	tsp. dried oregano
⅓	cup mayonnaise	1	(12-oz.) can refrigerated flaky
1	garlic clove, minced		biscuits

1. Preheat oven to 400°.

2. Combine first 6 ingredients in a small bowl; stir well.

3. Press each biscuit into a 4-inch circle on an ungreased baking sheet. Spread about 1 Tbsp. cheese mixture evenly on circles, leaving a ¼-inch border.

4. Bake at 400° for 8 to 10 minutes or until golden.   Jean McLain

A Taste of Gem Valley Country Living
North Gem Valley Development Corporation ~ Bancroft, Idaho

Hearty Oat and Walnut Bread

makes 1 loaf • prep: 30 min., cook: 40 min., other: 1 hr., 55 min.

There was a time when homemade bread loaves were baked everyday. Thanks to bread machines that knead the dough and allow it to rise without requiring attention (see directions at right), homemade yeast bread now fits into the lifestyle of hurried Southern cooks. Oats, walnuts, and brown sugar make this loaf a perfect partner with golden apricot or orange marmalade.

1¼	cups water	¾	cup chopped walnuts
¼	cup firmly packed light brown sugar	½	cup quick-cooking oats
1	Tbsp. butter or margarine	1½	tsp. active dry yeast
3	cups bread flour, divided	1½	tsp. salt

1. Combine water, sugar, and butter in a small saucepan; bring to a boil. Remove from heat, and let stand until mixture reaches a temperature between 120° and 130°.

2. Meanwhile, combine 2½ cups flour, walnuts, oats, yeast, and salt in a large mixing bowl; add water mixture, and stir until well blended. Turn dough out onto a heavily floured surface, and knead in enough of remaining flour to make a soft dough. Knead until smooth and elastic (about 10 minutes). Place in a well-greased bowl, turning to grease top.

3. Cover dough with plastic wrap, and let rise in a warm place (85°), free from drafts, 45 minutes or until double in bulk.

4. Punch dough down. Turn dough out onto a floured surface, and knead lightly 4 or 5 times. Roll dough into a 14- x 7-inch rectangle. Roll up dough, starting at narrow end, pressing firmly to eliminate air pockets; pinch ends to seal. Place dough, seam side down in a well-greased 8- x 4-inch loaf pan. Cover and let rise in a warm place, free from drafts, 1 hour or until doubled in bulk.

5. Preheat oven to 375°.

6. Bake at 375° for 40 minutes or until loaf sounds hollow when tapped. Remove bread from pan immediately; cool on wire racks.

test kitchen tip: This bread bakes beautifully in a bread machine. To do so, combine all ingredients in the bread machine according to the manufacturer's instructions. Select bake cycle, and start machine. When done, remove bread from pan, cool on a wire rack.

Onion and Rosemary Bread

makes 8 servings • prep: 15 min.; cook: 25 min.; other: 1 hr., 20 min.

Rosemary has become as much a part of the Southern landscape as of the regional cuisine. In gardens it's pruned into formal topiaries, and in recipes, such as this rustic round yeast loaf, it's sprinkled on top to impart a tantalizing herb flavor.

1	(¼-oz.) envelope rapid-rise yeast	4	cups all-purpose flour
1	Tbsp. sugar	2	Tbsp. vegetable or olive oil
1½	cups warm water (100° to 110°)	1½	Tbsp. fresh rosemary leaves
2	tsp. salt	½	tsp. coarse salt or ¼ tsp. salt
½	cup chopped onion		

1. Stir together first 3 ingredients in a large bowl, and let stand 5 minutes. Stir in 2 tsp. salt, onion, and enough flour to form a soft dough. Turn dough out onto a floured surface, and knead until smooth and elastic (about 10 minutes). Place in a well-greased bowl, turning to grease top. Cover and let rise in a warm place (85°), free from drafts, 45 minutes or until doubled in bulk.
2. Punch dough down. Shape into a 12-inch round on a greased baking sheet. Cover and let rise in a warm place, free from drafts, 30 minutes or until doubled in bulk. Drizzle with oil; sprinkle with rosemary and salt.
3. Preheat oven to 400°.
4. Bake at 400° for 25 minutes or until golden. Serve warm.

Always in Season
The Junior League of Salt Lake City, Utah

Herb Bread

makes 12 servings • prep: 10 min., cook: 25 min.

Store-bought French bread gives you a head start for this bread with a Middle Eastern-flavored topping. Olives, parsley, and herbs make it delicious with lamb or chicken.

1	(16-oz.) loaf French bread	1½	tsp. dried basil
1	cup butter or margarine, softened	½	tsp. garlic powder
1	(2¼-oz.) can chopped ripe olives	½	tsp. dried tarragon
½	cup chopped fresh parsley	¼	tsp. celery seeds
⅓	cup chopped green onions		

1. Preheat oven to 350°.
2. Slice bread in half horizontally; set aside.
3. Combine butter and remaining 7 ingredients; spread evenly over cut sides of bread. Place halves together; wrap in aluminum foil.
4. Bake at 350° for 25 minutes or until bread is thoroughly heated. Cut into slices to serve.

Annabelle Thomas

The Great Delights Cookbook
Genoa Serbart United Methodist Churches ~ Genoa, Colorado

South-of-the-Border Deviled Eggs

makes 24 servings • prep: 25 min., other: 1 hr.

With deviled eggs a mainstay of Southern picnics and parties, by the 1940s every household seemed to have an indented dish just for deviled eggs. This version shows how the famous recipe has evolved—the creamy filling includes avocado, chili powder, and dry Ranch dressing for a Southwest flavor.

1	dozen large hard-cooked eggs, peeled	2	Tbsp. sweet pickle juice	
1	small ripe avocado, peeled and coarsely chopped	2	Tbsp. mayonnaise	
2	green onions, finely chopped	1	Tbsp. dry Ranch dressing mix	
		½	tsp. chili powder (optional)	
		½	cup mild salsa	

1. Slice eggs in half lengthwise; carefully remove yolks, keeping egg white halves intact.

2. Mash together yolks and avocado in a medium bowl. Stir in green onions and next 3 ingredients until smooth. Spoon yolk mixture evenly into egg white halves. Sprinkle evenly with chili powder, if desired. Cover and chill at least 1 hour. Dollop with salsa just before serving.

make it ahead: Prepare this recipe as an appetizer or as a side dish, and refrigerate up to 2 days in advance.

Eggs Diablo

makes 12 servings • prep: 20 min.

In the 1920s serving hors d'oeuvres at lunches and showers became the rage and deviled eggs were a must. Green chiles, picante sauce, and Monterey jack cheese turn this stuffed egg recipe into a fiery favorite.

6	large hard-cooked eggs, peeled	2	Tbsp. mayonnaise	
2	Tbsp. finely shredded Monterey Jack cheese	2	Tbsp. picante sauce	
2	Tbsp. finely chopped green onions	¼	tsp. salt	
2	Tbsp. canned chopped green chiles, undrained	¼	tsp. pepper	
		Garnish: roasted red bell pepper strips		

1. Cut eggs in half lengthwise, and carefully remove yolks. Mash yolks; stir in cheese and next 6 ingredients. Spoon into egg whites. Garnish, if desired.

Savoring the Southwest Again
Roswell Symphony Guild ~ Roswell, New Mexico

test kitchen tip: Save time by using pre-cooked hard-cooked eggs available in the dairy department of larger supermarkets.

Easy Eggs Benedict

makes 4 to 8 servings • prep: 15 min., cook: 15 min.

Traditional Eggs Benedict consists of ham and poached eggs on English muffin halves topped with a time–consuming hollandaise sauce. This version is "easy" because the sauce is a simple blend of mayonnaise, fresh lemon, and whipping cream that takes about 5 minutes to make.

8	large eggs		1	Tbsp. fresh lemon juice
¾	cup mayonnaise		4	English muffins, split and toasted
¼	tsp. salt			Butter or margarine
¼	cup whipping cream, whipped		8	slices Canadian bacon or thinly
1	tsp. grated lemon rind			sliced ham

test kitchen tip: For a restaurant presentation, clean up the lacy edges of the poached eggs with kitchen shears before assembling the dish.

1. Lightly grease a large skillet; add water to a depth of 2 inches. Bring to a boil; reduce heat, and maintain a light simmer. Working in batches to poach 4 eggs at a time, break eggs, 1 at a time, into a cup; slip egg into water, holding cup close to water. Simmer 5 minutes or until done. Remove eggs with a slotted spoon; trim edges of eggs, if desired. Set aside.

2. Combine mayonnaise and salt in a small saucepan. Cook over low heat, stirring constantly, 3 minutes. Stir in whipped cream, lemon rind, and lemon juice; remove from heat, and keep warm.

3. Spread split sides of muffin halves with butter. Arrange bacon on muffin halves; top each bacon slice with a poached egg. Spoon reserved sauce over eggs.

Southern breakfast revolution

Today's fast-paced life has turned the family breakfast table once groaning with eggs, bacon, ham, biscuits, grits, gravy, and homemade jelly into furniture for holding papers while family members grab a cup of coffee and a sweet roll as they race out the door—if they eat at all. A sit-down breakfast with family is now a special occasion meal, perhaps for a holiday or celebration. But one place where breakfast hasn't changed is at Brennan's Restaurant in New Orleans. There, the 19th century three-hour breakfast custom was revived in the 1950s just as convenience food was on the rise. Lingering all morning over a multicourse breakfast of sauce-draped French specialties continues to be an everyday affair. And the phrase "breakfast at Brennan's" is heard as often as jazz notes trickling in the door.

Southwestern Eggs Benedict

makes 4 servings • prep: 30 min., cook: 30 min.

This southwestern twist on Eggs Benedict features corn tortillas instead of English muffins and a cilantro cream sauce rather than hollandaise.

make it a meal: Host a Tex-Mex brunch with Southwestern Eggs Benedict, ruby red grapefruit halves, and hot cocoa with cinnamon.

⅓ cup sour cream

3 Tbsp. whipping cream

2 Tbsp. chopped fresh cilantro

½ tsp. salt

¼ tsp. pepper

4 (6-inch) corn tortillas

Vegetable cooking spray

1½ lb. ground hot pork sausage

4 garlic cloves, chopped

2 Tbsp. chopped fresh chives

1 Tbsp. chopped fresh parsley

1 Tbsp. chopped fresh thyme

½ tsp. pepper

2 Tbsp. olive oil

¼ cup white vinegar

8 large eggs

Salsa

1. Preheat oven to 350°.

2. Stir together first 5 ingredients in a small bowl; cover and chill.

3. Lightly coat tortillas with cooking spray; place on a baking sheet. Bake 8 minutes or until golden, turning once; set aside.

4. Stir together sausage and next 5 ingredients in a medium bowl. Shape mixture into 8 (½-inch-thick) patties. Heat olive oil in a large skillet over medium heat until hot. Add patties, and cook 7 minutes on each side or until done. Set aside.

5. Lightly grease a large saucepan. Add water to a depth of 2 inches; add vinegar. Bring to a boil; reduce heat, and maintain at a light simmer. Break eggs, 1 at a time, into a measuring cup or saucer; slip eggs, 1 at a time, into water mixture, holding cup as close as possible to surface of water. Simmer 5 minutes or until done. Remove eggs with a slotted spoon. Trim edges, if desired.

6. To serve, place a tortilla on individual serving plates. Top each tortilla with 2 sausage patties and 2 poached eggs. Top with sour cream mixture. Serve with salsa.

Perennial Palette
Southborough Gardeners ~ Southborough, Massachusetts

Chicken-Pecan Quiche

makes 1 (9-inch) quiche • prep: 25 min.; cook: 1 hr., 7 min.; other: 10 min.

Chopped pecans are kneaded into the cheese crust, and pecan halves form a crunchy topping for the creamy filling to give it a Southern twist in flavor and texture.

1	cup all-purpose flour
1	cup (4 oz.) shredded sharp Cheddar cheese
¾	cup chopped pecans
½	tsp. salt
¼	tsp. paprika
⅓	cup vegetable oil
1	cup sour cream
½	cup chicken broth

¼	cup mayonnaise
3	large eggs, lightly beaten
2	cups finely chopped cooked chicken
½	cup (2 oz.) shredded sharp Cheddar cheese
¼	cup minced fresh onion
¼	tsp. dried dillweed
3	drops of hot sauce
¼	cup pecan halves

test kitchen tip: Typically, pie pastries are made with butter or shortening, but the pastry that lines the pie plate in this highly rated quiche is an oil pastry. There's no need to roll it with a rolling pin. Simply press it directly into the pie plate with your fingers.

1. Preheat oven to 350°.

2. Combine first 5 ingredients in a medium bowl; stir well. Add oil; stir well. Firmly press mixture on bottom and up sides of a 9-inch deep-dish pie plate. Bake at 350° for 12 minutes. Cool completely.

3. Combine sour cream, broth, mayonnaise, and eggs; stir with a wire whisk until smooth. Stir in chicken and next 4 ingredients. Pour chicken mixture over prepared crust. Arrange pecan halves over chicken mixture. Bake at 350° for 55 minutes or until set. Let stand 10 minutes before serving.

True Grits: Tall Tales and Recipes from the New South
The Junior League of Atlanta, Georgia

Artichoke and Smoked Ham Strata

makes 8 servings • prep: 25 min.; cook: 55 min.; other: 8 hr., 40 min.

This recipe takes ordinary ham and eggs upscale. Herbs, tangy sourdough bread cubes, and three cheeses, including goat, fontina, and Parmesan, make it a gourmet breakfast entrée you can assemble the night before.

test kitchen tip: A 1 lb. loaf of sourdough bread will give you just the right amount of bread cubes.

2	cups milk
¼	cup olive oil
8	cups (1-inch) sourdough bread cubes
1½	cups whipping cream
5	large eggs
3	garlic cloves, minced
1½	tsp. salt
¾	tsp. ground white pepper
½	tsp. ground nutmeg
3	(4-oz.) packages goat cheese, crumbled
2	Tbsp. chopped fresh sage
1	Tbsp. chopped fresh thyme
1½	tsp. herbes de Provence
¾	lb. smoked ham, chopped
3	(6½-oz.) jars marinated artichoke hearts, drained
1	cup (4 oz.) shredded fontina cheese
1½	cups grated Parmesan cheese

1. Combine milk and oil in a large bowl; add bread cubes, and let stand 10 minutes.

2. Whisk together whipping cream and next 5 ingredients in a large bowl. Stir in goat cheese.

3. Combine sage, thyme, and herbes de Provence in a small bowl.

4. Place half of bread mixture in a greased 13- x 9-inch baking dish.

5. Top with half each of ham, artichoke hearts, herb mixture, and cheeses. Pour half of cream mixture over cheeses. Repeat layers, ending with cream mixture. Cover and chill at least 8 hours.

6. Preheat oven to 350°.

7. Let stand at room temperature 30 minutes. Bake, uncovered, at 350° for 55 minutes or until set and lightly browned.

Dining by Design: Stylish Recipes, Savory Settings
The Junior League of Pasadena, California

Toulouse Tarts

makes 2 dozen • prep: 30 min.; cook: 1 hr., 10 min.

"Toulouse" is actually a French sausage made with wine, garlic, and seasonings. This mini quiche-style recipe baked in muffin pans uses regular sausage and features a buttery crust flavored with caraway seeds and mustard.

3 cups all-purpose flour	2 cups thinly sliced leek
1 Tbsp. caraway seeds	2 Tbsp. butter or margarine, melted
1 Tbsp. dry mustard	3 large eggs, beaten
1 cup butter or margarine, cut into 1-inch pieces	2 cups milk
¼ cup plus 3 Tbsp. ice water	⅓ cup butter or margarine, melted
¾ lb. ground pork sausage	½ cup (2 oz.) shredded Swiss cheese
2 Tbsp. freshly grated Parmesan cheese	¼ cup freshly grated Parmesan cheese
2 Tbsp. fine, dry breadcrumbs	1½ tsp. Dijon mustard
	1 tsp. salt

make it ahead: Get a head start on brunch by preparing tart crusts through Step 3. Cover tightly, and refrigerate overnight.

1. Preheat oven to 350°.

2. Process flour, caraway seeds, and dry mustard in a food processor until blended. Add 1 cup butter, processing until mixture is crumbly.

3. With processor running, slowly add ice water, 1 Tbsp. at a time; process just until pastry begins to form a ball and leaves sides of bowl. Shape dough into 24 balls; press into muffin pans to form crusts. Set aside.

4. Brown sausage in a large skillet, stirring until it crumbles; drain. Combine 2 Tbsp. Parmesan cheese and breadcrumbs; sprinkle over dough in muffin pans. Crumble sausage evenly over breadcrumb mixture.

5. Cook leeks in 2 Tbsp. melted butter in a large skillet over medium-high heat, stirring constantly until tender. Remove from heat. Add beaten eggs, milk, and remaining 5 ingredients, stirring well. Spoon egg mixture evenly into each muffin pan. Bake at 350° for 45 to 50 minutes or until lightly browned.

Lois Clark

Quad City Cookin'
Queen of Heaven Circle of OLV Ladies Council ~ Davenport, Iowa

Torta Rustica

makes 10 servings • prep: 40 min.; cook: 1 hr., 5 min.; other: 20 min.

This crispy puff pastry-encrusted torta makes a stately entrée layered with 4 kinds of cheese, spinach, and roasted red bell peppers.

test kitchen tip: Place thawed spinach between multiple layers of paper towels, and press to remove excess moisture.

1   (17.3-oz.) package frozen puff pastry sheets, thawed and divided
2   (10-oz.) packages frozen chopped spinach, thawed and squeezed dry
2   cups (8 oz.) shredded mozzarella cheese
1   cup ricotta cheese
2   (4-oz.) packages crumbled feta cheese

¾   cup freshly shredded Parmesan cheese
4   large eggs
½   cup fine, dry breadcrumbs
½   cup chopped onion
1   (15-oz.) jar roasted red bell peppers, drained and sliced
1   large egg, lightly beaten

1. Preheat oven to 425°.

2. Roll 1 pastry sheet into a 15-inch square on a lightly floured surface. Cut into a 15-inch circle, discarding excess pastry. Press into bottom and up sides of a lightly greased 8-inch springform pan, allowing pastry to overhang slightly.

3. Stir together spinach and next 7 ingredients. Spoon one-third of spinach mixture into prepared pan. Arrange half of sliced peppers on spinach mixture. Repeat with remaining spinach mixture and peppers, ending with spinach mixture.

4. Roll remaining pastry sheet slightly to remove creases. Cut into a 9-inch circle. Place on top of spinach mixture. Brush pastry with lightly beaten egg. Fold bottom pastry over top pastry, pressing lightly to seal. Brush again with egg. Place pan on a baking sheet.

5. Bake at 425° for 1 hour and 5 minutes, shielding edges with aluminum foil after 40 minutes to prevent excessive browning. Let stand 20 minutes before serving.

Patty Schexnaider

Recipes and Recollections
The Hitchcock Heritage Society ~ Hitchcock, Texas

Grits Soufflé With Caramelized Onions

(pictured on page 211)

makes 8 to 10 servings • prep: 30 min.; cook: 1 hr., 33 min.

Texas's 1015s and Georgia's Vidalias are onions known for their mild, sweet flavor that makes for extra rich-flavored caramelized rings. The onions top an easy cheese grits casserole for true sampling of a Southern breakfast.

4　cups milk

1　cup uncooked quick-cooking grits

3　cups (12 oz.) shredded smoked
　　Gouda or Cheddar cheese

½　cup butter or margarine, cut into
　　small pieces

½　tsp. salt

⅛　tsp. ground red pepper

3　large eggs, lightly beaten
　　Caramelized Onions

test kitchen tip: For individual presentations, bake in 8 buttered (6-oz.) soufflé dishes at 350° for 25 minutes or until puffed and golden brown. To serve, split the soufflés open, and spoon Caramelized Onions inside.

1. Preheat oven to 350°.

2. Bring milk to a simmer in a 4-qt. saucepan; add grits, stirring constantly. Reduce heat to medium, and cook, stirring constantly, 4 to 5 minutes or until mixture is thickened and bubbly. Add cheese and next 3 ingredients, stirring until cheese melts. Quickly whisk in eggs. Pour into a buttered 2½-qt. soufflé dish or baking dish. Bake, uncovered, at 350° for 55 minutes or until puffed and golden brown.

3. To serve, spoon grits onto serving plates; top with Caramelized Onions. Serve immediately.

Caramelized Onions

makes 2 cups • prep: 20 min., cook: 25 min.

¼　cup olive oil

5　large Texas 1015 onions, Vidalia
　　onions, or other sweet onions, thinly
　　sliced (about 10 cups)

2　Tbsp. sugar

1. Heat oil in a large skillet over high heat until hot; add onion, and cook over high heat 15 minutes, stirring often. Sprinkle with sugar; reduce heat to medium high, and cook 10 minutes or until golden.

Setting on the Dock of the Bay
Assistance League® of the Bay Area ~ Houston, Texas

Baked French Toast Casserole

makes 10 servings • prep: 25 min., cook: 40 min., other: 12 hr.

Here's a great recipe to make the night before when you need an impressive morning entrée for guests. A spicy egg mixture soaks into French bread overnight, then is topped with a cinnamon-pecan sugar topping before baking.

test kitchen tip: In Step 2, combine the egg mixture in a large bowl, and beat with a wire whisk or at medium speed with an electric mixer until blended. Or, if you prefer, combine the egg mixture in a blender, and process until smooth.

1	(16-oz.) loaf French bread		¼	tsp. ground nutmeg
8	large eggs, lightly beaten		1	cup firmly packed brown sugar
3	cups milk		1	cup chopped pecans
2	Tbsp. granulated sugar		½	cup butter or margarine, softened
1	tsp. vanilla extract		2	Tbsp. light corn syrup
¼	tsp. salt		½	tsp. ground cinnamon
¼	tsp. ground cinnamon		½	tsp. ground nutmeg

1. Butter a 13- x 9-inch baking dish. Cut bread into 20 equal slices. Arrange bread slices in 2 rows down length of dish, overlapping slices.

2. Combine eggs and next 6 ingredients; pour mixture over bread slices. Cover and chill overnight. Meanwhile, combine brown sugar and remaining 5 ingredients; cover and chill overnight.

3. Preheat oven to 350°.

4. Crumble brown sugar mixture evenly over bread slices. Bake at 350° for 40 minutes or until browned.

Greek Egg Casserole

makes 6 to 8 servings • prep: 20 min., cook: 32 min., other: 10 min.

Spinach, feta cheese, fresh mushrooms, and herbs make this breakfast dish hearty enough for lunch or supper.

test kitchen tip: This casserole needs to stand at room temperature to completely set or firm up before serving. Remove from the oven when the center barely jiggles.

12	large eggs, lightly beaten		⅓	cup milk
1	(10-oz.) package frozen chopped spinach, thawed and drained		1	tsp. salt
			1	tsp. dried dillweed
1	(8-oz.) package sliced fresh mushrooms		1	tsp. dried oregano
			½	tsp. pepper
1	(8-oz.) package feta cheese, crumbled		1½	cups (6 oz.) shredded mozzarella cheese
1	small onion, chopped		2	Tbsp. chopped fresh parsley

1. Preheat oven to 350°.

2. Combine first 10 ingredients in a large bowl; stir well. Pour into a greased 13- x- 9-inch baking dish. Sprinkle with mozzarella cheese and parsley. Bake at 350° for 30 to 32 minutes or until almost set. Let stand 10 minutes before serving.

Blueberry 'n' Cheese Coffee Cake

makes 16 servings • prep: 11 min., cook: 55 min.

The American tradition of serving coffee and sweet cake along with gossip actually evolved from the tradition of English tea. This moist blueberry cream cheese cake with a lemon–sugar topping is special enough for company.

½	cup butter, softened	2	cups fresh blueberries
1¼	cups sugar	1	(8-oz.) package cream cheese, cut into ¼-inch cubes
2	large eggs		
2	cups all-purpose flour	½	cup all-purpose flour
1	tsp. baking powder	½	cup sugar
1	tsp. salt	2	Tbsp. grated lemon rind
¾	cup milk	2	Tbsp. butter, softened
¼	cup water		

test kitchen tip: If you find it difficult to cut the cream cheese into such small cubes, place it in the freezer for about 20 minutes. But don't freeze it longer because partially frozen cream cheese will crumble.

1. Preheat oven to 375°.

2. Beat ½ cup butter at medium speed with an electric mixer until creamy; gradually add 1¼ cups sugar, beating well. Add eggs, 1 at a time, beating until blended after each addition.

3. Combine 2 cups flour, baking powder, and salt; stir well. Combine milk and water; stir well. Add flour mixture to butter mixture alternately with milk mixture, beginning and ending with flour mixture. Mix at low speed after each addition until mixture is blended. Gently stir in blueberries and cream cheese. Pour batter into a greased 9-inch square pan.

4. Combine ½ cup flour and remaining 3 ingredients; stir well with a fork. Sprinkle mixture over batter. Bake at 375° for 55 minutes or until golden. Serve warm, or let cool completely on a wire rack.

Cheese Blintz Muffins With Blueberry Sauce

makes 1 dozen • prep: 15 min., cook: 38 min., other: 5 min.

Like a traditional blintz pancake filling, these muffins are flavored with ricotta cheese and topped with a sweet fruit topping and a dollop of sour cream.

test kitchen tip: To save time, commercial lemon curd substitutes nicely for the homemade Blueberry Sauce prepared in Step 3.

1	(15-oz.) container part-skim ricotta cheese	⅔	cup sugar, divided
3	large eggs, lightly beaten	1	Tbsp. cornstarch
2	Tbsp. sour cream or yogurt	⅓	cup water
¼	cup butter or margarine, melted	2	Tbsp. lemon juice
½	cup reduced-fat biscuit mix	2	cups fresh or frozen blueberries
			Sour cream

1. Preheat oven to 350°.

2. Combine first 5 ingredients and ⅓ cup sugar in a large bowl; beat at medium speed with an electric mixer or with a wire whisk until blended. Spoon batter into a greased muffin pan, filling three-fourths full. Bake at 350° for 30 to 33 minutes or until edges are golden; cool muffins 5 minutes in pan. Run a small knife around edges of muffins in pan; turn muffins out onto a wire rack.

3. Stir together cornstarch and water in a medium saucepan. Stir in remaining ⅓ cup sugar, lemon juice, and blueberries. Bring to a boil over medium heat, stirring until mixture thickens.

4. To serve, top each muffin with blueberry sauce, and dollop with sour cream.

Caroline and Jim Lloyd

Flavors of Falmouth
Falmouth Historical Society ~ Falmouth, Massachusetts

desserts

New-Fashioned Blackberry Chocolate
Spice Cake, page 247

Peanut Butter-Lovers' Cake

makes 12 servings • prep: 30 min., cook: 28 min., other: 10 min.

Peanut butter, first popular in the late 1800s, flavors the 3 tall layers and the buttery frosting for this cake. Peanuts are an abundant cash crop for Virginia, Georgia, and Alabama, and this stately dessert is just one of hundreds of ways Southerners have found to savor peanut flavor.

test kitchen tip: Measure flour by spooning—not scooping—it into dry measuring cups, letting it mound slightly. Then level it off with a straight-edged spatula or knife. Measure liquids in glass-spouted measuring cups.

¾	cup butter or margarine, softened	½	tsp. salt
2	cups sugar	1	cup buttermilk
5	large eggs, separated	1	tsp. vanilla extract
1	cup creamy peanut butter		Peanut Butter Frosting
2	cups all-purpose flour	½	cup chopped peanuts
1	tsp. baking soda		

1. Preheat oven to 350°.

2. Beat butter at medium speed with an electric mixer until creamy; gradually add sugar; beating well. Add egg yolks, 1 at a time, beating until blended after each addition. Add peanut butter, and beat until smooth.

3. Combine flour, baking soda, and salt; add to butter mixture alternately with buttermilk, beginning and ending with flour mixture. Beat at low speed after each addition until blended. Stir in vanilla.

4. Beat egg whites at high speed until stiff peaks form. Gently fold one-third beaten egg white into batter; fold in remaining egg white. Pour batter into 3 greased and floured 9-inch round cake pans.

5. Bake at 350° for 25 to 28 minutes or until a wooden pick inserted in center comes out clean. Cool in pans on wire racks 10 minutes; remove from pans, and cool completely on wire racks.

6. Spread Peanut Butter Frosting between layers and on top and sides of cake. Sprinkle peanuts on top of cake.

Peanut Butter Frosting

makes 4 cups • prep: 15 min.

¾	cup butter or margarine, softened	⅓	cup milk
1	cup creamy peanut butter	1	tsp. vanilla extract
4½	cups sifted powdered sugar		

1. Beat butter at medium speed with an electric mixer until creamy; add peanut butter, beating until blended. Gradually add powdered sugar, beating until light and fluffy. Add milk, and beat until spreading consistency. Stir in vanilla.

Picnics, Potlucks & Prizewinners
Indiana 4-H Foundation ~ Indianapolis, Indiana

Mile-High White Chocolate Hummingbird Cake

(also pictured on front cover)

makes 16 to 24 servings • prep: 40 min.; cook: 36 min.; other: 25 hr., 10 min.

1	(8-oz.) can crushed pineapple in juice	2	tsp. ground cinnamon
2	(18.25-oz.) packages white cake mix (we tested with Duncan Hines)	1	(4-oz.) white chocolate baking bar, finely chopped (we tested with Ghirardelli)
2	(3.4-oz) packages vanilla instant pudding mix	1	cup flaked sweetened coconut
6	large eggs	2	cups chopped pecans, toasted
2½	cups milk, divided	2	cups chopped banana (about 3 medium)
2	cups canola oil		White Chocolate Cream Cheese Frosting
4	tsp. vanilla extract		Garnish: toasted pecans
1	tsp. almond extract		

1. Preheat oven to 350°.

2. Drain pineapple, reserving juice for another use. Squeeze pineapple well using several thicknesses of paper towels to remove excess moisture.

3. Combine cake mix and next 7 ingredients in an 8-qt. mixing bowl. Beat at low speed with an electric mixer 2 minutes; beat at medium speed 3 minutes. Fold in pineapple, white chocolate, and next 3 ingredients. Pour batter into 4 greased and floured 9-inch round cake pans.

4. Bake at 350° for 34 to 36 minutes or until a wooden pick inserted in center comes out clean. Cool in pans on wire racks 10 minutes. Remove from pans to wire racks, and cool completely. Wrap and chill cake layers at least 1 hour or up to 24 hours.

5. Using a serrated knife, slice cake layers in half horizontally to make 8 layers. Place 1 layer, cut side up, on cake plate. Spread with ½ cup White Chocolate Cream Cheese Frosting. Repeat procedure 6 times. Place final cake layer on top of cake, cut side down. Spread remaining frosting on top and sides of cake. Cover; chill in refrigerator overnight. Garnish, if desired. Store in refrigerator.

Note: Cover cake in an airtight container and freeze up to 1 month in advance. Thaw in refrigerator overnight before serving.

White Chocolate Cream Cheese Frosting

makes 9 cups • prep: 15 min., cook: 3 min.

3	cups white chocolate morsels	¾	cup butter, softened
3	(8-oz.) packages cream cheese, softened	7½	cups powdered sugar

1. Microwave white chocolate morsels in a microwave-safe bowl at MEDIUM (50% power) 3 minutes; stir until smooth.

2. Combine cream cheese and butter in a large mixing bowl; beat at medium speed with an electric mixer until creamy. Add melted chocolate, beating well. Gradually add powdered sugar, beating at low speed until blended. Beat at medium speed until mixture reaches desired spreading consistency.

test kitchen tip: To prepare a 4-layer White Chocolate Hummingbird Cake instead, use half of all ingredients in both cake and frosting recipes. Follow cake recipe as directed in Steps 1 through 4, except use only 2 greased and floured 9-inch round cake pans. In Step 5, slice the 2 cake layers in half horizontally to make 4 layers. Follow White Chocolate Cream Cheese Frosting recipe as directed except microwave white chocolate morsels in Step 1 for only 1½ minutes. Assemble cake as directed. Both the 8- and 4-layer versions of this delicious cake slice best after they have chilled overnight.

Chocolate Turtle Cake

makes 12 servings • prep: 40 min.; cook: 32 min.; other: 1 hr., 10 min.

Unsweetened cocoa
1 (18.25-oz.) package devil's food cake mix
1 (3.9-oz.) package chocolate instant pudding mix
3 large eggs
1¼ cups milk
1 cup canola oil
2 tsp. vanilla extract
1 tsp. chocolate extract
1 tsp. instant coffee granules
1 (6-oz.) package semisweet chocolate morsels

1 cup chopped pecans
1 (16-oz.) container ready-to-spread cream cheese frosting
½ cup canned dulce de leche
2 (7-oz.) packages turtle candies
1 (16-oz.) can ready-to-spread chocolate fudge frosting
1 (12-oz.) jar dulce de leche ice cream topping
¼ cup pecan halves, toasted

1. Preheat oven to 350°. Grease 2 (9-inch) round cake pans, and dust with cocoa. Set aside.

2. Beat cake mix and next 7 ingredients at low speed with an electric mixer 1 minute; beat at medium speed 2 minutes. Fold in chocolate morsels and chopped pecans. Pour batter into prepared pans.

3. Bake at 350° for 30 to 32 minutes or until a wooden pick inserted in center comes out clean. Cool in pans on wire racks 10 minutes. Remove from pans to wire racks, and cool completely. Wrap and chill cake layers at least 1 hour.

4. Whisk together cream cheese frosting and canned dulce de leche in a small bowl until well blended. Set aside. Cut 6 turtle candies in half, and set aside for garnish. Dice remaining turtle candies.

5. Using a serrated knife, slice cake layers in half horizontally to make 4 layers. Place 1 layer, cut side up, on cake plate. Spread with ½ cup cream cheese frosting mixture; sprinkle with one-third diced turtle candies. Repeat procedure twice. Place final cake layer on top of cake, cut side down. Spread chocolate-fudge frosting on top and sides of cake. Cover and chill in refrigerator until ready to serve. Just before serving, drizzle dulce de leche ice cream topping over top of cake. Garnish with remaining halved turtle candies and pecan halves. Store in refrigerator.

A simple caramel filling and turtle candies sandwiched between fudgy brownielike cake layers and frosted with dark chocolate come together in this ultimate dessert splurge. It's an ideal cake for a birthday bash.

Easy Black Forest Cake

makes 12 servings • prep: 35 min.; cook: 32 min.; other: 1 hr., 10 min.

Devil's food cake layers enriched with milk chocolate and a trio of extracts are sandwiched with the simplest and most decadent stuffing of them all—ready-to-eat cheesecake filling and cherry pie filling. Capped off with fudge frosting and gooey chocolate-covered cherries, it's a cinch to wow your guests.

test kitchen tip: We tested this recipe with Philadelphia ready-to-eat cheesecake filling. You'll find it in the dairy case with cream cheese products.

Unsweetened cocoa

1 (18.25-oz.) package devil's food cake mix

1 (3.4-oz.) package chocolate instant pudding mix

3 large eggs

1¼ cups milk

1 cup canola oil

1 Tbsp. vanilla extract

1½ tsp. chocolate extract

1 tsp. almond extract

3 (1.55-oz.) milk chocolate bars, chopped

1 (24.3-oz.) container ready-to-eat cheesecake filling, divided

1 (21-oz.) can cherry pie filling, divided

2 (16-oz.) cans chocolate fudge frosting

Garnish: chocolate covered cherries, halved (optional)

1. Preheat oven to 350°. Grease 2 (9-inch) round cake pans, and dust with cocoa. Set aside.

2. Beat cake mix and next 7 ingredients at low speed with an electric mixer 1 minute; beat at medium speed 2 minutes. Fold in chopped chocolate. Pour batter into prepared pans.

3. Bake at 350° for 30 to 32 minutes or until a wooden pick inserted in center comes out clean. Cool in pans on wire racks 10 minutes. Remove from pans to wire racks, and cool completely on wire rack. Wrap and chill cake layers at least 1 hour or up to 24 hours.

4. Using a serrated knife, slice cake layers in half horizontally to make 4 layers. Place 1 layer, cut side up, on cake plate. Spread one-third of cheesecake filling over cake; top with one-third of cherry pie filling. Repeat procedure twice with remaining cheesecake filling and cherry filling. Place final cake layer on top of cake; cut side down. Spread chocolate fudge frosting on top and sides of cake. Cover and chill in refrigerator until ready to serve. Garnish, if desired. Store in refrigerator.

New-Fashioned Blackberry Chocolate Spice Cake

(pictured on page 241)

makes 12 servings • prep: 35 min.; cook: 32 min.; other: 1 hr., 10 min.

Chocolate and spices mingle with sweet blackberries under a robe of chocolate fudge icing drizzled with blackberry sauce. Even grandmothers would be pleased with this updated classic.

Unsweetened cocoa

1   (18.25-oz.) package devil's food cake mix (we tested with Betty Crocker)

1   (3.4-oz.) package chocolate instant pudding mix

3   large eggs

1¼ cups milk

1   cup canola oil

1   Tbsp. vanilla extract

1   tsp. chocolate extract

½   tsp. almond extract

2   tsp. ground cinnamon

¼   tsp. ground ginger

¼   tsp. ground nutmeg

¼   tsp. ground cloves

2   (3.5-oz.) bittersweet dark chocolate with orange and spices candy bars, chopped (we tested with Green and Black's Organic)

1   (21-oz.) can blackberry pie filling

2   (16-oz.) cans chocolate fudge frosting

Garnish: fresh blackberries

test kitchen tip: As a general rule in cake baking, grease cake pans with shortening unless the recipe states otherwise.

1. Preheat oven to 350°. Grease 2 (9-inch) round cake pans, and dust with cocoa. Set aside.

2. Beat cake mix and next 11 ingredients at low speed with an electric mixer 1 minute; beat at medium speed 2 minutes. Fold in chopped chocolate. Pour batter into prepared pans.

3. Bake at 350° for 30 to 32 minutes or until a wooden pick inserted in center comes out clean. Cool in pans on a wire racks 10 minutes. Remove from pans to wire racks, and cool completely. Wrap and chill cake layers at least 1 hour or up to 24 hours.

4. Using a serrated knife, slice cake layers in half horizontally to make 4 layers. Place 1 layer, cut side up, on cake plate. Spread one-third of blackberry filling over cake. Repeat procedure twice. Place final cake layer on top of cake, cut side down. Spread chocolate fudge frosting on top and sides of cake. Drizzle remaining filling over top of cake, letting it drip down sides of cake. Cover and chill in refrigerator until ready to serve. Just before serving, garnish, if desired.

Cheesecake-Stuffed Luscious Lemon Cake

makes 12 servings • prep: 35 min., cook: 32 min., other: 1 hr.

test kitchen tip: If the lemon curd is a bit too thick to drizzle over the frosted cake, microwave it at HIGH for 30 seconds. Stir the warm lemon curd, and drizzle over cake using a small spoon.

1 (18.25-oz.) package white cake mix
1 (3.4-oz.) package vanilla instant pudding mix
3 large eggs
1¼ cups milk
1 cup canola oil
2 tsp. vanilla extract
1 (4-oz.) white chocolate bar, finely chopped
2 Tbsp. grated lemon rind (about 2 large lemons)

3 (16-oz.) cans homestyle cream cheese frosting
1 (19-oz.) package frozen cheesecake with strawberry topping, finely diced (we tested with Sara Lee)
2 cups fresh raspberries, divided
1 (10-oz.) jar premium lemon curd
1 cup halved fresh strawberries, halved
Fresh mint sprigs

1. Preheat oven to 350°.

2. Beat first 6 ingredients at low speed with an electric mixer 1 minute; beat at medium speed 2 minutes. Fold in chopped chocolate and lemon rind. Pour batter into 2 greased and floured 9-inch round cake pans.

3. Bake at 350° for 30 to 32 minutes or until a wooden pick inserted into center comes out clean. Cool in pans on wire racks 10 minutes. Remove from pans to wire racks, and cool completely. Wrap and chill cake layers at least 1 hour or up to 24 hours.

4. Using a serrated knife, slice cake layers in half horizontally to make 4 layers. Place 1 layer, cut side up, on cake plate. Spread with ½ cup cream cheese frosting; sprinkle with one-third of chopped cheesecake and ½ cup raspberries. Repeat procedure twice. Place final cake layer on top of cake, cut side down. Spread remaining frosting on top and sides of cake. Cover and chill in refrigerator until ready to serve. Store in refrigerator.

5. Just before serving, drizzle lemon curd over cake. Garnish with remaining raspberries, strawberries, and mint sprigs.

Apple Spice Cake With Caramel Glaze

makes 12 servings • prep: 15 min., cook: 38 min., other: 30 min.

test kitchen tip: In Step 3, pour the glaze over the sheet cake slowly so it will soak into the cake as much in the middle as in the corners.

1 (18.25-oz.) package spice cake mix without pudding
4 large eggs
½ cup vegetable oil

1 cup apple juice
1 (3.4-oz.) package butterscotch instant pudding mix
Caramel Glaze

1. Preheat oven to 350°.

2. Combine first 5 ingredients in a large bowl; beat at medium speed with an electric mixer 2 minutes or until blended. Pour batter into a greased and floured 13- x 9-inch pan.

3. Bake at 350° for 35 to 38 minutes or until a wooden pick inserted in center of cake comes out clean. Cool cake in pan on a wire rack 30 minutes. Pour Caramel Glaze evenly over cake.

Caramel Glaze

makes 1¼ cups • prep: 5 min., cook: 6 min.

1	cup firmly packed light brown sugar	½	cup evaporated milk
½	cup butter or margarine	1	tsp. vanilla extract

1. Combine first 3 ingredients in a medium saucepan over medium-high heat; bring to a boil. Boil 3 minutes, stirring constantly. Remove from heat; stir in vanilla. Cool completely.

Chocolate Sheet Cake

makes 12 servings • prep: 20 min., cook: 30 min.

You'll detect a hint of cinnamon in this cocoa-rich, bake-and-take sheet cake. Use a disposable pan if you're taking it to a friend or potluck dinner to save cleanup and to eliminate keeping track of the pan.

2	cups sugar	¼	cup unsweetened cocoa
2	cups all-purpose flour	1	cup water
1	tsp. baking soda	½	cup buttermilk
1	tsp. ground cinnamon	2	large eggs, lightly beaten
⅛	tsp. salt	1	tsp. vanilla extract
½	cup butter or margarine		Chocolate Icing
½	cup shortening		

test kitchen tip: Either unsweetened cocoa or Dutch process cocoa work well in this recipe. Dutch process has a more mellow flavor than unsweetened cocoa and is often used to dust desserts similar to the way powdered sugar is used for dusting.

1. Preheat oven to 350°.
2. Stir together first 5 ingredients in a large bowl.
3. Combine butter and next 3 ingredients in a small saucepan. Cook over medium-low heat, stirring constantly, 5 minutes or just until butter and shortening melt. Remove from heat; pour over sugar mixture, stirring until blended. Cool slightly.
4. Add buttermilk, eggs, and vanilla. Pour into a greased and floured 15- x 10-inch jelly-roll pan.
5. Bake at 350° for 25 minutes until a wooden pick inserted in center comes out clean. Spread Chocolate Icing over hot cake.

Chocolate Icing

makes 2½ cups • prep: 10 min., cook: 10 min.

½	cup butter or margarine	1	(16-oz.) package powdered sugar
¼	cup unsweetened cocoa	1	tsp. vanilla extract
6	Tbsp. milk	1	cup chopped pecans, toasted

1. Combine butter, cocoa, and milk in a medium saucepan. Cook over low heat 5 minutes or until butter melts. Bring to a boil over medium heat.
2. Remove from heat; stir in powdered sugar and vanilla. Beat at medium speed with an electric mixer until mixture is smooth. Stir in pecans.

Caramel-Nut Pound Cake

makes 16 servings • prep: 25 min.; cook: 1 hr., 20 min.; other: 15 min.

A pound of brown sugar and lots of butter give this cake a rich caramel flavor. Toasted slices are delicious served with coffee for breakfast.

test kitchen tip: The easiest and quickest way to grease a tube pan is to slip your hand into a plastic sandwich bag and then into the shortening. After coating the inside of the pan, turn the bag inside out and throw it away.

1	cup butter, softened	½	tsp. baking powder
½	cup shortening	½	tsp. salt
1	(16-oz.) package light brown sugar	1	cup milk
1	cup granulated sugar	1	tsp. vanilla extract
5	large eggs	1	cup walnuts, finely chopped
3	cups all-purpose flour		

1. Preheat oven to 325°.

2. Beat butter and shortening at medium speed with an electric mixer 2 minutes or until creamy. Gradually add sugars, beating 5 to 7 minutes. Add eggs, 1 at a time, beating just until yellow disappears.

3. Combine flour, baking powder, and salt; add to butter mixture alternately with milk, beginning and ending with flour mixture. Mix at low speed after each addition just until blended. Stir in vanilla and walnuts.

4. Pour batter into a greased and floured 10-inch tube pan. Bake at 325° for 1 hour and 15 to 20 minutes or until a long wooden pick inserted in center comes out clean. Cool in pan on a wire rack 15 minutes; remove from pan, and cool completely on wire rack.

From Black Tie to Blackeyed Peas: Savannah's Savory Secrets
St. Joseph's Foundation of Savannah, Inc. ~ Savannah, Georgia

famous Southern cakes

In Colonial days cakes were rated social status—those you made with available ingredients for family, like everyday pound cakes and upside-down skillet cakes, and those made with hard-to-get ingredients such as citrus fruit or coconut, which were reserved for holidays or weddings. Over time, a few recipes emerged with elite rankings—Charleston-inspired stately Lady Baltimore Cake with nuts and raisins, lemony Robert E. Lee Cake with meringue frosting named to honor General Lee, and Lane Cake with whiskey, raisins, and boiled icing. Other Southern-bred cakes include rich caramel cake, coconut cake, cocoa-based Red Velvet Cake, and more recently, Hummingbird Cake with mashed bananas, pineapple, pecans, and a cream cheese icing. Submitted to *Southern Living* in 1978 from a North Carolina reader, Hummingbird Cake has become the magazine's most requested recipe. The original recipe was the inspiration for our decadent but easy white chocolate version pictured on the front cover and also on page 243 (recipe on page 243).

Peanut Butter Cheesecake

makes 14 servings • prep: 30 min.; cook: 1 hr., 5 min.; other: 8 hr., 15 min.

Each creamy slice of this cheesecake is filled with chunks of peanut butter morsels and semisweet chocolate morsels. Chopped peanuts sprinkled on top leave no doubt about the flavor within.

1½ cups graham cracker crumbs

⅓ cup butter or margarine, melted

5 (8-oz.) packages cream cheese, softened

1½ cups granulated sugar

¾ cup creamy peanut butter

2 tsp. vanilla extract

3 large eggs

1 cup peanut butter morsels

1 cup semisweet chocolate morsels

1 (8-oz.) container sour cream

½ cup sifted powdered sugar

3 Tbsp. creamy peanut butter

½ cup finely chopped unsalted peanuts

make it ahead: Cheesecake is a great make-ahead dessert choice. Cover and refrigerate in the springform pan up to 1 week before serving.

1. Preheat oven to 350°.

2. Stir together graham cracker crumbs and melted butter. Firmly press mixture into bottom and 1 inch up sides of a 10-inch springform pan. Bake at 350° for 5 minutes; cool in pan on a wire rack.

3. Beat cream cheese at high speed with an electric mixer until creamy; gradually add 1½ cups sugar, beating well. Add ¾ cup peanut butter and vanilla, beating until blended. Add eggs, 1 at a time, beating until blended after each addition. Stir in morsels. Pour batter into prepared pan.

4. Bake at 350° for 55 minutes to 1 hour or until cheesecake is almost set. Remove from oven; cool in pan on wire rack 15 minutes.

5. Meanwhile, stir together sour cream, powdered sugar, and 3 Tbsp. peanut butter. Spread sour cream mixture over top of warm cheesecake; sprinkle with peanuts. Run knife around edge of pan to release sides; cool to room temperature. Cover and chill at least 8 hours. Store in refrigerator.   Teresa Austin

Sharing Our Best
Poyen Assembly of God Youth Ministry ~ Poyen, Arkansas

Uptown Banana Pudding Cheesecake

makes 10 to 12 servings • prep: 25 min., cook: 1 hr., other: 8 hr.

Though originally a family dessert, humble banana pudding
is now a favorite served in restaurants from barbecue shacks
to the top-tier eateries. Coffee liqueur adds sophisticated
flair to our top-rated cheesecake.

1½ cups finely crushed vanilla wafers	1 cup granulated sugar
¼ cup chopped walnuts, toasted	3 large eggs
¼ cup butter, melted	1 Tbsp. coffee liqueur
2 large ripe bananas, diced	2 tsp. vanilla extract
1 Tbsp. lemon juice	Meringue
2 Tbsp. light brown sugar	
3 (8-oz.) packages cream cheese, softened	

1. Preheat oven to 350°.
2. Combine first 3 ingredients in a bowl. Press into bottom of a greased
9-inch springform pan. Bake at 350° for 10 minutes. Cool on a wire rack.
3. Combine diced bananas and 1 Tbsp. lemon juice in a small saucepan. Stir in
2 Tbsp. brown sugar. Place over medium-high heat, and cook, stirring constantly, about 1 minute or just until sugar has melted. Set banana mixture aside.
4. Beat cream cheese at medium speed with an electric mixer 3 minutes or
until smooth. Gradually add 1 cup granulated sugar, beating until blended.
Add eggs, 1 at a time, beating until blended after each addition. Beat in
liqueur and vanilla. Pour into prepared pan. Spoon tablespoonfuls of banana
mixture evenly over top, and swirl gently into batter.

5. Bake at 350° for 35 to 40 minutes or until center is almost set. Remove cheesecake from oven, and increase oven temperature to 400°.

6. Drop spoonfuls of Meringue gently and evenly over hot cheesecake. Bake at 400° for 10 minutes or until Meringue is golden brown. Remove from oven, and run a knife around edge of cheesecake in springform pan to loosen. Cool cheesecake completely on a wire rack. Cover and chill 8 hours. Store in refrigerator.

Meringue

makes about 2 cups • prep: 12 min.

3   egg whites
¼   tsp. salt
6   Tbsp. sugar

1. Beat egg whites and salt at high speed with an electric mixer until foamy. Add sugar, 1 Tbsp. at a time, beating until stiff peaks form and sugar dissolves (about 1 to 2 minutes).

test kitchen tip: For maximum volume from beating egg whites, separate the eggs while cold, and then let whites sit at room temperature 20 minutes before whipping them. Use a glass or copper bowl, and make certain it's clean and grease-free.

Chocolate-Amaretto Cheesecake

makes 10 servings • prep: 20 min.; cook: 1 hr., 3 min.; other: 9 hr.

1¼ cups chocolate wafer crumbs
¼   cup butter or margarine, melted
2   Tbsp. sugar
2   (8-oz.) packages cream cheese, softened
½   cup sugar
2   large eggs
1   cup semisweet chocolate morsels, melted

⅔   cup sour cream
⅓   cup amaretto
1   tsp. vanilla extract
½   tsp. almond extract
½   cup semisweet chocolate morsels
1   Tbsp. butter or margarine
Garnishes: whipped cream, toasted sliced almonds

test kitchen tip: To quickly crush chocolate wafers into crumbs for the crust, place chocolate wafers in a zip-top plastic bag, and pound gently with a rolling pin.

1. Preheat oven to 300°.

2. Combine first 3 ingredients in a small bowl. Press into bottom and 1 inch up sides of a greased 8-inch springform pan. Chill.

3. Beat cream cheese at high speed with an electric mixer until creamy. Gradually add ½ cup sugar, beating well. Add eggs, 1 at a time, beating after each addition. Add melted chocolate and next 4 ingredients; beat until smooth. Pour into prepared crust.

4. Bake at 300° for 1 hour. Turn oven off; partially open oven door, and let cheesecake cool in oven 1 hour. Remove cheesecake from oven, and let cool to room temperature in pan on a wire rack; cover and chill at least 8 hours. Carefully remove sides of springform pan.

5. Combine ½ cup chocolate morsels and 1 Tbsp. butter in a small saucepan. Cook over low heat, stirring constantly, until chocolate melts. Cool slightly. Spread over cheesecake. Garnish, if desired.

Black-Bottom Pecan Cheesecake Pie

makes 8 servings • prep: 25 min., cook: 55 min.

This decadent pie has three irresistible layers. A rich chocolate ganache on the bottom, a creamy cheesecake filling in the middle, and a traditional pecan pie topping.

test kitchen tip: The pie plate will be very full so carefully transfer it to the oven.

½ (15-oz.) package refrigerated piecrusts
1 cup semisweet chocolate morsels
3 Tbsp. whipping cream
1 (8-oz.) package cream cheese, softened
4 large eggs

¾ cup sugar, divided
2 tsp. vanilla extract, divided
¼ tsp. salt
1 cup light corn syrup
3 Tbsp. butter or margarine, melted
1½ cups pecan halves
Chocolate syrup (optional)

1. Preheat oven to 350°.

2. Unroll piecrust; fit into a 9-inch pie plate according to package directions. Fold edges under, and crimp.

3. Microwave chocolate morsels and whipping cream in a small glass bowl at MEDIUM (50% power) for 1 to 1½ minutes or until morsels begin to melt. Whisk until smooth. Set aside.

4. Beat cream cheese, 1 egg, ½ cup sugar, 1 tsp. vanilla, and salt at medium speed with an electric mixer until smooth. Pour chocolate mixture into piecrust, spreading evenly. Pour cream cheese mixture over chocolate layer.

5. Whisk together corn syrup, melted butter, remaining 3 eggs, remaining ¼ cup sugar, and remaining 1 tsp. vanilla. Stir in pecans; pour over cream cheese layer.

6. Bake at 350° for 55 minutes or until set; shielding pie after about 45 minutes to prevent excessive browning. Cool completely on a wire rack. Drizzle each slice with chocolate syrup, if desired.

Crunchy Caramel Apple Pie

makes 8 servings • prep: 25 min., cook: 55 min., other: 25 min.

Tart Granny Smith apples are best for this nutty crumb-topped apple pie. Drizzle caramel topping over warm slices, and serve each slice with a scoop of vanilla ice cream.

½	cup granulated sugar	1	cup firmly packed light brown sugar
3	Tbsp. all-purpose flour	½	cup uncooked regular oats
1	tsp. ground cinnamon	½	cup all-purpose flour
⅛	tsp. salt	½	cup butter or margarine
6	cups peeled, thinly sliced Granny Smith apples	½	cup chopped pecans
		⅓	cup caramel topping
1	unbaked 9-inch pastry shell		Vanilla ice cream

test kitchen tip: Once cut, apples turn brown, so dip them in pineapple or orange juice if you're detained while assembling this recipe to prevent them from discoloring.

1. Preheat oven to 375°.

2. Combine first 4 ingredients in a large bowl; stir well. Add apple slices, and toss until coated. Spoon apple mixture into pastry shell; set aside.

3. Combine brown sugar, oats, and ½ cup flour; cut in butter with a pastry blender until crumbly. Stir in pecans. Sprinkle crumb topping over apple mixture. Bake at 375° for 55 minutes, shielding edges with aluminum foil after 25 minutes to prevent excessive browning. Drizzle with caramel topping. Let stand on a wire rack at least 25 minutes. Serve pie with vanilla ice cream.

apple picking time A cry of "the apples are in!" during late summer and early fall sends Southerners scurrying to the mountains from North Georgia to Virginia to get first pick of the season's harvest. In the weeks to follow, just as in hardscrabble days of the past, applesauce simmers on stovetops to "put up" for later. Meanwhile, church and community groups gather to stir apple butter in huge old-time copper kettles, while festivals complete with fried apple pies, fresh cider, and bluegrass music are in full swing. The air is rich with the scent of apple pies, apple spice cake, and even the famous Appalachian apple stack cake with layers soaked in applesauce or apple butter. Mountain stores and roadside stands sell home-dried apples and jellies. Despite chefs' upscale ways with apples across the South, at this time of year, Appalachia returns to its culinary roots, and it tastes mighty fine.

Chocolate Icebox Pie

makes 8 servings • prep: 20 min., cook: 12 min., other: 8 hr.

A chocolate crumb crust, silky chocolate filling, and chocolate candy bar pieces scattered over a whipped cream topping make this chilled pie a chocolate lover's dream.

test kitchen tip: For a silky chocolate filling, combine the cold water and cornstarch in Step 2, and whisk it gently until it makes a thin, smooth paste. And set a timer when cooking the filling in Step 3—it should boil only 1 minute.

⅔ cup milk

¾ cup semisweet chocolate morsels

¼ cup cold water

2 Tbsp. cornstarch

1 (14-oz.) can sweetened condensed milk

3 large eggs, beaten

1 tsp. vanilla extract

3 Tbsp. butter or margarine

1 (6-oz.) ready-made chocolate crumb piecrust

1 cup whipping cream

¼ cup sugar

½ cup chopped pecans, toasted

1 (1.55-oz.) milk chocolate candy bar, chopped

1. Heat milk until it just begins to bubble around the edges in a 3-qt. saucepan over medium heat (do not boil). Remove from heat, and whisk in chocolate morsels until melted. Cool slightly.

2. Whisk together cold water and cornstarch until dissolved.

3. Whisk cornstarch mixture, sweetened condensed milk, eggs, and vanilla into chocolate mixture. Bring to a boil over medium heat, whisking constantly. Boil 1 minute or until mixture thickens and is smooth. (Do not overcook.) Remove from heat, and add butter, whisking until melted. Spoon mixture into piecrust. Cover and chill at least 8 hours.

4. Beat whipping cream at high speed with an electric mixer until foamy; gradually add sugar, beating until soft peaks form. Spread whipped cream evenly over pie filling, and sprinkle with pecans and chopped candy bar. Store in refrigerator.

Rancher's Buttermilk Pie

makes 8 servings • prep: 15 min., cook: 45 min., other: 30 min.

This dessert is much like chess pie with its gooey egg and buttermilk filling and a spoonful of cornmeal to give it a little crunch. Pineapple, coconut, and fresh lemon juice stirred in make the traditional Southern pie a little fancier.

test kitchen tip: A balloon whisk is the simplest cooking tool to blend the ingredients for this pie.

½ (15-oz.) package refrigerated piecrusts

2 cups sugar

2 Tbsp. cornmeal

5 large eggs, lightly beaten

⅔ cup buttermilk

½ cup crushed pineapple, drained

½ cup sweetened flaked coconut

¼ cup butter, melted

2 tsp. grated lemon rind

2 tsp. fresh lemon juice

1 tsp. vanilla extract

1. Preheat oven to 350°.

2. Fit piecrust into a 9-inch pie plate according to package directions; fold edges under, and crimp.

3. Combine sugar and cornmeal in a large bowl. Whisk in beaten eggs and buttermilk until combined. Stir in pineapple and next 5 ingredients. Pour filling into piecrust.

4. Bake at 350° for 45 minutes or until pie is set and top is lightly browned. Cool at least 30 minutes on a wire rack. Serve warm or at room temperature.

Coconut Meringue Pie

makes 8 servings • prep: 20 min., cook: 40 min.

A slice of custardlike coconut pie is a must with any Southern barbecue dinner. This one is topped with meringue and sprinkled with toasted coconut.

1	(3-oz.) can flaked coconut, divided	2	Tbsp. light corn syrup
1½	cups sugar	1½	tsp. vanilla extract
¼	cup cornstarch	1	baked 9-inch pastry shell
Dash of salt		4	large egg whites
2½	cups milk	½	tsp. cream of tartar
4	large egg yolks, lightly beaten	¼	tsp. salt
¼	cup butter or margarine	½	cup sugar

test kitchen tip: Use a knife dipped first in hot water to cut meringue pies neatly.

1. Preheat oven to 350°.

2. Sprinkle 2 Tbsp. coconut on a baking sheet; reserve remaining coconut. Bake at 350° for 3 to 4 minutes or until lightly toasted. Set toasted coconut aside.

3. Combine 1½ cups sugar, cornstarch, and dash of salt in a large saucepan. Add remaining coconut, milk, and next 4 ingredients; stir well. Cook over medium heat, stirring constantly, until butter melts and mixture thickens. Spoon into prepared pastry shell.

4. Reduce oven temperature to 325°.

5. Beat egg whites, cream of tartar, and ¼ tsp. salt at high speed with an electric mixer until soft peaks form. Gradually add ½ cup sugar, 1 Tbsp. at a time, beating until stiff peaks form and sugar dissolves (2 to 4 minutes). Spread meringue over filling, sealing to edge of pastry.

6. Bake at 325° for 25 to 28 minutes or until golden. Sprinkle toasted coconut on top of pie. Cool completely on a wire rack. Cover and chill. Store in refrigerator.

Mrs. Judy Waldorff

Bay Leaves
The Junior Service League of Panama City, Inc. ~ Panama City, Florida

Mocha Pecan Mud Pie

makes 8 servings • prep: 20 min.; cook: 15 min.; other: 8 hr., 10 min.

Two store-bought ice creams pack lots of flavor into this frozen dessert.

1   cup cream-filled chocolate sandwich cookie crumbs (12 cookies)
3   Tbsp. butter or margarine, melted
1   egg white, lightly beaten
1¼ cups chopped pecans

¼   cup sugar
1   pt. coffee ice cream, softened
1   pt. chocolate ice cream, softened
12 cream-filled chocolate sandwich cookies, coarsely chopped and divided

1. Preheat oven to 350°.

2. Stir together cookie crumbs and butter. Press into a 9-inch pie plate. Brush with egg white.

3. Bake at 350° for 5 minutes. Cool on a wire rack.

4. Place pecans on a lightly greased baking sheet; sprinkle with sugar. Bake at 350° for 8 to 10 minutes. Cool.

5. Stir together ice creams, 1 cup coarsely chopped cookies, and 1 cup pecans; spoon into crust. Freeze 10 minutes. Press remaining coarsely chopped cookies and pecans on top. Cover and freeze at least 8 hours.

Grasshopper Delight Frozen Pie

makes 12 servings • prep: 15 min.; other: 9 hr., 40 min.

Traditional grasshopper pie is made with crème de menthe liqueur, but this easy pie with a chocolate cookie crust gets flavor from mint chocolate chip ice cream.

30	cream-filled chocolate sandwich cookies	1	(8-oz.) container frozen whipped topping, thawed
⅓	cup butter or margarine, melted	½	cup sifted powdered sugar
½	gal. mint chocolate chip ice cream, softened	½	tsp. vanilla extract

test kitchen tip: Soften the ice cream at room temperature for about 10 to 15 minutes so it will spread easily over the crust. If time is tight, soften it in the microwave at MEDIUM LOW (30% power) for about 20 to 30 seconds.

1. Process cookies in a food processor or blender until ground; add butter, and process until blended. Reserve ½ cup crumb mixture. Firmly press remaining crumb mixture in an ungreased 13- x 9-inch pan. Chill 30 minutes.

2. Spoon ice cream over crust; cover and freeze 1 hour. Stir together whipped topping, powdered sugar, and vanilla; spread over ice cream layer. Sprinkle remaining ½ cup crumb mixture over whipped topping mixture. Cover and freeze at least 8 hours.

Bavarian Rhubarb Tart

makes 12 servings • prep: 30 min., cook: 40 min., other: 1 hr.

Chopped cherry-colored rhubarb stalks, which are shaped a lot like celery, are caramelized and cinnamon-spiced for a sweet gooey filling that soaks into the cakelike crust of this tart.

1¼	cups all-purpose flour	1	large egg, well beaten
1	tsp. baking powder	4	cups chopped fresh rhubarb
1	tsp. sugar	2¼	cups sugar, divided
½	tsp. salt	1½	Tbsp. all-purpose flour
½	cup butter or margarine	1	tsp. ground cinnamon
2	Tbsp. milk	5	Tbsp. butter or margarine

test kitchen tip: The large green leaves on the tips of rhubarb stalks contain oxalic acid and can be toxic. Always trim and discard them.

1. Preheat oven to 350°.

2. Combine first 4 ingredients; cut in ½ cup butter with a pastry blender until crumbly. Combine milk and egg; add to flour mixture. Stir with a fork until dry ingredients are moistened. Press into a greased 13- x 9-inch pan.

3. Combine rhubarb and 1½ cups sugar; spoon over crust. Combine remaining ¾ cup sugar, 1½ Tbsp. flour, and cinnamon; cut in 5 Tbsp. butter with a pastry blender until crumbly. Sprinkle over rhubarb mixture. Bake at 350° for 40 minutes or until crust is lightly browned and rhubarb is tender. Remove from oven, and cool 1 hour on a wire rack.

Pear Crisp With Lemon Sauce

makes 6 servings • prep: 15 min., cook: 35 min., other: 10 min.

Sliced fresh pears are topped with a crisp layer of crunchy brown sugar, oats, and almonds for an easy autumn dessert. Spoon warm Lemon Sauce over each serving.

test kitchen tip: Commercially prepared lemon curd is available in most supermarkets and makes a speedy substitution for the Lemon Sauce.

⅔ cup uncooked regular oats

⅓ cup all-purpose flour

⅓ cup firmly packed brown sugar

¼ tsp. ground cardamom

¼ cup butter or margarine, cut into ½-inch pieces

⅓ cup sliced almonds

5 firm, ripe pears, peeled and sliced (we tested with Bosc)

1 Tbsp. granulated sugar

½ tsp. grated lemon rind

Lemon Sauce

1. Preheat oven to 375°.

2. Combine first 4 ingredients; cut in butter with a pastry blender until crumbly. Stir in almonds; set aside.

3. Combine pear slices, 1 Tbsp. sugar, and lemon rind. Spoon mixture into a lightly greased 2-qt. baking dish. Sprinkle oat mixture evenly over fruit mixture.

4. Bake at 375° for 35 minutes or until golden. Let stand 10 minutes. Serve with warm Lemon Sauce.

Lemon Sauce

makes ⅔ cup • prep: 10 min., cook: 8 min.

½ cup water

¼ cup sugar

2 tsp. cornstarch

1 egg yolk, beaten

1 Tbsp. butter or margarine

¼ tsp. grated lemon rind

1 Tbsp. fresh lemon juice

1. Whisk together first 3 ingredients in a medium saucepan. Bring to a boil over medium heat, stirring constantly; cook, stirring constantly, 2 minutes or until mixture thickens. Remove from heat. Gradually stir about one-fourth of hot mixture into egg yolk; add to remaining hot mixture, stirring constantly.

2. Bring to a boil over low heat; cook, stirring constantly, 1 minute or until thickened. Remove from heat; stir in butter, lemon rind, and lemon juice.

Blueberry Cobbler With Cookie Dough Topping

makes 8 servings • prep: 20 min., cook: 35 min.

Cobbler toppings usually vary between a biscuitlike sweet-ened dough and piecrusts. Drop spoonfuls of cookie dough over the juicy blueberry filling for this version.

4	cups fresh blueberries	½	tsp. vanilla extract
¼	cup plus 1 Tbsp. sugar	1	cup all-purpose flour
¾	cup orange juice	½	tsp. baking powder
1	cup butter or margarine, softened	⅛	tsp. salt
1	cup sugar	½	tsp. ground cinnamon
1	large egg		Vanilla ice cream

test kitchen tip: Create a mixed berry cobbler by substituting 4 cups blueberries with a combination of blueberries, black-berries, and raspberries.

1. Preheat oven to 375°.

2. Combine first 3 ingredients, stirring gently. Spoon into a lightly greased 13- x 9-inch baking dish.

3. Beat butter at medium speed with an electric mixer until creamy; gradu-ally add 1 cup sugar, beating well. Add egg and vanilla; beat well. Combine flour, baking powder, and salt; add to butter mixture, beating well. Drop batter by tablespoonfuls over blueberry mixture; sprinkle with cinnamon.

4. Bake at 375° for 35 minutes or until lightly browned and bubbly. Serve warm or at room temperature with ice cream.

Berry Tart With Mascarpone Cream

makes 12 servings • prep: 35 min.; cook: 40 min.; other: 1 hr., 45 min.

Mascarpone is a soft double or triple cream cheese known for delicately enhancing the flavor of fresh fruits. The creamy filling for this tart is topped with patriotic looking strawberries, raspberries, blueberries, and blackberries for a stunning Fourth of July meal finale.

Sweet Pastry Dough

1   cup mascarpone cheese

⅓   cup whipping cream

¼   cup sugar

1½   cups small strawberries, quartered

1   cup fresh raspberries

1   cup fresh blueberries

1   cup fresh blackberries

2   Tbsp. orange marmalade

2   Tbsp. blackberry or crème de cassis liqueur

1. Roll Sweet Pastry Dough into an 11-inch circle on a lightly floured surface. Fit into a 9-inch tart pan with removable bottom; trim off excess pastry along edges. Prick bottom and sides of pastry with a fork; chill 30 minutes.

2. Preheat oven to 375°.

3. Line pastry with aluminum foil, and fill with pie weights or dried beans. Bake at 375° for 20 minutes. Remove weights and foil; bake 10 more minutes. Cool completely on a wire rack.

4. Beat mascarpone cheese, whipping cream, and sugar at medium speed with an electric mixer until stiff peaks form. Spoon into prepared crust. Chill 45 minutes. Meanwhile, combine strawberries and next 3 ingredients in a medium bowl; toss gently.

5. Combine marmalade and liqueur in a small saucepan. Bring to a boil; reduce heat, and simmer 5 minutes or until reduced to 3 Tbsp. Pour over berry mixture, and toss gently. Cover and chill 30 minutes. Spoon berry mixture over cheese mixture.

Sweet Pastry Dough

makes enough pastry for 1 (9-inch) tart shell • prep: 10 min., other: 1 hr.

1⅓   cups all-purpose flour

½   cup unsalted butter, cut into pieces

2   Tbsp. sugar

¼   tsp. salt

1   egg yolk, lightly beaten

2½   Tbsp. ice water

1. Combine first 4 ingredients with a pastry blender until crumbly. Combine egg yolk and water. Sprinkle yolk mixture, 1 Tbsp. at a time, evenly over surface; stir with a fork until dry ingredients are moistened. Shape into a ball.

2. Gently press pastry into a 6-inch circle on a sheet of plastic wrap; cover dough with plastic wrap, and chill 1 hour.

A Sensational Encore
The Junior League of Greater Orlando, Florida

test kitchen tip: Pie weights, used in Step 3, are small metal pellets used to keep the pastry shell from puffing up and bursting as it's baked. Dried beans are an inexpensive and effective substitute.

Five-Nut Caramel Tart

makes 10 servings • prep: 30 min., cook: 45 min., other: 1 hr.

Pecan pie, step aside. One bite of the buttery, honey-soaked filling of cashews, macadamia nuts, almonds, pistachios, and pine nuts is so rich you'll need only a small slice.

1½	cups all-purpose flour
½	cup unsalted butter, cut into 1-inch pieces
¼	cup plus 1 Tbsp. granulated sugar, divided
2	egg yolks, lightly beaten
1	Tbsp. cold water
½	cup unsalted butter
½	cup firmly packed dark brown sugar
¼	cup honey
1	cup salted roasted whole cashews
⅔	cup macadamia nuts
½	cup whole blanched almonds
⅓	cup pistachio nuts
¼	cup pine nuts
2	Tbsp. whipping cream
¼	cup semisweet chocolate morsels (optional)

test kitchen tip: Freeze any extra nuts in a zip-top plastic freezer bag, a jar, or any airtight container for up to a year.

1. Position knife blade in a food processor bowl; add flour, ½ cup butter pieces, and 3 Tbsp. sugar. Pulse 12 times or until mixture is crumbly. Combine egg yolks and water; add to flour mixture, and process just until dough begins to leave sides of bowl and forms a ball. Cover and chill 30 minutes.

2. Preheat oven to 375°.

3. Roll dough to ⅛-inch thickness on a floured surface. Fit pastry into a 9-inch tart pan; trim off excess pastry. Cover and chill 30 minutes.

4. Line pastry shell with aluminum foil; fill with pie weights or dried beans. Bake at 375° for 10 minutes. Remove pie weights and aluminum foil; bake 10 more minutes.

5. Combine remaining 2 Tbsp. sugar, ½ cup butter, brown sugar, and honey in a medium-size heavy saucepan. Cook over medium heat, stirring constantly, until mixture comes to a boil. Remove from heat. Stir in nuts and whipping cream. Pour mixture into prepared tart pan.

6. Bake at 350° for 20 minutes or until lightly browned and bubbly. If desired, sprinkle with chocolate morsels; let stand until softened enough to spread. Let cool completely on a wire rack.

Special Selections of Ocala
Ocala Royal Dames for Cancer Research, Inc. ~ Ocala, Florida

Coffee-Coconut Tart

makes 8 servings • prep: 20 min.; cook: 29 min.; other: 1 hr., 10 min.

Coconut and coffee are ground together to make a luscious crust for this tart with coffee filling. Sweetened whipped cream spooned on top and sprinkled with toasted coconut and chocolate-covered espresso beans turn this tart into a stunningly beautiful dessert to cap off an elegant meal.

test kitchen tip: Delicious chocolate-covered espresso beans make a beautiful garnish and add a welcomed texture contrast to the creamy filling. Find them at specialty grocery stores and specialty coffee stores.

½ cup all-purpose flour
¼ cup sweetened shredded coconut, toasted
¼ cup sifted powdered sugar
¼ cup unsalted butter, cut into pieces
¾ tsp. instant coffee granules
⅛ tsp. salt
¼ cup granulated sugar
2 Tbsp. cornstarch

2 Tbsp. instant coffee granules
½ cup plus 2 Tbsp. whipping cream
¼ cup plus 2 Tbsp. cream of coconut
4 large egg yolks, lightly beaten
½ tsp. vanilla extract
Whipped cream
Garnishes: chocolate-covered espresso beans, shredded coconut

1. Preheat oven to 350°.

2. Process first 6 ingredients in a food processor 1 minute or until crumbly. Firmly press dough in bottom and up sides of a 8-inch tart pan with removable bottom; freeze 10 minutes. Pierce crust with fork; place on a baking sheet. Bake at 350° for 25 minutes or until crust is golden brown. Remove from oven, and cool completely in pan on a wire rack.

3. Whisk together granulated sugar, cornstarch, and 2 Tbsp. instant coffee granules in a heavy saucepan. Gradually stir in whipping cream and cream of coconut. Stir in egg yolks; bring to a boil over medium-high heat, stirring constantly. Cook 3 to 4 minutes or until mixture thickens. Stir in vanilla. Remove from heat, and cool to room temperature, stirring occasionally. Spoon coffee filling into prepared crust. Cover and chill 1 hour. Serve with whipped cream, and garnish, if desired.

Victorian Thymes and Pleasures
The Junior League of Williamsport, Pennsylvania

Chocolate Turtle Tart

makes 12 servings • prep: 20 min.; cook: 35 min.; other: 3 hr., 30 min.

Any dessert with "turtle" in the title lets you know that you're in for a chocolate-caramel-pecan treat. This decadent tart has a pecan crust, a creamy chocolate filling, and is draped with Warm Caramel Sauce.

1¾ cups coarsely chopped pecans
⅓ cup sugar
¼ cup unsalted butter, melted
1½ cups whipping cream

12 (1-oz.) semisweet chocolate squares, chopped
½ cup finely chopped pecans
Warm Caramel Sauce

1. Preheat oven to 350°.
2. Process 1¾ cups pecans and sugar in a food processor until finely ground; add melted butter, and process until combined. Press mixture firmly in bottom and up sides of a 9-inch tart pan with removable bottom. Bake at 350° for 20 to 23 minutes or until golden brown; cool completely in pan on a wire rack.
3. Bring whipping cream to a simmer in a medium saucepan; reduce heat to low, and add chocolate, whisking until smooth. Remove from heat; cool.
4. Pour chocolate mixture into prepared crust; chill 30 minutes. Sprinkle ½ cup finely chopped pecans around edges. Chill 3 hours or until firm.
5. Loosen tart pan sides, and remove. Serve tart with Warm Caramel Sauce.

Warm Caramel Sauce

makes 1⅔ cups • prep: 5 min., cook: 8 min.

½ cup unsalted butter
1 cup sugar
1 cup whipping cream

1. Melt butter in a saucepan over medium heat; add sugar, and cook, stirring often, 8 minutes or until deep golden brown. Whisk in whipping cream until smooth.

Creating a Stir
The Fayette County Medical Auxiliary ~ Lexington, Kentucky

test kitchen tip: Cook the butter and sugar mixture for the Warm Caramel Sauce until it's a deep golden brown similar to the color of pecan shells.

Angel food cake squares, fresh summer berries, and a sweet creamy sauce in a tall trifle bowl make a layered and lovely chilled dessert. It usually tastes even better a day later when the sauce and berry juices fully soak the sweet cake.

Lemon Trifle

Lemon Trifle

makes 8 to 10 servings • prep: 25 min., other: 8 hr.

1	(14-oz.) can sweetened condensed milk	⅓	cup fresh lemon juice (about 1½ lemons)
1	(8-oz.) container lemon yogurt	2	cups sliced fresh strawberries
1	Tbsp. grated lemon rind	1	cup fresh blueberries
1	(8-oz.) container whipped topping, thawed	1	cup fresh raspberries
1	(1-lb.) angel food cake, cut into bite-size pieces	½	cup flaked coconut, lightly toasted

1. Combine first 3 ingredients in a large bowl; fold in whipped topping. Toss cake pieces with lemon juice. Layer one-third of cake pieces and one-third of whipped topping mixture in a 6-qt. trifle bowl. Top with sliced strawberries.

2. Layer half each of remaining cake, whipped topping mixture, blueberries, and raspberries. Repeat layers once. Sprinkle with coconut. Cover and chill at least 8 hours.

Sweet Pickin's
The Junior League of Fayetteville, North Carolina

Frozen Mocha Torte

makes 8 servings • prep: 35 min.; other: 16 hr., 15 min.

Put on the coffee, and pull out this cheesecakelike frozen mocha dessert to celebrate a birthday, a promotion, or just the end of the work week. Chocolate wafer crumbs on top, like the ones in the crust, dress it up.

1¼	cups chocolate water crumbs (about 25 wafers), divided	1	(14-oz.) can sweetened condensed milk
¼	cup sugar	⅔	cup chocolate syrup
¼	cup butter or margarine, melted	2	Tbsp. hot water
1	(8-oz.) package cream cheese, softened	2	Tbsp. instant coffee granules
		1	cup whipping cream, whipped

test kitchen tip: If you don't keep coffee granules on hand, substitute 3 Tbsp. strong, brewed coffee in place of hot water and coffee granules mixture in Step 3.

1. Stir together 1 cup wafer crumbs, sugar, and butter; press mixture into bottom and 1 inch up sides of a 9-inch springform pan. Cover and freeze 8 hours or until firm.

2. Beat cream cheese in a large bowl at medium speed with an electric mixer until creamy. Gradually add condensed milk and chocolate syrup, beating 5 minutes or until smooth.

3. Combine hot water and coffee granules, stirring until granules dissolve. Add to cream cheese mixture, stirring well. Fold in whipped cream. Pour into prepared pan. Sprinkle with remaining ¼ cup chocolate wafer crumbs. Cover and freeze 8 hours or until firm.

4. To serve, remove from freezer, and let stand 15 minutes at room temperature; remove sides of pan before serving.

Apricot-Cheese-Rum Turnovers

makes 8 servings • prep: 20 min., cook: 15 min., other: 30 min.

freeze it: Cool these turnovers completely before sprinkling with powdered sugar in Step 5. Freeze up to 1 month in an airtight container. Thaw overnight in refrigerator, then before serving, warm them at 325° for about 10 minutes to crisp pastry. Don't forget to sprinkle with powdered sugar.

1 (8-oz.) package cream cheese, softened	½ cup apricot preserves
1¼ cups sifted powdered sugar, divided	1 egg yolk, beaten
1 tsp. rum flavoring	1 Tbsp. milk
1 (17.3-oz.) package frozen puff pastry sheets, thawed	Vegetable cooking spray

1. Preheat oven to 400°.

2. Beat cream cheese at medium speed with an electric mixer until creamy. Add 1 cup powdered sugar and rum flavoring, beating until smooth.

3. Cut each sheet of puff pastry into 4 squares. Spoon cream cheese mixture into center of each square of pastry; top each with 1 Tbsp. apricot preserves.

4. Combine egg yolk and milk in a small bowl; stir well. Brush edges of pastry squares lightly with egg mixture. Fold each square of pastry into a triangle; press edges together with a fork to seal. Place tarts on a baking sheet lightly coated with cooking spray. Brush tarts with remaining egg mixture.

5. Bake at 400° for 10 to 15 minutes or until puffed and golden. Remove tarts to wire racks; cool 30 minutes. Sprinkle with remaining ¼ cup powdered sugar.

H.C. Muller

In the Breaking of Bread
Catholic Committee on Scouting and Camp Fire ~ Lake Charles, Louisiana

Chocolate Bread Pudding With Chocolate Liqueur Cream

makes 6 servings • prep: 20 min., cook: 1 hr., other: 15 min.

test kitchen tip: If you're entertaining and want to do as much as possible ahead, spoon the beaten cream mixture in Step 4 into 6 mounds on a baking sheet lined with wax paper, and freeze up to 6 hours. Let thaw 3 minutes before placing on top of each serving.

5 cups diced white bread	½ tsp. ground cinnamon
1 cup semisweet chocolate morsels	¼ tsp. salt
3 cups milk	1 tsp. vanilla extract
3 Tbsp. chocolate liqueur or crème de cacao	1 cup whipping cream
3 large egg yolks	2 Tbsp. chocolate liqueur or crème de cacao
⅓ cup sugar	Ground cinnamon

1. Preheat oven to 350°.

2. Combine bread and chocolate morsels in a greased 11- x 7-inch baking dish. Stir together milk and next 6 ingredients; pour milk mixture over bread mixture. Let stand 15 minutes.

3. Bake at 350° for 1 hour or until puffy and set.

4. Beat whipping cream until foamy; gradually add 2 Tbsp. chocolate liqueur, beating until soft peaks form. Cut bread pudding into squares, top with whipped cream, and sprinkle with ground cinnamon.

At Your Service: Southern Recipes, Places and Traditions
The Junior League of Gwinnett and North Fulton Counties ~ Duluth, Georgia

Chocolate liqueur and semisweet chocolate turn humble bread pudding made with slices of white bread into an uptown dessert fit for company. Whipped cream spiked with chocolate liqueur adds the crowning touch.

Chocolate Bread Pudding
With Chocolate Liqueur Cream

Cinnamon Pudding

makes 12 servings • prep: 20 min., cook: 46 min., other: 5 min.

English pudding recipes brought to America were traditionally savory and served as sides. But ingenious Southerners found ways to use the same culinary technique for sumptuous desserts. Here's a creamy baked pudding spiced with warm cinnamon flavor and topped with a rich syrup of brown sugar and butter.

test kitchen tip: To measure brown sugar, pack it firmly into a measuring cup until it's more than full, then scrape away the excess with a flat spatula.

2	cups firmly packed light brown sugar		2	tsp. baking powder
1½	cups water		2	tsp. ground cinnamon
2	Tbsp. butter or margarine		½	tsp. salt
⅛	tsp. salt		1	cup milk
2	tsp. vanilla extract, divided		2	Tbsp. butter or margarine, melted
2	cups all-purpose flour		1	cup chopped pecans
1	cup sugar			

1. Combine first 4 ingredients in a medium saucepan. Bring to a boil over medium heat, and cook, uncovered, 5 minutes. Remove from heat; stir in 1 tsp. vanilla. Set syrup aside.

2. Preheat oven to 350°.

3. Combine flour and next 4 ingredients in a large bowl; set aside. Combine milk, melted butter, and remaining 1 tsp. vanilla; add to flour mixture all at once, stirring until well blended. Pour batter into a greased 13- x 9-inch pan; pour syrup evenly over batter. Sprinkle with pecans.

4. Bake at 350° for 38 minutes or until edges are golden and pull away from sides of pan. Let stand 5 minutes. Serve warm.

Rebecca Rollins Boudreaux

Atchafalaya Legacy
Melville Women's Club ~ Melville, Louisiana

White Chocolate Crème Brûlée

makes 6 servings • prep: 30 min.; cook: 1 hr., 10 min.; other: 8 hr., 5 min.

Smooth-textured sweet brûlée isn't as hard to prepare as you might think. In this version, white chocolate adds an updated twist to the classic recipe.

test kitchen tip: If you don't have a kitchen blow torch, you can make the sugar topping on the stovetop. Place ¼ cup sugar and 1 Tbsp. water in a small heavy saucepan. Cook over medium heat 5 to 8 minutes or until golden. Resist the urge to stir, since doing so may cause the sugar to crystallize. Immediately pour the sugar mixture evenly over cold custards, spreading to form a thin layer.

¾	cup sugar, divided		3	(1-oz.) squares white chocolate,
5	egg yolks, lightly beaten			coarsely chopped
2	cups whipping cream		¼	tsp. vanilla extract

1. Preheat oven to 300°.

2. Combine ¼ cup sugar and egg yolks, stirring with a wire whisk until smooth; set aside.

3. Combine ¼ cup sugar and whipping cream in a heavy saucepan; cook over medium heat, stirring constantly, until sugar melts and mixture comes to a simmer (do not boil). Remove from heat; add chocolate, stirring until chocolate melts.

4. Gradually stir about one-fourth of hot cream mixture into egg yolk mixture; add to remaining cream mixture, stirring constantly. Add vanilla. Pour mixture into 6 (4-oz.) soufflé cups or custard cups. Place cups in a 13- x 9-inch pan; add hot water to pan to depth of ½ inch.

5. Bake, uncovered, at 300° for 1 hour and 10 minutes or until almost set. Remove cups from water; let cool completely on a wire rack. Cover and chill at least 8 hours or until ready to serve.

6. Sift remaining ¼ cup sugar evenly over each custard. Holding a kitchen blow torch about 2 inches from the top of each custard, heat the sugar, moving the torch back and forth, until sugar is completely melted and caramelized (about 1 minute). Let stand 5 minutes before serving to allow sugar to harden.

Lemon Ice Cream

makes 5 qt. • prep: 15 min.

Triple lemon flavor from lemon extract and fresh juice and rind perks up homemade ice cream.

5½	cups heavy whipping cream	2	tsp. lemon extract
5½	cups milk	2	cups fresh lemon juice (about 8
4	cups sugar		large lemons)
1	Tbsp. grated lemon rind		

1. Pour all ingredients into freezer container of a 5-qt. electric ice cream maker. Freeze according to manufacturer's instructions. (Instructions and times will vary.)

Jim Watkins

Bread from the Brook
The Church at Brook Hills ~ Birmingham, Alabama

test kitchen tip: After the ice cream has frozen, most electric ice cream makers that use ice and salt instruct you to cover the ice cream and let it "ripen" for about 1 hour. Newer ice cream makers using no salt or ice suggest transferring ice cream to an airtight container and freezing at least 1 hour to ripen. If you make it days in advance, take it out of the freezer 10 minutes before serving to soften.

Fresh Mango Sorbet

makes 1 qt. • prep: 20 min.

Fresh, sweet mango blended with mango nectar and tangy fresh lime juice in this creamy frozen dessert will make visions of a tropical island vacation dance in your head.

2	large ripe mangoes, peeled and	¾	cup sugar
	chopped	1	Tbsp. grated lime rind
1	cup mango nectar	½	cup fresh lime juice

1. Process all ingredients in a food processor until smooth. Pour mixture into freezer container of a 2-qt. electric ice cream maker. Freeze according to manufacturer's instructions. (Instructions and times will vary.)

Gracious Gator Cooks
The Junior League of Gainesville, Florida

test kitchen tip: Look for unblemished mangoes with yellow skin and a pretty red blush. Ripe ones will hold for a couple of days in a plastic bag in the refrigerator.

Oatmeal–Molasses Cookies

makes about 6 dozen • prep: 15 min., cook: 10 min. per batch

Tangy, dark-colored molasses in these coconut-oatmeal cookies keeps them soft.

freeze it: Make cookie dough through Step 3, omitting Step 1. Seal dough in an airtight container. Freeze up to 3 months. Let dough thaw in refrigerator overnight before proceeding with Step 4. Or if you prefer, freeze the baked cookies in an airtight container, and freeze up to 1 month.

2	cups sugar	1	tsp. baking soda
1	cup vegetable oil	1	tsp. salt
⅓	cup molasses	1	tsp. ground cinnamon
2	large eggs	2	cups quick-cooking oats, uncooked
2	cups all-purpose flour	1	cup raisins
1	tsp. baking powder	1	cup flaked coconut

1. Preheat oven to 350°.

2. Combine first 4 ingredients in a large mixing bowl. Beat at medium speed with an electric mixer until smooth.

3. Combine flour and next 4 ingredients; stir well. Add to sugar mixture, mixing well. Stir in oats, raisins, and coconut.

4. Drop dough by heaping teaspoonfuls onto lightly greased baking sheets. Bake at 350° for 10 minutes. Cool slightly on baking sheets; remove cookies to wire racks, and let cool completely.

Rum-Kissed Chocolate Cookies

makes 5 dozen • prep: 20 min., cook: 10 min.

The cookies are reminiscent of holiday rum balls with a combination of chocolate, dark rum, and pecans.

make it ahead: Everyone knows the wonder of eating a warm cookie from the oven. To make oven-fresh cookies from this recipe spontaneously, prepare the recipe through Step 3. Refrigerate the dough in an airtight container up to 2 weeks. Bake desired number of cookies as directed for 10 to 12 minutes.

12	(1-oz) squares semisweet chocolate, finely chopped	1	tsp. vanilla extract
		½	cup all-purpose flour
4	(1-oz) squares unsweetened chocolate, finely chopped	½	tsp. baking powder
		½	tsp. baking soda
¼	cup unsalted butter, softened	⅛	tsp. salt
2	cups sugar	2	cups semisweet chocolate morsels
4	large eggs	2	cups chopped pecans
1	Tbsp. dark rum		

1. Preheat oven to 350°.

2. Combine chocolate squares in a large glass bowl. Microwave at HIGH 2 minutes or until melted. Set aside.

3. Beat butter at medium speed with an electric mixer until creamy; gradually add sugar, beating well. Add eggs, 1 at a time, beating after each addition. Stir in rum and vanilla. Combine flour and next 3 ingredients; add to butter mixture, beating well. Stir in melted chocolate, chocolate morsels, and pecans, stirring well.

4. Drop dough by heaping tablespoonfuls onto ungreased baking sheets. Bake at 350° for 8 to 10 minutes. Cool slightly on baking sheets; remove to wire racks to cool completely.

10-Cup Cookies

makes 5½ dozen • prep: 20 min., cook: 12 min. per batch

These cookies are chock-full of all the pantry's best flavors—nutty-tasting oats, pecans, coconut, raisins, and chocolate morsels. The recipe yields more than 5 dozen, so it's a great choice for taking to a cookie exchange party.

1	cup granulated sugar		2	tsp. baking soda
1	cup firmly packed light brown sugar		1	tsp. baking powder
1	cup shortening		1	cup chopped pecans
1	cup peanut butter		1	cup flaked coconut
3	large eggs, lightly beaten		1	cup raisins
1	cup all-purpose flour		1	cup semisweet chocolate morsels
1	cup uncooked quick-cooking oats			

1. Preheat oven to 350°.

2. Combine first 4 ingredients in a large mixing bowl; beat at medium speed with an electric mixer until creamy. Add eggs, beating well.

3. Combine flour and next 3 ingredients; add to peanut butter mixture, and beat well. Stir in pecans and remaining ingredients. Drop dough by level teaspoonfuls onto lightly greased baking sheets.

4. Bake at 350° for 10 to 12 minutes or until golden. Immediately remove to wire racks to cool.

Texas-sized Almond Cookies

makes 3½ dozen • prep: 35 min., cook: 12 min. per batch

Almonds, toffee bits, and almond extract intensify the almond flavor of these hand-sized cookies, which reflect the "bigger-is-better" reputation of Texas.

test kitchen tip: Gather the family to shape the buttery dough for these big cookies into 3-inch balls. That's about the size of a tennis ball.

1	cup butter or margarine, softened	1	cup whole wheat flour
1	cup granulated sugar	1	tsp. baking soda
1	cup sifted powdered sugar	1	tsp. salt
1	cup vegetable oil	1	tsp. cream of tartar
2	large eggs	2	cups coarsely chopped almonds
1	tsp. almond extract	1	(6-oz.) package toffee bits
3½	cups all-purpose flour		Granulated sugar

1. Preheat oven to 350°.

2. Beat butter at medium speed with an electric mixer until creamy; gradually add 1 cup granulated sugar and powdered sugar, beating well. Add oil, eggs, and almond extract; beat well.

3. Combine flours, baking soda, salt, and cream of tartar; add to butter mixture, beating well. Stir in almonds and toffee bits.

4. Shape cookie dough into 3-inch balls; roll in additional granulated sugar. Place 5 inches apart on ungreased baking sheets. Flatten cookies in a criss-cross pattern with a fork dipped in granulated sugar.

5. Bake at 350° for 10 to 12 minutes. Cool slightly on baking sheets; remove to wire racks, and let cool completely.

White Chocolate Cherry Cookies

makes 5 dozen • prep: 25 min., cook: 15 min. per batch

test kitchen tip: For another flavor, substitute walnuts for pecans, and dried sweetened cranberries for cherries. If you'd like to dress up these as a gift or for a special occasion, drizzle each cookie with melted dark chocolate.

9	oz. white chocolate, coarsely chopped	⅔	cup firmly packed light brown sugar
1	cup coarsely chopped pecans	2	large eggs
1	cup dried tart cherries	1½	tsp. vanilla extract
1	cup unsalted butter, softened	2⅓	cups all-purpose flour
⅔	cup granulated sugar	1	tsp. baking soda
		½	tsp. salt

1. Preheat oven to 350°.

2. Combine first 3 ingredients in a bowl; set aside.

3. Beat butter and sugars at medium speed with an electric mixer until light and fluffy. Add eggs, 1 at a time, beating after each addition. Stir in vanilla. Combine flour, baking soda, and salt; add to butter mixture, beating just until blended. Stir in white chocolate mixture.

4. Shape dough into 1½-inch balls, and place 3 inches apart on prepared baking sheets. Bake at 350° for 13 to 15 minutes or until golden. Remove cookies to wire racks to cool.

Date Nugget Cookies

makes 3 dozen • prep: 20 min., cook: 12 min. per batch

If you like chewy cookies, here's your recipe. Dates, brown sugar, and walnuts make every bite a taste of heaven.

1	cup shortening	½	tsp. salt
1¼	cups firmly packed brown sugar	3	tsp. ground cinnamon
3	large eggs	2	cups chopped walnuts
2½	cups all-purpose flour	1½	cups chopped dates
1	tsp. baking soda	1	tsp. vanilla extract

1. Preheat oven to 350°.

2. Beat shortening at medium speed with an electric mixer until fluffy; gradually add sugar, beating well. Add eggs; beat well.

3. Combine flour and next 3 ingredients; gradually add to shortening mixture, beating well. Stir in walnuts, dates and vanilla. Shape dough into 1-inch balls; place 2 inches apart on greased baking sheets.

4. Bake at 350° for 12 minutes or until lightly browned. Cool slightly on baking sheets; remove to wire racks, and let cool completely.

test kitchen tip: Purchase chopped dates for this cookie, or chop whole dates. It's easier to chop whole dates if you dip your knife in water as you go. The water helps keep the dates from sticking to the knife.

Browned Butter-Pecan Shortbread

makes about 10½ dozen • prep: 30 min., cook: 18 min. per batch, other: 5 hr.

Buttery shortbread cookies are so tender they melt in your mouth. Toasted pecans and butter cooked until browned add a warm, cozy flavor that calls for a cup of hot tea or coffee and a few minutes to savor every bite.

1½	cups butter	3	cups all-purpose flour
¾	cup firmly packed brown sugar	1½	cups chopped toasted pecans
¾	cup powdered sugar		

1. Cook butter in a small heavy saucepan over medium heat, stirring constantly, 6 to 8 minutes or until butter begins to turn golden brown. Remove pan from heat immediately, and pour butter into a small bowl. Cover and chill 1 hour or until butter is cool and begins to solidify.

2. Beat browned butter at medium speed with an electric mixer until creamy. Gradually add sugars, beating until smooth. Gradually add flour to butter mixture, beating at low speed just until blended. Stir in pecans.

3. Shape dough into 4 (8-inch) logs. Wrap logs tightly in plastic wrap, and chill 4 hours or until firm.

4. Preheat oven to 350°.

5. Cut logs into ¼-inch-thick rounds; place on lightly greased baking sheets. Bake at 350° for 8 to 10 minutes or until lightly browned. Transfer to wire racks to cool.

test kitchen tip: Finely chopping the pecans make the logs easier to cut in Step 4.

Peanut Butter Fingers

makes 4 dozen • prep: 20 min., cook: 22 min., other: 35 min.

Pour a glass of cold milk to enjoy with these peanut butter bars topped with a marbled chocolate-peanut butter frosting.

1	cup all-purpose flour	⅓	cup creamy peanut butter
1	cup uncooked quick-cooking oats	1	large egg
½	cup granulated sugar	½	tsp. vanilla extract
½	cup firmly packed light brown sugar	1	cup semisweet chocolate morsels
½	tsp. baking soda	½	cup sifted powdered sugar
¼	tsp. salt	½	cup creamy peanut butter
½	cup butter or margarine, softened	6	Tbsp. milk

1. Preheat oven to 350°.

2. Combine first 10 ingredients in a large bowl. Beat at medium speed with an electric mixer until well blended. Firmly press mixture into a greased 13- x 9-inch pan. Bake at 350° for 20 to 22 minutes or until golden. Remove pan to wire rack; sprinkle immediately with chocolate morsels. Let stand 5 minutes, and spread to cover.

3. Whisk together powdered sugar, ½ cup peanut butter, and milk in a small bowl. Spoon mixture over melted chocolate layer in pan. Gently swirl chocolate and peanut butter with a knife to create a marbled effect. Cool at least 30 minutes in pan on a wire rack. Cut into bars.

freeze it: Bake these ultra-rich bars in a baking pan that includes a tight-fitting lid for storage. Once cooked and cut into bars, cover with lid, and freeze up to 2 months.

Chocolate-Peppermint Brownies

makes 16 • prep: 15 min., cook: 40 min. other: 45 min.

Peppermint extract flavors the dough and frosting for these brownies. If you're making them for the holidays, sprinkle crushed peppermint candy on top to offer a hint of the refreshing flavor.

½	cup plus 3 Tbsp. butter or margarine, divided	½	cup all-purpose flour
			Dash of salt
3½	(1-oz.) squares unsweetened chocolate, divided	1	tsp. peppermint extract, divided
1	cup granulated sugar	1	cup sifted powdered sugar
2	large eggs, lightly beaten	1	Tbsp. whipping cream

1. Preheat oven to 350°.

2. Melt ½ cup butter and 2 chocolate baking squares in a heavy saucepan over low heat; stirring occasionally. Gradually add granulated sugar and next 3 ingredients, stirring until blended. Stir in ¼ tsp. peppermint extract.

3. Pour batter into a lightly greased 8- x 8-inch square pan. Bake at 350° for 24 minutes or until a wooden pick inserted in center comes out clean. Cool completely in pan on a wire rack.

4. Melt 2 Tbsp. butter in a saucepan over low heat; stir in remaining ¾ tsp. peppermint extract, powdered sugar, and whipping cream. Spread over

test kitchen tip: For picture-perfect brownies, line the pan with aluminum foil, allowing edges to extend over the edges of pan before adding the batter. Continue as directed. After brownies have chilled, carefully lift the brownies from the pan using the foil as handles, and transfer to a cutting board. Cut the brownies into squares, pressing straight down with a sharp knife.

brownies. Chill 15 minutes. Melt remaining 1 Tbsp. butter and remaining 1½ baking squares in a small saucepan; cook over low heat until butter and chocolate melt, stirring occasionally. Drizzle chocolate mixture evenly over powdered sugar mixture, spreading into a smooth layer. Cover and chill at least 30 minutes. Cut into squares.

Loving Spoonfuls
Covenant House of Texas ~ Houston, Texas

Citrus Bars

makes 2 dozen • prep: 15 min., cook: 52 min.

If you like traditional ooey, gooey lemon bars topped with powdered sugar, you'll love this version that also includes fresh orange juice and rind.

1	cup butter, softened	1	tsp. finely grated orange rind
2¼	cups all-purpose flour, divided	4	large eggs, beaten
½	cup powdered sugar	1	tsp. baking powder
1¾	cups granulated sugar	¼	tsp. salt
⅓	cup fresh lemon or lime juice	1	Tbsp. powdered sugar
⅓	cup fresh orange juice		

test kitchen tip: Grate and measure the orange rind before squeezing the fresh juice. If you prefer an extra-tart flavor, add 1 tsp. of finely grated lemon or lime rind.

1. Preheat oven to 350°.

2. Beat butter at medium speed with an electric mixer until creamy; add 2 cups flour and ½ cup powdered sugar. Beat until mixture forms a smooth dough. Press mixture into a lightly greased 13- x 9-inch pan.

3. Bake at 350° for 20 to 22 minutes or until lightly browned.

4. Meanwhile, whisk together remaining ¼ cup flour, granulated sugar, and next 6 ingredients; pour over baked crust. Bake at 350° for 28 to 30 more minutes or until set. Cool in pan on a wire rack. Sprinkle evenly with 1 Tbsp. powdered sugar, and cut into bars.

the key to flavor

Though a 1926 hurricane wiped out citrus groves in the Florida Keys and ended the commercial success of Key limes there, the famous cool, creamy pie named for the Ping-Pong-sized fruit has become a recognized symbol of this southernmost tip of the United States. Scrubby, thorned Key lime trees grow in almost every backyard in the subtropical Keys, but after the storm, growers found less temperamental and thornless Persian lime trees easier to grow. Still, the juice from the newer varieties can't replace that of the small, tart, seedy Key limes necessary for the traditional pie that is pale yellow, *never* green. Locally, the juice also is popular in jams and with seafood, but it will forever be relished as the essential ingredient of one of the South's most famous desserts.

Oatmeal Carmelitas

Oatmeal Carmelitas

makes 2 dozen • prep: 25 min., cook: 36 min.

Cubes of chewy caramels provide the distinctive flavor for bar cookies also packed with chocolate morsels and pecans.

2 cups all-purpose flour
2 cups uncooked quick-cooking oats
1½ cups firmly packed light brown sugar
1 tsp. baking soda
¼ tsp. salt
1 cup butter, melted

1 (12-oz.) package semisweet chocolate morsels
½ cup chopped pecans or walnuts, toasted (optional)
1 (14-oz.) package caramels
⅓ cup half-and-half

1. Preheat oven to 350°.

2. Stir together first 5 ingredients in a large bowl. Add butter, stirring until mixture is crumbly. Set aside half of mixture (about 2¾ cups). Press remaining half of mixture into bottom of a lightly greased 13- x 9-inch pan. Sprinkle evenly with chocolate morsels, and, if desired, pecans.

3. Microwave caramels and half-and-half in a microwave-safe bowl at MEDIUM (50% power) 3 minutes. Stir and microwave at MEDIUM 1 to 3 more minutes or until mixture is smooth. Let stand 1 minute. Pour evenly over chocolate morsels. Sprinkle with reserved crumb mixture.

4. Bake at 350° for 30 minutes or until light golden brown. Cool completely in pan on a wire rack. Cut into bars.

make it ahead: Have Oatmeal Carmelitas on hand for unexpected guests. Layer the bar cookies in between sheets of parchment or wax paper, and seal in an airtight container. Store at room temperature up to a week, or freeze up to 1 month.

Simply Heaven Fudge

makes about 64 pieces • prep: 10 min., cook: 12 min.

Make this fudge with or without a handful of roasted, salted pecans to suit the flavor preference of your family or gift recipients.

1⅔ cups sugar
⅔ cup evaporated milk
2 Tbsp. butter

2 cups miniature marshmallows
1½ cups semisweet chocolate morsels
2 tsp. vanilla extract

1. Bring first 3 ingredients to a boil in a large heavy saucepan over medium heat; boil, stirring constantly, until a candy thermometer registers 234° (soft ball stage) (about 7 minutes).

2. Remove from heat; stir in marshmallows and chocolate morsels until smooth. Stir in vanilla.

3. Pour chocolate mixture into a buttered 8-inch square pan; cool completely. Cut into 1-inch squares.

test kitchen tip: A candy thermometer simplifies the process of bringing the sugar, evaporated milk, and butter to the soft ball stage (234°). Make sure the thermometer isn't touching the bottom of the pot, and be sure to read the temperature at eye level.

Mildred's Toffee

makes about 1½ lb. • prep: 15 min., cook: 20 min., other: 1 hr.

Break this chocolate-coated candy into bite-sized pieces. Chopped toasted almonds stand in for pecans for a delicious variation.

test kitchen tip: Use butter to prepare this classic candy. Don't substitute margarine.

1½ cups chopped toasted pecans, divided
1 cup sugar
1 cup butter
1 Tbsp. light corn syrup
¼ cup water
1 cup semisweet chocolate morsels

1. Spread 1 cup pecans into a 9-inch circle on a lightly greased baking sheet or a marble candy slab.

2. Bring sugar and next 3 ingredients to a boil in a heavy saucepan over medium heat, stirring constantly. Cook until mixture is golden brown and a candy thermometer registers 290° to 310° (about 15 minutes). Pour sugar mixture over pecans on baking sheet.

3. Sprinkle with morsels; let stand 30 seconds. Spread melted morsels evenly over top; sprinkle with remaining ½ cup chopped pecans. Let stand 1 hour or until cool. Break into bite-size pieces. Store in an airtight container.

Macadamia Nut Brittle

makes 1 lb. • prep: 20 min., cook: 15 min., other: 1 hr.

Peanut and pecan brittle candies are longtime Southern treats. Now that macadamia nuts are easy to come by, use this recipe to make another nutty version.

test kitchen tip: Test the accuracy of your candy thermometer before cooking by letting it stand in boiling water for 10 minutes. If the thermometer registers 212°, it's in good condition. If it measures above or below 212°, make adjustments when cooking.

1 cup sugar
½ cup light corn syrup
¼ cup water
¾ cup whole macadamia nuts
½ cup chopped macadamia nuts
1 Tbsp. butter or margarine
½ tsp. vanilla extract
⅛ tsp. baking soda

1. Combine first 3 ingredients in a large saucepan. Cook over medium heat, stirring constantly, until sugar dissolves. Cover and cook over medium heat 2 to 3 minutes to wash down sugar crystals from sides of pan.

2. Add whole and chopped macadamia nuts; cook over medium heat, stirring constantly until a candy thermometer registers 300° (hard crack stage). Remove from heat. Stir in butter, vanilla, and soda.

3. Working rapidly, pour mixture into a buttered 15- x 10-inch jelly-roll pan, spreading thinly. Let stand 1 hour or until cool. Break into pieces. Store in an airtight container.

main dishes

Ham-and-Greens Pot Pie With Cornbread Crust, page 288

Beef With Red Wine Sauce

makes 6 servings • prep: 25 min., cook: 6 hr.

Flavorful chuck roast cooks all day in a slow-cooker while it soaks in the flavors of red wine, onion, and beef broth. Serve it over egg noodles or rice. Best of all, dinner is done when you arrive home.

test kitchen tip: Substitute ½ cup beef broth and ½ cup water in place of the red wine, if you prefer.

3   lb. boneless beef chuck roast, cut into 1-inch pieces
1   medium onion, sliced
1   lb. fresh mushrooms, halved
1   (1.61-oz.) package brown gravy mix
1   (10½-oz.) can beef broth
1   cup red wine
2   Tbsp. tomato paste
1   bay leaf
Hot cooked egg noodles or rice

1. Place first 3 ingredients in a 6-qt. slow cooker.

2. Whisk together gravy mix and next 3 ingredients; pour evenly over beef and vegetables. Add bay leaf.

3. Cover and cook on HIGH 6 hours. Discard bay leaf. Serve over noodles.

Sloppy Joe Shepherd's Pie

makes 8 to 10 servings • prep: 15 min., cook: 45 min., other: 5 min.

An old time English favorite, shepherd's pie is a meat casserole traditionally made with lamb and topped with mashed potatoes. This updated version uses a beef barbecue base and mashed potatoes on top that include Cheddar cheese and green onions.

test kitchen tip: We considered this mildly hot. Adjust the amount of pickled jalapeños (and liquid from the jar) to suit your family's tastes.

1½   lb. lean ground beef
1   (14½-oz.) can diced tomatoes
1¼   cups ketchup
½   cup bottled barbecue sauce
1   Tbsp. Worcestershire sauce
2   Tbsp. chopped pickled jalapeños (optional)
1   Tbsp. liquid from pickled jalapeños (optional)
1   (22-oz.) package refrigerated or frozen mashed potatoes
2   cups (8 oz.) shredded Cheddar cheese, divided
⅓   cup sliced green onions
½   tsp. salt
¼   tsp. pepper

1. Preheat oven to 350°.

2. Cook ground beef in a large skillet over medium-high heat, stirring until beef crumbles and is no longer pink; drain well. Return cooked beef to skillet.

3. Stir in tomatoes, next 3 ingredients, and, if desired, jalapeños and liquid. Spoon into a lightly greased 13- x 9-inch baking dish.

4. Prepare mashed potatoes according to package directions. Stir in 1 cup shredded Cheddar cheese, green onions, salt, and pepper. Spread evenly over meat mixture in casserole dish, spreading potatoes to edge of dish.

5. Bake at 350° for 25 minutes; sprinkle 1 cup shredded Cheddar cheese on potatoes. Bake 5 more minutes or until cheese is melted. Let stand 5 minutes before serving.

Festive Cajun Pepper Steak

makes 4 to 6 servings • **prep: 20 min.; cook: 1 hr., 25 min.**

Cajun seasoning kicks up the flavor of saucy sirloin beef tips spooned over mashed potatoes.

1½ lb. sirloin beef tips
1 tsp. salt-free Cajun seasoning
1 Tbsp. vegetable oil
1 medium-size green bell pepper, chopped
1 onion, chopped
3 garlic cloves, minced
1 (14½-oz.) can beef broth
1 (14½-oz.) can diced tomatoes, undrained
2 tsp. Worcestershire sauce
1 tsp. white wine vinegar
½ tsp. dried basil
¼ tsp. salt
⅛ tsp. pepper
1 (22-oz.) package refrigerated or frozen mashed potatoes
2 Tbsp. cornstarch
2 Tbsp. cold water

make it a meal: Round out the meal with a side of steamed broccoli spears tossed with lemon-pepper and melted butter.

1. Sprinkle beef tips with Cajun seasoning.

2. Cook beef in hot oil in large skillet over medium–high heat 10 minutes or until browned. Add bell pepper, onion, and garlic; sauté 3 minutes.

3. Stir in broth and next 6 ingredients. Bring to a boil; reduce heat, cover, and simmer 1 hour or until meat is tender.

4. Prepare mashed potatoes according to package directions.

5. Stir together cornstarch and water until smooth; stir into meat mixture. Bring to a boil; cook, stirring constantly, 2 minutes or until thickened. Serve over mashed potatoes.

Boarding House Meat Loaf

makes 6 servings • prep: 15 min.; cook: 1 hr., 12 min.

Miss Mary Bobo's Boarding House in Lynchburg, Tennessee, is no longer a boarding house, but it's still known for serving up Southern family-style meals. This sauce-topped meat loaf is a delicious example of the cuisine served there for 100 years.

½	green bell pepper, chopped	¾	cup uncooked regular oats
½	small onion, chopped	¼	cup ketchup
1½	lb. lean ground beef	1½	tsp. salt
2	large eggs, beaten		Meat Loaf Sauce

1. Preheat oven to 350°.

2. Microwave green bell pepper and onion in a microwave-safe bowl at HIGH 2 minutes.

3. Combine onion mixture, ground beef, and next 4 ingredients. Shape into a loaf. Place in a lightly greased 9- x 5-inch loaf pan.

4. Bake at 350° for 45 minutes. Remove from oven, and pour off pan juices. Spread half of Meat Loaf Sauce evenly over meat loaf; bake 25 more minutes. Remove from pan, and serve with remaining Meat Loaf Sauce.

Meat Loaf Sauce

makes about 1 cup • prep: 10 min., cook: 10 min.

test kitchen tip: For a spicier sauce, substitute ¾ cup chili sauce for ketchup.

2	Tbsp. butter	¾	cup ketchup
½	small onion, chopped	1	Tbsp. cider vinegar
½	green bell pepper, chopped		

1. Melt butter in a large skillet over medium-high heat; add onion and bell pepper, and sauté 5 minutes or until vegetables are tender. Stir in ketchup and vinegar, and simmer, stirring constantly, until sauce thickens.

Creamy Dijon Lamb Chops

makes 4 servings • prep: 15 min., cook: 30 min., other: 5 min.

A smooth sauce of whipping cream, mustard, and fresh herbs blankets juicy baked lamb chops. Rosemary and lamb have been a traditional duo for centuries.

8	(2-inch-thick) lamb chops, trimmed	½	cup whipping cream
½	tsp. salt	⅓	cup Dijon mustard
¼	tsp. freshly ground pepper	2	Tbsp. chopped fresh thyme
1	Tbsp. olive oil	1	to 2 Tbsp. chopped fresh rosemary
2	garlic cloves, pressed		

make it a meal: Creamy Dijon Lamb Chops served with couscous and fresh baby carrots make an easy and delicious meal for company.

1. Preheat oven to 400°.

2. Sprinkle lamb chops evenly with salt and pepper.

3. Brown chops in hot oil in a heavy skillet over medium-high heat 2 minutes on each side; place chops in a 13- x 9-inch baking dish, reserving drippings in skillet.

4. Bake at 400° for 15 minutes or until a meat thermometer inserted into thickest portion registers 150° (medium rare). Let lamb chops stand 5 minutes before serving.

5. Sauté garlic in reserved drippings over medium heat 3 minutes or until lightly browned.

6. Stir together cream and next 3 ingredients in a small bowl. Add mixture to skillet, and bring to a boil over medium heat, stirring occasionally. Reduce heat, and simmer 5 minutes. Serve sauce with chops.

Talk about impressive—a sausage-pear-fig stuffing is rolled into this roast, which is served with a tangy-sweet sauce of fig preserves, Madeira, and balsamic vinegar. It's a stunning centerpiece for any holiday table.

Fig-Balsamic Roasted Pork Loin

makes 8 to 10 servings • **prep: 35 min.; cook: 1 hr., 45 min.; other: 15 min.**

½	lb. ground pork sausage	1	(4-lb.) boneless pork loin roast
1¾	cups herb-seasoned stuffing mix	1	tsp. salt
1	large ripe Bartlett pear, peeled and chopped	1	to 2 Tbsp. cracked pepper
		1	(11.5-oz.) jar fig preserves
½	red bell pepper, finely chopped	1	cup Madeira wine
⅓	cup chopped dried figs	2	Tbsp. balsamic vinegar
½	cup hot chicken broth	¼	cup butter or margarine
1	Tbsp. fresh minced thyme	¼	cup all-purpose flour

test kitchen tip: Purchase a pork loin, not a rolled pork loin roast (which has 2 loins tied together with netting). Don't trim away the entire fat cap on top of the loin; leaving a thin layer prevents the meat from drying out.

1. Preheat oven to 375°.

2. Cook sausage in a large skillet over medium-high heat, stirring often, 4 to 5 minutes or until lightly browned. Drain well. Stir together sausage, stuffing mix, and next 5 ingredients. Set aside.

3. Butterfly pork loin roast by making a lengthwise cut down center of 1 flat side, cutting to within ½ inch of the bottom. (Do not cut all the way through roast.) Open roast, forming a rectangle, and place between 2 sheets of heavy-duty plastic wrap. Flatten to ½-inch thickness using a meat mallet or rolling pin. Sprinkle evenly with salt and pepper. Spoon sausage mixture evenly over pork loin roast, leaving a ½-inch border. Roll up roast, and tie with string at 1½-inch intervals. Place roast, seam side down, in a greased shallow roasting pan.

4. Bake at 375° for 55 to 60 minutes or until a meat thermometer inserted into thickest portion registers 145°. Remove roast from pan, reserving drippings in pan. Stir together fig preserves, Madeira, and balsamic vinegar. Spoon half of preserves mixture evenly over roast.

5. Bake at 375° for 20 to 30 more minutes or until meat thermometer registers 155°. Let roast stand 15 minutes before slicing.

6. Melt butter in a medium saucepan; whisk in flour until smooth. Cook, whisking constantly, 3 minutes. Whisk in reserved pan drippings and remaining fig preserves mixture, and cook over medium-high heat 5 minutes. Serve sauce with roast.

Ham-and-Greens Pot Pie With Cornbread Crust

(pictured on page 281)

makes 8 to 10 servings • prep: 15 min., cook: 1 hr., other: 10 min.

make it ahead: To get a head start on this recipe, make it a day in advance through Step 3; cover and refrigerate. The following day, simply reheat the filling in the microwave; uncover and continue with Step 4.

4	cups chopped cooked ham	1	(16-oz.) package frozen chopped
2	Tbsp. vegetable oil		collard greens
3	Tbsp. all-purpose flour	1	(16-oz.) can black-eyed peas, rinsed
3	cups chicken broth		and drained
1	(16-oz.) package frozen seasoning	½	tsp. dried crushed red pepper
	blend		Cornbread Crust Batter

1. Preheat oven to 425°.

2. Sauté ham in hot oil in a Dutch oven over medium-high heat 5 minutes or until lightly browned. Add flour, and cook, stirring constantly, 1 minute. Gradually add chicken broth, and cook, stirring constantly, 3 minutes or until broth begins to thicken.

3. Bring mixture to a boil, and add seasoning blend and collard greens; return to a boil, and cook, stirring often, 15 minutes. Stir in black-eyed peas and crushed red pepper; spoon hot mixture into a lightly greased 13- x 9-inch baking dish.

4. Pour Cornbread Crust Batter evenly over hot filling mixture. Bake at 425° for 20 to 25 minutes or until cornbread is golden brown and set. Let stand 10 minutes before serving.

Cornbread Crust Batter

makes enough batter for 1 (13- x 9-inch) crust • prep: 10 min.

1½	cups white cornmeal mix	2	large eggs, lightly beaten
½	cup all-purpose flour	1½	cups buttermilk
1	tsp. sugar		

1. Combine first 3 ingredients; make a well in the center of mixture. Add eggs and buttermilk to cornmeal mixture, stirring just until moistened.

the country ham tradition Like the Jamestown colonists who were the first to cure and smoke hams for preservation, you can find Southerners in Virginia, North Carolina, Georgia, Kentucky, and Missouri who still cure the salty, mahogany hams just to carry on family tradition. Says TV personality Willard Scott in *The Ultimate Guide to Country Ham, An American Delicacy,* "It's the romance of it, it's our culture...." That's why he continued the family tradition for years on his Virginia farm despite a jet-set lifestyle. In the old days curing involved months, and baking a brown sugar crusted ham meant days of work. Today, a cooked and sliced one can be shipped to your door. You can buy just a few slices at the grocery store to fry and serve with red eye gravy and biscuits. Or you can enjoy it in upscale restaurants where noted chefs know the value of bringing history to life on their tables.

Sausage-and-Wild Rice Casserole

makes 8 to 10 servings • prep: 20 min.; cook: 1 hr., 30 min.; other: 5 min.

Wild rice lends a nutty flavor and chewy texture to a hot, hearty casserole topped with chopped toasted pecans.

½   cup chopped pecans
1   (1-lb.) package sage ground pork sausage
1   Tbsp. butter
1   large onion, chopped
1   cup chopped celery
2   (6-oz.) packages long-grain and wild rice mix

2   Tbsp. chopped fresh flat-leaf parsley
1   Tbsp. chopped fresh or 1 tsp. dried rubbed sage
½   tsp. freshly ground pepper
3½   cups low-sodium chicken broth

make it a meal: Round out a complete meal by adding Brussels sprouts and baked apples.

1. Preheat oven to 325°.

2. Heat ½ cup chopped pecans in a large nonstick skillet over medium-low heat, stirring often, 5 minutes or until toasted. Remove pecans from skillet; set aside.

3. Brown sausage in same skillet over medium-high heat, stirring often, 10 minutes or until meat crumbles and is no longer pink. Remove sausage from skillet using a slotted spoon; reserve drippings in skillet.

4. Melt butter in hot drippings over medium heat. Add onion and celery, and sauté 10 to 15 minutes or until celery is tender.

5. Remove 1 seasoning packet from rice mixes; reserve for another use. Combine sausage, vegetable mixture, remaining seasoning packet, rice, and next 3 ingredients in a lightly greased 13- x 9-inch baking dish. Stir in chicken broth until well blended.

6. Bake, covered, at 325° for 1 hour or until liquid is almost absorbed. Let stand 5 minutes. Sprinkle with reserved pecans.

Oven-Fried Parmesan Chicken Strips

makes 5 servings • prep: 15 min., cook: 30 min.

Make your own crunchy chicken strips; they're easy and better than store-bought or carry-out. The hot, crisp strips take only 15 minutes to get into the oven. And it's easy to freeze leftovers for later.

2   Tbsp. butter
⅓   cup reduced-fat baking mix
⅓   cup grated Parmesan cheese

1½   tsp. Old Bay seasoning
⅛   tsp. black pepper
2   lb. chicken breast strips

freeze it: Cool baked chicken strips completely, and place in a large zip-top plastic freezer bag; seal and freeze up to 1 month. To reheat, bake strips (still frozen) at 425° for 20 minutes or until hot and crisp.

1. Preheat oven to 425°.

2. Melt butter in a 15- x 10-inch jelly-roll pan in a 425° oven.

3. Place baking mix and next 3 ingredients in a large zip-top plastic bag; shake well to combine. Add chicken, several pieces at a time, shaking well to coat. Arrange chicken in melted butter in hot baking dish.

4. Bake at 425° for 30 minutes or until chicken is done, turning once. Serve immediately.

Peppery Chicken Fried Chicken

makes 8 to 10 servings • prep: 35 min., cook: 42 min.

Like the famous chicken fried steak of Texas, flattened chicken breasts are breaded, skillet-fried, and served with cream gravy for this family favorite.

test kitchen tip: Cut leftover chicken into strips, and serve over salad greens drizzled with creamy Ranch or blue cheese dressing.

8   (6-oz.) skinned and boned chicken breasts
3½   tsp. salt, divided
2½   tsp. freshly ground black pepper, divided
76   saltine crackers (2 sleeves), crushed

2½   cups all-purpose flour, divided
1   tsp. baking powder
1   tsp. ground red pepper
8   cups milk, divided
4   large eggs
Peanut oil

1. Place chicken breasts between 2 sheets of heavy-duty plastic wrap, and flatten to ¼-inch thickness using a meat mallet or rolling pin.

2. Sprinkle ½ tsp. salt and ½ tsp. black pepper evenly over chicken. Set aside.

3. Combine cracker crumbs, 2 cups flour, baking powder, 1½ tsp. salt, 1 tsp. black pepper, and ground red pepper.

4. Whisk together 1½ cups milk and eggs. Dredge chicken in cracker crumb mixture; dip in milk mixture, and dredge in cracker mixture again.

5. Pour oil to a depth of ½ inch in a 12-inch skillet (do not use a nonstick skillet). Heat to 360°. Fry chicken, in batches, 10 minutes, adding oil as needed. Turn and fry 4 to 5 more minutes or until golden brown. Remove to a wire rack in a jelly-roll pan. Keep chicken warm in a 225° oven. Carefully drain hot oil, reserving cooked bits and 2 Tbsp. drippings in skillet.

6. Whisk together remaining ½ cup flour, remaining 1½ tsp. salt, remaining 1 tsp. black pepper, and remaining 6½ cups milk. Pour mixture into reserved drippings in skillet; cook over medium-high heat, whisking constantly, 10 to 12 minutes or until thickened. Serve gravy with chicken.

Oven-Fried Bacon-Wrapped Chicken Thighs

makes 8 servings • prep: 20 min.; cook: 1 hr.

Two Southern favorites—bacon and cornmeal—add flavor and crunch to boned chicken thighs. Wrap bacon around the chicken and dredge it in cornmeal before baking until crisp.

8	bacon slices	1	Tbsp. salt
8	skinned and boned chicken thighs	1	tsp. paprika
1	cup yellow cornmeal	1	tsp. pepper

test kitchen tip: Substituting yellow cornmeal mix for regular yellow cornmeal works great, too.

1. Preheat oven to 350°.

2. Arrange bacon slices on paper towels on a microwave-safe plate in microwave. Top with paper towel. Microwave at HIGH 30 seconds to 1 minute or just until bacon is limp and heated through. (Do not fully cook bacon.)

3. Wrap each chicken thigh with a piece of bacon; secure with a wooden pick, if desired.

4. Combine cornmeal and next 3 ingredients in a bowl. Dredge chicken in cornmeal mixture. Arrange on a wire rack coated with cooking spray in a lightly greased broiler or roasting pan.

5. Bake at 350° for 50 minutes to 1 hour or until chicken is done.

Stuffed Peppers With Chicken and Corn

makes 8 servings • prep: 25 min., cook: 40 min.

Mix chicken and a convenient package of corn soufflé with taco seasoning and green chiles for a Southwestern-style filling to bake in bell peppers.

4	large red bell peppers	½	medium-size sweet onion, finely chopped
1	(12-oz.) package frozen corn soufflé, thawed	1	Tbsp. taco seasoning
3	cups chopped cooked chicken	2	cups (8 oz.) shredded Monterey Jack cheese with peppers, divided
1	cup fresh corn kernels		
¾	cup soft breadcrumbs	Garnish: chopped fresh cilantro	
1	(4.5-oz.) can chopped green chiles, drained		

make it a meal: Entertain friends for dinner with Stuffed Peppers With Chicken and Corn, Spanish rice, and an avocado salad. Cap off the meal with coffee ice cream drizzled with dulce de leche ice cream topping.

1. Preheat broiler.

2. Cut peppers in half lengthwise, leaving stems intact; remove seeds. Place, cut sides down, on a lightly greased baking sheet. Broil 6 inches from heat 4 to 5 minutes or until peppers begin to blister. Set aside.

3. Reduce oven temperature to 375°.

4. Combine corn soufflé and next 6 ingredients; stir in 1 cup cheese.

5. Turn peppers cut sides up; spoon corn mixture evenly into peppers.

6. Bake at 375° for 25 minutes. Top evenly with remaining 1 cup cheese; bake 5 to 10 more minutes or until cheese melts. Garnish, if desired.

Grilled Chicken With White Barbecue Sauce

makes 5 servings • prep: 15 min., cook: 20 min., other: 4 hr.

Aromatic herb flavors scent the air when you grill this chicken seasoned with a dry rub. The flavors go well with a creamy white barbecue sauce spiced with tangy brown mustard and a spoonful of horseradish.

make it a meal: Serve Grilled Chicken With White Barbecue Sauce alongside a red cabbage slaw, marinated potato salad, and freshly squeezed lemonade.

3	lb. chicken thighs and drumsticks		1	tsp. onion powder
1	Tbsp. dried thyme		½	tsp. salt
1	Tbsp. dried oregano		½	tsp. pepper
1	Tbsp. ground cumin			White Barbecue Sauce
1	Tbsp. paprika			

1. Rinse chicken, and pat dry with paper towels. Combine thyme and next 6 ingredients; rub mixture evenly over chicken. Place chicken in a large zip-top plastic freezer bag. Seal and chill 4 hours.

2. Preheat grill to medium-high heat (350° to 400°). Remove chicken from bag, discarding bag.

3. Grill, covered with grill lid, over medium-high heat (350° to 400°) for 8 to 10 minutes on each side or until a meat thermometer inserted into thickest portion registers 165° or to desired doneness. Serve with White Barbecue Sauce.

bring on the barbecue

The fastest way to start an argument in the South is to bring up college football or barbecue, two subjects on which no one agrees. The first barbecue discrepancy is the meat. Pork is preferred in most parts of the South. You'll find brisket and sometimes goat in Texas, lamb in Kentucky, and chicken in Maryland. Then there is the sauce, most of which is ketchup-based, but in eastern North Carolina and Virginia, the favorite is a clear vinegar type. In central South Carolina, mustard rules. Alabama has a favorite mayonnaise-based white barbecue sauce. And in Texas, sauce is optional. There the definition of "barbecue" simply means the act of slowly roasting the meat in a deeply dug pit. Memphis is famous for pork ribs and the World Championship Barbecue Contest each May, where you can sample it all and pick your favorite.

White Barbecue Sauce

makes 1¾ cups • prep: 10 min., other: 2 hr.

1½ cups mayonnaise

¼ cup white wine vinegar

1 garlic clove, minced

1 Tbsp. coarse ground pepper

1 Tbsp. spicy brown mustard

1 tsp. sugar

1 tsp. salt

2 tsp. horseradish

1. Stir together all ingredients until well blended. Store in an airtight container in refrigerator at least 2 hours and up to 1 week.

Lime Chicken With Grilled Pineapple

makes 6 servings • prep: 35 min.; cook: 18 min.; other: 2 hr., 5 min.

A smoky grilled flavor seasons the chicken breasts as well as pineapple and orange slices for a honey-kissed fruit salsa. Jalapeño adds a little heat to both the chicken and salsa.

make it a meal: Serve Lime Chicken With Grilled Pineapple with Spanish rice from a mix and a green salad. Finish the meal with a purchased berry sorbet.

6	skinned and boned chicken breasts
1	tsp. salt, divided
1	tsp. pepper, divided
1	cup fresh lime juice, divided
2	jalapeño peppers, seeded, minced, and divided
½	cup pineapple juice
2	garlic cloves, minced
½	cup tequila (optional)
1	pineapple, peeled, cored, and cut horizontally in half
1	orange, sliced (¼ inch thick)
2	Tbsp. honey
½	tsp. grated lime rind

1. Place chicken between 2 sheets of plastic wrap, and flatten to a ¼-inch thickness, using a meat mallet or rolling pin. Sprinkle evenly with ½ tsp. salt and ½ tsp. pepper.

2. Whisk together remaining ½ tsp. salt, remaining ½ tsp. pepper, ¾ cup lime juice, 1 minced jalapeño pepper, pineapple juice, garlic, and tequila, if desired, in a medium bowl.

3. Place chicken and lime mixture in a shallow bowl or a large zip-top plastic freezer bag. Cover or seal, and chill 2 hours.

4. Preheat grill to medium-high heat (350° to 400°).

5. Drain chicken, discarding marinade. Grill, covered with grill lid, over medium-high heat (350° to 400°) 4 minutes on each side or until done. Let stand 5 minutes before serving.

6. Grill pineapple and orange slices 5 minutes on each side, watching to prevent burning; coarsely chop pineapple, and place in a medium bowl. Stir in remaining ¼ cup lime juice, remaining 1 minced jalapeño, honey, and lime rind. Serve with chicken and grilled orange slices.

Chicken Cobbler With Caramelized Onions

makes 6 servings • prep: 40 min.; cook: 1 hr., 18 min.

Pecans and Parmesan cheese are smashed between two layers of pastry used for the lattice top strips to make this savory main dish company-fancy.

⅓ cup butter or margarine

2 large sweet onions, diced

¼ cup all-purpose flour

1 (12-oz.) can evaporated milk

1 cup chicken broth

½ cup dry white wine

1 Tbsp. chicken bouillon granules

¼ tsp. pepper

3 cups coarsely chopped cooked chicken

3 Tbsp. chopped fresh parsley

1 (15-oz.) package refrigerated piecrusts

½ cup finely chopped pecans, toasted

½ cup grated Parmesan cheese

make it a meal: For easy entertaining, serve Chicken Cobbler With Caramelized Onions alongside a purchased spinach salad kit complete with salad dressing.

1. Preheat oven to 425°.

2. Melt butter in a large skillet over medium heat; add onion, and sauté 20 minutes or until caramel colored. Add flour, and cook, stirring constantly, 1 minute. Gradually stir in evaporated milk, chicken broth, and wine; cook, stirring constantly, 5 minutes or until thickened. Add bouillon and pepper. Remove from heat; stir in chicken and parsley. Pour chicken mixture into a lightly greased 10-inch deep-dish pie plate.

3. Unroll piecrusts on a lightly floured surface. Sprinkle 1 piecrust with pecans and Parmesan cheese. Top with remaining piecrust. Roll into a 14-inch circle; press edges to seal. Cut into ½-inch-wide strips. Arrange strips in a lattice design over filling, reserving any extra strips; fold edges under, and crimp.

4. Bake at 425° for 35 to 40 minutes or until golden brown. Place remaining strips on a lightly greased baking sheet. Bake at 425° for 10 to 12 minutes or until golden brown. Serve with cobbler.

Citrus-and-Herb Turkey With Cranberry Salsa

makes 18 servings • prep: 20 min., cook: 2 hr.

Rubbing a fresh herb butter under the skin and anchoring citrus slices in those same pockets before baking helps to keep turkey breast meat moist and delicious. Serve it with a colorful cranberry, orange, and bell pepper salsa for a unique twist on holiday tradition.

test kitchen tip: Use leftovers to make a delicious sandwich. Spread 1 side of a whole wheat bread slice with cream cheese. Top with thin slices of turkey and a spoonful of Cranberry Salsa. Top with remaining bread slice.

1	(7½-lb.) bone-in turkey breast	2	oranges, thinly sliced
1	tsp. salt	2	lemons, thinly sliced
1	tsp. freshly ground pepper		Vegetable cooking spray
1	Tbsp. butter or margarine, softened	1	large onion, quartered
3	Tbsp. chopped fresh rosemary	3	cups Riesling
3	Tbsp. chopped fresh sage		Cranberry Salsa

1. Preheat oven to 325°.

2. Sprinkle turkey breast evenly with salt and pepper.

3. Stir together butter, rosemary, and sage. Loosen skin from turkey without detaching it; spread butter mixture under skin. Arrange one-fourth of orange and lemon slices over butter mixture. Gently pull skin over fruit. Coat with cooking spray. Place turkey in an aluminum foil-lined baking pan coated with cooking spray. Place onion and remaining orange and lemon slices in pan. Drizzle with wine.

4. Bake at 325° for 2 hours or until a meat thermometer inserted in thickest portion registers 165° or to desired doneness, basting every 30 minutes. Cover loosely with aluminum foil coated with cooking spray to prevent excessive browning after 1 hour and 30 minutes, if necessary. Serve with Cranberry Salsa.

Cranberry Salsa

makes 1¾ cups • prep: 10 min., other: 8 hr.

1½	cups fresh cranberries	2	Tbsp. orange juice
1	tsp. grated orange rind	¼	to ½ tsp. ground allspice
1	orange, peeled and chopped	¼	tsp. salt
½	yellow bell pepper, diced	2	tsp. olive oil
⅓	cup sugar		

1. Pulse cranberries in a blender or food processor 5 or 6 times until coarsely chopped, and place in a bowl. Stir in orange rind and remaining ingredients. Cover and chill 8 hours.

Cornish Hens With Toasted Pecan-Cornbread Stuffing

makes 8 servings • prep: 20 min., cook: 55 min.

Toasted Pecan-Cornbread Stuffing

8   (1- to 1½-lb.) Cornish hens

Melted butter or margarine

test kitchen tip: To toast pecans, arrange them in a single layer on a baking sheet. Bake at 350° for 8 to 10 minutes. A darkened brown color and a nutty aroma are giveaways that they're ready.

1. Preheat oven to 450°.

2. Spoon about 1 cup Toasted Pecan-Cornbread Stuffing into each hen; tie legs together with kitchen string. Place hens, breast side up, in a roasting pan. Brush with butter.

3. Bake, covered, at 450° for 5 minutes. Reduce heat to 350°, and bake 50 more minutes or until a meat thermometer inserted in meaty part of breast and stuffing registers 165°.

Toasted Pecan-Cornbread Stuffing

makes 8 cups • prep: 20 min., cook: 48 min.

10   bacon slices
1⅓   cups yellow cornmeal
1⅓   cups all-purpose flour
2   tsp. baking powder
1   tsp. garlic powder
¾   tsp. baking soda
½   tsp. salt
½   to 2 cups chicken broth
2   large eggs
2   Tbsp. butter or margarine

1½   cups coarsely chopped pecans, toasted
1   large onion, diced
2   Tbsp. vegetable oil
3   celery ribs, diced
1   red bell pepper, chopped
¾   cup diced mushrooms
2   tsp. dried thyme
2   tsp. dried sage
3   to 4 large eggs, lightly beaten

1. Cook bacon in a 9-inch skillet until crisp; remove bacon, and drain on paper towels, reserving 2 Tbsp. drippings in skillet. Keep skillet warm. Crumble bacon, and set aside.

2. Preheat oven to 400°.

3. Combine cornmeal and next 5 ingredients in a large bowl. Whisk together broth, 2 eggs, and butter; add to dry ingredients, stirring just until moistened. Pour mixture into hot skillet with drippings.

4. Bake at 400° for 25 minutes or until golden around edges. Crumble cornbread onto a baking sheet; reduce oven temperature to 350°, and bake, stirring occasionally, 15 minutes or until lightly toasted. Transfer cornbread to a large bowl, and stir in crumbled bacon and pecans.

5. Sauté diced onion in hot oil in a large skillet over medium-high heat 5 minutes or until tender. Add diced celery, chopped bell pepper, and diced mushrooms, and cook 3 minutes; stir in thyme and sage. Stir vegetable mixture into cornbread mixture; stir in lightly beaten eggs.

Hush puppy mix and egg form a thick batter for coating catfish pieces before frying to make these crispy bite-sized nuggets. The delicate flavor is enhanced by a fiery tartar sauce heated by jalapeño, chili powder, and hot sauce.

Hush Puppy–Battered Catfish Nuggets With Spicy Tartar Sauce

makes 4 servings • prep: 35 min., cook: 8 min. per batch, other: 5 min.

1	(8-oz.) package hush puppy mix	1	Tbsp. hot sauce
½	cup milk	½	tsp. ground red pepper
½	cup water		Vegetable oil
1	large egg, beaten	1¼	lb. farm-raised catfish fillets
1	Tbsp. sliced pickled jalapeño peppers, minced	1	cup all-purpose flour
			Spicy Tartar Sauce

test kitchen tip: A garlic press works great for finely mincing the pickled jalapeño peppers.

1. Stir together first 7 ingredients in a medium bowl; let stand 5 minutes.

2. Pour oil to a depth of ½ inch in a large deep skillet; heat oil to 350°.

3. Pat catfish fillets dry with paper towels, and cut into bite-size pieces. Dredge catfish pieces in flour, and then dip in hush puppy batter mixture. Drop catfish pieces into hot oil, and fry, in batches, 3 to 4 minutes on each side or until golden. Serve with Spicy Tartar Sauce.

Spicy Tartar Sauce

makes about 1 cup • prep: 5 min.

1	cup mayonnaise	1	tsp. hot sauce
1	Tbsp. sliced pickled jalapeño peppers, finely minced	½	tsp. lemon juice
1	Tbsp. finely minced onion	¼	tsp. chili powder
1	garlic clove, finely minced		Pinch of salt

1. Stir together all ingredients in a medium bowl. Cover and chill until ready to serve.

catfish cuisine

It was a trash fish, a slick-skinned whiskered fish that ate anything and was eaten mostly by poor Southerners who spent days at the Mississippi riverbanks catching dinner for the family. Today, it's a delicacy served on tables topped with white linen and is a major cash crop in Mississippi's Delta region where catfish farms dot the landscape. It has become the largest selling farm-raised fish in the country. Wild catfish has a musky taste due to its indiscriminate diet, but farm-fed fillets taste delicate and mild, which make them ideal for whatever flavors the chef wants to pair with them. Still, many Southerners prefer catfish the old-fashioned way—cornmeal-coated, fried, and savored in their local fish camp-style restaurant perched on a river's edge with a giant glass of sweet tea.

Broiled Mahi-Mahi With Parsleyed Tomatoes

makes 6 servings • prep: 15 min., cook: 29 min.

With this recipe, serve up a dinner that's beautiful, delicious, and fast. The fish broils in just 10 minutes and is served nestled inside a Greek-inspired bed of onions, tomatoes, and garlic. Sprinkle crumbly feta cheese on top.

test kitchen tip: The second to the top shelf of an oven is typically 5 inches from the broiler. If your shelf is any closer, the cook time will likely be less.

2	medium onions, sliced	2	garlic cloves, chopped
2	Tbsp. olive oil, divided	½	tsp. salt, divided
1	pt. cherry tomatoes, seeded and chopped	½	tsp. pepper, divided
		6	(6- to 8-oz.) mahi-mahi fillets
2	Tbsp. chopped fresh parsley	1	(4-oz.) package crumbled feta cheese
¼	cup white wine		
1	Tbsp. tomato paste		Cracked black pepper

1. Preheat broiler.

2. Sauté sliced onions in 1 Tbsp. olive oil over medium-high heat 8 minutes or until tender. Remove from pan, and set aside. Add remaining oil and cherry tomatoes; cook over medium-high heat until tomatoes begin to burst. Return onion to pan. Add parsley, wine, tomato paste, garlic, and ¼ tsp. each of salt and pepper. Simmer, stirring occasionally, 5 minutes. Set tomato mixture aside.

3. Place fish in a single layer on a lightly greased rack in an aluminum foil-lined broiler pan; sprinkle with remaining ¼ tsp. each of salt and pepper.

4. Broil 5 inches from heat 10 minutes or until lightly browned and fish flakes with a fork.

5. Spoon tomato mixture evenly onto a platter; top with fish fillets. Sprinkle with crumbled feta cheese and cracked pepper.

Spicy Salmon Fillets With Avocado Mayonnaise

makes 6 servings • prep: 15 min., cook: 14 min.

A chili powder–brown sugar topping on broiled salmon imparts a spicy-sweet layer of flavor. Serve the creamy mayo–avocado mixture with the fillets.

1	small very ripe avocado, peeled and cubed	1½	tsp. salt
2	tsp. fresh lemon juice	½	tsp. ground cumin
5	Tbsp. mayonnaise	½	tsp. chili powder
1	Tbsp. brown sugar	½	tsp. ground black pepper
2	tsp. paprika	6	(6- to 8-oz.) salmon fillets
		2	Tbsp. olive oil

1. Preheat broiler.

2. Mash avocado until smooth; stir in lemon juice. Whisk in mayonnaise until very smooth. Cover and chill until ready to serve.

3. Combine brown sugar and next 5 ingredients in a small bowl; set aside.

4. Rinse fillets, and dry well. Place, skin side down, in broiler pan; brush each top with 1 tsp. oil. Sprinkle evenly with brown sugar mixture.

5. Broil 5 inches from heat 1½ to 2 minutes or until brown sugar mixture begins to caramelize. Reduce oven temperature to 425°, and bake 8 to 12 more minutes or until fish flakes with a fork.

6. Serve avocado mayonnaise with fillets.

Skillet Grits With Seasoned Vegetables

makes 6 to 8 servings • prep: 10 min., cook: 25 min.

In this nontraditional meatless main dish, sautéed potatoes, turnips, carrots, and zucchini are spooned over mounds of cheesy grits.

test kitchen tip: Spoon any leftover grits evenly into a plastic wrap-lined container to about a 2-inch depth. Cover and chill overnight or up to 3 days. Remove grits from pan, peel off the plastic wrap, and cut into ½-inch-thick slices. Slices can be pan-fried or baked.

1   (32-oz.) container chicken broth
3   Tbsp. butter
1   tsp. salt
1½ cups uncooked regular grits
1   cup (4 oz.) shredded Cheddar
    cheese
⅓   cup (1.5 oz.) shredded Parmesan
    cheese
½   tsp. pepper
Seasoned Vegetables

1. Bring first 3 ingredients to a boil in a large saucepan over medium-high heat. Gradually whisk in grits; return to a boil. Reduce heat to medium-low, and simmer, stirring occasionally, 10 to 12 minutes or until thickened.

2. Whisk in cheeses and pepper until cheeses are melted. Spoon Seasoned Vegetables evenly over grits, and serve immediately.

Seasoned Vegetables

makes 6 to 8 servings • prep: 25 min., cook: 35 min.

1   medium onion, chopped
2   garlic cloves, minced
2   Tbsp. olive oil
4   carrots, chopped
3   small red potatoes, diced
2   small turnips (about ½ lb.), peeled
    and chopped
2   celery ribs, diced
1   medium zucchini, chopped
1   (14-oz.) can chicken broth
1   tsp. salt
1   tsp. dried thyme
½   tsp. pepper
1   tsp. cornstarch
1   Tbsp. water

1. Sauté onion and garlic in hot oil in a large skillet over medium heat 5 minutes or until caramelized. Add carrots and next 4 ingredients, and sauté 12 to 15 minutes or until vegetables are tender. Increase heat to medium-high; stir in chicken broth and next 3 ingredients. Bring to a boil. Reduce heat to medium-low, and simmer, stirring occasionally, 5 minutes.

2. Whisk together cornstarch and 1 Tbsp. water until smooth. Whisk into vegetable mixture in skillet, and cook, stirring constantly, 3 to 5 minutes or until thickened.

salads and salad dressings

Grilled Pork Salad With Spicy Peanut Dressing, page 322

Uptown Bluegrass Salad

makes 10 to 12 servings • prep: 20 min.

A tangy mustard dressing tops this upscale salad of romaine, bacon, artichoke hearts, and avocado.

1   lb. bacon, cooked and crumbled
2   heads romaine lettuce, torn
1   (14-oz.) can artichoke hearts, drained and chopped

1   large avocado, cut into bite-size pieces
6   oz. freshly grated Parmesan cheese
Spicy Mustard Dressing

1. Combine first 5 ingredients in a large bowl. Drizzle with Spicy Mustard Dressing, and toss gently to coat. Serve immediately.

Spicy Mustard Dressing

makes 1 cup • prep: 10 min.

⅓   cup chopped onion
3   Tbsp. cider vinegar
2   tsp. spicy brown mustard
½   tsp. sugar

½   tsp. salt
¼   tsp. freshly ground pepper
¾   cup olive oil

1. Process first 6 ingredients in a food processor until pureed. With processor running, slowly pour olive oil through food chute, processing until blended.

Creating a Stir
The Fayette County Medical Auxiliary ~ Lexington, Kentucky

test kitchen tip: This dressing can be mixed by hand if you don't have a food processor. Finely mince the onion, and whisk together the remaining ingredients.

Hearts of Palm Salad

makes 6 servings • prep: 15 min., other: 4 hr.

Hearts of palm, the edible inner portion of Florida's state tree, turn a plate of baby greens into a stately first course.

test kitchen tip: Hearts of palm have a delicate flavor similar to artichokes. They're expensive and rarely available fresh. Canned hearts of palm are sold in gourmet markets and large supermarkets. Rinse and drain canned hearts of palm before using.

1   garlic clove, minced
⅓   cup olive oil
2   Tbsp. white wine vinegar
1   Tbsp. Dijon mustard
½   tsp. salt
½   tsp. pepper
⅛   tsp. dried tarragon

⅛   tsp. dried basil
⅛   tsp. dried thyme
6   cups mixed baby salad greens
1   (14.4-oz.) can hearts of palm, rinsed, drained, and cut into bite-size pieces
1   medium tomato, cut into wedges

1. Combine first 9 ingredients in a small bowl; stir with a wire whisk until blended. Cover and chill dressing at least 4 hours.
2. Combine salad greens, hearts of palm, and tomato in a large bowl. Pour dressing over salad; toss well. Serve salad immediately.   Ann Thellefson

A Cook's Tour of Libertyville
Main Street Libertyville ~ Libertyville, Illinois

Romaine Salad With Blue Cheese, Chili Toasted Pecans, and Pears

makes 4 to 6 servings • prep: 30 min.

The first layer is a mix of lettuce, blue cheese, goat cheese, and an herbed buttermilk dressing. This tangy layer is topped with sweet fresh pears, then sprinkled with toasted pecans that are dusted with chili powder for a surprising flavor combination you'll love.

½ cup sour cream
½ cup buttermilk
¼ cup half-and-half
¼ cup fresh orange juice
1 Tbsp. minced fresh mint
2 tsp. minced fresh basil
½ small shallot, minced
¼ tsp. salt

¼ tsp. ground red pepper
4 oz. blue cheese, crumbled
2 oz. goat cheese, crumbled
1 head romaine lettuce, torn
2 Bartlett pears, cut into thin wedges
3 Tbsp. fresh lemon juice
Chili-Toasted Pecans
¼ tsp. freshly ground black pepper

test kitchen tip: Chilling the salad plates and serving bowl will keep the salad greens crisper longer.

1. Combine first 9 ingredients in a bowl; stir well. Add cheeses; stir well. Place lettuce in a large bowl; add cheese mixture, and toss gently.

2. Combine pears and lemon juice; toss to coat. Arrange pears over salad. Sprinkle with Chili-Toasted Pecans and freshly ground black pepper. Serve immediately.

Chili-Toasted Pecans

makes 1 cup • prep: 10 min., cook: 25 min.

2 Tbsp. vegetable oil
2 tsp. coffee liqueur
1 cup pecan halves

1 Tbsp. chili powder
¼ tsp. ground red pepper
2 tsp. sugar

1. Preheat oven to 300°.

2. Combine vegetable oil and liqueur. Add pecan halves, and toss to coat. Stir in chili powder, red pepper, and sugar. Spread on an ungreased baking sheet. Bake at 300° for 25 minutes or until toasted, stirring often. Cool in pan on a wire rack.

From Black Tie to Blackeyed Peas: Savannah's Savory Secrets
St. Joseph's Foundation of Savannah, Inc. ~ Savannah, Georgia

Winter Salad With Raspberry Vinaigrette

makes 8 servings • prep: 20 min.

Fresh spinach, sweet apples, juicy kiwifruit, and toasted walnuts make a quick-to-fix salad that's beautiful and refreshing.

make it a meal: Top this no-fuss salad with grilled chicken for a main dish that's easy enough to serve any night of the week.

1	(7-oz.) bag fresh spinach, washed, trimmed, and torn	2	Red Delicious apples, thinly sliced
1	head Bibb lettuce, torn	1	kiwifruit, peeled and thinly sliced
2	oranges, peeled and sectioned	½	cup chopped walnuts, toasted
			Raspberry Vinaigrette

1. Combine spinach, lettuce, orange, apple, kiwifruit, and walnuts in a large bowl; toss gently. Pour Raspberry Vinaigrette over spinach mixture just before serving; toss gently.

Raspberry Vinaigrette

makes about 1 cup • prep: 5 min.

½	cup vegetable oil	½	tsp. grated orange rind
¼	cup raspberry vinegar	¼	tsp. salt
1	Tbsp. honey	⅛	tsp. pepper

1. Combine all ingredients in a jar; cover tightly, and shake vigorously. Cover and chill thoroughly.

The Bess Collection
The Junior Service League of Independence, Missouri

foraged food: they eat what?

Some guy weekends are for hunting or fishing. In the southern Appalachians, one group retreats to a mountain cabin to eat garliclike ramps, the mountain leek whose appearance heralds spring. Retreat is necessary, says Howard Matherly of Elizabethton, Tennessee. "The smell comes out of your pores for days!" he says. Once eaten only by those who foraged native foods to fill their tables, today, top restaurants like The Inn at Blackberry Farm in Walland, Tennessee, proudly put it on the menu. Other favorites gathered from the moist woodlands include dandelion greens, wild mustard, and poke weed, often called poke sallet. Only young poke sallet leaves can be harvested; the big ones are toxic. Boiled and fried, the iron-rich leaves taste somewhat like asparagus or spinach and are traditionally served with vinegar or hot pepper sauce. To sample these foraged foods for yourself, catch the Ramp Festival in Crosby, Tennessee, or the Poke Sallet Festival in Harland, Kentucky, each May.

Chopped Cilantro Salad

makes 8 servings • prep: 25 min.

Romaine lettuce, cabbage, tomatoes, crispy jicama, and corn are tossed with a tomatillo-cilantro dressing for a Southwest-inspired salad.

6	fresh tomatillos, husked
⅔	cup loosely packed fresh cilantro leaves
6	Tbsp. fresh lime juice (about 3 limes)
2	garlic cloves, halved
2	tsp. chopped jalapeño pepper (about 1 small)
¾	cup vegetable oil
1	cup finely chopped green onions
1	tsp. salt
½	tsp. pepper

5	cups loosely packed, coarsely chopped romaine lettuce
4	cups loosely packed, coarsely chopped cabbage
2	medium tomatoes, seeded and chopped (about 1½ cups)
1½	cups chopped, peeled jicama
1½	cups fresh corn kernels (about 3 ears)
½	cup crumbled feta cheese
2	ripe avocados, chopped
	Tortilla chips (optional)

test kitchen tip: To get the most juice from citrus fruits, start with fruits that are heavy for their size; they contain more juice. Leave the fruit at room temperature, and roll it on the counter under the palm of your hand a few seconds before you start juicing it.

1. Cut tomatillos into quarters. Process tomatillos, cilantro, and next 3 ingredients in a blender 20 seconds or until pureed; pour into a medium bowl. Whisk together cilantro puree and oil; add green onions, salt, and pepper, stirring well.

2. Stir together romaine lettuce and next 5 ingredients in a large bowl. Gently toss avocado and lettuce mixture with cilantro mixture. Serve with tortilla chips, if desired.

Sounds Delicious: The Flavor of Atlanta in Food & Music
Atlanta Symphony Orchestra ~ Atlanta, Georgia

Apple-Pear Salad With Lemon-Poppy Seed Dressing

makes 6 to 8 servings • prep: 10 min.

For an easy fall salad with lots of color, team fruit slices with Swiss cheese, cashews, and a lemon dressing.

test kitchen tip: A vegetable peeler quickly shaves paper-thin slices from a block of Swiss cheese.

1 (16-oz.) package romaine lettuce	1 large apple, thinly sliced
1 (6-oz.) block Swiss cheese, shaved	1 large pear, thinly sliced
1 cup roasted, salted cashews	Lemon-Poppy Seed Dressing
½ cup sweetened dried cranberries	

1. Toss together first 6 ingredients in a large bowl; serve with Lemon-Poppy Seed Dressing.

Lemon-Poppy Seed Dressing

makes 1¼ cups • prep: 10 min.

⅔ cup olive oil	2 tsp. finely chopped onion
½ cup sugar	1 tsp. Dijon mustard
⅓ cup fresh lemon juice	½ tsp. salt
1½ Tbsp. poppy seeds	

1. Process all ingredients in a blender until smooth. Store in an airtight container in the refrigerator up to 1 week; serve at room temperature.

Summer Fruit Bowl With Almond-Mango Sauce

makes 6 servings • prep: 25 min., other: 3 hr.

Nearly the whole produce stand goes into this juicy fruit salad—nectarines, peaches, plums, mango, and summer berries. Toss with a smooth mango sauce for a spectacular buffet salad.

test kitchen tip: Leaving the skin on the nectarines adds another dimension of color and distinguishes them from the peaches. Add the blueberries and raspberries just before serving to keep the colors distinctly separate.

3 ripe nectarines, sliced	¼ cup fresh lime juice
2 ripe peaches, peeled and sliced	½ cup fresh blueberries
2 plums, sliced	½ cup fresh raspberries
1 firm ripe mango, peeled and coarsely chopped	Almond-Mango Sauce
½ small honeydew melon, peeled, seeded, and cubed	Garnish: fresh mint sprigs

1. Combine first 5 ingredients in a large serving bowl; toss with lime juice. Cover and chill up to 3 hours before serving.

2. Drizzle ½ cup Almond-Mango Sauce over fruit; toss to coat. Spoon blueberries and raspberries over fruit. Garnish, if desired. Serve with remaining Almond-Mango Sauce.

Almond–Mango Sauce

makes 1⅓ cups • prep: 15 min.

1	large mango, peeled and chopped	2	Tbsp. sugar
1	Tbsp. grated orange rind	1	drop almond extract
¾	cup fresh orange juice (about 2 oranges)		

1. Process all ingredients in a blender until pureed, stopping to scrape down sides. Pour mixture through a wire-mesh strainer into a bowl, discarding solids. Cover and chill.

Cranberry Relish Salad

makes 10 servings • prep: 30 min.; other: 8 hr., 30 min.

This salad calls for a traditional roast turkey or baked ham beside it. The fruity mixture is suspended in gelatin and then poured into an attractive gelatin mold for a make-ahead holiday salad.

2	(3-oz.) packages cherry-flavored gelatin	3	Red Delicious apples, peeled and quartered
2	cups boiling water	3	oranges, peeled and sectioned
1	cup sugar	1	(8¼-oz.) can crushed pineapple in heavy syrup, undrained
1	cup cold water		Toppings: sweetened whipped cream, toasted chopped pecans
1	(12-oz.) package fresh or thawed frozen cranberries		
1	cup pecans, toasted		

test kitchen tip: For best results, be sure the salad is firm before unmolding. To remove it easily from the mold, dip the bottom of the mold into warm water for 15 seconds before unmolding.

1. Stir together gelatin, 2 cups boiling water, and 1 cup sugar in a large bowl 2 minutes or until gelatin and sugar dissolve. Add 1 cup cold water, and chill 30 minutes or until consistency of unbeaten egg white.

2. Process cranberries and pecans in a food processor 30 seconds or until coarsely chopped, stopping to scrape down sides. Set cranberry mixture aside in a small bowl.

3. Process apples and oranges in food processor 30 to 45 seconds or until coarsely chopped, stopping to scrape down sides. Add cranberry mixture and apple mixture to gelatin mixture. Stir in pineapple. Spoon into a lightly greased 10- to 12-cup mold; cover and chill 8 hours or until firm.

4. Invert onto a serving plate, and serve with desired toppings.

Apple-Broccoli Salad

makes 6 servings • prep: 15 min.

Classic broccoli-apple salad, chock-full of raisins, pecans, and bacon in a creamy dressing, is a relatively new "must" at Southern potlucks.

4	cups small fresh broccoli florets		1	small red onion, chopped
½	cup raisins		1	cup mayonnaise
½	cup chopped pecans, toasted		½	cup sugar
6	bacon slices, cooked and crumbled		2	Tbsp. cider vinegar
2	large Red Delicious apples, diced			

1. Combine first 6 ingredients in a large bowl. Combine mayonnaise, sugar, and vinegar; add to broccoli mixture, stirring to coat. Cover and chill.

Fresh Corn Salad

(pictured on page 3)

makes 6 cups • prep: 15 min., cook: 4 min., other: 2 hr.

Use Silver Queen or another sweet corn variety for this sugary-sweet salad with an oil and vinegar dressing. Using corn freshly cut from the cob yields the sweetest kernels.

6	ears white or yellow corn, husks removed	½	tsp. salt	
¼	cup sugar	½	tsp. pepper	
¼	cup cider vinegar	1	medium-size red onion, diced	
¼	cup olive oil	1	medium-size red bell pepper, diced	
		¼	cup coarsely chopped fresh parsley	

1. Cook corn in boiling salted water in a large stockpot 3 to 4 minutes; drain. Plunge corn into ice water to stop the cooking process; drain. Cut kernels from cobs.
2. Whisk together ¼ cup sugar and next 4 ingredients in a large bowl; add corn, onion, bell pepper, and parsley, tossing to coat. Cover and chill at least 2 hours.

test kitchen tip: As an alternative to cooking the corn in boiling water in Step 1, grill it to add a nutty flavor to the salad. To do so, remove all but the innermost layers of husks, and snip off the silk tassels with kitchen shears. Place the ears on the grill and cook, turning often, until you see the silhouette of the kernels through the husks, and the husk begins to pull away from the tip of the ear. Set it aside until cool enough to peel away the husks and silk.

Carrot-Raisin Salad With Honey-Orange Dressing

makes 6 servings • prep: 15 min.

Crisp apples, honey, orange juice concentrate, and raisins enhance the natural sweetness of carrots in this chilled salad. It's ideal for a summer picnic because it's perfectly portable and holds up well outdoors.

¾	cup vegetable oil	¼	tsp. celery salt	
⅓	cup honey	¼	tsp. paprika	
3	Tbsp. frozen orange juice concentrate, thawed	3	cups shredded carrot	
		2	medium apples, peeled and diced	
3	Tbsp. lemon juice	½	cup raisins	
½	tsp. dry mustard			

1. Combine first 7 ingredients in a large bowl; stir well with a wire whisk.
2. Add carrot, apple, and raisins; toss gently to combine. Cover salad, and chill thoroughly.

Kelley L. Wright

Southern Elegance: A Second Course
The Junior League of Gaston County ~ Gastonia, North Carolina

test kitchen tip: Galas, Fuji, Cameo, Cripps Pink, and Red Delicious are excellent apple choices for salads.

Black-eyed Pea Salad

makes 8 to 10 servings • prep: 25 min., other: 8 hr.

Bacon, the traditional seasoning for simmered black-eyed peas, is the crunchy topper for this chilled salad mixed with fresh bell peppers, tomatoes, and mushrooms.

make it a meal: Serve this bacon- and bell pepper-studded salad alongside collard greens, a rotisserie pork loin roast, or barbecue-flavored chicken.

⅔ cup extra virgin olive oil
⅓ cup white wine vinegar
3 garlic cloves, minced
½ tsp. salt
½ tsp. Dijon mustard
¼ tsp. pepper
1 large tomato, seeded and chopped
1 green bell pepper, chopped
1 yellow bell pepper, chopped

6 fresh mushrooms, chopped
2 (16-oz.) cans black-eyed peas, rinsed and drained
1 (4-oz.) jar diced pimiento, drained
3 Tbsp. chopped fresh cilantro
Lettuce leaves
Red cabbage leaves
2 Tbsp. cooked and crumbled bacon
⅓ cup chopped green onions

1. Whisk together first 6 ingredients until blended; set vinaigrette aside.
2. Combine tomato, bell peppers, and mushrooms in a large bowl. Stir in peas, pimiento, and cilantro. Add vinaigrette, and toss gently to coat. Cover and chill at least 8 hours.
3. Line a serving platter with lettuce and cabbage leaves. Spoon salad onto leaves, using a slotted spoon. Sprinkle with bacon and green onions.

bean cuisine

Travel across the Southern regions from the sandy coast to the arid Texas plains, and the beans of preference change with the landscape. In areas of heavy Hispanic influence, black beans mixed with rice are tradition. Along the eastern coast, black-eyed peas (really a bean) and limas are part of the soul food standard. Creamy butter beans are the favorite in the Deep South. The preference is red pinto beans in New Orleans's recipes, Texas cowboy cuisine, and Appalachian "soup beans" served with sliced fresh onion, and cornbread. Mountain folks found stringing and drying green beans, called "leather britches," preserved summer flavor for later months when they wanted to cook up a "mess of beans" for supper. Traditionally, fat back seasoned them all. Now, a variety of seasonings replace the fat back, still preserving the historic roots and the nutritional benefits in soups, salads, sides, salsas, and savory entrées.

Two Shades of Red Salad

makes 8 servings • prep: 25 min., other: 1 hr.

Baked sweet beets and tomato are the shades of red in this salad. Feta cheese and cilantro flavor it with a salty tang.

1 lb. fresh beets	½ cup fresh lemon juice
1¼ cups seeded, coarsely chopped tomato	2 Tbsp. extra virgin olive oil
½ medium-size red onion, minced	½ tsp. salt
¼ cup chopped fresh flat-leaf parsley	¼ tsp. freshly ground black pepper
¼ cup chopped fresh cilantro	½ cup crumbled feta cheese (optional)
1 garlic clove, minced	Garnish: flat-leaf parsley sprig

1. Preheat oven to 400°.
2. Leave roots and 1 inch of stem on beets; discard greens. Scrub beets with a vegetable brush. Wrap beets tightly in aluminum foil; bake at 400° with for 1 hour or until tender. Cool completely. Trim off roots and stems; rub off skins. Dice beets.
3. Place beets, tomato, and next 4 ingredients in a small bowl; toss well. Whisk together lemon juice and next 3 ingredients in a large bowl. Drizzle over beet mixture, and toss gently. Sprinkle with feta cheese, if desired. Garnish, if desired.

test kitchen tip: Leaving about 1 inch of stem attached to beets prevents loss of nutrients and color as they cook.

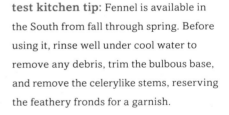

Minted Fennel Salad With Olives

makes 8 to 10 servings • prep: 25 min., other: 3 hr.

The sweet, delicate flavor of fennel bulbs gets a kiss of mint in this crisp salad that's ideal to serve with grilled lamb.

2 medium fennel bulbs (about 1 lb. each)	¼ cup chopped red onion
1 cup loosely packed fresh mint leaves	3 Tbsp. fresh lemon juice
	3 Tbsp. olive oil
¾ cup chopped Mediterranean-style olives (we tested with kalamata)	2 tsp. grated lemon rind
	½ tsp. salt
	¼ tsp. pepper

1. Trim stems and base from fennel bulbs, reserving fronds. Remove tough outer layer from each bulb. Cut each bulb in half through base. Cut out the small, pyramid-shaped core from each half. Place cored fennel, cut side down, and slice crosswise into 4 thick slices. Slice lengthwise into ¼-inch-wide strips. Chop enough of the reserved fronds to measure 1 Tbsp.
2. Combine fennel strips, fronds, mint, olives, and onion in a large bowl; toss gently.
3. Stir together lemon juice and remaining 4 ingredients in a small bowl. Pour over fennel mixture, and toss gently. Cover and chill up to 3 hours.

test kitchen tip: Fennel is available in the South from fall through spring. Before using it, rinse well under cool water to remove any debris, trim the bulbous base, and remove the celerylike stems, reserving the feathery fronds for a garnish.

Spectacular Overnight Slaw

makes 12 cups • prep: 15 min., cook: 5 min., other: 8 hr.

When you're hosting a party, make this crowd-pleaser the night before. Chilling it for several hours blends the flavors. Pimiento-stuffed olives add a unique flavor twist.

make it a meal: Serve this make-ahead dish at your next backyard cookout alongside burgers, oven-baked fries, and wedges of sweet watermelon.

1	medium cabbage, finely shredded	½	cup vegetable oil
1	medium-size red onion, thinly sliced	½	cup white wine vinegar
½	cup chopped green bell pepper	1	tsp. salt
½	cup chopped red bell pepper	1	tsp. celery seeds
½	cup sliced pimiento-stuffed olives	1	tsp. mustard seeds
½	cup sugar	2	tsp. Dijon mustard

1. Combine first 5 ingredients in a large bowl; stir well. Combine sugar and remaining 6 ingredients in a small saucepan, and bring to a simmer. Reduce heat, and cook 3 minutes, stirring frequently, until sugar dissolves. Boil 1 minute. Pour dressing over cabbage mixture; toss well. Cover and chill 8 hours. Toss well before serving.

Roasted Sweet Potato Salad

makes 6 to 8 servings • prep: 30 min., cook: 45 min.

Roasting sweet potatoes, garlic, and onions together makes for a sweet, caramelized mixture to serve over fresh spinach. Drizzle Warm Bacon Dressing over all for a savory salad.

1½	lb. sweet potatoes	½	tsp. pepper
2	large onions	1	(6-oz.) bag baby spinach
2	garlic cloves, crushed		Warm Bacon Dressing
2	Tbsp. olive oil		Garnish: cooked, crumbled bacon
½	tsp. salt		

test kitchen tip: Cook 2 or 3 more bacon slices in Step 1 of Warm Bacon Dressing, and reserve to use as garnish for salad just before serving.

1. Preheat oven to 400°.

2. Peel sweet potatoes, and cut into 1-inch cubes. Cut onions into quarters, and cut each quarter in half.

3. Toss together sweet potatoes, onions, crushed garlic, and 2 Tbsp. olive oil; place on a lightly greased aluminum foil-lined 15- x 11-inch jelly-roll pan. Sprinkle evenly with salt and pepper.

4. Bake at 400° for 45 minutes or until tender and lightly browned, stirring occasionally. Serve over spinach, and drizzle with Warm Bacon Dressing. Garnish, if desired.

Warm Bacon Dressing

makes ½ cup • prep: 10 min., cook: 10 min.

4	bacon slices	2	Tbsp. honey
⅓	cup red wine vinegar	¼	tsp. salt
3	Tbsp. orange juice	⅛	tsp. pepper

1. Cook bacon slices in a large skillet until crisp. Remove bacon, and drain on paper towels, reserving 1 Tbsp. drippings in skillet. Crumble bacon.

2. Stir vinegar and next 4 ingredients into hot drippings in skillet; cook over medium heat, stirring until thoroughly heated. Stir in bacon.

Potato Salad With Goat Cheese and Roasted Red Peppers

makes 10 to 12 servings • prep: 13 min., cook: 32 min., other: 10 min.

No matter which ingredients you use, potato salad is a universal must at any Southern cookout. This version will have your guests talking—it features basil, dried tomatoes, bacon, and crumbled goat cheese.

test kitchen tip: To keep potatoes from discoloring as you're prepping them, keep the sliced or cut potatoes in a bowl of cold water.

3	lb. red potatoes, peeled and cut into ¼-inch-thick slices	2	tsp. salt
3	large red bell peppers	1	tsp. freshly ground black pepper
⅓	cup olive oil	⅓	cup chopped dried tomatoes in oil, drained
1	Tbsp. balsamic vinegar	8	slices bacon, cooked and crumbled
½	cup thinly sliced green onions	6	oz. goat cheese, crumbled
⅓	cup chopped fresh basil		

1. Cook potatoes in boiling, salted water to cover 12 minutes or until tender; drain well. Cool slightly, and set aside.

2. Preheat broiler.

3. Cut peppers in half lengthwise; discard seeds and membranes. Place peppers, skin side up, on an ungreased baking sheet; flatten with palm of hand. Broil peppers 3 inches from heat 15 minutes or until charred. Place peppers in a zip-top plastic freezer bag; seal and let stand 10 minutes to loosen skins. Peel peppers, and discard skins; cut peppers into ½-inch pieces.

4. Combine warm potato, olive oil, and next 5 ingredients in a large bowl; toss gently. Add reserved peppers, tomatoes, and bacon; toss gently. Sprinkle with goat cheese, and serve immediately.

Black Bean and Rice Salad

makes 10 servings • prep: 20 min., cook: 35 min.

With Cuban flair, black beans and rice are seasoned with cilantro, cumin, and chili powder in this chilled salad. Serve it with grilled meat or fish.

test kitchen tip: For a quick sandwich, roll up leftover Black Bean and Rice Salad with grilled chicken strips in a flour tortilla.

1   (16-oz.) package long-grain rice
2   (14½-oz.) cans ready-to-serve chicken broth
½   cup water
2   bay leaves
2   (15-oz.) cans black beans, rinsed and drained
1   medium-size red bell pepper, diced
1   medium-size green bell pepper, diced

1   medium onion, diced
½   cup olive oil
½   cup chopped fresh cilantro
3   Tbsp. orange juice
2   Tbsp. red wine vinegar
2   tsp. ground cumin
1⅛   tsp. chili powder
Lettuce leaves

1. Combine first 4 ingredients in a medium saucepan. Bring to a boil; cover, reduce heat, and simmer 25 minutes or until liquid is absorbed and rice is tender. Discard bay leaves. Transfer rice to a bowl. Stir in beans and next 9 ingredients. Cover and chill. Serve on a lettuce-lined plate.

the story of rice

Rice grains poured into the port cities of South Carolina and Louisiana early in the region's history, taking root in the marshy coastal areas and becoming entwined in the cuisines introduced to the area by the Africans, Acadians, French, and Spanish. As rice flourished, it developed a pairing relationship in the coastal kitchens. It's evident with red rice (with tomatoes), seafood pilafs, and hoppin' John in Charleston and Savannah. Or in Louisiana's dirty rice made with chicken livers and gizzards, jambalaya, red beans-and-rice, étouffée, boudin (a hot, spicy Cajun sausage that contains rice), paella, and famous rice fritters called calah, once sold by Creole street vendors in the French Quarter. Now flavorful, aromatic varieties—basmati, wild pecan, and jasmine—offer a nutty, popcornlike flavor that gives even more reason for creative Southern chefs to continue the renaissance of rice in croquettes, timbales, salads, and savory rice cakes.

Couscous and Chickpea Salad

makes 8 servings • prep: 1 hr., 15 min.; cook: 6 min.; other: 5 min.

Garbanzo beans—also called chickpeas—mixed with vegetables, feta cheese, and a Mint Vinaigrette make a delicious salad served at room temperature or chilled.

1½ cups water	⅔ cup sliced green onions
½ tsp. salt	½ cup chopped carrot
1 cup couscous, uncooked	½ cup kalamata olives, pitted
1 (15-oz.) can garbanzo beans (chickpeas), drained	Mint Vinaigrette
	6 oz. crumbled feta cheese
1¼ cups diced red bell pepper	

test kitchen tip: For a fun serving variation, roll up scoops of this salad in romaine lettuce leaves and eat out of hand.

1. Combine water and ½ tsp. salt in a medium saucepan; bring to a boil. Stir in couscous. Cover, remove from heat, and let stand 5 minutes or until liquid is absorbed.

2. Combine couscous, garbanzo beans, and next 4 ingredients in a large bowl; toss gently.

3. Pour Mint Vinaigrette over couscous mixture; add feta cheese, and toss gently. Serve immediately, or cover and chill.

Mint Vinaigrette

makes about 1 cup • prep: 10 min.

¾ cup fresh mint sprigs	¼ tsp. sugar
3 Tbsp. white wine vinegar	¼ tsp. salt
2 garlic cloves	⅛ tsp. pepper
1 tsp. Dijon mustard	⅔ cup olive oil

1. Process first 7 ingredients in a food processor until mint and garlic are finely chopped. Pour olive oil through food chute with processor running; process until blended.

Fiesta Salad

makes 8 servings • prep: 20 min., cook: 20 min.

You'll love this easy taco salad that's anchored with a base of crushed tortilla chips, followed with salad greens, chili-spiced ground beef and pork, buttery avocado, pico de gallo, cheese, and olives that layer on flavor and color.

test kitchen tip: Some avocados are rock-hard when purchased. Place these in a paper bag, and leave them at room temperature; they'll soften in 2 to 5 days.

1   lb. lean ground beef
1   lb. ground pork
¾   cup water
½   (2-oz.) package onion soup-and-dip mix
1   Tbsp. chili powder
2   large ripe avocados
1   (8-oz.) container French onion dip
1½ tsp. lemon juice
1   (9-oz.) bag tortilla chips, divided

2   (5-oz.) packages mixed salad greens
1   (12-oz.) jar pico de gallo or chunky salsa
1   cup (4 oz.) shredded Cheddar cheese
1   (2¼-oz.) can sliced ripe black olives, drained
Garnish: tomato wedges

1. Cook ground beef and pork in a large skillet over medium-high heat, stirring until meat crumbles and is no longer pink; drain and return to skillet. Stir in ¾ cup water, onion soup–and–dip mix, and chili powder; reduce heat, and simmer 6 minutes or until liquid evaporates. Remove from heat, and set aside.

2. Cut avocados in half. Scoop pulp into a bowl; mash with a fork just until slightly chunky. Stir in onion dip and lemon juice.

3. Coarsely crush half of tortilla chips. Divide crushed chips evenly in 8 serving bowls; top with salad greens, meat mixture, and avocado mixture. Spoon ¼ cup pico de gallo onto each salad, and sprinkle with cheese and olives. Garnish, if desired. Serve immediately with remaining half of chips.

Asian Beef Salad

makes 8 servings • prep: 15 min.; cook: 14 min.; other: 1 hr., 5 min.

Grilled flank steak marinated in teriyaki sauce gives this salad an Asian flair. Sliced strips tossed with napa cabbage and lettuce and drizzled with Soy-Sesame Dressing add to the Asian flavor.

¼	cup teriyaki sauce	2	large tomatoes, cut into wedges
2	Tbsp. olive oil	2	cucumbers, thinly sliced
2	(1-lb.) flank steaks	½	small red onion, thinly sliced
1	(1¾-lb.) napa cabbage, chopped	½	cup loosely packed fresh cilantro
1	large head romaine lettuce, chopped		Soy-Sesame Dressing

test kitchen tip: Napa cabbage may be called Chinese cabbage in some grocery stores.

1. Combine teriyaki sauce and oil in a shallow dish or large zip-top plastic freezer bag; add steaks, turning to coat. Cover or seal, and chill 1 hour, turning steaks occasionally.

2. Preheat grill to medium-high heat (350° to 400°). Remove steaks from marinade, discarding marinade.

3. Grill steaks, covered with grill lid, over medium-high heat (350° to 400°) 5 to 7 minutes on each side or to desired degree of doneness. Let stand 5 minutes; cut diagonally across the grain into thin slices.

4. Toss together steak slices, cabbage, and next 5 ingredients; drizzle with desired amount of dressing, tossing gently to coat.

Soy-Sesame Dressing

makes ¾ cup • prep: 5 min.

¼	cup fresh lime juice	3	Tbsp. sesame oil
1	Tbsp. light brown sugar	2	Tbsp. lite soy sauce
3	Tbsp. olive oil	1	to 2 tsp. Asian garlic-chili sauce

1. Whisk together all ingredients.

Grilled Pork Salad With Spicy Peanut Dressing

(pictured on page 303)

makes 6 servings • prep: 20 min., cook: 21 min., other: 15 min.

This creative combination of grilled pork tenderloin, sugar snap peas, salad greens, and mango slices is deliciously captivating and unexpected.

test kitchen tip: Marinate and grill twice the amount of pork tenderloins needed for this salad. Wrap half, and chill up to 3 days. Thinly slice the tenderloin, and serve on buns with barbecue sauce and deli coleslaw.

⅓ cup ketchup
3 Tbsp. firmly packed brown sugar
1 Tbsp. cider vinegar
¾ tsp. garlic salt
¾ tsp. chili powder
1 (1½-lb.) package pork tenderloins

½ lb. sugar snap peas, trimmed
8 cups mixed salad greens
2 peaches, nectarines, or mangoes, peeled and sliced
½ cup roasted, unsalted peanuts
Spicy Peanut Dressing

1. Preheat grill to medium-high heat (350° to 400°).

2. Stir together first 5 ingredients until blended; brush evenly over pork.

3. Grill pork, covered with grill lid, over medium-high heat (350° to 400°) 10 minutes on each side or until a meat thermometer inserted in thickest portion of tenderloins registers 155°. Remove from grill; let stand 15 minutes before slicing.

4. Cook sugar snap peas in boiling salted water to cover 1 minute or until crisp-tender; drain. Plunge into ice water to stop the cooking process; drain and pat dry.

5. Arrange salad greens on a large serving platter; top evenly with sugar snap peas, peaches, sliced pork, and peanuts. Serve with Spicy Peanut Dressing.

Spicy Peanut Dressing

makes about 1¾ cups • prep: 5 min.

¾ cup creamy peanut butter
¾ cup water
1 Tbsp. brown sugar

3 Tbsp. soy sauce
1½ Tbsp. fresh lemon juice
½ tsp. crushed red pepper flakes

1. Whisk together all ingredients in a large bowl until smooth.

Louise Mathew's Chutney Chicken Salad

makes 6 to 8 servings • prep: 15 min.

Grapes, chutney, and a dash of curry powder make this chicken salad spicy-sweet and fruity tasting. Add almonds for crunch, then serve in pita pockets or on croissants for a sandwich, or over lettuce leaves for a hearty luncheon salad.

¾	cup mayonnaise	4	cups cubed cooked chicken breast
½	cup chutney	2	celery ribs, chopped
½	cup sour cream	¾	cup seedless green grapes, halved
¼	cup fresh lime juice	½	cup chopped green onions
1	tsp. curry powder	1	(2.25-oz.) package slivered natural
½	tsp. salt		almonds, toasted

make it ahead: Combine all ingredients as directed except almonds. Cover and chill overnight. Stir in almonds just before serving.

1. Stir together first 6 ingredients in a large bowl. Stir in chicken and remaining ingredients. Serve immediately, or cover and chill.

Cookin' with Friends

National Presbyterian School Class of 2000 ~ Washington, D.C.

Chicken Tabbouleh

makes 6 servings • prep: 20 min., other: 30 min.

Instead of a side salad, this version with deli-roasted chicken serves as a main dish. It's a handy make-ahead meal if you prefer it chilled.

1	cup bulgur wheat, uncooked	½	cup sliced red onion
4	cups boiling water	¼	cup pitted, chopped kalamata olives
4	cups cubed deli-roasted chicken (about 2 chickens)	¼	cup thinly sliced fresh basil leaves
3	medium tomatoes, seeded and chopped (about 3 cups)	¼	cup chopped fresh parsley
		⅓	cup fresh lemon juice
1	cup crumbled feta cheese	3	Tbsp. olive oil
		¾	tsp. salt

test kitchen tip: Chicken Tabbouleh makes a great sandwich filling, too. Just spoon it into pita pockets with mayonnaise and tomato slices.

1. Place bulgur in a large bowl. Add boiling water; stir well. Cover and let stand 30 minutes. Drain well, and return bulgur to bowl. Add chicken and remaining ingredients; toss well. Serve immediately, or cover and chill.

Layered Cornbread-and-Turkey Salad

makes 6 servings • prep: 45 min., other: 8 hr.

Normally served as a family supper side salad with no lettuce, this version of cornbread salad is a whole meal. Smoked turkey, Swiss cheese, vegetables, crumbled cornbread, and crisp bacon make a colorful layered salad to serve in a clear bowl or dish.

test kitchen tip: To cook a big batch of bacon, preheat oven to 425°. Arrange bacon in a single layer on a wire rack in an aluminum foil-lined broiler or jelly-roll pan. Bake at 425° for 25 to 30 minutes or until done.

1	(6-oz.) package buttermilk cornbread mix
1	(12-oz.) bottle Parmesan-peppercorn dressing
½	cup mayonnaise
¼	cup buttermilk
1	(9-oz.) package romaine lettuce, shredded
2½	cups chopped smoked turkey (about ¾ pound)
2	large yellow bell peppers, chopped
2	large tomatoes, seeded and chopped
1	red onion, chopped
1	cup diced celery (about 3 celery ribs)
2	cups (8 oz.) shredded Swiss cheese
10	bacon slices, cooked and crumbled
2	green onions, sliced

1. Prepare cornbread according to package directions; cool and crumble. Set aside.

2. Stir together dressing, mayonnaise, and buttermilk until blended.

3. Layer half each of crumbled cornbread, shredded lettuce, and next 7 ingredients in a large glass bowl; spoon half of dressing mixture evenly over top. Repeat layers ending with dressing mixture. Cover and chill at least 8 hours or up to 24 hours. Sprinkle top with green onions just before serving.

Note: For testing purposes only, we used Martha White Buttermilk Cornbread Mix and Girard's Parmesan-Peppercorn Dressing.

Grilled Salmon Louis

makes 6 servings • prep: 25 min., cook: 10 min.

Flakes of rich–tasting grilled salmon top layers of romaine, garlic croutons, and Parmesan for a classic seafood salad.

test kitchen tip: Cook fresh salmon within 24 hours of purchase. It should be wrapped in plastic wrap or placed in a zip-top plastic bag and refrigerated until time to cook.

⅓ cup olive oil

6 garlic cloves, minced

3 anchovies

3 Tbsp. red wine-garlic vinegar

2 Tbsp. water

1 Tbsp. fresh lemon juice

1 tsp. Worcestershire sauce

⅛ tsp. hot sauce

1 (6-oz.) salmon fillet (about 1 inch thick)

¼ tsp. salt

¼ tsp. pepper

Vegetable cooking spray

2 large heads romaine lettuce, torn

1 cup garlic- or Caesar-flavored croutons

½ cup freshly grated Parmesan cheese

1. Combine first 8 ingredients in a blender; process until blended, stopping to scrape down sides. Set aside.

2. Preheat grill to medium–high heat (350° to 400°).

3. Sprinkle salmon with salt and pepper. Coat grill rack with cooking spray, and grill, covered with grill lid, over medium-high heat (350° to 400°) 5 minutes on each side or until fish flakes with a fork. Let salmon cool slightly; remove and discard skin. Flake salmon with a fork.

4. Place lettuce in a large bowl; add croutons and cheese, and toss gently. Drizzle dressing over salad. Top with flaked salmon. Serve immediately.

Greek Orzo Salad With Shrimp

makes 4 servings • prep: 25 min., cook: 20 min.

Kalamata olives, feta cheese, cherry tomatoes, dill, and lemon juice combine with shrimp for a bold-flavored main dish. Every favorite Greek flavor is found in this salad that you can serve at room temperature.

1	lb. unpeeled, large raw shrimp	3	Tbsp. chopped fresh dill or 1 Tbsp. dried dillweed
3	cups water	3	Tbsp. olive oil
¾	cup uncooked orzo	3	Tbsp. fresh lemon juice
1	(4-oz.) package crumbled feta cheese	1½	Tbsp. red wine vinegar
1	cup cherry tomatoes, quartered	2	garlic cloves, minced
12	kalamata olives, pitted and halved	½	tsp. salt
2	green onions, thinly sliced	¼	tsp. pepper

1. Peel shrimp, and devein, if desired. Bring water to a boil; add shrimp, and cook 3 to 5 minutes or just until shrimp turn pink. Drain.

2. Cook orzo according to package directions; drain. Rinse with cold water; drain well. Combine shrimp, orzo, feta cheese, and next 3 ingredients in a large bowl.

3. Stir together dill and remaining 6 ingredients. Drizzle dressing over shrimp mixture; toss to coat.

test kitchen tip: Deveining shrimp is mostly an aesthetic choice rather than a necessity. It's an easy process to remove the sandy vein that runs along the back of shrimp, particularly with a special deveining tool. However, a knife can be used; just slit the shrimp lengthwise down its back, and pull away the vein with the tip of the knife.

Creamy Basil Dressing

makes 2 cups • prep: 10 min.

The mellow flavor of balsamic vinegar pairs well with the assertive flavors of basil and tarragon in this mayonnaise-based dressing.

make it a meal: This dressing tastes amazing on BLTs or as a dip for fresh vegetables.

2	cups firmly packed chopped fresh basil		2	large garlic cloves
¼	cup olive oil		¼	tsp. dried tarragon
1	cup mayonnaise		½	tsp. dry mustard
¼	cup chopped fresh parsley		3	green onions, chopped
3	Tbsp. balsamic vinegar		½	tsp. freshly ground pepper

1. Process all ingredients in a food processor until smooth, stopping to scrape down sides.

Caesar Salad Dressing

makes 1½ cups • prep: 15 min.

Here's a classic Parmesan and anchovy-seasoned version of the famous salad dressing. Though romaine lettuce is traditional, any crisp salad greens will welcome the dressing.

make it a meal: Typically Caesar salad is served as a side; add chicken, however, and it moves up to main-dish status.

⅓	cup grated Parmesan cheese		1	tsp. sugar
⅓	cup fresh lemon juice		1	tsp. Worcestershire sauce
1	(2-oz.) can anchovy fillets		1	cup olive oil
3	garlic cloves		2	Tbsp. chopped fresh parsley
2	Tbsp. Dijon mustard			

1. Process first 7 ingredients in a blender or food processor until smooth, stopping to scrape down sides as necessary. Turn blender on high; gradually add oil in a slow, steady stream. Add parsley; process until blended. Serve over salad greens.

Denise Dunkin

Doggone Good Cookin'
Support Dogs, Inc. ~ St. Louis, Missouri

sandwiches
and soups

Stuffed Focaccia With Roasted Red
Pepper Vinaigrette, page 341

The Ultimate Grilled Cheese

makes 5 sandwiches • prep: 15 min., cook: 8 min.

Three cheeses nestle between slices of golden skillet-grilled sourdough bread for a grilled cheese that beats all others.

¾ cup mayonnaise

1 (3-oz.) package cream cheese, softened

1 cup (4 oz.) shredded Cheddar cheese

1 cup (4 oz.) shredded mozzarella cheese

½ tsp. garlic powder

⅛ tsp. seasoned salt

10 (½-inch) slices sourdough bread

2 Tbsp. butter or margarine, softened

1. Beat mayonnaise and cream cheese at medium speed with an electric mixer until light and fluffy. Stir in Cheddar cheese and next 3 ingredients. Spread each of 5 bread slices evenly with cheese mixture. Top with remaining bread slices.

2. Spread butter on both sides of sandwiches. Cook, in batches, in skillet over medium heat until lightly browned on both sides. Serve immediately.

Cooking with the Original Search Engine
Fort Worth Public Library All Staff Association ~ Fort Worth, Texas

test kitchen tip: Preheat your griddle or skillet to medium heat before adding a sandwich to get crispy golden crusts everytime.

Italian Cheese Bites

makes 8 servings • prep: 15 min., cook: 6 min. per batch

Provolone and Italian bread give these grilled cheese sandwiches their Italian accent. Marinara sauce is a must for dipping the griddle-toasted sandwiches.

½ cup butter, softened

½ cup freshly grated Parmesan cheese

16 Italian bread slices

16 provolone cheese slices

Marinara sauce

1. Stir together butter and Parmesan cheese; spread on 1 side of each bread slice. Place 8 bread slices, buttered sides down, on wax paper; layer with 2 provolone cheese slices. Top with remaining bread slices, buttered sides up.

2. Cook sandwiches, in batches, on a hot griddle or in a nonstick skillet over medium heat, gently pressing with a spatula, 3 minutes on each side or until golden brown and cheese melts. Cut each sandwich into fourths, and serve with marinara sauce for dipping.

make it a meal: If your family likes spaghetti and lasagna, they'll love one of these sandwiches for supper. Serve it with carrot and celery sticks or fresh fruit on the side.

Turkey and Ham Pine-Berry Sandwiches

makes 6 servings • prep: 8 min.

Sweet raisin bread pairs deliciously with a sandwich filling of pineapple, ham, turkey, and cranberry relish.

1   (3-oz.) package cream cheese, softened

⅓   cup drained crushed pineapple

12 raisin bread slices

1   (6-oz.) package low-fat smoked turkey breast slices

6   Tbsp. cranberry-orange relish, drained

1   (6-oz.) package low-fat cooked ham slices

test kitchen tip: Save the pineapple juice from canned pineapple to use to keep cut fruit such as apples and bananas from discoloring. Just toss the cut fruit in the juice, then discard.

1. Stir together cream cheese and pineapple. Spread 2 tsp. cream cheese mixture on each bread slice. Top 6 bread slices with turkey. Spread relish over turkey slices. Top with ham and remaining bread slices.

BLTs With a Twist

makes 4 servings • prep: 20 min., cook: 20 min.

The "twist" in this sandwich is the addition of goat cheese, dried tomatoes instead of fresh, and a sprinkle of fresh basil on a French bread loaf.

8	bacon slices	½	cup (about 3 oz.) dried tomatoes in oil, drained and chopped
1	(1-lb.) French bread loaf (not baguette)	4	lettuce leaves
¼	cup chopped fresh basil	½	small red onion, thinly sliced
6	oz. goat cheese		

1. Preheat oven to 325°.

2. Cook bacon in a large skillet until crisp; drain on paper towels. Set aside.

3. Slice bread in half horizontally. Sprinkle basil over cut side of bottom half of loaf; crumble goat cheese over basil. Sprinkle tomatoes over goat cheese. Top with top half of loaf. Place loaf on a baking sheet; bake at 325° for 10 minutes.

4. Remove loaf from oven; remove top half of loaf. Arrange bacon, lettuce, and onion over tomatoes; replace top half of loaf.   Gary Moon

Bread from the Brook
The Church at Brook Hills ~ Birmingham, Alabama

Chicken Salad Croissants

makes 20 sandwiches • prep: 25 min., other: 30 min.

Bridal showers, summer tea parties, and wedding receptions call for fresh fruity chicken salad sandwiches. Toasted pecans and sweet grapes flavor this chicken salad.

1	cup mayonnaise	1	cup seedless green or red grapes
1	cup sour cream	¾	cup pecans, toasted and coarsely chopped
1	tsp. salt		
1	tsp. pepper	20	croissants
¼	to ½ tsp. fresh tarragon		Red leaf lettuce
3	cups chopped cooked chicken		Fresh tarragon sprigs

1. Stir together first 5 ingredients in a large bowl. Add chicken, grapes, and chopped pecans, tossing to coat. Cover and chill at least 30 minutes.

2. Cut a slit horizontally on 1 side of each croissant; fill evenly with lettuce and chicken salad. Skewer sandwiches with fresh tarragon sprigs to hold together.

Old Bay Shrimp Salad Rolls

makes 6 to 8 servings • prep: 20 min., cook: 2 min., other: 2 hr.

In 1939, German immigrant Gustav Brunn settled in Baltimore among the seafood lovers of Maryland. With only a handheld spice grinder, he developed the secret recipe that would become the legendary Old Bay seasoning. In this recipe, the seasoning imparts a distinctive bold flavor to the shrimp and lemony mayonnaise dressing.

3	qt. water	2	Tbsp. lemon juice
¼	cup Old Bay seasoning	¾	tsp. Old Bay seasoning
2	lb. unpeeled, medium-size raw shrimp	¼	tsp. seasoned pepper
		8	green leaf lettuce leaves (optional)
½	cup finely chopped celery	8	(8-inch) soft taco-size flour tortillas
⅓	cup finely chopped onion	2	large avocados, thinly sliced
⅓	cup light mayonnaise		

make it a meal: Serve these tasty sandwiches alongside Wild Berry Soup on page 345.

1. Bring 3 qt. water and ¼ cup Old Bay seasoning to a boil in a Dutch oven; add shrimp, and cook, stirring occasionally, 2 minutes or until shrimp turn pink. Drain. Place shrimp into a 13- x 9-inch dish to cool. Peel shrimp, and devein, if desired; chop shrimp.

2. Stir together celery and next 5 ingredients; stir in shrimp. Cover and chill 2 hours.

3. Place 1 lettuce leaf on top of each tortilla. Top each evenly with ½ cup shrimp salad and 3 or 4 avocado slices. Roll up tortillas, and secure with thick, round wooden picks. Cut in half.

Fried Green Tomato Po'boys

makes 3 servings • prep: 20 min., cook: 18 min.

The New Orleans traditional po' boy sandwich usually filled with ham, fried oysters, shrimp, or beef gets a new twist with a fried green tomato and crispy bacon filling.

test kitchen tip: Like many Louisiana specialties, this sandwich is spicy. If you prefer to tone down the heat, reduce the amount of Cajun seasoning, and omit the hot sauce.

2 cups self-rising flour	9 ready-to-serve bacon slices
3 Tbsp. Cajun seasoning	3 center-split deli rolls
2 cups canola oil	6 Tbsp. mayonnaise
3 large green tomatoes, cut into ¼-inch-thick slices	1 ripe avocado, sliced
	1½ cups shredded iceberg lettuce
1 cup buttermilk	Hot sauce (optional)

1. Preheat broiler.

2. Combine flour and Cajun seasoning in a shallow dish.

3. Heat oil in a large nonstick skillet over medium–high heat to 360°. Dip tomato slices in buttermilk, and dredge in flour mixture. Fry tomatoes, in batches, 2 minutes on each side or until golden. Drain on a wire rack over paper towels; set aside.

4. Heat bacon according to package directions; keep warm.

5. Split rolls, and arrange, split sides up, on a baking sheet. Broil 5 inches from heat 2 minutes or until lightly toasted; remove from oven.

6. Spread cut sides of rolls with mayonnaise; place fried green tomatoes on bottom roll halves. Top evenly with bacon, avocado, and lettuce; sprinkle with hot sauce, if desired. Top with remaining roll halves, and serve immediately.

Melted Avocado Club

makes 4 sandwiches • prep: 20 min., cook: 12 min.

Buttery homemade guacamole gives grilled club sandwiches a unique flavor. It blends well with nutty, delicate provolone cheese slices.

2	ripe avocados, mashed	½	lb. thinly sliced deli ham	
1	Tbsp. fresh lime juice	½	lb. thinly sliced deli roast beef	
1	Tbsp. mayonnaise	4	tomato slices	
1	Tbsp. yellow mustard	8	bacon slices, cooked	
¼	tsp. hot sauce	¼	lb. provolone cheese slices	
⅛	tsp. ground red pepper	3	Tbsp. butter, softened and divided	
8	whole wheat bread slices			

test kitchen tip: To effortlessly pit an avocado, slice all the way around the pit and through both ends of the avocado with a large knife. Then twist the halves in opposite directions, and pull them apart. If the avocado flesh is firm, tap the pit sharply with a knife, and twist the blade to lift out the pit.

1. Stir together first 6 ingredients. Spread avocado mixture evenly on 1 side of each of 4 bread slices. Top each evenly with ham, next 4 ingredients, and remaining bread slices. Spread butter on both sides of each sandwich.

2. Cook sandwiches in a nonstick skillet or on a griddle over medium heat 6 minutes on each side or until golden.

essence of Tabasco sauce
After the Civil War, Edmund McIlhenny brought more than his family back to his Avery Island, Louisiana, home. He returned with hot pepper seeds given to him by a traveler from Central America. These seeds soon yielded sizzling hot little peppers that grew well on the island's salt dome. Edmund mashed, fermented, cooked, and experimented with the peppers until his creation, Tabasco Sauce, now graces tables around the world as a favorite condiment. The incendiary sauce is still produced by McIlhenny's descendants only on the tiny island and is now an undisputed icon of Louisiana cuisine. But the variations on the original red sauce offer cooks more options than ever. In order of the greatest heat, now look for the following green or red sauce Tabasco variations: habanero, original, chipotle, garlic, green, and sweet & spicy. They flavor everything from soups to ice cream with as much heat as you can stand.

Open-Faced Philly Sandwiches

makes 2 servings • prep: 20 min., cook: 32 min.

Juicy steak with sautéed mushrooms, peppers, and onions makes this a sandwich to eat with a knife and fork.

test kitchen tip: Reserve tops of submarine rolls and hollowed out bread to make fresh breadcrumbs. Tear the bread into 1-inch chunks, and pulse in a food processor until breadcrumbs form.

2	(8-inch) submarine rolls, unsliced
½	lb. boneless top round steak
2	Tbsp. Italian dressing
¼	tsp. dried crushed red pepper
2	Tbsp. butter
1	large onion, thinly sliced
1½	cups sliced fresh mushrooms
1	green bell pepper, cut into thin strips
1	garlic clove, pressed
2	(¾-oz.) slices provolone cheese

1. Preheat broiler.

2. Make a 1½- to 2-inch deep vertical cut around outside edge of each roll, leaving a ½-inch border. Remove tops of rolls, and discard. Hollow out about 1½ inches of each bread roll, forming a boat. Set boats aside.

3. Cut steak diagonally across grain into ⅛-inch-thick strips; place in a small shallow bowl. Add dressing and crushed red pepper, tossing to coat; set aside.

4. Melt butter in a nonstick skillet over medium-high heat; add onion and mushrooms, and sauté 15 minutes or until onions are golden brown. Add bell pepper; sauté 8 to 10 minutes or until bell pepper is tender. Add garlic, and sauté 1 minute. Remove mixture from skillet, and set aside.

5. Stir-fry steak mixture in skillet over medium-high heat 2 to 3 minutes or until steak strips are no longer pink.

6. Layer bread boats with steak mixture and onion mixture; top with cheese. Broil 5½ inches from heat 3 minutes or until cheese is lightly browned.

Sloppy José Sandwiches With Broccoli-Cilantro Slaw

makes 4 serving • prep: 15 min., cook: 19 min.

Kids will love the chili-spiced filling with or without the slaw.

make it a meal: Serve these sandwiches with apple wedges and stovetop baked beans for an easy weeknight supper.

1	medium onion, finely chopped
1	Tbsp. vegetable oil
1	lb. lean ground beef
2	(8-oz.) cans tomato sauce
1	Tbsp. ground cumin
1	Tbsp. dried oregano
1	Tbsp. chili powder
½	tsp. pepper
¼	tsp. salt
4	honey wheat hamburger buns, toasted
	Broccoli-Cilantro Slaw

1. Cook onion in hot oil in a large skillet over medium heat about 4 minutes or until onion is tender. Stir in ground beef and next 6 ingredients, and cook, stirring occasionally, 15 minutes or until beef crumbles and is no longer pink.

2. Spoon beef mixture on bottom halves of toasted buns; top each with about 3 Tbsp. Cilantro Slaw and remaining bun halves. Serve with remaining Cilantro Slaw.

Broccoli–Cilantro Slaw

makes 4 cups • prep: 10 min.

¼   cup finely chopped fresh cilantro

¼   cup Dijon mustard

3   Tbsp. mayonnaise

1   Tbsp. white wine vinegar

1   (12-oz.) package broccoli slaw mix

1. Whisk together first 4 ingredients in a large bowl; add broccoli slaw, tossing to coat.

Stuffed Border Burgers

makes 6 servings • prep: 20 min., cook: 10 min.

Beef patties mixed with olives, chili powder, and fajita seasoning encase a slice of Monterey Jack cheese in the centers of these grilled burgers.

test kitchen tip: Toast the cut sides of rolls directly on grill rack alongside burgers during the last 2 to 3 minutes of cooking.

1½	lb. lean ground beef	6	(1-oz.) slices Monterey Jack cheese
½	cup finely chopped onion		with peppers
1	(4.25-oz.) can chopped ripe olives,	6	onion rolls, split and toasted
	drained		Tex-Mex Secret Sauce
2	Tbsp. ketchup		Toppings: shredded lettuce, sliced
1	tsp. chili powder		tomatoes, guacamole
1	tsp. fajita seasoning		

1. Preheat grill to medium–high heat (350° to 400°).

2. Combine first 6 ingredients. Shape mixture into 12 (4-inch) patties. Fold cheese slices into quarters; place cheese on each of 6 patties. Top with remaining 6 patties, pressing to seal edges.

3. Grill, covered with grill lid, over medium–high heat (350° to 400°) for 4 to 5 minutes on each side or until done. Serve on rolls with Tex-Mex Secret Sauce and desired toppings.

Note: For testing purposes only, we used McCormick Fajita Seasoning and Sargento Monterey Jack Cheese with Peppers.

Tex-Mex Secret Sauce

makes ¾ cup • prep: 5 min.

½	cup sour cream	1	(4.5-oz.) can chopped green chiles
⅓	cup ketchup	1	Tbsp. minced fresh cilantro

1. Stir together all ingredients. Cover and chill until ready to serve.

Barbecue Pork Sandwiches

makes 12 servings • prep: 30 min., cook: 9 hr.

A slow cooker is a good way to simmer a pork roast so that the meat is juicy and tender. The sauce for these sandwiches is tomato-based with a hint of mustard.

freeze it: Prepare barbecue pork up to a month in advance, and freeze in an airtight container. Thaw overnight in refrigerator before reheating in microwave.

2	Tbsp. barbecue seasoning, divided	1	Tbsp. Worcestershire sauce
1½	tsp. salt, divided	¼	cup firmly packed brown sugar
1	(5-lb.) bone-in pork loin center rib	2	Tbsp. spicy brown mustard
	roast	1	tsp. black pepper
1	(15-oz.) can no-salt-added diced	2	tsp. dried crushed red pepper
	tomatoes	12	multigrain buns
⅓	cup cider vinegar		Dill pickles (optional)
¼	cup no-salt-added tomato paste		

1. Combine 1 Tbsp. barbecue seasoning and 1 tsp. salt; rub evenly over pork roast.

2. Stir together tomatoes, next 7 ingredients, remaining 1 Tbsp. barbecue seasoning, and remaining ½ tsp. salt in a 6½-qt. slow cooker. Add roast; cover and cook on LOW 9 hours or until meat shreds easily.

3. Remove roast; remove and discard bone. Shred meat using the tines of 2 forks. Return to slow cooker, and stir together with sauce; spoon over multi-grain buns. Serve with pickles, if desired.

Note: For testing purposes only, we used Chef Paul Prudhomme's Magic Barbecue Seasoning.

Balsamic-Blue Cheese Portobello Burgers

makes 2 servings • prep: 15 min., cook: 8 min., other: 1 hr.

Burger-sized portobello mushrooms have a firm texture and rich flavor similar to beef and make a delicious meatless sandwich.

2	large portobello mushroom caps, stemmed	¼	cup crumbled blue cheese or Gorgonzola cheese
3	Tbsp. balsamic vinegar	2	Tbsp. light mayonnaise
1	Tbsp. olive oil	1	tsp. balsamic vinegar
1	tsp. minced fresh garlic	2	whole wheat hamburger buns, split
½	tsp. pepper		Romaine lettuce leaves
¼	tsp. salt	2	tomato slices

1. Scrape gills from mushroom caps, if desired.

2. Combine 3 Tbsp. vinegar, oil, and next 3 ingredients in a shallow dish or large zip-top plastic freezer bag; add mushrooms, turning to coat. Cover or seal, and chill 1 hour, turning occasionally. Remove mushrooms from marinade, discarding marinade.

3. Preheat grill to medium-high heat (350° to 400°).

4. Grill mushrooms, covered with grill lid, over medium-high heat (350° to 400°) 3 to 4 minutes on each side or until tender. Remove mushrooms from grill, and immediately sprinkle undersides evenly with blue cheese.

5. Stir together mayonnaise and 1 tsp. vinegar. Spread mixture evenly on cut sides of buns; place lettuce, mushrooms, and tomato slices on bottom halves of buns, and cover with tops. Serve immediately.

test kitchen tip: The brownish-black walls on the underside of mushroom caps are called gills. Scrape them off gently using a spoon. Removing gills keeps other ingredients from turning a grayish brown.

Hot Brown

makes 4 servings • prep: 15 min., cook: 20 min.

This Kentucky tradition is so gooey and bubbly you'll need to eat it with a fork.

test kitchen tip: This rich and creamy Cheese Sauce also tastes great over steamed veggies and pasta.

8	bacon slices		4	tomato slices
8	bread slices, crusts removed and toasted			Cheese Sauce
1	lb. sliced cooked turkey breast		½	cup grated Parmesan cheese

1. Preheat oven to 425°.

2. Cook bacon in a large skillet over medium heat until partially crisp; remove bacon, and set aside.

3. Cut 4 slices of toast in half diagonally. Place 2 slices, cut side in, with 1 whole slice in the center, on an ovenproof plate or a 15- x 10-inch jelly-roll pan. Repeat with remaining toast. Top with turkey, tomato, Cheese Sauce, bacon, and Parmesan cheese. Bake at 425° for 15 minutes or until bacon is crisp and sauce is bubbly.

Cheese Sauce

makes 3 cups • prep: 10 min., cook: 10 min.

2	Tbsp. butter or margarine		¼	tsp. salt
2	Tbsp. all-purpose flour		¼	cup (1 oz.) shredded sharp Cheddar cheese
2	cups milk			
½	tsp. Worcestershire sauce		¼	cup grated Parmesan cheese

1. Melt butter in a heavy saucepan over low heat; add flour, stirring until smooth. Cook 1 minute, stirring constantly. Gradually add milk, Worcestershire sauce, and salt; cook over medium heat, stirring constantly, until mixture is thickened and bubbly. Add cheeses, stirring until cheeses melt.

Recipes and Remembrances
Newport Bicentennial Commission ~ Newport, Kentucky

solely Southern sandwiches

When it comes to sandwiches with Southern roots, opportunity was the mother of invention. In New Orleans, working-class Greeks enjoyed lunches of deli meats, olive salad, cheeses, and Italian bread—all served separately. Before long, muffulettas, a sandwich combining it all, were made to order. A few years later, two restaurant owners sympathizing with striking New Orleans streetcar workers felt sorry for the "poor boys" and gave away sandwiches of French bread filled with ham, deep-fried oysters, shrimp, sausage, or beef sauced with rich gravy. Thus, the "po' boy" was born. But probably no Southern sandwich is as famous as the Hot Brown, Kentucky's broiled sandwich of sliced turkey or chicken and bacon topped with tomato and a hot cheese sauce. Originally made for high society patrons at Louisville's Brown Hotel in 1923, it's still served to upscale diners at the hotel as well as to visitors at every state park restaurant in Kentucky.

Stuffed Focaccia With Roasted Pepper Vinaigrette

(pictured on page 329)

makes 4 servings • prep: 20 min., cook: 8 min.

Pick up the ingredients from the grocery on the way home from work, and you can have this impressive sandwich ready for the oven in about 20 minutes. A filling of goat cheese, pine nuts, and deli-roasted chicken makes a delicious filling.

1   (9-inch) loaf focaccia bread
Roasted Pepper Vinaigrette, divided
1   (4-oz.) log goat cheese, crumbled
¼   cup pine nuts or slivered almonds,
    toasted

1   deli-roasted chicken
3   cups mixed baby lettuces
½   pt. grape or cherry tomatoes,
    halved

test kitchen tip: To slice the focaccia in half horizontally, place it on a cutting board, and hold it securely, being careful to keep your fingers out of the knife's way. As you cut the loaf in half, move the serrated knife using a sawing motion, away from your body.

1. Preheat oven to 400°.

2. Cut bread in half horizontally, using a serrated knife; place, cut sides up, on a baking sheet. Drizzle evenly with 1 cup Roasted Pepper Vinaigrette. Sprinkle evenly with goat cheese and pine nuts.

3. Bake at 400° for 6 to 8 minutes or until lightly browned. Remove meat from chicken, and coarsely chop. Sprinkle chicken over bottom bread half. Top with lettuce and tomatoes; cover with top bread half. Cut into quarters. Serve immediately with remaining ½ cup Roasted Pepper Vinaigrette.

Note: We used focaccia topped with peppers, onions, mushrooms, and cheese from a local bakery.

Roasted Pepper Vinaigrette

makes 1½ cups • prep: 5 min.

1   cup oil-and-vinegar dressing
1   (5.2-oz.) jar roasted red bell
    peppers, drained

1. Process dressing and roasted peppers in a blender or food processor until smooth.

Note: For testing purposes only, we used Newman's Own Olive Oil & Vinegar dressing.

Roasted Vegetable Sandwiches

makes 4 sandwiches • prep: 20 min., cook: 12 min.

Provolone cheese melts over sweet roasted vegetables in these sandwiches. Serve a chilled soup or fruit salad in contrast with the oven-warmed sandwiches.

test kitchen tip: French hamburger rolls are made with French bread dough and are much sturdier than ordinary hamburger buns. Substitute an onion or kaiser roll if French buns are not available.

¼ cup butter, softened	4 tsp. mayonnaise
1 garlic clove, pressed	Roasted Summer Vegetables
¼ tsp. dried Italian seasoning	4 provolone cheese slices
4 French hamburger buns, split	

1. Preheat oven to 400°.

2. Stir together first 3 ingredients.

3. Spread butter mixture evenly on cut sides of top bun halves; spread mayonnaise evenly on cut sides of bottom bun halves. Place ¾ cup Roasted Summer Vegetables evenly on each bottom bun half; top each with 1 provolone cheese slice and remaining bun halves. Wrap each sandwich lightly in aluminum foil, and place on a baking sheet.

4. Bake at 400° for 10 to 12 minutes or until cheese melts.

Note: For testing purposes only, we used Publix Deli French Hamburger Buns.

Roasted Summer Vegetables

makes 3 cups • prep: 30 min., cook: 20 min., other: 20 min.

1 medium eggplant	1 medium-size sweet onion, halved
1 tsp. salt, divided	3 Tbsp. olive oil
2 medium zucchini (about 1 lb.)	½ tsp. pepper
3 yellow squash (about 1¼ lb.)	3 Tbsp. chopped fresh basil
1 red bell pepper	1 Tbsp. chopped fresh parsley

1. Cut eggplant into ¼-inch-thick slices, and place in a single layer on paper towels. Sprinkle with ½ tsp. salt, and let stand 20 minutes.

2. Preheat oven to 450°.

3. Cut zucchini and yellow squash into ¼-inch-thick slices. Cut bell pepper into ½-inch strips. Cut onion halves into ½-inch slices.

4. Toss together vegetables, olive oil, remaining ½ tsp. salt, and pepper; place in 3 lightly greased broiler pans or jelly-roll pans.

5. Bake at 450° for 20 minutes or until vegetables are tender, stirring once. Remove from oven, and sprinkle evenly with basil and parsley.

Spinach, Blue Cheese, Pecan, and Cranberry Wraps

makes 8 servings • prep: 20 min.

These wraps are like a fruity spinach salad in a tortilla, and they're an easy pack-and-go sandwich for work or picnics.

1	(8-oz.) container light spreadable cream cheese
2	Tbsp. nonfat buttermilk
¼	tsp. garlic powder
¼	tsp. onion powder
1	(4-oz.) package crumbled blue cheese

½	cup chopped toasted pecans
½	cup sweetened dried cranberries
8	(8-inch) flour tortillas
1	Granny Smith apple, thinly sliced
4	cups baby spinach leaves

1. Stir together first 4 ingredients until blended; stir in blue cheese, pecans, and cranberries. Spread about ⅓ cup cream cheese mixture over each tortilla. Layer with apple slices and spinach. Roll up; secure with wooden picks.

Cream of Butternut Squash and Leek Soup

makes 14 cups • prep: 40 min., cook: 56 min.

Sweet butternut squash and delicate leeks are herb-seasoned, then pureed for a smooth, creamy soup topped with Parmesan and chives.

test kitchen tip: To save time, look for prepeeled and cubed butternut squash in the produce department. It's typically available while butternut squash is at its peak during fall and winter months.

2	small leeks		Pepper to taste
⅓	cup butter, melted	1	cup whipping cream
4	lb. butternut squash, peeled, seeded, and cubed (about 9 cups)	1	cup milk
		⅓	cup grated Parmesan cheese
6	cups chicken broth	¼	cup chopped fresh chives or
1	tsp. salt		parsley
¼	tsp. dried thyme		

1. Remove and discard roots, tough outer leaves, and tops of leeks to where dark green begins to pale. Cut leeks in half lengthwise; rinse well. Chop leeks.
2. Cook leek in butter in a Dutch oven over medium-high heat 4 minutes, stirring constantly. Stir in squash and next 4 ingredients; bring to a boil. Cover, reduce heat, and simmer 40 minutes or until squash is tender. Remove from heat, and let cool slightly.
3. Position knife blade in food processor bowl; add squash mixture, in batches, and process until smooth, stopping to scrape down sides. Return pureed mixture to Dutch oven; stir in whipping cream and milk. Ladle soup into individual bowls; sprinkle with cheese and chives.

Gazpacho

makes 12 cups • prep: 20 min., other: 4 hr.

Whirl all the fresh vegetables in the blender, and chill to make refreshing summertime gazpacho. Croutons and diced hard-cooked eggs are common garnishes for the cold Spanish soup.

test kitchen tip: This is a great recipe to make in the summer when fresh tomatoes are abundant. In the winter, use Roma or plum tomatoes. They are juicier and meatier than out-of-season beefsteak tomatoes.

2	large ripe tomatoes, chopped	¼	cup lime juice
2	yellow onions, chopped	¼	cup red wine vinegar
2	medium cucumbers, peeled, seeded, and chopped	2	Tbsp. olive oil
		1½	tsp. salt
2	garlic cloves, minced	½	tsp. black pepper
1	(7-oz.) jar roasted red bell peppers, drained	2	tsp. hot sauce
			Sour cream (optional)
½	cup chopped fresh cilantro		Ground red pepper (optional)
1	(46-oz.) can tomato juice		

1. Process first 6 ingredients in a food processor until smooth, stopping to scrape down sides.
2. Stir together vegetable puree, tomato juice, and next 6 ingredients. Cover and chill at least 4 hours. Top gazpacho with sour cream, if desired, and sprinkle with red pepper, if desired.
Odessa Fells

Wild Berry Soup

makes 8 cups • prep: 20 min., cook: 13 min., other: 3 hr.

Pureed strawberries, blueberries, and raspberries are thickened with vanilla yogurt and rich whipping cream, then sweetened with honey for this easy, but sophisticated-looking chilled soup.

2	cups quartered fresh strawberries	1	(32-oz.) container vanilla yogurt
1	cup fresh blueberries	1	cup heavy whipping cream
1	cup fresh raspberries	⅓	cup honey
½	cup pineapple juice		Orange-Ginger Sauce

1. Process first 4 ingredients in a blender until smooth. Press berry mixture through a wire-mesh strainer into a large bowl, discarding seeds. Stir in yogurt and remaining ingredients. Cover and chill 3 hours.

Orange-Ginger Sauce

makes ½ cup • prep: 5 min., cook: 15 min.

½	cup fresh orange juice	2	Tbsp. honey
½	cup white Zinfandel or blush wine	2	slices fresh ginger

1. Bring all ingredients to a boil in a small saucepan over medium-high heat. Reduce heat, and simmer, uncovered, 10 minutes or until juice mixture is reduced by half. Discard ginger. Cool.

make it ahead: To get a head start on this delicate recipe, prepare the Orange-Ginger Sauce up to a week in advance, and refrigerate in an airtight container.

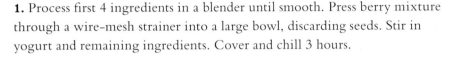

Lobster and Chive Bisque

makes 6 cups • prep: 10 min., cook: 30 min.

Chunks of lobster and sherry flavor this velvety bisque.

3	Tbsp. butter	1	tsp. salt
1	Tbsp. minced onion	⅛	tsp. paprika
3	Tbsp. all-purpose flour	1	cup chopped cooked lobster
3	cups milk		(about 12 oz.)
1	cup heavy whipping cream	2	Tbsp. chopped fresh chives
½	cup dry sherry		

1. Melt butter in a Dutch oven over medium heat; add onion, and sauté 1 minute or until tender. Add flour, stirring until blended. Cook 1 minute, stirring constantly. Gradually add milk and next 4 ingredients. Bring just to a simmer; cook, uncovered, 3 to 4 minutes or until slightly thickened (do not boil). Stir in lobster and chives.

Secret Ingredients
The Junior League of Alexandria, Louisiana

make it a meal: Serve this luxurious soup with breadsticks and a simple green salad for an impressive luncheon.

Crème de Brie Soup

makes 7½ cups • prep: 35 min., cook: 27 min.

Imagine French onion soup with mushrooms and a broth enriched with Brie and whipping cream. For added richness, top crusty baguette slices with Brie slices for an impressive special-occasion soup.

test kitchen tip: Brie has a fairly short shelf life, so use it within a few days.

6	oz. Brie	1	bay leaf
¼	cup butter or margarine	2	cups heavy whipping cream
1	lb. onions, finely chopped	1	Tbsp. chopped fresh thyme
1	(8-oz.) package sliced fresh mushrooms	1	Tbsp. dry sherry
4	tsp. minced garlic	¼	tsp. salt
1	cup dry white wine	¼	tsp. pepper
¼	cup all-purpose flour	12	slices French baguette, toasted
3½	cups chicken broth	4	oz. Brie, cut into 12 slices

1. Discard rind from 6 oz. of Brie. Cut Brie into cubes; set aside.

2. Melt butter in a Dutch oven over medium heat; add onion, mushrooms, and garlic, and sauté 5 minutes. Add wine, and cook 9 to 11 minutes or until wine has almost evaporated. Add flour, stirring until thoroughly blended. Add chicken broth and bay leaf. Bring to a boil, stirring constantly. Reduce heat, and simmer, uncovered, 5 to 6 minutes or until mixture thickens. Stir in whipping cream and thyme. Add cubed Brie, and stir until cheese melts. Stir in sherry, salt, and pepper. Discard bay leaf.

3. Preheat broiler.

4. Place 6 large ovenproof soup bowls on a 15- x 10-inch jelly-roll pan. Fill bowls with soup. Top each serving with 2 slices bread and 2 slices Brie. Broil 2 to 3 minutes or until Brie is melted and bubbly.

Ham-and-Bean Soup

makes 9½ cups • prep: 6 min.; cook: 2 hr., 13 min.; other: 8 hr.

In the Appalachian region, this recipe is known simply as "soup beans," and each bowl is topped with chopped fresh onion. This version is sprinkled with crispy cornbread croutons; most Southerners say that cornbread is a must with a bowl of soup beans.

1 (16-oz.) package dried great Northern beans	2 Tbsp. olive oil
3 cups chopped cooked ham (about 1 lb.)	10 oz. smoked ham hocks
1 large sweet onion, diced	2 (32-oz.) containers chicken broth
2 garlic cloves, minced	2 cups water
	½ tsp. dried crushed red pepper

test kitchen tip: Some old recipes add baking soda to the water when soaking dried beans. Today we know that step reduces the nutritional value. Skip the soda.

1. Rinse and sort beans according to package directions. Cover with water 2 inches above beans; let soak 8 hours. Drain.

2. Sauté ham, onion, and garlic in hot oil in a Dutch oven over medium-high heat 5 minutes or until onion is tender.

3. Add beans, ham hocks, chicken broth, 2 cups water, and red pepper. Bring to a boil; cover, reduce heat, and simmer 1 hour. Uncover and mash some of the beans with a potato masher. Simmer, uncovered, 1 more hour or until beans are tender. Remove ham hocks before serving.

Potato Soup

makes 13 cups • prep: 25 min., cook: 45 min.

Just like a baked potato, dress up servings of Potato Soup with crumbled bacon, Cheddar cheese, and chopped green onions.

5 large baking potatoes, peeled and cubed (about 4½ lb.)
¼ cup chopped onion
2 celery ribs, chopped
2 carrots, thinly sliced
1 (8-oz.) package cream cheese, softened
½ cup butter, softened
1 (10¾-oz.) can cream of chicken soup, undiluted

2 cups milk
2 cups water
1 tsp. salt
½ tsp. freshly ground pepper
8 bacon slices, cooked and crumbled
Shredded Cheddar cheese
Chopped green onions

1. Combine first 4 ingredients in a large Dutch oven; add water to cover. Bring to a boil; cover, reduce heat, and simmer 12 minutes or until potatoes are tender. Drain.

2. Beat cream cheese and butter in a medium bowl at medium speed with an electric mixer until creamy. Add cream of chicken soup, beating well. Gradually add milk, beating until smooth; add milk mixture to vegetable mixture. Stir in 2 cups water, salt, and pepper. Bring to a boil; reduce heat, and simmer, uncovered, 15 minutes, stirring occasionally. Mash with potato masher to desired consistency.

3. Top each serving with bacon, Cheddar cheese, and green onions.

Simple Pleasures: From Our Table to Yours
Arab Mothers' Club ~ Arab, Alabama

test kitchen tip: Refrigerate any leftovers in an airtight container, and save for evenings when everyone's schedules are different.

Sweet Potato-Corn Chowder

makes 8 cups • prep: 20 min., cook: 45 min.

Indulge in this Southern vegetable version of a New England chowder. It's velvety and cream-colored with chunks of sweet potatoes and corn throughout.

6 bacon slices, diced
1 medium onion, chopped
1 cup frozen whole kernel corn
½ cup chopped red bell pepper
½ cup chopped leek
1 tsp. chopped fresh thyme
1 tsp. chopped fresh marjoram
2 sweet potatoes, peeled and chopped

2½ cups water
1 (14½-oz.) can chicken broth
2 tsp. cornstarch
½ cup cold water
½ cup whipping cream
Salt and freshly ground pepper to taste

1. Cook bacon in a Dutch oven until crisp; remove bacon, reserving drippings in pan. Set bacon aside.

test kitchen tip: If fresh marjoram is unavailable, substitute about ¼ tsp. dried marjoram.

2. Cook onion and next 5 ingredients in drippings in Dutch oven over medium-high heat, stirring constantly, until tender. Add sweet potato, 2½ cups water, and chicken broth; cook, uncovered, 18 minutes or until sweet potato is tender.

3. Combine cornstarch and ½ cup cold water, stirring until smooth. Stir cornstarch mixture into soup. Bring to a boil; cook over medium heat, stirring constantly, until slightly thickened and bubbly. Reduce heat to low; add bacon, whipping cream, and salt and pepper to taste. Cook, uncovered, until thoroughly heated, stirring occasionally.

Gwen Smith

Blue Stocking Club Forget-Me-Not Recipes
Blue Stocking Club ~ Bristol, Tennessee

Creole Beef Stew

makes 8 cups • prep: 25 min.; cook: 2 hr., 50 min.

Seasoned chuck roast simmers with vegetables for this stew where molasses and raisins add a flavor surprise. Spoon it into bowls over cornbread squares or hot rice for a one-dish meal.

3	Tbsp. all-purpose flour
1	tsp. salt
½	tsp. ground ginger
½	tsp. celery salt
¼	tsp. garlic salt
¼	tsp. pepper
3	lb. chuck roast, cut into 2-inch cubes
2	Tbsp. vegetable oil
1	(16-oz.) can whole tomatoes, undrained and chopped
3	medium onions, sliced
½	cup molasses
⅓	cup red wine vinegar
6	medium carrots, cut diagonally into 1-inch pieces
½	cup raisins

1. Combine first 6 ingredients in a large zip-top plastic freezer bag; add meat. Seal bag securely, and shake until meat is coated.

2. Brown meat in oil in a large Dutch oven over medium-high heat. Add tomatoes and next 3 ingredients; bring to a boil. Cover, reduce heat, and simmer 2 hours, stirring occasionally. Add carrot and raisins; bring to a boil. Cover, reduce heat, and simmer 30 minutes or until carrot is tender.

test kitchen tip: Be sure to scrape any browned bits from the bottom of the Dutch oven after browning the meat. These browned particles give the stew a rich, complex flavor.

Cioppino

makes 19 cups • prep: 20 min.; cook: 1 hr., 29 min.

Having a party? This one-pot fish stew makes enough for a crowd and is swimming with clams, shrimp, grouper, scallops, and crabmeat.

test kitchen tip: Littleneck clams are the smallest, hard-shell East Coast clams measuring in at less than 2 inches in diameter. Fresh clams are actually living mollusks. When purchasing, check to see that the shells are moist and tightly closed or that they snap closed when tapped. Discard any suspicious-looking clams as instructed in Step 1.

24 fresh littleneck clams in shells
2 large onions, chopped
2 green bell peppers, chopped
4 garlic cloves, minced
¼ cup olive oil
¼ cup butter
½ lb. fresh mushrooms, quartered
1 (28-oz.) can Italian-style tomatoes, undrained and chopped
1 (15-oz.) can tomato sauce
2 cups dry red wine
1 bay leaf
2 tsp. salt
1 tsp. pepper
1 tsp. dried basil
1 tsp. dried oregano
½ tsp. hot sauce
2 lb. grouper or snapper fillets, cut into bite-size pieces
1 lb. unpeeled, large raw shrimp, peeled and deveined
½ lb. sea scallops
½ lb. fresh lump crabmeat, drained

1. Scrub clams thoroughly; discard any opened, cracked, or heavy clams; set clams aside.

2. Cook onion, green pepper, and garlic in oil and butter in a large stockpot over medium-high heat 5 minutes or just until vegetables are tender. Add mushrooms, and cook 5 minutes. Add tomatoes and next 8 ingredients; bring to a boil. Cover, reduce heat, and simmer 1 hour.

3. Add reserved clams; cover and simmer 3 minutes. Add grouper, shrimp, and scallops; cover and simmer 3 more minutes or until clams open and shrimp turn pink. Gently stir in crabmeat, and cook just until crabmeat is heated (do not overcook). Discard bay leaf.

Italian Sausage Soup

makes 13 cups • prep: 25 min.; cook: 1 hr., 35 min.

freeze it: Package leftover soup in pt. or qt. plastic freezer containers or zip-top plastic freezer bags. Label with recipe name, date, and amount and freeze up to 3 months.

1½	lb. Italian sausage links, cut into ½-inch slices	3	Tbsp. fresh parsley
2	medium onions, chopped	½	tsp. dried basil
2	garlic cloves, minced	3	cups uncooked farfalle (bow tie pasta)
3	(10½-oz.) cans beef broth	2	zucchini, cut in half lengthwise and sliced
1	(28-oz.) can whole tomatoes, undrained and chopped		Grated Parmesan cheese
1½	cups dry red wine		
1	medium-size green bell pepper, chopped		

1. Brown sausage in a large skillet over medium heat; remove sausage, and drain well, reserving 1 Tbsp. drippings in skillet.

2. Sauté onion and garlic in drippings in skillet over medium-high heat 3 minutes or until tender. Combine sausage, onion mixture, broth, and next 5 ingredients. Bring to a boil; cover, reduce heat, and simmer 1 hour. Add pasta and zucchini. Cover and simmer 12 minutes.

3. To serve, ladle soup into individual bowls, and sprinkle with cheese.

Smoky Jambalaya

makes 10 cups • prep: 20 min.; cook: 1 hr., 5 min.; other: 5 min.

Shrimp, chicken, smoked pork, and smoked sausage simmer together in this quick version of Louisiana's famous meaty rice stew.

test kitchen tip: There's a big difference in the saltiness among Creole seasonings. If using a different brand than we tested with, we recommend reducing the seasoning to 1 Tbsp., then season to taste at the table, if necessary.

1	onion, finely chopped	1½	cups uncooked long-grain rice
1	green bell pepper, finely chopped	1	cup shredded smoked pork
1	celery rib, finely chopped	1	(14-oz.) can low-sodium beef broth
1	cup sliced smoked sausage (about 4½ oz.)	2	cups water
½	lb. boneless, skinless chicken thighs, cubed	2	Tbsp. Creole seasoning
¼	cup vegetable oil	1	bay leaf
		½	lb. peeled and deveined medium-size raw shrimp

1. Preheat oven to 325°.

2. Cook first 5 ingredients in hot oil in a 4- to 5-qt. cast-iron Dutch oven over medium-high heat 10 minutes or until vegetables are tender. Stir in rice and next 5 ingredients.

3. Bake, covered, at 325° for 45 minutes. (Do not remove lid or stir). Remove from oven; stir in shrimp. Bake, covered, 10 more minutes or just until shrimp turn pink. Let stand 5 minutes before serving. Discard bay leaf.

Note: For testing purposes only, we used Zatarain's Creole Seasoning.

Southwestern Chicken-and-Rice Soup With Tortilla Strips

makes about 6 servings • prep: 30 min., cook: 1 hr.

Cilantro, cumin, and fresh lime juice add earthy flavor to traditional southwestern chicken soup. Crunchy baked corn tortilla strips and buttery avocado top the brothy mixture.

1	medium onion, chopped	1	tsp. cumin
1	large carrot, chopped	¼	tsp. black pepper
½	medium-size red bell pepper, chopped	8	cups chicken broth
1	Tbsp. vegetable oil	¼	cup loosely packed cilantro leaves, chopped
2	garlic cloves, minced		Juice of 1 lime (about 2 Tbsp.)
2	cups shredded cooked chicken	6	(6-in.) corn tortillas
¾	cup uncooked white rice	1	ripe avocado, chopped
2	medium plum tomatoes, chopped		
1	to 2 Tbsp. chopped pickled jalapeño slices		

test kitchen tip: Substitute ¾ cup brown rice for white rice, if you'd like. Prepare recipe as directed, increasing simmer time to 45 minutes or until rice is tender.

1. Sauté chopped onion, carrot, and bell pepper in hot oil in a large Dutch oven over medium heat 7 minutes or until vegetables are tender. Add minced garlic, and sauté 1 minute.

2. Stir in chicken and next 5 ingredients. Stir in chicken broth. Bring to a boil, reduce heat, and simmer 20 minutes or until rice is tender. Stir in cilantro and lime juice.

3. Preheat oven to 400°.

4. Cut tortillas into strips, and place on a baking sheet coated with vegetable cooking spray. Spray cooking spray over tops of strips. Bake at 400° for 10 to 15 minutes or until crisp, stirring occasionally.

5. Serve soup topped with tortilla strips and avocado.

Chili Con Carne

makes 6½ cups • prep: 10 min.; cook: 1 hr., 20 min.

Texans don't take kindly to beans in their chili. If they do, they add them separately. This traditional chili is also served as a meaty sauce to smother enchiladas and burritos.

test kitchen tip: If you can't find coarsely ground beef in your supermarket, use a regular grind.

3 lb. coarsely ground beef	1 (8-oz.) can tomato sauce
4 garlic cloves, minced	2½ cups water
7 Tbsp. chili powder, divided	3 Tbsp. masa harina
1 Tbsp. ground cumin	Toppings: shredded Cheddar cheese,
1 tsp. ground red pepper	chopped green onions, chopped
1 Tbsp. paprika (optional)	tomatoes, shredded lettuce
½ tsp. salt	

1. Cook ground beef in a Dutch oven over medium-high heat about 8 minutes, stirring until it crumbles and is no longer pink. Drain well and return to Dutch oven.

2. Add garlic, reduce heat to medium, and cook, stirring frequently, 2 minutes. Stir in 6 Tbsp. chili powder, cumin, red pepper, paprika, if desired, and salt. Add tomato sauce and 2½ cups water. Bring to a boil; cover, reduce heat, and simmer 1 hour. Stir 1 Tbsp. masa harina at a time into meat mixture, allowing chili to thicken between additions to desired consistency.

3. Cook, uncovered, 5 minutes. Stir in remaining 1 Tbsp. chili powder, and cook 5 more minutes before serving. Serve with desired toppings.

do you know beans about chili?

Texans will tell you that if you know beans about chili, you'll know there ain't no beans in a real bowl of red. That story stems from the cowboy cuisine of years ago when cooks added beans on the cattle trail to stretch the chili as the meat was getting low. Starting in the late 1800s fiery stews sold by Mexican women in San Antonio plazas became a tourist attraction. The chilis of today are now a blend of Mexican, Native American, and Anglo tastes with as many variations as there are chili cook-offs around the region. The choice is beans or no beans, chunks or ground meat, gravy thick as paste or more like stew, and three-alarm spicy or mildly hot. Even "white" chilis with chicken in a white broth have emerged. There is one consensus, however—every bowl needs a wedge of buttery cornbread to go with it.

Turkey Chili

makes 8 cups • prep: 15 min., cook: 50 min.

This quick and easy chili uses canned tomatoes, canned beans, and a chili seasoning mix to stir in with ground turkey and ground turkey sausage. Top the chili with sour cream and Cheddar cheese for extra flavor.

1	onion, chopped	2	cups tomato juice
1	green bell pepper, chopped	1	garlic clove, minced
1	lb. ground turkey	1	(1.75-oz.) envelope chili seasoning mix
1	lb. ground turkey sausage		
1	tsp. vegetable oil	1	(10-oz.) can diced tomatoes and green chiles
1	(16-oz.) can chili beans		
2	cups tomato sauce	1	tsp. sugar

make it a meal: Serve Turkey Chili with a grilled cheese sandwich and green grapes for a casual evening meal.

1. Cook onion, bell pepper, ground turkey, and sausage in hot oil in a Dutch oven over medium heat, stirring until meat crumbles and is no longer pink. Drain well.

2. Add chili beans and remaining ingredients to Dutch oven; bring to a boil, stirring frequently. Reduce heat, and simmer 30 minutes, stirring occasionally.

Black Beans 'n' Vegetable Chili

makes 6 cups • prep: 30 min., cook: 45 min.

This vegetarian chili filled with black beans, bell peppers, squash, and tomatoes served over rice is hearty and filling.

1 large onion, coarsely chopped

1 Tbsp. vegetable oil

1 (28-oz.) can diced tomatoes, undrained

⅔ cup picante sauce

1½ tsp. ground cumin

1 tsp. salt

½ tsp. dried basil

1 (15-oz.) can black beans, rinsed and drained

1 medium-size green bell pepper, cut into ¾-inch pieces

1 medium-size red bell pepper, cut into ¾-inch pieces

1 large yellow squash or zucchini, cut into ½-inch pieces

Hot cooked rice

Shredded Cheddar cheese

Sour cream

Chopped fresh cilantro

Picante sauce (optional)

test kitchen tip: Other good choices for chili toppings include salsa, diced plum tomatoes, shredded lettuce or spinach, diced onion, sliced green onions, chopped avocado, cornbread croutons, oyster crackers, and tortilla chips.

1. Cook onion in oil in a Dutch oven over medium-high heat, stirring constantly, until tender. Add tomatoes and next 4 ingredients; stir well. Bring to a boil; cover, reduce heat, and simmer 5 minutes.

2. Stir in beans, peppers, and squash. Cover and cook over medium-low heat 25 minutes or until vegetables are tender, stirring mixture occasionally.

3. To serve, ladle chili over rice in individual bowls. Top each serving with cheese, sour cream, and cilantro. Serve with additional picante sauce, if desired.

Michele Farri

"Show-me" Fine Dining
United Guardsman Foundation ~ St. Joseph, Missouri

Corn and White Bean Chili

makes 13 cups • prep: 20 min.; cook: 2 hr., 35 min.; other: 8 hr.

This family favorite uses great Northern beans, chicken, white corn, and half-and-half resulting in a hearty chili. It's unlike a traditional bowl of red—this version is creamy and white. The toppings add more flavor and a punch of color, making the chili ideal for casual entertaining, too.

test kitchen tip: To quick-soak beans, combine 8 cups water and beans in a large Dutch oven. Bring to a boil, cover, and cook 2 minutes. Remove from heat; let stand 1 hour. Drain, rinse, and proceed with Step 2 of recipe.

1   lb. dried great Northern beans
2   medium onions, chopped
1   Tbsp. olive oil
2   (4½-oz.) cans chopped green chiles, undrained
1   (16-oz.) package frozen shoepeg white corn
4   garlic cloves, minced
2   tsp. ground cumin
1½ tsp. dried oregano
Dash of ground red pepper

3   cups chicken broth
3   cups half-and-half
5   cups chopped cooked chicken breast
1   cup (4 oz.) shredded Monterey Jack cheese, divided
Salt and pepper to taste
Toppings: chopped tomato, chopped fresh cilantro, shredded Cheddar cheese

1. Sort and wash beans; place in a large Dutch oven. Cover with water 2 inches above beans; let soak overnight. Drain; set beans aside.

2. Cook onion in oil in Dutch oven over medium-high heat, stirring constantly, until tender. Add green chiles and next 5 ingredients; cook 5 minutes, stirring constantly. Add beans and chicken broth. Bring to a boil; cover, reduce heat, and simmer 2 hours or until beans are tender, stirring occasionally. Add chicken, 1 cup cheese, and salt and pepper to taste.

3. Bring to a boil; reduce heat, and simmer, 10 minutes, stirring often. To serve, ladle chili into individual soup bowls. Top each serving with desired toppings.

side dishes

Savory Sweet Potato Hash, page 376

Asparagus Dressed With Feta and Sun-dried Tomatoes

makes 4 servings • prep: 10 min., cook: 10 min.

Feta cheese and sun-dried tomatoes in a tangy vinaigrette give flavor to crisp-tender spears of spring asparagus.

test kitchen tip: Substitute broccoli florets for the asparagus if you'd like.

1	lb. fresh asparagus	¼ cup chopped oil-packed sun-dried tomatoes
2	Tbsp. olive oil	Ground white pepper
2	tsp. fresh lemon juice	
4	oz. crumbled feta cheese	

1. Snap off tough ends of asparagus. Add water to a medium skillet to a depth of 1 inch, and bring to a boil. Add asparagus in a single layer; cook 6 to 8 minutes or until crisp-tender. Drain asparagus, and arrange on a serving plate.

2. Combine oil and lemon juice in a small bowl; stir well with a wire whisk. Add cheese and sun-dried tomatoes; stir well. Pour lemon juice mixture over hot asparagus. Sprinkle with pepper.

Grilled Asparagus With Parmesan Salsa

makes 4 to 6 servings • prep: 20 min., cook: 10 min.

Two to three minutes on the grill is all it takes to add a smoky flavor to fresh asparagus. A tomato salsa drapes the grilled spears.

test kitchen tip: If the asparagus spears available to you are larger in diameter than a pencil, they might have tough scales at the bases. Remove them with a vegetable peeler.

1	lb. fresh asparagus	1 tsp. vegetable oil
1	Tbsp. vegetable oil	1 small tomato, finely chopped
1	garlic clove, minced	¼ cup shredded Parmesan cheese
⅛	tsp. salt	Dash of salt
1	(½-inch-thick) sweet onion slice	Dash of pepper

1. Preheat grill to medium heat (300° to 350°).

2. Snap off and discard tough ends of asparagus, if necessary.

3. Stir together 1 Tbsp. vegetable oil and garlic. Combine asparagus with vegetable oil mixture in a large bowl, tossing to coat. Sprinkle with ⅛ tsp. salt.

4. Brush onion slice evenly on both sides with 1 tsp. vegetable oil.

5. Grill onion slice and asparagus, uncovered, over medium heat (300° to 350°). Grill onion slice 4 to 5 minutes on each side or until tender. Grill asparagus 2 to 3 minutes on each side or until tender.

6. Finely chop onion. Stir together onion, tomato, and next 3 ingredients. Serve salsa with warm asparagus.

Oven-Roasted Asparagus With Thyme

makes 4 servings • prep: 10 min., cook: 20 min.

Roasting asparagus with garlic, thyme, and olive oil adds an herby sweet flavor to the delicate-tasting spears.

1½ lb. fresh asparagus
1 large garlic clove, halved
2 tsp. olive oil

½ tsp. salt
¼ tsp. freshly ground pepper
¼ tsp. dried thyme

make it a meal: This recipe is an ideal accompaniment for entertaining with a roasted beef tenderloin and buttery mashed potatoes.

1. Preheat oven to 400°.
2. Snap off and discard tough ends of asparagus. Rub cut sides of garlic over bottom and sides of an ungreased 13- x 9-inch baking dish. Place asparagus and garlic in dish. Drizzle with olive oil. Sprinkle with salt, pepper, and thyme; toss gently. Bake, uncovered, at 400° for 20 minutes, stirring once.   Elizabeth Morrison Pilgrim

Beyond Cotton Country
The Junior League of Morgan County ~ Decatur, Alabama

Creamy-and-Crunchy Green Bean Casserole

makes 8 servings • prep: 10 min., cook: 45 min.

Since its inception in the mid-seventies, cheesy green bean casseroles have played supporting roles in important Southern meals, from the Thanksgiving buffet and Easter dinner to summertime family reunions. Sautéed onion, bean sprouts, and water chestnuts give this version an updated twist.

¼ cup butter
1 large onion, chopped
2 (10¾-oz.) cans cream of mushroom soup
2 (16-oz.) packages frozen French-cut green beans, thawed
1 (14-oz.) can bean sprouts, rinsed and drained

2 (8-oz.) cans diced water chestnuts, drained
¼ tsp. salt
1 cup (4 oz.) shredded sharp Cheddar cheese
2 (2.8-oz.) cans French fried onions

make it ahead: Prepare recipe through Step 2; cover tightly with foil and refrigerate up to 2 days in advance. When ready to cook, let stand at room temperature 20 minutes; proceed as directed in Step 3.

1. Preheat oven to 375°.
2. Melt butter in a Dutch oven over medium-high heat; add onion, and sauté 8 minutes or until tender. Stir in soup, and bring to a boil. Stir in beans and next 3 ingredients. Spoon into a lightly greased 13- x 9-inch baking dish. Sprinkle evenly with shredded Cheddar cheese.
3. Bake, covered, at 375° for 25 minutes. Uncover and sprinkle evenly with French fried onions, and bake 10 more minutes or until bubbly.

Sautéed Green Beans

makes 6 to 8 servings • prep: 10 min., cook: 15 min.

A simple seasoning of garlic and Creole seasoning lets the garden-fresh flavor of green beans shine through.

2   lb. small fresh green beans, trimmed
1   red bell pepper, sliced
2   Tbsp. olive oil
2   garlic cloves, minced
1   tsp. Creole seasoning

1. Cook green beans in boiling salted water to cover 8 to 10 minutes or until crisp-tender. Drain and plunge into ice water to stop the cooking process; drain.
2. Sauté sliced red bell pepper in 2 Tbsp. hot oil in a large skillet over medium heat 2 minutes or until crisp-tender; add minced garlic, and sauté 2 more minutes. Add green beans; sprinkle with Creole seasoning, and cook, stirring constantly, until vegetable mixture is thoroughly heated.

Roasted Beets With Warm Dijon Vinaigrette

makes 8 servings • prep: 40 min.; cook: 1 hr., 52 min.

Place the cooked green tops and the sweet beet roots on serving plates as you would a salad. Then drizzle with Dijon-dill dressing.

3	lb. medium beets with greens	⅓	cup olive oil
½	tsp. salt	½	tsp. salt
⅓	cup sliced green onions	½	tsp. freshly ground pepper
2	Tbsp. balsamic vinegar	2	to 3 Tbsp. minced fresh dill
2	Tbsp. Dijon mustard		

1. Preheat oven to 400°.

2. Leave root and 1 inch stem on beets; reserve greens. Scrub beets with a vegetable brush; wrap in aluminum foil. Bake at 400° for 1 hour and 30 minutes or until tender. Unwrap beets; pour cold water over beets, and drain. Trim off roots and stems, and rub off skins. Cut cooked beets into ¼-inch slices. Set aside, and keep warm.

3. Wash greens thoroughly; pat dry with paper towels. Cut greens into thin strips. Place greens in a large saucepan; cover with water, and add ½ tsp. salt. Bring to a boil; reduce heat, and simmer, uncovered, 10 minutes or until tender. Drain well. Set aside, and keep warm.

4. Position knife blade in food processor bowl; add green onions, vinegar, and mustard. Process until smooth, stopping to scrape down sides. Pour olive oil through food chute with processor running, processing until smooth. Place vinegar mixture in a small saucepan; cook over medium heat until thoroughly heated, stirring occasionally.

5. Place greens and beets on individual serving plates; top evenly with vinegar mixture. Sprinkle with ½ tsp. salt, pepper, and dill.

test kitchen tip: When cut, beets stain everything they touch. To help remove these stains from cutting boards, sprinkle stained area with salt; then rinse and scrub with soap. Wear disposable gloves to keep beets from staining your hands.

Smoky Speckled Butterbeans

makes 8 to 10 servings • prep: 15 min.; cook: 3 hr., 15 min.

Butterbeans and other fresh summer vegetables get a flavor boost with chowchow—a zesty mustard-flavored vegetable relish once referred to as "Indian pickle."

3	qt. water	1	tsp. pepper
1	lb. smoked pork shoulder	1	jalapeño pepper, sliced
2	lb. fresh or frozen speckled butterbeans		Hot cooked rice (optional)
2	tsp. salt		Toppings: chowchow, chopped sweet onion

1. Bring first 6 ingredients to a boil in a Dutch oven. Reduce heat to medium. Cover and simmer 3 hours or until beans are tender, stirring occasionally.
2. Remove pork, and shred. Return to Dutch oven. Serve with rice and toppings, if desired.

test kitchen tip: You'll know when this dish is ready—the pork shreds easily, and the beans are creamy on the inside.

Elegant Broccoli and Walnuts

makes 6 to 8 servings • prep: 20 min., cook: 20 min.

Three simple ingredients combine to make steamed broccoli a standout side—crumbled bacon, green onions, and sautéed walnuts.

2	lb. fresh broccoli	1	cup chopped walnuts
1	lb. bacon	¾	cup sliced green onions

1. Remove leaves from broccoli; cut off tough ends of stalks, and discard. Cut off broccoli florets. Place florets in a steamer basket over boiling water; cover and steam 6 minutes or until crisp-tender. Set aside, and keep warm.
2. Cook bacon in a skillet until crisp; remove bacon, and drain on paper towels, reserving 1 Tbsp. drippings in skillet. Crumble bacon, and set aside. Cook walnuts in reserved drippings, stirring constantly, over medium heat 3 minutes. Add green onions, and cook 1 minute or until soft.
3. Transfer warm broccoli to a serving platter; spoon walnut mixture over broccoli. Sprinkle with bacon, and serve immediately.

Creating a Stir
The Lexington Medical Society Auxiliary ~ Lexington, Kentucky

test kitchen tip: Get a head start on this recipe by cooking and crumbling the bacon up to 2 days in advance. Store the crumbled bacon and drippings separately in the refrigerator.

Broccoli Soufflés

makes 8 servings • prep: 20 min., cook: 55 min.

These individually portioned side dishes are classic Cheddar cheese soufflés enhanced with broccoli. When they come out of the oven, they'll be puffed and at their peak of perfection— plan to serve them immediately.

2	(10-oz.) packages frozen chopped broccoli, thawed		5	large eggs, separated
¼	cup butter or margarine		1½	tsp. salt
¼	cup all-purpose flour		¼	tsp. minced garlic
1¼	cups milk		2	Tbsp. lemon juice
⅔	cup (2.6 oz.) shredded sharp Cheddar cheese			

freeze it: Prepare Broccoli Soufflés through Step 5. Seal each dish in aluminum foil, and freeze up to 1 month. Unwrap soufflés, and bake frozen at 400° for 10 minutes; reduce heat to 350°, and bake 35 to 40 more minutes or until browned and puffed. Serve immediately.

1. Preheat oven to 350°.

2. Cook broccoli in a small amount of boiling water 5 minutes, and drain.

3. Melt butter in a heavy saucepan over low heat; add flour, whisking until smooth. Cook, whisking constantly, 1 minute. Gradually add milk, and cook over medium heat, whisking constantly, until thickened and bubbly. Add cheese, stirring until it melts. Remove cheese mixture from heat.

4. Beat egg yolks at medium speed with an electric mixer until thick and pale. Add cooked broccoli, salt, garlic, and lemon juice, beating until blended. Gradually stir about one-fourth of hot cheese mixture into yolk mixture; add to remaining hot mixture, stirring constantly.

5. Beat egg whites at high speed until stiff but not dry; fold one-third of egg whites into broccoli mixture. Fold in remaining egg whites. Pour into 8 buttered individual soufflé dishes or 6-ounce custard cups.

6. Place soufflés in a 13- x 9-inch pan, and add hot water to pan to a depth of 1 inch. Bake at 350° for 35 to 40 minutes or until puffed and browned. Serve soufflés immediately.

Cabbage Casserole

makes 8 servings • prep: 20 min.; cook: 1 hr., 5 min.

Cooked cabbage, a Southern favorite, is baked with a creamy cheese sauce splashed with chili sauce.

1	medium cabbage, cut into thin wedges	½	tsp. pepper
½	cup water	⅔	cup (2.6 oz.) shredded Cheddar cheese
¼	cup butter or margarine	½	cup chopped green pepper
¼	cup all-purpose flour	½	cup chopped onion
2	cups milk	½	cup mayonnaise
½	tsp. salt	1	Tbsp. chili sauce

make it a meal: Serve Cabbage Casserole with either grilled smoked sausages, baked brisket or roast pork, and crusty sourdough bread.

1. Preheat oven to 375°.

2. Combine cabbage wedges and water in a large saucepan; bring to a boil. Cover, reduce heat, and cook 15 minutes. Drain well; place cabbage wedges in an ungreased 13- x 9-inch baking dish.

3. Melt butter in a heavy saucepan over low heat; add flour, stirring until smooth. Cook 1 minute, stirring constantly. Gradually add milk; cook over medium heat, stirring constantly, until mixture is thickened and bubbly. Stir in salt and pepper; pour over cabbage. Bake, uncovered, at 375° for 20 minutes.

4. Increase oven temperature to 400°.

5. Combine cheese and remaining 4 ingredients; stir well. Spread over cabbage. Bake, uncovered, at 400° for 20 minutes.

Bea Phillips

BMC on Our Menu
Baptist Medical Center Auxiliary of Volunteers ~ Columbia, South Carolina

Hunter's-Style Carrots

makes 4 servings • prep: 24 min., cook: 25 min., other: 2 hr.

Carrots were never so sophisticated. Sweet Madeira wine, woodsy-flavored porcini mushrooms, and prosciutto (Italy's version of country ham) season sweet carrot slices for this upscale dish.

test kitchen tip: Country ham is an excellent substitute for prosciutto. If you make the switch, leave out the salt.

½	oz. dried porcini mushrooms	1	oz. prosciutto, cut into very thin strips
½	cup Madeira		
1½	lb. small carrots, cut diagonally into ½-inch pieces	2	large garlic cloves, minced
		3	Tbsp. chopped fresh flat-leaf parsley
3	Tbsp. olive oil	⅛	tsp. freshly ground pepper
⅛	tsp. salt		

1. Rinse mushrooms thoroughly with cold water; drain well. Combine mushrooms and Madeira in a small bowl; let stand 2 hours. Drain, reserving liquid. Finely chop mushrooms, and set aside.

2. Cook carrot in oil in a large skillet over medium-high heat 15 minutes, stirring frequently. Add reserved liquid, mushrooms, and salt; reduce heat to medium-low, and cook, stirring constantly, 8 minutes or until carrot is lightly browned. Add prosciutto and garlic, and cook 1 minute or until thoroughly heated. Stir in parsley and pepper. Serve immediately.

Gratin of Cauliflower With Gingered Crumbs

makes 4 to 6 servings • prep: 20 min., cook: 40 min., other: 5 min.

Nutty-flavored Swiss cheese is melted into a creamy nutmeg sauce to flavor tender cooked cauliflower. Before baking, sprinkle soft, buttery bread crumbs with a hint of ginger on top.

1	(1½-lb.) cauliflower, broken into florets	¼	cup (1 oz.) shredded Swiss cheese
3	Tbsp. unsalted butter, divided	1	tsp. lemon juice
2	Tbsp. all-purpose flour	3	drops of hot sauce
¼	tsp. salt	¼	cup soft breadcrumbs
¼	tsp. ground nutmeg	⅛	tsp. ground ginger
1	cup half-and-half	2	Tbsp. freshly grated Parmesan cheese

1. Preheat oven to 350°.

2. Cook cauliflower in a small amount of boiling water 10 minutes or until tender; drain. Place cauliflower in a lightly greased 11- x 7-inch baking dish.

3. Melt 2 Tbsp. butter in a medium saucepan over low heat; add flour, salt, and nutmeg, stirring until smooth. Cook 1 minute, stirring constantly. Gradually add half-and-half; cook over medium heat, stirring constantly, until mixture is thickened and bubbly. Stir in Swiss cheese, lemon juice, and hot sauce. Pour sauce mixture over cauliflower, and set aside.

4. Melt remaining 1 Tbsp. butter in a small skillet over medium heat; stir in breadcrumbs and ginger. Cook, stirring constantly, until golden. Spoon crumb mixture over cauliflower; sprinkle with Parmesan cheese. Bake, uncovered, at 350° for 20 minutes. Let stand 5 minutes before serving.

test kitchen tip: Make soft breadcrumbs by tearing fresh bread into small pieces and pulsing it in a food processor until very finely chopped. Freeze any leftover crumbs in an airtight container up to 6 months. Use soft breadcrumbs as a filler for meat loaf and meatballs or to top a casserole.

Buttermilk Fried Corn

makes 2 cups • prep: 15 min., cook: 15 min., other: 30 min.

Soaked in buttermilk, floured, and then fried, corn kernels are a crispy side or topping for salads, soups, and casseroles.

test kitchen tip: Use a slotted spoon to remove these golden nuggets from the hot oil, allowing excess oil to drain before transferring to paper towels.

2 cups fresh corn kernels
1½ cups buttermilk
⅔ cup all-purpose flour
⅔ cup cornmeal
1 tsp. salt
½ tsp. pepper
Corn oil

1. Combine corn kernels and buttermilk in large bowl; let stand 30 minutes. Drain.

2. Combine flour and next 3 ingredients in large zip-top plastic bag. Add corn to flour mixture, a small amount at a time, and shake bag to coat corn.

3. Pour oil to a depth of 1 inch in a Dutch oven; heat to 375°. Fry corn, a small amount at a time, in hot oil 2 minutes or until golden. Drain on paper towels. Serve as a side dish, or sprinkle on salads and soups.

Sweet Corn Pudding

makes 6 servings • prep: 10 min.; cook: 1 hr., 5 min.; other: 10 min.

In colonial America, unexpected visitors stopping by would be offered whatever was simmering in a pot over a fire. The "potluck" hospitality still means an informal gathering but now guests bring a dish to the host home for a meal. Sweet Corn Pudding is perfect for such an occasion. It travels and reheats well.

make it a meal: Serve Sweet Corn Pudding alongside barbecued pork chops and marinated cucumbers and tomatoes. Serve strawberry shortcake as the finale.

1 cup soft, fresh breadcrumbs
6 Tbsp. self-rising white cornmeal mix
1½ Tbsp. sugar
½ tsp. salt
3 large eggs
1¼ cups milk
½ cup half-and-half
2 Tbsp. butter, melted
1 (20-oz.) package frozen cream-style corn, thawed
Garnish: sliced green onions

1. Preheat oven to 325°.

2. Combine breadcrumbs and next 3 ingredients in a large bowl.

3. Whisk eggs in a large bowl until pale and foamy; whisk in milk, half-and-half, and butter. Whisk egg mixture into breadcrumb mixture; stir in corn. Pour into a lightly greased 9-inch square baking dish.

4. Bake, uncovered, at 325° for 1 hour to 1 hour and 5 minutes or until set. Let stand 10 minutes before serving. Garnish, if desired.

Grilled Okra and Tomatoes

makes 8 servings • prep: 16 min., cook: 10 min.

Fresh garden vegetables get a smoky flavor from the grill and no further enhancement than salt and pepper.

5	plum tomatoes	10	(10-inch) metal skewers
1	lb. small fresh okra	½	tsp. salt
2	Tbsp. olive oil	¼	tsp. freshly ground pepper

1. Preheat grill to medium heat (300° to 350°).

2. Toss tomatoes and okra with oil in a large bowl. Evenly thread okra onto double skewers (2 skewers side-by-side). Grill tomatoes and okra, covered with grill lid, over medium heat (300° to 350°) 7 minutes or until okra chars slightly and tomato skins blister and split, turning occasionally.

3. Remove vegetables from grill. Peel tomatoes, and cut into chunks. Combine tomatoes, okra, salt, and pepper in a large serving bowl, tossing gently. Serve immediately.

test kitchen tip: Peel grilled tomatoes over a large serving bowl to catch the juices. They cut easily into chunks using kitchen shears.

corn, the Southern staple

It was corn shared by Native Americans that saved the lives of many early settlers, so it's no wonder that in the cuisine of every region of the South, there's a corn specialty that has survived the test of time. In the Southwest, it's the base of crispy ground corn tortillas and the moist paste that encases tamales filling. In the Deep South, sweet corn pudding, creamy spoonbread, succotash, hominy, grits, and cornbread are still part of everyday meals. Nearly every Atlantic coastal seafood boil includes corn on the cob, and juicy "roastin' ears" slathered with butter—especially the sweet white corn varieties—are a favorite summertime family and celebration food. Today, the delicate white or yellow kernels are popular hot or cold in salsas, salads, and dips. But maybe the most famous use of corn in the South was for clear and potent moonshine whiskey, a home-distilled liquor illegal then—and now.

Fried Okra

Fried Okra

makes 4 servings • prep: 15 min., cook: 4 min. per batch, other: 45 min.

Called "country popcorn," fried okra is on the menu of some Southern restaurants that serve big bowls of the crunchy nuggets for folks to eat as you would popcorn, a handful at a time.

1	lb. fresh okra	1	tsp. salt
2	cups buttermilk	¼	tsp. ground red pepper
1	cup self-rising cornmeal		Vegetable oil
1	cup self-rising flour	¼	cup bacon drippings

1. Cut off and discard tip and stem ends from okra; cut okra into ½-inch-thick slices. Stir into buttermilk; cover and chill 45 minutes.

2. Combine cornmeal and next 3 ingredients in a bowl.

3. Remove okra from buttermilk with a slotted spoon, and discard buttermilk. Dredge okra, in batches, in the cornmeal mixture.

4. Pour oil to a depth of 2 inches into a Dutch oven or cast-iron skillet; add bacon drippings, and heat to 375°. Fry okra, in batches, 4 minutes or until golden; drain on paper towels.

test kitchen tip: You'll need to cook about 4 slices of bacon to get ¼ cup bacon drippings. Refrigerate the cooked bacon, and use it later to sprinkle over salads or soups.

Sweet Onion Bake

makes 4 to 6 servings • prep: 20 min., cook: 45 min.

Sauté onion before layering with Swiss cheese, cracker crumbs, and a rich cream sauce for a baked casserole that's delicious with any entrée.

6	Tbsp. butter, divided	2	large eggs
3	medium-size sweet onions, chopped (about 2 cups)	1	cup half-and-half
1	(8-oz.) block Swiss cheese, shredded	1	tsp. salt
¾	cup finely crushed saltine crackers, divided (about 20 crackers)	⅛	tsp. freshly ground pepper

1. Preheat oven to 350°.

2. Melt 4 Tbsp. butter in a large skillet over medium heat; add onions, and sauté 20 minutes or until golden brown. Place half of cooked onions in a lightly greased 8-inch square baking dish. Sprinkle evenly with half of cheese and ¼ cup cracker crumbs. Top with remaining onions and cheese.

3. Whisk together eggs and next 3 ingredients in a medium bowl; pour over onion mixture.

4. Melt remaining 2 Tbsp. butter in skillet over medium heat; add remaining ½ cup cracker crumbs, and cook, stirring often, until crumbs are lightly browned. Sprinkle crumbs evenly over mixture in dish. Bake at 350° for 20 minutes or until lightly browned and set.

test kitchen tip: For an upscale twist on this comfort food recipe, substitute shredded Gruyère cheese. It's a specialty Swiss cheese with very few holes and a rich, sweet, nutty flavor that's sharper than that of regular Swiss cheese.

Onions Parmesan

makes 6 servings • prep: 30 min., cook: 30 min.

A large heavy skillet helps keep the heat even for cooking the onions long enough to develop the sweet caramelized flavor.

lighten up: Using 2% low-fat or whole milk in place of half-and-half saves calories and still keeps the side dish rich and creamy tasting.

6	small sweet onions		2	Tbsp. all-purpose flour
1	Tbsp. butter		2	tsp. salt
½	cup freshly grated Parmesan cheese		¼	tsp. Worcestershire sauce
1	cup half-and-half		⅛	tsp. freshly ground pepper
				Paprika

1. Cook onions in boiling water to cover 1 minute; remove onions from water, and immediately plunge into ice water to stop the cooking process. Peel onions; cut into ¼-inch-thick slices.

2. Melt butter in a large heavy skillet over low heat. Arrange half of onion slices in skillet; sprinkle with ¼ cup Parmesan cheese. Layer with remaining half of onions; sprinkle with remaining ¼ cup Parmesan cheese. Combine half-and-half and next 4 ingredients; stir well, and pour evenly over onions.
3. Preheat broiler.
4. Cover and cook over medium heat 20 minutes or until onion is tender. Uncover and cook 10 more minutes or until thickened and bubbly. Sprinkle with paprika. Broil 6 inches from heat 3 minutes or until browned.

Caramelized Onion Pudding

makes 6 servings • prep: 15 min.; cook: 1 hr., 6 min.

Tangy goat cheese melts into the creamy sweet pudding, which makes a good substitute for mashed potatoes. Use sweet Vidalia or Texas Sweet onions for extra sugary caramelized flavor.

¼	cup butter	2	Tbsp. sugar
3	cups sliced onion (about 2 small	1	tsp. salt
	onions)	1	tsp. baking powder
3	large eggs	1	(4-oz.) package crumbled goat
2	cups heavy whipping cream		cheese
2	Tbsp. all-purpose flour		

1. Preheat oven to 350°.
2. Melt butter in a large skillet over medium heat. Add onion; sauté 28 minutes or until onion is browned. Remove from heat, and set aside.
3. Beat eggs and next 5 ingredients with an electric mixer until smooth. Stir in goat cheese and onion. Pour onion mixture into a greased 11- x 7-inch baking dish. Bake, uncovered, at 350° for 35 minutes or until golden.   Kathy Cary

Splendor in the Bluegrass
The Junior League of Louisville, Kentucky

test kitchen tip: After slicing or chopping onions, rub your hands with a little lemon juice, or try rubbing fingertips on the bowl of a stainless steel spoon under warm, running water to rescue hands from an onion smell.

Honey-Orange Parsnips

makes 3 to 4 servings • prep: 10 min., cook: 18 min.

A honey and orange juice glaze coats slices of sweet parsnips for a delicious winter side dish.

1	cup water	1	Tbsp. honey
1	lb. parsnips, peeled and sliced	1	tsp. grated orange rind
3	Tbsp. butter or margarine	1	Tbsp. fresh orange juice

1. Bring water to a boil in a medium saucepan. Add parsnips; cover and cook 8 minutes or just until tender. Drain. Return parsnips to pan; add butter and remaining ingredients, stirring gently until butter melts.
2. Place pan over medium heat, and cook, uncovered, 1 to 2 minutes or until parsnips are glazed, stirring occasionally.

make it a meal: Pair Honey-Orange Parsnips with a spiral baked ham and a cranberry congealed salad for a traditional holiday meal.

Peppery Peas o' Plenty

Peppery Peas o' Plenty

makes 4 to 6 servings • prep: 15 min., cook: 40 min.

Five types of peas, hickory-smoked bacon and drippings, and garlic-chili sauce simmer together for hearty side servings. These will require biscuits or cornbread—handy for "pea pushers" so you can scoop up every bite.

4	bacon slices	1	cup frozen field peas with snaps
1	large onion, chopped	1	(32-oz.) container chicken broth
1	cup frozen black-eyed peas	1	Tbsp. Asian garlic-chili sauce
1	cup frozen purple hull peas	¾	to 1 tsp. salt
1	cup frozen crowder peas	1	Tbsp. freshly ground pepper
1	cup frozen butter peas		

test kitchen tip: Find Asian garlic-chili sauce in Asian food markets or the Asian foods section of your supermarket. It's the same color and similar to hot sauce but with a greater depth of flavor.

1. Cook bacon in a Dutch oven until crisp; remove bacon, and drain on paper towels, reserving drippings in pan. Crumble bacon.

2. Sauté onion in hot drippings in Dutch oven over medium-high heat 8 minutes or until translucent. Add black-eyed peas and next 8 ingredients, and cook, uncovered, 20 to 25 minutes. Top with crumbled bacon.

Better-Than-Grandma's Mashed Potatoes

makes 8 servings • prep: 25 min.; cook: 1 hr., 35 min.

They're better than Grandma's because sour cream makes them richer, carrots turn them golden, and dillweed adds a fresh herb taste.

3	lb. baking potatoes, peeled	1	tsp. dried dillweed
2½	qt. chicken broth	1½	cups sour cream
4	small carrots, cut into ½-inch pieces	3	Tbsp. chopped fresh parsley
		1	tsp. salt
1	small onion, chopped	¼	tsp. pepper
¼	cup butter or margarine	1	Tbsp. butter or margarine

make it a meal: Serve these unique mashed potatoes with a roasted pork loin roast and Brussels sprouts.

1. Preheat oven to 325°.

2. Combine potatoes and chicken broth in a Dutch oven; bring to a boil. Reduce heat, and simmer 15 minutes. Add carrot and onion, and simmer 20 minutes or until potatoes are tender; drain.

3. Mash vegetables, ¼ cup butter, and dillweed in a large bowl. Add sour cream and next 3 ingredients, stirring well. Spoon mixture into a greased 11- x 7-inch baking dish; dot with 1 Tbsp. butter. Cover and bake at 325° for 1 hour.

Savory Sweet Potato Hash

(pictured on page 359)

makes 4 to 6 servings • prep: 20 min., cook: 20 min.

Chopped sweet potatoes and tart Granny Smith apples mingle in a savory skillet side topped with parsley and pecans.

test kitchen tip: Remove cooked bacon from skillet in Step 1 using a slotted spoon to leave the flavor-rich drippings behind.

4	bacon slices, diced	½	cup chicken broth
1	Tbsp. olive oil	¼	tsp. dried thyme
½	medium onion, diced	¼	tsp. ground allspice
2	large sweet potatoes, peeled and chopped	½	cup chopped toasted pecans
1	large Granny Smith apple, peeled and chopped		Garnish: chopped fresh parsley

1. Sauté bacon in hot oil in a large skillet over medium-high heat 3 minutes or until brown. Remove bacon, and set aside; reserve drippings in skillet. Add onion, and sauté 2 minutes. Stir in sweet potatoes, and sauté over medium-high heat 5 minutes. Stir in apple and next 3 ingredients, and cook, stirring often, 8 to 10 minutes or until potatoes and apple are tender.
2. Spoon mixture into a serving dish, and sprinkle with pecans and reserved bacon. Garnish, if desired.

the saga of sweet potatoes

Candied yams, sweet potato pie, crunchy chips, muffins, pancakes, biscuits, and ever popular sweet potato soufflé topped with marshmallows or a buttery sugar-pecan crust. That's a list of Southern soul food traditions if there ever was one. Fat-free and loaded with nutrients such as Vitamins A, E, and C; iron; and potassium, sweet potatoes have kept Southerners healthy and well-fed for centuries. Even these days, Southern cooks have found new ways to serve them in recipes such as tacos and yam-and-catfish wraps. They're not truly "yams," the name that came from African-Americans, who found sweet potatoes to be similar to their native tuber called "nyami." A 1930s marketing campaign for "Louisiana yams" added to the name confusion. But no matter what you call them, the sweet, orange-fleshed sweet potato remains an icon of Southern cuisine.

Apricot-Glazed Sweet Potatoes

makes 6 servings • prep: 20 min., cook: 1 hr.

Cooked slices of sweet potatoes glisten with a glaze of brown sugar, apricot nectar, cinnamon, and pecans.

3	lb. medium-size sweet potatoes	¼	tsp. salt
1	cup firmly packed brown sugar	⅛	tsp. ground cinnamon
1	cup apricot nectar	½	cup chopped pecans
1½	Tbsp. cornstarch	2	Tbsp. butter
2	Tbsp. hot water		

test kitchen tip: Nectar is thicker and sweeter than fruit juice. Find apricot nectar among canned fruit juices in large supermarkets.

1. Preheat oven to 350°.

2. Cook potatoes in boiling water to cover 10 minutes. Let cool to touch; peel potatoes, and cut into ½-inch-thick slices. Arrange potato slices in a lightly greased 2-qt. casserole.

3. Combine brown sugar and next 5 ingredients in a small saucepan, stirring with a wire whisk. Cook, uncovered, over medium heat until thickened and bubbly, stirring often. Stir in pecans and butter. Pour sauce over potato. Bake, uncovered, at 350° for 45 minutes or until potato is tender.

Creamed Spinach

makes 4 servings • prep: 15 min., cook: 30 min.

Pine nuts and Parmesan perk up simple creamed spinach.

¼	cup pine nuts	½	tsp. freshly ground pepper
½	cup butter or margarine	½	tsp. freshly grated nutmeg
2	cups whipping cream	2	(10-oz.) packages fresh spinach, shredded
⅔	cup grated Parmesan cheese		
½	tsp. salt		

make it a meal: For a hearty Southern-style main dish, serve Creamed Spinach over grits or cornbread with a fresh peach and strawberry salad.

1. Preheat oven to 350°.

2. Bake pine nuts in a shallow pan at 350°, stirring occasionally, 5 minutes or until toasted. Set aside.

3. Bring butter and whipping cream to a boil over medium-high heat; reduce heat to medium, and cook, stirring often, 15 minutes or until thickened.

4. Stir in Parmesan cheese and next 3 ingredients. Add shredded spinach, and cook over low heat, stirring often, until wilted. Sprinkle with pine nuts.

Spinach Casserole

makes 4 to 6 servings • prep: 20 min., cook: 40 min., other: 5 min.

This easy spinach casserole starts with frozen chopped spinach. Serve it hot from the oven, or spoon the creamy mixture into ready-to-serve crêpes.

make it a meal: Serve Spinach Casserole with pan-seared chicken, prepared cranberry-orange relish, and icebox rolls.

1   (10-oz.) package frozen chopped spinach, thawed
2   Tbsp. butter
1   medium onion, chopped (about ¾ cup)
2   garlic cloves, minced
3   large eggs

2   Tbsp. all-purpose flour
½   tsp. salt
¼   tsp. nutmeg
¼   tsp. pepper
1   cup milk
1   cup freshly grated Parmesan or Romano cheese

1. Preheat oven to 350°.

2. Drain spinach well, pressing between paper towels to remove all excess liquid.

3. Melt butter in a large skillet over medium heat; add onion and garlic, and sauté 5 minutes or until garlic is lightly browned and onions are tender. Remove from heat, and stir in spinach until well blended; cool.

4. Whisk together eggs and next 4 ingredients in a large bowl. Whisk in milk and freshly grated Parmesan cheese; stir in spinach mixture, and pour into a lightly greased 8-inch square baking dish. Bake at 350° for 33 to 35 minutes or until set. Let stand 5 minutes before serving.

Squash Casserole

makes 8 servings • prep: 25 min., cook: 55 min.

Have you ever been to a family reunion or church supper where there wasn't a squash casserole? Take this version with Cheddar cheese and a buttery cracker crumb crust to your next one.

3	lb. yellow squash, sliced	¼	cup mayonnaise
5	Tbsp. butter or margarine, divided	2	tsp. sugar
1	small onion, chopped (about ½ cup)	1	tsp. salt
1	cup (4 oz.) shredded sharp Cheddar cheese	20	round buttery crackers, crushed (about ¾ cup)
2	large eggs, lightly beaten		

1. Preheat oven to 350°.

2. Cook squash in boiling water to cover in a large skillet 8 to 10 minutes or just until tender. Drain well; gently press between paper towels.

3. Melt 4 Tbsp. butter in a skillet over medium-high heat; add onion, and sauté 5 minutes or until tender. Remove skillet from heat; stir in squash, cheese, and next 4 ingredients. Spoon mixture into a lightly greased 11- x 7-inch baking dish.

4. Melt remaining 1 Tbsp. butter. Stir together melted butter and crushed crackers; sprinkle evenly over casserole. Bake at 350° for 30 to 35 minutes or until set.

lighten up: These simple steps will save calories and grams of fat. Reduce butter to 3 Tbsp., using 2 Tbsp. to sauté onion. Substitute ½ cup egg substitute for the 2 eggs and low-fat versions of cheese, mayonnaise, and crackers. Proceed as directed.

Glazed Butternut Squash

makes 4 servings • prep: 30 min., cook: 36 min.

A buttery apple cider-pecan glaze coats chunks of butternut squash for a sweet side that goes great with ham.

3	lb. butternut squash, peeled	1	tsp. salt
½	cup apple cider	½	tsp. pepper
¼	cup water	¼	cup chopped, toasted pecans
2	Tbsp. butter	1	Tbsp. chopped fresh or 1 tsp. dried sage
1	Tbsp. sugar		

1. Cut squash in half lengthwise; remove and discard seeds. Cut each half into 4 wedges; cut wedges into 2-inch pieces.

2. Stir together squash, apple cider, and next 5 ingredients in a 12-inch, deep-sided, nonstick skillet; bring to a boil over medium-high heat. Cover, reduce heat, and simmer, stirring occasionally, 25 minutes. Uncover and cook 5 minutes or until liquid thickens and squash is tender. Gently stir in pecans and sage.

test kitchen tip: If butternut squash isn't available, an equal amount of sweet potatoes substitutes nicely in this recipe. Peel sweet potatoes using a paring knife or vegetable peeler, and cut into 2-inch pieces.

Grilled Summer Squash and Tomatoes

makes 6 servings • prep: 5 min., cook: 10 min., other: 30 min.

test kitchen tip: When selecting yellow squash and green tomatoes, be sure to look at the stem ends; they can indicate the quality of the vegetables. If the stems are hard, dry, shriveled or dark, the vegetables aren't fresh.

¼	cup olive oil	4	medium-size green tomatoes, cut into ¼-inch-thick slices
2	Tbsp. balsamic vinegar	1	lb. yellow squash, cut diagonally into ½-inch-thick slices
1	tsp. salt		
½	tsp. pepper		
4	garlic cloves, minced		

1. Preheat grill to medium-high heat (350° to 400°).

2. Combine first 5 ingredients in a shallow dish or zip-top plastic bag; add tomato and squash. Cover or seal; chill 30 minutes.

3. Remove vegetables from marinade, reserving marinade. Grill vegetables, covered with grill lid, over medium-high heat (350° to 400°) 10 minutes, turning occasionally. Toss with reserved marinade.

Cheesy Tomato Casserole

makes 4 to 6 servings • prep: 15 min., cook: 30 min.

Buttery cracker crumbs, Cheddar cheese, onion, and canned tomatoes are simply stirred together and baked for a tangy tomato side good with pork, chicken, or beef.

make it a meal: Grill pork chops or chicken breasts while this side dish bakes. Add ready-to-serve rice for an easy weeknight meal.

1	(35-oz.) can whole tomatoes, drained and chopped	1	Tbsp. butter, melted
½	cup round buttery cracker crumbs (about 15 crackers)	½	small onion, finely chopped
		1	large egg, well beaten
½	cup (2 oz.) shredded sharp Cheddar cheese	½	tsp. salt
		¼	tsp. paprika

1. Preheat oven to 325°.

2. Stir together all ingredients. Spoon mixture into a lightly greased 8-inch square baking dish. Bake at 325° for 30 minutes or until golden.

Sweet, smoke-seasoned tomatoes and squash will turn this side dish into the star of the menu. Add a few hickory chips to the fire for extra flavor.

Grilled Summer Squash
and Tomatoes

Crunchy Fried Green Tomatoes

makes 4 to 6 servings • prep: 25 min., cook: 8 min. per batch

Jewish cooks have found ways to enjoy favorite Southern recipes and still maintain kosher guidelines. With kosher salt and a matzo meal coating, these crispy fried green tomatoes still meet the rules of Jewish law.

test kitchen tip: Look for matzo meal in the kosher section of the supermarket.

½ cup matzo meal
1 tsp. kosher salt
½ tsp. ground red pepper
⅛ tsp. sugar
4 to 5 large green tomatoes, cut into ½-inch-thick slices

2 large eggs, lightly beaten
Vegetable oil
Kosher salt (optional)

1. Combine first 4 ingredients in a shallow dish.

2. Dip tomatoes into eggs, allowing excess to drip off. Dredge in matzo mixture, pressing it into the surfaces. Place on a wax paper–lined baking sheet.

3. Pour oil to a depth of ½ inch into a large, deep cast–iron or heavy skillet; heat over medium heat to 360°. Fry tomatoes, in batches, 3 to 4 minutes on each side or until golden. Drain on paper towels. Sprinkle with additional salt, if desired. Serve immediately.

summertime is tomato time
Even Southerners living in tiny apartments are apt to have a staked tomato plant growing on the porch. Store-bought varieties can't compare to the sweet squirt of tiny grape tomatoes in a salad, slices of juicy plum or Romas on a sandwich, or juice dribbling down your chin from a bite of a sun-warmed Better Boy fresh off the vine. Every region in the South includes the juicy orbs in recipes from appetizers to desserts. Brought into American cuisine from the Italians, Spanish, and Mexicans, tomatoes found their way on Southern tables in tomato gravy over biscuits, between slices of white bread slathered with mayo, in vegetable soups, and sprinkled with salt on a relish tray with cucumbers and pickles; this only after a brave soul in the early 1800s reported that tomatoes weren't poisonous. Thank goodness he did! Can you imagine the South without barbecue sauce, chili, cornmeal-crusted fried green tomatoes, or a home-grown gift to take to the neighbors?

Pecan Wild Rice

makes 6 servings • prep: 15 min., cook: 55 min.

This side couldn't be simpler. After the rice cooks, stir in onions, pecans, raisins, orange juice, and rind, and then serve.

5½	cups chicken broth	¼	cup chopped fresh parsley
1	cup wild rice, uncooked	¼	cup olive oil
4	green onions, thinly sliced	1	Tbsp. grated orange rind
1	cup pecan halves, toasted	1½	tsp. salt
1	cup golden raisins	¼	tsp. freshly ground pepper
⅓	cup orange juice		

1. Combine broth and rice in a medium saucepan. Bring to a boil; reduce heat, and simmer, uncovered, 45 minutes. Drain and place in a medium bowl. Add green onions and remaining ingredients; toss gently. Serve immediately.

make it a meal: Serve Pecan Wild Rice with a deli-roasted chicken and roasted green beans. Or, if wild game is on your menu, team it with this side for an irresistible and eye-catching combination.

Risotto

makes 6 servings • prep: 15 min.; cook: 1 hr., 12 min.

Super-starchy Arborio rice is used for Italian risottos to achieve the desired creamy texture.

½	cup butter or margarine	2	bay leaves
1	medium onion, chopped	5½	cups hot chicken broth, divided
2¼	cups uncooked Arborio rice	¼	tsp. salt
2	garlic cloves, chopped	¼	tsp. pepper
2	cups dry white wine	⅛	tsp. hot sauce

1. Melt butter in a Dutch oven over medium-high heat; add onion, and sauté 5 to 7 minutes or until tender.
2. Stir in rice and garlic; sauté 2 minutes. Reduce heat to medium; add wine and bay leaves. Cook 5 minutes or until liquid is reduced by half. Add 1 cup chicken broth, salt, pepper, and hot sauce; cook, stirring often, until liquid is absorbed.
3. Repeat procedure with remaining broth, ½ cup at a time. (Cooking time is about 45 minutes.) Discard bay leaves.

test kitchen tip: Substitute chicken broth for white wine, if you prefer. Plan for at least 40 to 45 minutes of hands-on cooking in Step 3.

Pine Nut–Barley Bake

makes 4 servings • prep: 25 min., cook: 1 hr.

Barley, mushrooms, and pine nuts team up for a hearty, rustic-tasting side. Serve it instead of rice or pasta.

½ cup chopped green onions
¼ cup chopped celery
¼ cup sliced fresh mushrooms
⅓ cup butter or margarine, melted
1 cup pearl barley, uncooked

2 cups chicken broth, divided
⅓ cup chopped fresh parsley
½ cup pine nuts, toasted
Salt and pepper to taste

1. Preheat oven to 350°.

2. Cook first 3 ingredients in butter in a large skillet over medium-high heat, stirring constantly, until vegetables are tender. Add barley; cook, stirring constantly, until barley is golden.

3. Combine barley mixture, 1 cup broth, and parsley in an ungreased 2-qt. casserole. Cover and bake at 350° for 30 minutes. Stir in remaining 1 cup broth and pine nuts.

4. Bake, uncovered, 30 more minutes or until liquid is absorbed and barley is tender. Stir in salt and pepper to taste. Serve immediately.

test kitchen tip: Test barley for doneness by taking a small bite. It should be chewy, not soft, with a rich, nutty flavor.

Lemon Vermicelli

makes 4 servings • prep: 10 min., cook: 22 min.

Instead of mashed potatoes or rice, serve this lemon-kissed buttered pasta topped with Parmesan cheese. It's especially good with fish or chicken.

⅓ cup whipping cream
3 Tbsp. butter
1 (7-oz.) package dried vermicelli

¼ cup fresh lemon juice
⅓ cup freshly grated Parmesan cheese

1. Combine cream and butter in a small saucepan; cook over medium-low heat until butter melts. Set aside, and keep warm.

2. Cook vermicelli according to package directions; drain. Place in a bowl, and toss with lemon juice; let stand 1 minute. Add cheese and warm cream mixture; toss to coat. Serve immediately.

Project Open Hand Cookbook
Project Open Hand ~ Atlanta, Georgia

test kitchen tip: Substitute an aged Asiago cheese in place of Parmesan, if you'd like. The side dish will look the same but will have a distinctly nutty flavor.

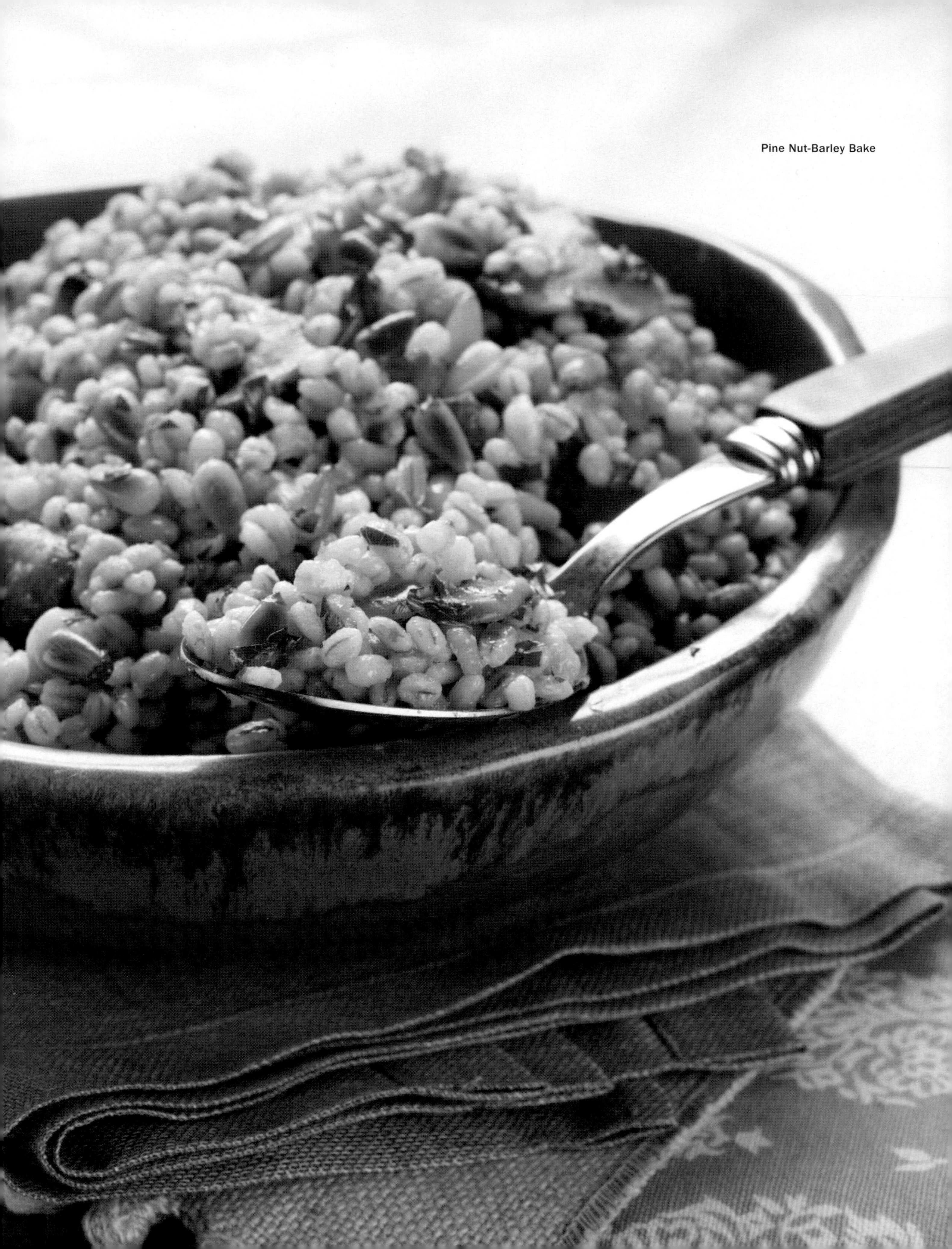

Pine Nut-Barley Bake

Classic Baked Macaroni and Cheese

makes 4 servings • prep: 15 min., cook: 25 min., other: 10 min.

It's worth shredding the cheese yourself for this classic dish.
A sprinkle of red pepper adds a surprise kick.

1	(8-oz.) package elbow macaroni	½	tsp. salt
2	Tbsp. butter or margarine	½	tsp. freshly ground black pepper
2	Tbsp. all-purpose flour	¼	tsp. ground red pepper
2	cups milk		
1	(8-oz.) block sharp Cheddar cheese, shredded and divided		

lighten up: Switching to 1% reduced-fat milk and 2% reduced-fat Cheddar cheese saves 48 calories and a whopping 16.4 grams fat per serving.

1. Preheat oven to 400°.

2. Prepare pasta according to package directions. Keep warm.

3. Melt butter in a large saucepan or Dutch oven over medium-low heat; whisk in flour until smooth. Cook, whisking constantly, 2 minutes. Gradually whisk in milk, and cook, whisking constantly, 5 minutes or until thickened. Remove from heat. Stir in 1 cup shredded cheese, salt, peppers, and cooked pasta.

4. Spoon pasta mixture into 4 lightly greased (8-oz.) ovenproof ramekins; top with remaining 1 cup cheese.

5. Bake at 400° for 15 minutes or until bubbly. Let stand 10 minutes before serving.

Note: For one-pot macaroni and cheese, prepare recipe as directed, stirring all grated cheese into thickened milk mixture until melted. Stir in cooked pasta, salt, and peppers, and serve immediately.

metric equivalents

The recipes that appear in this cookbook use the standard U.S. method for measuring liquid and dry or solid ingredients (teaspoons, tablespoons, and cups). The information in the following charts is provided to help cooks outside the United States successfully use these recipes. All equivalents are approximate.

Metric Equivalents for Different Types of Ingredients

A standard cup measure of a dry or solid ingredient will vary in weight depending on the type of ingredient. A standard cup of liquid is the same volume for any type of liquid. Use the following chart when converting standard cup measures to grams (weight) or milliliters (volume).

Standard Cup	Fine Powder (ex. flour)	Grain (ex. rice)	Granular (ex. sugar)	Liquid Solids (ex. butter)	Liquid (ex. milk)
1	140 g	150 g	190 g	200 g	240 ml
¾	105 g	113 g	143 g	150 g	180 ml
⅔	93 g	100 g	125 g	133 g	160 ml
½	70 g	75 g	95 g	100 g	120 ml
⅓	47 g	50 g	63 g	67 g	80 ml
¼	35 g	38 g	48 g	50 g	60 ml
⅛	18 g	19 g	24 g	25 g	30 ml

Useful Equivalents for Liquid Ingredients by Volume

¼ tsp				=	1 ml
½ tsp				=	2 ml
1 tsp				=	5 ml
3 tsp	= 1 Tbsp		= ½ fl oz	=	15 ml
	2 Tbsp	= ⅛ cup	= 1 fl oz	=	30 ml
	4 Tbsp	= ¼ cup	= 2 fl oz	=	60 ml
	5⅓ Tbsp	= ⅓ cup	= 3 fl oz	=	80 ml
	8 Tbsp	= ½ cup	= 4 fl oz	=	120 ml
	10⅔ Tbsp	= ⅔ cup	= 5 fl oz	=	160 ml
	12 Tbsp	= ¾ cup	= 6 fl oz	=	180 ml
	16 Tbsp	= 1 cup	= 8 fl oz	=	240 ml
	1 pt	= 2 cups	= 16 fl oz	=	480 ml
	1 qt	= 4 cups	= 32 fl oz	=	960 ml
			33 fl oz	=	1000 ml = 1 l

Useful Equivalents for Dry Ingredients by Weight

(To convert ounces to grams, multiply the number of ounces by 30.)

1 oz	=	1/16 lb	=	30 g
4 oz	=	¼ lb	=	120 g
8 oz	=	½ lb	=	240 g
12 oz	=	¾ lb	=	360 g
16 oz	=	1 lb	=	480 g

Useful Equivalents for Length

(To convert inches to centimeters, multiply the number of inches by 2.5.)

1 in			=	2.5 cm
6 in	= ½ ft		=	15 cm
12 in	= 1 ft		=	30 cm
36 in	= 3 ft	= 1 yd	=	90 cm
40 in			=	100 cm = 1 m

Useful Equivalents for Cooking/Oven Temperatures

	Fahrenheit	Celsius	Gas Mark
Freeze water	32° F	0° C	
Room temperature	68° F	20° C	
Boil water	212° F	100° C	
Bake	325° F	160° C	3
	350° F	180° C	4
	375° F	190° C	5
	400° F	200° C	6
	425° F	220° C	7
	450° F	230° C	8
Broil			Grill

recipe index

subject index

Elvis, 190
   pimiento cheese, 190
   Worcestershire sauce, 190
étouffée, 12, 318
   crawfish, 12

Fairhope, Alabama, 104
family meals, 119, 130, 231
fast food track, 113
fat back, 312
festivals, 147, 155
   Chitlin' Strut, 147
   Country Ham Festival, 147
   Crawfish Festival, 147
   Florida Strawberry Festival, 147
   International Chili Championship, 147
   International Rice Festival, 147
   Maryland Seafood Festival, 147
   Memphis-in-May, 147
   National Cornbread Festival, 147
   National Peanut Festival, 147
   Poke Sallet Festival, 306
   Ramp Festival, 306
   World Catfish Festival, 147
Florida, 22, 30, 147
   Central, 22
   Gulf Coast, 22
   Keys, 22, 277
   Miami, 22
   Panhandle, 22
   Plant City, 147
Florida's Catch, 22
flounder, 22, 104
   "flounder light," 104
   "gig," 104
food gifts, 186
fox hunt club, 46
French cuisine, 46
French Quarter, 12
fried chicken, 24, 42, 77, 130, 213
Frogmore stew, 30, 155
front porch, 207

Game, 12, 30, 46
Georgia, 36, 155, 288
   Augusta, 190
   Brunswick stew, 155
   Savannah, 30, 318
German heritage, 55
gifts of food, 186
gigging, for flounder, 22, 104
gravy, 213
greens, 72, 306
   dandelion, 306
   poke weed (poke sallet), 306
   wild mustard, 306

grillades and grits, 84
grits, 26, 84, 369
   grillades and, 84
   "grits belt," 84
   shrimp-'n'-grits, 84
Gruene, Texas, 42
Gullah women, 30
gumbo, 155

Ham, 26
   country, 46, 288
   Country Ham Festival, 147
   tasso, 12
   Ultimate Guide to Country Ham,
      An American Delicacy, The, 288
Harland, Kentucky, 306
Heart of Dixie, The, 26
Hilton Head, South Carolina, 30
"hoe cakes," 218
hominy, 369
honey, 36
hoppin' John, 30
Hot Brown, 340
huevos rancheros, 42
Hummingbird Cake, 250
Huntsville, Alabama, 55
hush puppies, 218

Ice cream, 94
Inn at Blackberry Farm, The, 306
International Chili Championship, 147
International Rice Festival, 147

Jambalaya, 155, 318
Jefferson, Thomas, 46
jubilee, 104

Kentucky, 55, 147, 155, 288, 292,
     306, 340
   barbecue, 292
   burgoo, 155
   Cadiz, 147
   Covington, 55
   Harland, 306
   Hot Brown, 340
   Louisville, 340
Key limes, 277
   Key lime pie, 22, 277
King Cake, 72
kosher cooking, 69
   and Southern cuisine, 69

"Leather britches," 312
leeks, mountain, 306
   ramps, 306
lemonade, 94, 207

limeade, 94
Louisiana, 12, 84, 147, 155, 318
   Breaux Bridge, 147
   Crowley, 147
   gumbo, 155
   jambalaya, 155
   New Orleans, 12, 30, 312, 340
Louisville, Kentucky, 340
   Brown Hotel, 340
Lowcountry Cookin', 30
luck, foods that ensure good, 72

Mardi Gras, 72
mariachi music, 42
Maryland, 18, 147, 292
   barbecue, 292
   Chesapeake Bay, 147
Master's Golf Tournament, 190
   Augusta, Georgia, 190
   pimiento cheese, 190
Memphis, Tennessee, 174, 292
   Memphis-in-May, 147
   Mississippi Delta, 174
   pork ribs, 292
   World Championship Barbecue
      Contest, 292
Memphis-in-May, 147
menudo, 72
Miami, Florida, 22
mint julep, 207
Mississippi, 147
   Belzoni, 147
   Vicksburg, 174
   World Catfish Festival, 147
Mississippi River, 174
   Delta, 174, 299
Missouri, 288
   country ham, 288
Mobile Bay, Alabama, 104
mojitos, 22
Moravian, 52
   bakery, 52
   sugar cake, 52
mountain heritage, 36
muffuletta, 340
mullet, 22
mustard, wild, 306

Natchez pilgrimage, 26
National Cornbread Festival, 147
National Peanut Festival, 147
   Dothan, Alabama, 147
Native Americans, 18, 22, 155, 354, 369
   Cherokees, 36
New Braunfels, Texas, 42, 55
New Orleans, Louisiana, 12, 30, 312, 340